DIRECTORY OF SCOTS
in the
CAROLINAS

1680-1830

Volume 1

By

David Dobson

CLEARFIELD

Reprinted for
Clearfield Company by
Genealogical Publishing Co.
Baltimore, Maryland
2007

ISBN-13: 978-0-8063-1143-2
ISBN-10: 0-8063-1143-6

Made in the United States of America

Introduction

Early attempts at establishing Scottish colonies in the Carolinas ended in failure, to illustrate which we need only note that the emigrant ship the *James of Ayr* was wrecked off the coast of Carolina in 1680 and the short-lived colony at Stewarts Town was overrun by the Spanish in 1686. There were, however, a number of Scots to be found in various English settlements in the late seventeenth century, including a group of recently-banished Covenanters. Although a number of Jacobite Highlanders were exiled to the Carolinas as early as 1716, the main thrust of Highland immigration to the Carolinas began in the 1730s and continued into the nineteenth century, much of this from Argyll to the Cape Fear Valley.

While Scottish names abound in the historical annals of the Carolinas, it is virtually impossible in the majority of cases to distinguish the established population from the immigrant population, or the Scots from the Scotch-Irish. Despite these obstacles sufficient evidence exists to identify thousands of Scottish immigrants of the period 1680 to 1830, as this work attests. Since this directory attempts to identify permanent settlers, it excludes Scots who may have settled in the Carolinas temporarily, such as the Loyalists who returned to Britain or moved to Canada or the West Indies after the American Revolution.

Acknowledgements

I should like to express my appreciation to the following for their help and for permission to quote from their records: Duke University, London Record Office, Public Record Office (London), Scottish Record Office (Edinburgh), North Carolina State Archives and Library, University of St. Andrews (Scotland), and, in particular, Ransom and Janet McBride of the North Carolina Genealogical Society and Mrs. Lee Albright, Genealogy Librarian of the North Carolina State Archives and Library.

David Dobson

References

AABB	American Armoury and Blue Book (London, 1903)
AB	Annals of Banff (Aberdeen, 1891)
ALR	All Roads Lead to Little Rock (1981)
AMC	Miscellaneous Ancestral Records of Moore Co., N.C. (1971)
ANY	Register of the Saint Andrew's Society of New York (N.Y., 1911)
AP	American Presbyterianism (Edinburgh, 1885)
APB	Aberdeen Propinquity Books (MS)
ASCB	Argyll Sheriff Court Book
BAF	Burke's American Families with British Ancestry (London, 1939)
BM	*Blackwood's Edinburgh Magazine*
C	U.S. Census of 1850
CCAI	Clan Cameron Ancestral Index (Raleigh, N.C.)
CCG	*Charleston City Gazette*
CCMC	Colonial Clergy of the Middle Colonies (1957)
CCVC	Colonial Clergy of Virginia, North Carolina and South Carolina (1955)
CFM	*Cape Fear Mercury*
CFR	*Cape Fear Recorder*
ChO	*Charleston Observer*
CI	Clan Iver (Dingwall)
CJ	*Camden Journal*
CLM	*Clan Lachlan Magazine*
CMM	*Clan MacMillan Magazine*
CMN	Clan MacNeil (N.Y., 1923)
CMR	History of the Clan MacRae (Dingwall, 1899)
CTB	Calendar of Treasury Books (London, *Series*)
CV	A Carolina-Virginia Genealogy (Aldershot, 1962)
DAM	Descendants of Duncan and Ann Cameron MacRae of South Carolina and North Carolina (Greensboro, 1932)

DD	Dunlops of Dunlop (London, 1939)
DNCB	Dictionary of North Carolina Biography
DP	Darien Papers (Edinburgh, 1849)
DPCA	*Dundee, Perth and Cupar Advertiser*
DU	Duke University
E	The Elliots (1974)
EA	*Edinburgh Advertiser*
ECJ	Erskins of Carnock's Journal, 1683/87 (Edinburgh, 1893)
EEC	*Edinburgh Evening Courant*
EF	Early Founders of the North Carolina Counties of Rockingham and Stokes, with Revolutionary Service (Madison, 1977)
EHG	Erskine-Halcro Genealogy (Edinburgh, 1895)
EMA	A List of Emigrant Ministers to America, 1690-1811 (London, 1904)
EMR	Edinburgh Marriage Register (Edinburgh, 1908)
ESG	A List of the Early Settlers of Georgia (1967)
ESSC	Early Settlers of South Carolina, 1670-1680
ETR	Edinburgh Tolbooth Records (MS)
F	Fasti Ecclesiae Scoticanae (Edinburgh, 1915)
FA	Family of Abercromby (Aberdeen, 1927)
FC	Family of Cassels (Edinburgh, 1870)
FKC	From Kintyre to Carolina (Glasgow, 1976)
GaR	*Georgia Republican*
GBF	Genealogy of the Blue Family (Montgomery, 1886)
GBG	Burgesses and Gildbrethren of Glasgow (Edinburgh, 1931)
GC	*Glasgow Courier*
GG	A Roll of the Graduates of Glasgow University, 1727-1897 (Glasgow, 1898)
GH	*Genealogical Helper*
GL	Gordons of Craichlaw (Dalbeattie, 1924)
GMG	Geddie-McPhail Genealogy (Forth Worth, 1959)
GWS	*Glasgow and West Scotland Family History Society Newsletter*

H	*The Highlander*
HD	History of Dumfries (Edinburgh, 1867)
HGP	Hayden Guest Papers (MS 377284), St. Andrews University
HHF	Genealogy and History of the Haliburton Family (1959)
HOJ	History of the Johnstones (Edinburgh, 1909)
HOM	History of the Mathesons (Stirling, 1900)
HSNC	Highland Scots of North Carolina (Durham, 1957)
INC	Index of North Carolina Ancestors (Raleigh, 1981)
INE	Immigrants to New England (1931)
JC	Records of the High Court of Justiciary (MS)
JPC	John Paul Jones
KCA	Records of the University and King's College, Aberdeen (Aberdeen, 1854)
LGR	London Guildhall Record Office
LJ	Letters and Journals, 1663-1889 (London, 1953)
LJM	Letters of James Murray, Loyalist (Boston, 1901)
LOS	List of Soldiers of North Carolina in the American Revolution (High Point, 1948)
LRS	Lumber River Scots
MCA	Records of Marischal College and the University of Aberdeen, 1593-1860 (Aberdeen, 1898)
MCF	The McCaskill Family, 1770-1984 (Irmo, 1984)
MOK	The McCormicks of Kintyre (Texas, 1955)
MOT	*Mirror of the Times*
MQQ	The MacQueens of Queensdale (Charlotte, 1916)
MRM	Miscellaneous Records of Moore County
NCA	North Carolina Archives
NCHGR	*North Carolina Historical and Genealogical Register*
NCSJ	*North Carolina Genealogy Society Journal*
NHP	Nisbet's Heraldic Plates (Edinburgh, 1892)
NRAS	National Register of Archives in Scotland
NWI	New World Immigrants (Baltimore, 1979)
OCM	Our Clan of McCormicks (Laurinburg, 1950)
OL	Original Lists of Protestant Immigrants to South Carolina, 1763-73 (1939)

PC	Register of the Privy Council of Scotland (Edinburgh, *Series*)
PCC	Prerogative Court of Canterbury
PCM	PC Mordecai Papers, Raleigh
PMQ	Ancestors and Descendants of Peter McQueen (1976)
PP	*People's Press*
Pr	Probate
PRO	Public Record Office, London
RaNCSw	Raleigh, North Carolina . . . Weekly
RCCR	Richmond County Court Records (MS)
REA	Register of Apprentices of the City of Edinburgh (Edinburgh, 1963)
REB	Register of Edinburgh Burgesses and Gild Brethren (Edinburgh, 1933)
RM	*Raleigh Minerva*
RR	*Raleigh Register*
RRW	*Raleigh Register Weekly*
RS	Register of Sasines, Scottish Record Office, Edinburgh
RSA	Rose-Steele Anthology (Richmond, 1982)
RTI	Rutherford of That Ilk (Edinburgh, 1884)
RTRA	Roster of Texas Daughters of Revolutionary Ancestry (Texas, 1976)
S	*The Scotsman*
SA	Scotus Americanus (Edinburgh, 1982)
SAA	History of the Society of Advocates in Aberdeen (Aberdeen, 1912)
SC	*Southern Chronicle*
SCA	South Carolina Archives
SC GAZ	*South Carolina Gazette*
SCHGM	*South Carolina Historical and Genealogical Magazine*
SFG	Stewarts of Forthergill (Edinburgh, 1879)
SFV	The Story of Fayetteville (Fayetteville, 1950)
SG	*Scottish Genealogist*
SH	Services of Heirs, Scottish Record Office, Edinburgh
SHA	Scotch Highlanders in America (Cleveland, 1900)

SHC	The Scottish Highlander Carmichaels of the Carolinas (Washington, 1935)
SHR	*Scottish Historical Review*
SM	*Scots Magazine*
SNC	Silversmiths of North Carolina, 1696-1850 (Raleigh, 1973)
SO	Scots Overseas (London, 1966)
SP	The Scots Peerage (London, 1904)
SPC	State Papers: Colonial (America and the West Indies)
SRA	Strathclyde Regional Archives, Glasgow
SRO	Scottish Record Office, Edinburgh
STK	Scots and Their Kin (Enterprise, 1984)
TC	The Covenanters (Glasgow, 1908)
TML	The MacLeods—Genealogy of a Clan (Edinburgh, 1969)
TOF	The Thanage of Fermartyn (Aberdeen, 1894)
TSA	The Scots in America (N.Y., 1896)
UNC	University of North Carolina
UPC	Records of the United Presbyterian Church (Edinburgh, 1904)
VG	Virginia Genealogies (Wilkes-Barre, Pa., 1891)
VI	Viri Illustres Universitatum Abredonensium (Aberdeen, 1923)
VMHB	*Virginia Magazine of History and Biography*
VOS	Valley of the Scots (1985)
VSA	Virginia State Archives
WA	Who Was Who in America (Chicago, 1967)
WC	*Western Carolinian*
WCF	The William Cromarty Family (Clarkton)
WI	*Winyaw Intelligencer*
WS	History of the Society of Writers to H. M. Signet (Edinburgh, 1890)
WTB	Wilmington Town Book, 1743-78 (Raleigh, 1973)
ZFH	Zetland Family Histories (Lerwick, 1907)
1812	British Aliens in U.S. During War of 1812 (Baltimore, 1979)

'S ged rachadh iad Charolina
No do thir tha fo'n ghréin
Cha b'urrainn iadsan tachairt
Ach ann nan talamh féin

*and though they would go to Carolina
or to any other land under the sun, they
would not be able to meet except in their
own land*

From *Baird na Gaidhealtachd mu Thuath*,
by Donald Matheson (1851)

DIRECTORY OF SCOTS
in the
CAROLINAS

1680-1830

SCOTS IN THE CAROLINAS

ABERCROMBY WILLIAM
Born 1723 son of Alexander Abercromby and Mary Duff,
Skeith. Died during 1741 in Georgetown, N.C.   (FA)

ADAMS ANDREW
Born c1726 in Scotland. An indentured servant who
absconded during March 1744.   (SCGaz 12.3.1744)

ADAMS JAMES
Aberdeen. Clerk. Settled in N.C.   (Pr 9.1711 PCC)

ADAMS JOHN
40. Machinist. Born in Scotland. Mary 40. Born in Scotland.
James 14. Born in NC. Mary 12. Born in NC. Ann 10. Born in
SC. Eleanor 8. Born in SC. John 8. Born in SC. Gracy 4.
Born in SC. Jennette 3. Born in SC. William 1. Born in SC.
Greenville County, SC.   (C)

ADAM ROBERT
Born during 1759 son of Rev. Adam, minister of West
Kilbride and New Parish of Greenock, Renfrewshire.
Co-partner in the firm of Archibald Fleming and Company
of Greenock. Merchant in Fayetteville and Wilmington, NC.
Father of John, Eliza Ann and Margaret Jane. Died on
11 June 1801. Buried Cross Creek. Pr. July 1801 NC.
                                    (SFV)(NCA.CR.029.801)

ADAMS ROBERT
55. Farmer. Born in Scotland. Jane 55. Born in Scotland.
Jennette 23. Born in Scotland. Robert 14. Born in NC.
David 11. Born in NC. Greenville County, SC.   (C)

AFFLECK THOMAS
Dunbar, Scotland. Merchant in Prince William parish, SC.
                                              (Pr 1758 SC)

AINSLEY ALEXANDER
Born in Aberdeen during 1776. Mariner. Nat. 24 July 1804
in Charleston, SC Court of Admiralty.   (Nat Arch M1183.1)

AINSLEY JOHN
Married Lady Mary, daughter of the Earl of Cromartie, and
widow of Hon. Thomas Drayton, in Charleston, SC, 17 June 1762.
                                              (SM.24.451)

AIR CHARLES JAMES
Member of the House of Representatives in SC. Murdered on
6 March 1803.   (EA.4105.03)

SCOTS IN THE CAROLINAS

AITCHISON ROBERT
Born in Roxburghshire during 1784. Merchant in Charleston,
Merchant in Charleston, SC. Nat. 11 December 1813 Charleston.
(Nat Arch M1183.1)

AITCHISON WILLIAM
Born in Hawick, Roxburghshire during 1781. Merchant.
Nat. 2 January 1806 Charleston, SC.   (Nat Arch M1183.1)

ALEXANDER JOHN
Born in Scotland. Merchant in Carolina. Died 8 October 1699.
(SRO.CC8.8.83)

ALEXANDER WILLIAM
Born during 1715 in Greenock, Renfrewshire, son of John
Alexander and his wife Janet Kerr. Died in October 1766.
Buried in Halifax Colonial Cemetery, NC.   (Halifax Gs.)

ALISON PATRICK
Carnwath, Lanarkshire. Covenanter. Prisoner in Edinburgh
Tolbooth. Banished to Carolina on 2 July 1684. Transported
by Robert Malloch on 1 August 1684.   (PC)(ETR)

ALLEN ALEXANDER
Resident in US for over five years. Settled in NC by 1803.
Nat. January 1805 Craven County, NC.   (Craven Co Ct Rec)

ALLEN ARCHIBALD SMYTH
Native of Great Britain. Resident in NC over five years.
Nat. October 1815 New Hanover Co, NC.   (New Han Sup Ct Mins)

ALLAN ANDREW
Merchant in Charleston, SC. Admitted a Burgess and Gilds-
Brother of Glasgow, gratis, 20 February 1723.   (GBG)

ALLAN JAMES
Born in Scotland on 21 October 1765. Married (1) Isabella,
born in Scotland, and died on 22 August 1792. Parents of
Nancy and Isabella. (2) Mary. Parents of Charlotte. Died
on 14 August 1811. Buried in St James' Cemetery, Wilmington,
NC.   (Wilmington Gs)(RR)

ALLAN JOHN
Born in Edinburgh. Nat. 29 November 1797 Charleston, SC.
Court of Admiralty.   (Nat Arch M1183.1)

ALLAN WILLIAM
Born in Glasgow. Merchant. Nat. 16 January 1798 Charleston,
SC. Court of Admiralty.   (Nat Arch M1183.1)

SCOTS IN THE CAROLINAS

ALSTON GEORGE
Merchant in Granville County, NC. Died on 8 July 1811.
(DPCA.480)

ANCRUM JOHN
Born in Scotland during 1724. Patriot. Died on
10 October 1779 in Wilmington, NC.   (LOS)

ANDERSON ALEXANDER
Emigrated from Scotland to Charleston, SC, with his wife
Elizabeth on 1 December 1817. Nat. 30 March 1825 Chester
County, SC.   (Nats. Chester A216)

ANDERSON ANGUS
Born in Scotland during 1768. Emigrated to America in 1802.
Nat. Richmond County, NC, 20 September 1813.   (RCCR)

ANDERSON EDWARD K.
Born in Galloway during 1803. Settled in Charleston, SC.
Nat. Charleston 5 August 1830.   (Nat Arch M1183.1)

ANDERSON GEORGE
Born in Scotland. Emigrated to South Carolina during 1750.
Presbyterian minister in Sc from 1750 to 1751. Died in
Walterborough, SC, on 20 November 1751.   (CCVC)

ANDERSON HUGH
With his wife Elizabeth and their children Alexander,
Catherine and Moira(?) emigrated from Cromarty, Scotland,
to Georgia during 1737. Landed in Georgia on 27 June 1737.
Allocated a 50 acre land grant in Savannah on 2 June 1736.
Inspector General of Public Gardens. Moved to Carolina
during 1739.   (SPC)(ESG)

ANDERSON HUGH
Born in Glasgow. Nat 11 May 1821 SC.(Circuit Ct Jl V.9.164)

ANDERSON JAMES
Born in Scotland. Died in Halifax Town, NC, on
30 October 1813.   (RM)

ANDERSON JAMES
Born in Kilmarnock, Ayrshire, on 4 June 1796. Died in
Morganton, NC, on 15 June 1874. Buried in Judge John
William Cemetery, Henderson, Vance County, NC. (Henderson Gs)

SCOTS IN THE CAROLINAS

ANDERSON JAMES
54. Farmer. Born in Scotland. Elisabeth 52. Born in
NC. Robert B. 17. Student. Born in NC. Lincoln
County, NC.   (C)

ANDERSON JOHN
Born in Scotland during 1765. Emigrated to United States
c1802. Described in 1812 as a farmer in Richmond County,
NC, with a wife and seven children. Nat. Richmond County
20 September 1813.   (RCCR)(1812)

ANDREW WILLIAM
Linlithgow, West Lothian. Covenanter. Prisoner in the
Tolbooth of Edinburgh. Banished to the Plantations by
the Privy Council on 27 May 1684. Though originally
destined to be transported from Greenock, Renfrewshire,
to Carolina by Walter Gibson, merchant in Glasgow, later
sailed on Robert Malloch's ship from Leith.   (PC)

ARBUCKLE JOHN
Emigrated from Scotland or Ireland to South Carolina on
the Pearl, Walter Buchanan, landing December 1767.
Allocated 100 acres on 12 December 1767.   (OL)

ARCHIBALD ROBERT
Dalyshire(?), Scotland. Cabinetmaker. Nat. 17 June 1799
Charleston, SC. Court of Admiralty.   (Nar Arch M1183.1)

ARMSTRONG THOMAS
Emigrated from Scotland to Brunswick, NC, during September
1739.   (VOS)

ARNOT WILLIAM
Son of Thomas Arnot, Fife. Settled in SC.(Pr 17 11 1790 SC)

ATCHISON GEORGE
Probably from Dumfries. Merchant in Charleston, NC.
                                           (Pr 9 1728 PCC)

ATKINS Lady ANNE
Widow of Hon Edmond Atkins, and a daughter of George,
Earl of Cromartie, married John Murray MD, in Charleston,
SC on 16 February 1764.   (SM.26.166)

AUSTIN ADAM
Merchant in Charleston, SC. Serviced as Heir to his father
Captain Joseph Austin of Kilspindie, Scotland, 3 July 1782.
                                               (SRO/SH)

4

SCOTS IN THE CAROLINAS

BACHOP WILLIAM
Glasgow. Settled in Cumberland County, NC. Died 1792.
(NCA.CR.029.801)

BAILEY WILLIAM
Born in Scotland. Planter on Little River, Laurens
County, SC. Died on 16 June 1791. (CCG 23 9 1791)

BAIN WILLIAM
37. Shop-keeper. Widower. Wick, Caithness. Emigrated
from Wick to Wilmington, NC, on the Bachelor of Leith
during April 1774. (PRO/T47.12)

BAIRD ARCHIBALD
Husband of Winifred Irving. Georgetown, SC.
(RS Dumfries 1779)(Pr1777PCC)

BAIRD JAMES
Calderwater, Lanarkshire. Covenanter. Prisoner in the
Tolbooth of Edinburgh or the Canongate. Banished to the
Plantations on 2 July 1684. Transported from Leith to
Carolina by Robert Malloch, merchant in Edinburgh, in
August 1684. (PC)

BAKER DUNCAN
55. Born in Scotland. Sarah 48. Born in Robeson County.
Daniel 30. Born in Robeson County. Helen 21. Born in
Robeson County. Sarah 18. Born in Robeson County. Archibald
17. Born in Robeson County. James P. 15. Born in Robeson
County. Matilda 7. Born in Robeson County. Robeson County,
NC. (C)

BAKER JAMES FOWLER
Charleston, SC. Student of Physic at University of
Edinburgh, married Ann, daughter of Francis Pringle deceased,
Lieutenant in the Royal American Regiment, now resident in
College Kirk parish, married in Edinburgh on 15 March 1772.
(EMR)

BAKER MARY
80. Born in Scotland. Alexander 41. Born in Robeson County,
NC. John 32. Born in Robeson County, NC. Archibald 30. Born
in Robeson County, NC. Catherine 35. Born in Scotland.
Sarah 25. Born in Robeson County, NC. Robeson County, NC.(C)

BALFOUR ANDREW
Merchant in Edinburgh. Purchased land in St Andrew's parish,
SC, on 4 August 1741. (SC Deeds,W.469)

BALFOUR ANDREW
Born in Edinburgh during 1737, son of Andrew Balfour and his wife Margaret Robertson. Emigrated from Greenock, Renfrewshire, to Boston, Massachusetts, in 1772. Married (1) in Scotland (2) Elizabeth Dayton, Newport, Rhode Island, who died in 1816. Father of Tibbie, born in Scotland c1771. Salt manufacturer in Charleston, SC. Planter in Rowan County, NC. Patriot. Died on 10 March 1782. Buried in Balfour Cemetery, Randolph County, NC.
(LOS)(DNCB)

BALFOUR CHARLES
Born during 1770. Emigrated to America in 1793, with his wife and six children. Farmer in Richmond County, NC.
(1812)

BALFOUR HENRY
Youngest son of Major Balfour. Died in Charleston, SC, on 7 August 1794. (EA.3216.262)

BALFOUR JOHN
Born in Edinburgh after 1737, eldest son of Andrew Balfour of Braidwood and his wife Margaret Robertson. Married Mary Ann Gray. Father of Isabella. Merchant and planter on the Peedee River and in Charleston, SC. Died in SC on 15 November 1781. (DNCB)(SRO/CC8/8/126)

BALLANTINE DAVID
Born in Campbelltown, Argyllshire, during 1772. Mariner. Nat. 21 March 1798 Charleston, SC. (Nat Arch M.1183.1)

BALLANTINE JOHN
Born in Ayrshire during 1800. Housecarpenter in Charleston, SC. Nat. 26 August 1830 Charleston, SC. (Nat Arch M.1183.1)

BALLANTYNE SUSAN STEWART
Second daughter of Charles Ballantyne, Burntisland, Fife, married Rev. Arthur Buist, Charleston, SC, in Edinburgh on 31 July 1820. (BM.7.583)

BALVERD JAMES
Born near Dundee, Angus. Sailor. Settled in SC c1729. Sought via an advertisement. (SC Gaz 19.4.1739)

BANKS CHARLES
Born in Ross-shire. Merchant in Charleston, SC, for 30
years. Nat. 2 April 1788 Charleston, SC. Died in
Philadelphia, Pennsylvania, on 28 May 1812. His wife
died in Charleston on 14 May 1812. (SC Cit Book)(EA.5164.13)

BANKS JOHN
Merchant 43. Born in Scotland, H.L.(f) 34. Born in
Connecticut. L.P.(f) 13. Born in NC. C. 11. Born in NC.
R. 9. Born in NC. M(f) 7. Born in NC. J 4. Born in NC.
W. 2 months. Born in NC. Wilmington, NC.   (C)

BANKS SAMUEL
Planter 87. Born in Scotland. Nat. 19 April 1808 Fairfield
County, SC.   (C)

BANNATYNE THOMAS
Born in Glasgow during 1773. Mariner. Nat. 6.9.1804
Charleston, SC.   (Nat Arch M.1183.1)

BARCLAY WILLIAM
68. Born in Scotland. Agnes 64. Born in Scotland. Jeanette
22. Born in SC. Margaret 7. Born in SC. Mary 5. Born in SC.
Richland County, SC.   (C)

BARON ALEXANDER
Born in Aberdeen. Educated at Marischal College, Aberdeen,
c1745. Emigrated to SC during 1748. Schoolmaster in
Charleston, SC. Episcopalian minister in SC from 1753 to
1759. Died in St Helena's parish, SC, in 1759.   (CCVC)

BARON ALEXANDER
Born in Scotland during 1745. Educated at the University of
Edinburgh - graduated MD in 1768. Settled in Charleston,
SC. Died in 1819.   (SA)

BARRY ANN
Emigrated from Scotland or Ireland to South Carolina on the
Pearl, master Walter Buchanan, in December 1767. Allocated
a 100 acre land grant in SC on 12 December 1767.   (OL)

BASS JAMES
51. Born in Scotland. Elizabeth 35. Born in NC. Robeson
County, NC.   (C)

SCOTS IN THE CAROLINAS

BAXTER JOHN
Born in Scotland during 1766. Emigrated to America in
1802. Described as a tavern-keeper with a wife and
five children in 1812. Died in Fayetteville, NC, on
16 April 1823.   (1812)(RaNCSw 25.4.1823)

BEATON DAVID
28. Farmer. Wife Flora McBride. Kintyre, Argyllshire.
Emigrated from Greenock, Renfrewshire, to Wilmington, NC,
on the Ulysses, Captain Chalmers, in August 1774.
                                                 (PRO/T47.12)

BEATTIE FRANCIS
22. Farmer. Dumfries-shire. Emigrated from Greenock,
Renfrewshire, to Charleston, SC, on the Countess, R Eason,
in October 1774.   (PRO/T47.12)

BEGBIE ELIZABETH
Wife of Captain G Yarrel, Carolina. Serviced as Heir to her
granduncle William Begbie of Gifford Vale, Scotland, on
6 November 1829.   (SRO/SH)

BEGBIE THOMAS
Williamston, NC. Serviced as Heir to his granduncle William
Begbie of Gifford Vale, Scotland, on 6 November 1827.(SRO/SH)

BELL ANDREW
Born in Scotland. Emigrated to Georgia as an indentured
servant to Patrick Houston - landed 1 August 1734.
Allocated a land grant in Savannah, Georgia, during 1736.
Moved to Carolina in 1737. Married Mrs Elizabeth Dunlop,
a widow, on 8 September 1739. Buried in St Helena's,
Beaufort, SC, on 27 August 1752.   (ESG)(St Helena's OPR)

BELL ANDREW
Partner in William Marshall and Company. Died in
Charleston, SC, on 27 October 1807.   (SM.70.78)

BELL ELIZABETH
Probably Scottish. St Helena's parish, Granville County,
SC.   (Pr.11.8.1769 SC)

BELL ROBERT
Born in Scotland. Resident in Georgia. Buried St Helena's
parish, Beaufort, SC. 17 November 1737.   (St Helena's OPR)

BELL WILLIAM
Edinburgh. Died in South Carolina.   (Pr. 5.1827 PCC)

BENNET GEORGE
Eldest son of Rev Patrick Bennet, Polmont, Stirlingshire.
Settled in Charleston, SC, c1783.   (SRO/RD4.236.795)

BENNETT Captain ROBERT
Born in Fort George, Inverness-shire during 1752. Died in
Charleston, SC, on 19 October 1816.   (CCG 31.10.1816)

BENNET ROBERT
Born in Inverness during 1761. Mariner. Nat. 13.4.1805
Charleston, SC.   (Nat Arch M.1183.1)

BERNIE WILLIAM
Born in Aberdeen during 1782. Merchant. Nat. 29.9.1806
Charleston, SC.   (Nat Arch M.1183.1)

BERRIE JAMES
Glasgow. Merchant in Charleston, SC, c1745. (SRA/B10.15.7105)

BETHUNE CATHERINE
70. Born in Scotland. Sarah 65. Born in Scotland.
Richmond County, NC.   (C)

BETHUNE COLIN
Born in Scotland during 1756. Emigrated from Greenock,
Renfrewshire, to Wilmington, NC, during 1772. Died on
29 March 1820. Buried in Bethesda Cemetery, Aberdeen,
Moore County, NC.   (MQQ)(Bethesda Gs)

BETHUNE JOHN
77. Farmer. Born in Scotland. Christian 70. Born in NC.
Elizabeth 40. Born in NC. Mary 38. Born in NC. Hazell 32.
Born in NC. Malcolm 30. Born in NC. Richmond County, NC. (C)

BETHUNE JOHN
Born in Scotland. Emigrated to NC with his father. Tailor.
Married (1) Penny McGeady (2) Sallie McMillan. Settled in
Robeson County. Died 26 June 1854.   (St Paul's Presb Ch Rec)

BETHUNE MURDOCH
Born in Scotland. Settled in Moore County, NC. Died in
Fayetteville, NC, on 15 April 1814.   (RR)

BIBBIE GEORGE
Born in Scotland. Apprentice to Mr Pringle. Buried on
21 April 1785 in St Helena's parish, Beaufort, SC.
                                         (St Helena's OPR)

9

BIRNIE GEORGE
Born in Aberdeen during 1789. Merchant in Charleston.
Nat. 19 October 1818 Charleston, SC.   (Nat Arch M.1183.1)

BIRNIE JOHN
Born in Aberdeenshire during 1787. Millwright in
Charleston. Nat. 11 October 1828 Charleston, SC.
                                            (Nat Arch M.1183.1)

BIRNIE WILLIAM
48. Merchant. Born in Scotland. Mary E. 40. Born in SC.
Jane S. 25. Born in SC. Charleston, SC.   (C)

BISSETT WILLIAM
Son of Kenneth Bissett, gentleman in Edinburgh. Tailor
in Charleston, SC.   (Pr.1754.SC)

BLACK ALEXANDER
59. Farmer. Born in Scotland. Sylvia 50. Born in NC.
Moore County, NC.   (C)

BLACK DONALD
45. Labourer. With wife Janet 34, and children Christian 8,
Ann 4, Ewen 4, and Duncan 2, in Lismore, Argyllshire.
Emigrated from Scotland to Wilmington, NC, on the Jupiter of
Larne, master Samuel Brown, in September 1775.
                                            (PRO/T47.12)

BLACK FLORA
75. Born in Scotland. Hugh 45. Farmer. Born in NC. Sarah 50.
Born in NC. Moore County, NC.   (C)

BLACK G.
Son of Michael Black, Elgin, Morayshire. Tailor. Sought via
an advertisement.   (SCGaz 11.3.1745)

BLACK ISABEL
65. Born in Scotland. William A Savage 31. Farmer. Born in
NC. Lucy A Savage 25. Born in NC. Sarah A Savage 5. Born in
NC. Ann E Savage. Born in NC. William A Savage 1. Born in NC.
Bladen County, NC.   (C)

BLACK JOHN
14. Servant to Kenneth Stewart, Breadalbane, Perthshire.
Emigrated from Scotland to Wilmington, NC, on the Jupiter of
Larne, master Samuel Brown, in September 1775. (PRO/T47.12)

BLACK JOHN
Born 1752. Emigrated to America during 1790. Described as
a farmer in Richmond County, NC, with a wife and two children
in 1812.   (1812)

BLACK JOHN
Born in Scotland. Settled in Georgia c1799.
Nat. 18 11 1806 Laurens, SC.   (Laurens Court Roll 3)

BLACK JOSEPH
Nat. 1 1806 Craven County, NC.   (Craven Co Ct Rec)

BLACK MARY
16. Servant to Kenneth Stewart, Breadalbane, Perthshire.
Emigrated from Scotland to Wilmington, NC, on the Jupiter
of Larne, master Samuel Brown, in September 1775.
                                                (PRO/T47.12)

BLACK MARY
70. Born in Scotland. Kenneth 42. Labourer. Born in NC.
Moore County, NC.   (C)

BLACK MARY
65. Born in Scotland. Mary S Atkins 33. Born in NC.
Maria Atkins 18. Born in NC. Amelia Atkins 16. Born in
NC. George Atkins 14. Born in NC. Cumberland County, NC. (C)

BLACK WILLIAM jr
Son of Nellie Black, daughter of George Martlan, merchant in
Aberdeen, purchased land on the Peedee River, SC, 24 April
1759.   (SC Deeds C3,314)

BLACK WILLIAM
Born in Scotland. Emigrated from Scotland to Charleston,
SC, on 1 November 1803. Settled in Laurens County, SC.
Nat. 19 November 1811 Laurens, SC.   (Laurens Co Roll 46)

BLACK WILLIAM
Born in Fife during 1794. Settled in Charleston, SC.
Nat. 10 October 1828 Charleston.   (Nat Arch M.1183.1)

BLACK WILLIAM
55. Farmer. Born in Scotland. Nancy 48. Born in NC.
Alexander 22. Labourer. Born in NC. Elizabeth 17. Born in
NC. David 14. Born in NC. Mary 11. Born in NC. Maryann 8.
Born in NC. Nancy 5. Born in NC. Ashe County, NC.   (C)

BLACK WILLIAM
Born in Glasgow on 2 April 1793. Died on 20 February 1877.
Buried at Mount Zion Methodist Episcopal Church Cemetery,
Piney Creek, Alleghany County, NC.   (Alleghany Gs)

11

BLACKLOCK WILLIAM
23 Farmer. Dumfries-shire. Emigrated from Greenock,
Renfrewshire, to Charleston, South Carolina, on the
Countess, master S. Eason, during October 1774. (PRO/T47.12)

BLAIN ANDREW
Born in Galloway during 1775. Wheelwright in Charleston,
SC. Nat. 27 August 1813 Charleston, SC. Serviced as Heir to
his sister Margaret, wife of D McNish, merchant in Newton
Stewart, Wigtonshire, on 20 May 1828.
(SRO/SH)(Nat Arch M.1183.1)

BLAIR HUGH
Born in Galloway during 1808. Settled in Charleston.
Nat. 5 August 1830 Charleston, SC.   (Nat Arch M.1183.1)

BLAIR JAMES
Born in Scotland. Nat. 7 July 1794 Charleston, SC.
(Nat Arch M.1183.1)

BLAIR JOHN
Born in Paisley, Renfrewshire. Nat. 29 November 1797
Charleston, SC.   (Nat Arch M.1183.1)

BLAIR WADE
Son of Rev William and Lucy Blair, Invernessshire. Settled
Craven County, SC.   (Pr 4 10 1763 SC)

BLAIR WILLIAM
Born in Kirkcudbright during 1805. Settled in Charleston.
Nat. 21 March 1828 Charleston, SC.   (Nat Arch M.1183.1)

BLAKSWIK JAMES
21. Clerk. Born in Scotland. Emigrated from London to NC
on the Margaret and Mary during February 1774.   (PRO/T47.12)

BLUE CHRISTIAN
45. Born in Scotland. Malcolm 40. Farmer. Born in NC.
Catherine 80. Born in Scotland. Richmond County, NC.   (C)

BLUE DANIEL
65. Born in Scotland. Elizabeth 58. Born in Robeson Co.,
NC. Jane 35. Born in Robeson Co., NC. Flora 33. Born in
Robeson Co.,NC. Margaret 31. Born in Robeson Co.,NC.
Archibald 28. Born in Robeson Co.,NC. Robeson County,NC. (C)

SCOTS IN THE CAROLINAS

BLUE DUNCAN
Born in Scotland during 1734. Married Margaret Campbell.
Emigrated to America in 1767. Died in Moore County, NC,
during 1814. Buried Lakeview Cemetery, Moore County, NC.
(INC 22005)(Lakeview Gs)

BLUE DUNCAN
Son of Malcolm Blue. Born in North Knapdale, Argyllshire,
during 1741. Emigrated to America in 1748. Settled in
Cumberland County, NC. Married Margaret Graham. Father of
Daniel, Neil and Flora. Died in Cumberland County during
September 1828. (GBF)

BLUE JOHN
Son of Malcolm Blue. Born in Scotland during 1745. Married
Mary McKay. Father of John, Mary, Effie, Sarah, and
Catherine. Died in Cumberland County, NC, in 1781. (GBF)

BLUE JOHN
Born in Scotland(?) c1754. Settled in America c1803, with
his wife and five children. Farmer in Robeson County, NC.
(1812)

BLUE JOHN
54. Farmer. Born in Scotland. Margaret 45. Born in Scotland.
Flora 28. Born in NC. Angus 22. Born in NC. Catherine 17.
Born in NC. Daniel 14. Born in NC. Sarah 12. Born in NC.
Margaret 7. Born in NC. Richmond County, NC. (C)

BLUE JOHN
50. Born in Scotland. Mary 52. Born in Scotland. Christian
45. Born in Scotland. Robeson County, NC. (C)

BLUE MALCOLM
Born in Kintyre, Argyllshire. Emigrated from North Knapdale,
Argyllshire, to Wilmington, NC, during 1748. Settled in
Cumberland County, NC. Married Sarah Smith. Father of
Duncan, Daniel, John, James, Dugald, Neil, Malcolm, and
Sarah. Died in 1770. (BAF)(GBF)

BLUE WILLIAM
Born in Kintyre, Argyllshire, c1756. Emigrated to America
c1768. Revolutionary soldier. Presbyterian Elder in
Ashpole, NC. Died 25 March 1829. (RR 24 4 1829)

BLUE Mrs
Born in Scotland during 1712. Died in Richmond County, NC,
during April 1814. (RR 29 4 1814)

SCOTS IN THE CAROLINAS

BOGLE ROBERT
Born c1751. Merchant. Died on 13 December 1785. Buried
in St James's Cemetery, Wilmington, NC.   (Wilmington Gs)

BOGE ARCHIBALD
Probably from Argyllshire. Emigrated from Scotland to NC
during 1739. Settled in Bladen County where he was given a
land grant of 320 acres on 4 June 1740.   (SHA.105)

BONTHRON JOHN
Born during 1777, son of James Bonthron, builder.
Merchant. Nat. 15 September 1806 Charleston, SC. Died in
Charleston on 20 June 1817.   (BM.1.671)(Nat Arch M.1183.1)

BOSTON CHRISTINA
Born c1750, daughter of Rev Thomas Boston, Jedburgh,
Roxburghshire, grand-daughter of Rev Thomas Boston,
Ettrick, Selkirkshire, and wife of Tucker Harris MD.
Died in Charleston, SC, on 10 March 1818.   (BM.3.364)

BOTHWELL JOHN
Aberdeen. Perukemaker in Charleston, SC, pre 1777.
                         (SC Will Book 13 10 1777)

BOWLING EDWARD
Emigrated from Scotland or Ireland to South Carolina on the
Pearl, master Walter Buchanan, in December 1767. Allocated
a 100 acres land grant on 12 December 1767.   (OL)

BOLIN JAMES
Born in Scotland c1767. Married (1) ... Ferguson in North
Carolina c1794 (2) Lucretia Bell in North Carolina c1802.
Died in Cumberland County, NC, during 1843.   (INC 60769)

BOWDEN ROBERT
SC, married Miss C Fullarton, daughter of Alexander
Fullarton, land surveyor, Perth, in Ellisbank, Glasgow, on
1 February 1802.   (SM 64 181)

BOWMAN JOHN
Son of John Bowman, Ashgrove, Ayr. Died in Charleston, SC,
on 2 July 1807.   (SM 69 958)

BOYCE JOHN
60. Born in Scotland. Sarah F. 55. Born in SC. May 24. Born
in SC. James Y. 3. Born in SC. Richland County, SC.   (C)

SCOTS IN THE CAROLINAS

BOYD JOHN
Educated at the University of Glasgow. Physician in Virginia.
Episcopalian missionary in North Carolina. Died in Bertie,
NC, on 19 May 1738.   (CCVC)

BOYD MAITLAND WILSON
Serviced as Heir to his father William Boyd, merchant in
Charleston, SC, on 24 August 1829.   (SRO/SH)

BOYD WILLIAM
Charleston, North America. Father of Maitland Boyd.
                                              (Pr 7 1817 PCC)

BRADLEY JOHN
Born in Scotland. Married Margaret Witherspoon. Died
during 1785 in Salem, Black River, Sumter County, SC.   (GH)

BRADLEY MARY
83. Born in Scotland. Moore County, NC.   (C)

BRADLEY PETER
Born in Campbelltown, Argyllshire, during 1786. Mariner.
Nat. 10 June 1806 Charleston, SC.   (Nat Arch M.1183.1)

BRAID MATTHEW
Born in Dunbartonshire during 1779. Carpenter in Charleston,
SC. Nat. 27 August 1813 Charleston, SC. (Nat Arch M.1183.1)

BRAIDY JAMES
Born in Scotland. Nat. 14 May 1822. SC. (Circuit Ct Jl 9.231)

BREBNER ARCHIBALD
Born in Aberdeen during 1770. Merchant. Nat. 16 May 1805
Charleston, SC.   (Nat Arch M.1183.1)

BRIDIE ROBERT
Perth. Gentleman in Charleston, SC.   (Pr 31 3 1790 SC)

BRIDIE ROBERT
Born in Perth during 1784. Cooper. Nat. 13 September 1807
Charleston, SC.   (Nat Arch M.1183.1)

15

SCOTS IN THE CAROLINAS

BRISBANE ROBERT
Born in 1707, third son of William Brisbane and his wife
Catherine Patterson, Glasgow. Educated at the University
of Glasgow c1723. Emigrated to South Carolina during 1733.
Co-founder of the Charleston Library Society in 1748.
Member of the St Andrews Society. Died in December 1781.
(SCHGM 14 123)

BRISBANE WILLIAM
Born in 1710, fourth son of William Brisbane and his wife
Catherine Patterson, Glasgow. Educated at the University
of Glasgow c1726. Surgeon. Emigrated to South Carolina
during 1732. Allocated land grants at Kingston, 250 acres,
on 10 April 1738, and in Granville County, 450 acres, on
16 September 1738. Married (1) Margaret Stewart in
Charleston on 18 October 1733 (2) Hannah Staples before
October 1760 (3) Eunice Stevens. Father of James, William,
Alexander, Catherine, Adam, Margaret, and Hannah. Baptist.
Planter on the Ashley River. Died during 1771. (SCHGM 14 125)

BROADFOOT ANDREW
Born in Scotland. Merchant in Fayetteville, NC. Died on
29 March 1810.   (RR 5 4 1810)

BROADFOOT WILLIAM
Born in Galloway. Merchant. Nat. 2 April 1798 Charleston, SC.
(Nat Arch M.1183.1)

BROADFOOT WILLIAM
Born in Scotland(?) c1786. Settled in America c1808.
Merchant in Fayetteville, NC.   (1812)

BRODIE ALEXANDER
Born in Scotland. Nat. 25 May 1792 Charleston, SC.
(Nat Arch M.1183.1)

BRODIE THOMAS
Aberdeen. Factor in Charleston, SC.   (Pr 27 7 1798 SC)

BROKE ROBERT
Born in Scotland c1708. Indentured servant who absconded
from his master James Smallwood in Charleston, SC, during
July 1733.   (SC Gaz 14 7 1733)

BROTHERSON JAMES
Born in Scotland c1794. Died in Wilmington, NC, during
December 1831.   (St James' OPR)

BROWN ABRAHAM
78. Born in Scotland. Catherine 50. Born in NC. Jennett 29.
Born in NC. Peter 28. Born in NC. Catherine 24. Born in NC.
Archibald 21. Born in NC. Robeson County, NC.   (C)

16

SCOTS IN THE CAROLINAS

BROWN ADAM
Born in Edinburgh during 1781. Mariner. Nat. 11 October
1804 Charleston, SC.   (Nat Arch M.1183.1)

BROWN ALEXANDER
47. Tailor. Born in Scotland. Grace 47. Born in Scotland.
Charles 18. Merchant. Born in NC. Ellen 14. Born in NC.
Alexander 9. Born in NC. Sampson County, NC.   (C)

BROWN ANGUS
'A passenger with Mr Simpson' - emigrated from Scotland
to North Carolina during July 1770.
          (McAlister/Boyd letters 10.1771; McAllister pp,SHC/UNC)

BROWN BUIE ARCHIBALD
Emigrated from Scotland to America before 1775. Settled in
Cumberland County, NC.   (SHC)

BROWN DUNCAN
'The Scotch weaver' Died at Cheraw Hill, NC, during
September 1804.   (MAJ)

BROWN GEORGE
45. Wine-merchant. Born in Scotland. Margaret 32. Born in
Scotland. Charleston, SC.   (C)

BROWN ISABELL
Emigrated from Scotland or Ireland to South Carolina on the
Pearl, master Walter Buchanan, during December 1767.
Allocated a 100 acre land grant on 12 December 1767.   (OL)

BROWN JOHN
18. Joiner. Dumfries-shire. Emigrated from Greenock,
Renfrewshire, to Charleston, SC, on the Countess, master
R Eason, during October 1774.   (PRO/T47.12)

BROWN MALCOLM
Possibly from Stirlingshire. Died in Charleston, SC.
                                        (Pr 3 7 1795 SC)

BROWN Mrs
Born in Scotland. Settled in Columbia, SC. Nat. 14 October
1830 SC.   (SC Cit Bk 124)

BROWN PETER
Carpenter in Dundee. Indentured for four years service with
John Rutherford and Company, merchants at Cape Fear, NC, in
their shipyards there - contract signed at Leith 1 November
1752. Possibly emigrated on the snow Grenadier from Leith
to NC.   (SRO/RD4.178.2)

17

BROWN ROBERT
Born in Glasgow during 1775. Emigrated from Scotland
to America in 1796. Factor and planter in Charleston by
1800. Stated to have six in his family in 1812. Nat.
29 September 1812 Charleston, SC. Catharine 43. Born in
SC. James 47. Planter. Born in SC. Robert C. 45. Planter.
Born in SC. Charleston, SC.   (Nat Arch M.1183.1)(C)(1812)

BROWN SAMUEL S.
Born in Scotland. Merchant. Nat. 9 March 1798 Charleston,SC.
                                        (Nat Arch M.1183.1)

BRYCE HENRY
Born in Edinburgh during 1783. Merchant. Nat. 29 January 1806
Charleston, SC.   (Nat Arch M.1183.1)

BRYCE JANE C.
49. Teacher. Born in Glasgow, Scotland. Lexington County, SC.
                                                         (C)

BRYCE NICHOL
Born in Edinburgh during 1780. Merchant. Nat. 16 September
1805 Charleston, SC.   (Nat Arch M.1183.1)

BRYCE PETER
57. Merchant. Born in Scotland. Mary C. 26. Born in SC.
John Y. 24. Clerk. Born in SC. Peter 16. Born in SC.
Ellen 12. Born in SC. Robert 10. Born in SC. William 6.
Born in SC. Richland County, SC.   (C)

BRYCE NICHOL
52. Merchant. Born in Scotland. Caroline 33. Born in SC.
Harriet 19. Born in SC. Richland County, SC.   (C)

BRYCE WILLIAM
Born in Scotland. Nat. October 1808 Union, SC.   (SCA)

BUCHANAN ARCHIBALD
Born in Scotland c1797. Settled in Charleston, SC.
Died on 18 August 1823 in Camden, SC.   (SC 27.8.1823)

BUCHANAN DUNCAN
Born in Scotland(?) c1766. Settled in America c1792. Wife
and child. Farmer in Richmond County, NC.   (1812)

BUCHANAN DUNCAN
Born in Scotland(?) c1767. Settled in America c1792. Wife.
Farmer in Richmond County, NC.   (1812)

BUCHANAN GEORGE
Covenanter. Prisoner transported from Gourock, Renfrew-
shire to Port Royal, South Carolina, on the Carolina
Merchant, by Walter Gibson on 21 July 1684.   (ECJ)

BUCHANAN HUGH
Born in Greenock, Renfrewshire, during 1773. Mariner.
Nat. 8 May 1805 Charleston, SC.   (Nat Arch M.1183.1)

BUCHANAN JOHN
Born in Scotland(?) c1763. Emigrated to America in 1792.
Wife and four children. Farmer in Richmond County, NC.(1812)

BUCHANAN JOHN
79. Farmer. Born in Scotland. Sarah 70. Born in NC.
Elizabeth 55. Born in NC. Richmond County, NC.   (C)

BUCHANAN Mrs MARY
50. Born in Scotland. William 56. Born in NC. Margaret 25.
Born in NC. George 19. Born in NC. Elizabeth 16. Born in NC.
Mary I. 14. Born in NC. Melinda 12. Born in NC. Isabel 10.
Born in NC. Catherine 5. Born in NC. Richard 8. Born in NC.
Person County, NC.   (C)

BUCHANAN PETER
Possibly from Callender, Perthshire. Merchant in Charleston,
SC. Nat. 10 February 1818 SC. Died 10 September 1819.
                    (SC Misc. Rec. 04.278)(SRO/CC8.8.146)

BUCHANAN WILLIAM
Son of John Buchanan jr., merchant in Glasgow. Planter in
Granville County, SC. Received a 500 acre land grant in
Craven County on 12 August 1737.   (Pr 11.8.1758 SC)

BUIE ARCHIBALD
Emigrated from Scotland to Brunswick, NC, September 1739.(VOS)

BUIE ARCHIBALD
Smith. Emigrated from Jura, Argyllshire, with his family
to North Carolina before 1764.   (NCA.PC20.1)

BUEA ARCHIBALD
Emigrated from Jura, Argyllshire, to America (probably) on
the General Wolfe, master J MacLean, with his wife and son.
Landed at Brunswick, NC, on 4 November 1767. Allocated
a 300 acre land grant. Settled Cumberland or Mecklenburg
Counties, NC.   (SCGaz 1671)(SHA.111)

19

BUIE DANIEL
Emigrated from Scotland to Brunswick, North Carolina,
during September 1739.   (VOS)

BUIE DUNCAN
Emigrated from Scotland to Brunswick, North Carolina,
during September 1739.   (VOS)

BUEA DUNCAN
Emigrated, with his wife and son, from Jura, Argyllshire,
(probably) on the General Wolfe, master J MacLean, to
America. Landed at Brunswick, NC, on 4 November 1767.
Allocated a land grant of 300 acres. Settled in
Cumberland or Mecklenburg Counties, NC.
                                        (SHA.111)(SCGaz.1671)

BUEA DUNCAN
Emigrated from Jura, Argyllshire, (probably) on the
General Wolfe, master J MacLean. Landed at
Brunswick, NC, on 4 November 1767. Allocated a land grant
of 100 acres. Settled in Cumberland or Mecklenburg,
Counties, NC.   (SHA.111)(SCGaz.1671)

BUIE DUNCAN
Born in Scotland c1724. Emigrated to North Carolina. Died
in Cumberland County, NC, on 10 October 1819. (RR 5.11.1819)

BUIE MALCOLM
Emigrated, with his family, from Jura, Argyllshire, to
North Carolina before 1764.   (NCA/PC20.1)

BUEA MALCOLM
Emigrated from Jura, Argyllshire, (probably) on the
General Wolfe, master J MacLean, to America. Landed at
Brunswick, NC, on 4 November 1767. Allocated a land grant
of 100 acres. Settled in Cumberland or Mecklenburg
Counties, NC.   .   (SHA.111)(SCGaz.1671)

BUEA MARY
Emigrated from Jura, Argyllshire, (probably) on the
General Wolfe, master J MacLean, to America. Landed at
Brunswick, NC, on 4 November 1767. Allocated a land grant
of 100 acres. Settled in Cumberland or Mecklenburg
Counties, NC.   (SHA.111)(SCGaz.1671)

BUEA NEILL
Emigrated from Jura, Argyllshire, (probably) on the
General Wolfe, master J MacLean, to America. Landed at
Brunswick, NC, 4 November 1767. Allocated a land grant
of 100 acres. Settled Cumberland or Mecklenburg
Counties, NC.   (SHA.111)(SCGaz.1671)

BUIE WILLIAM
Born in Scotland during 1770. Married Margaret McIver.
Settled in Anson County, NC. Died Moore County, NC.
                                                    (INC 27697)

BUIST Rev ARTHUR
Charleston, SC, married Susan Stewart Ballantyne, second
daughter of Charles Ballantyne, Burntisland, Fife, in
Edinburgh on 31 July 1820.   (BM 7.583)

BUIST GEORGE
Born in Fife during 1778. Educated at the University of
Edinburgh. Minister in Charleston, SC, from 1793 to 1808.
Principal of Charleston College in 1805. Died in July 1852.
                                                      (F)(SA)

BULLOCH JAMES
Born in Glasgow during 1701. Emigrated from Scotland to
Charleston, SC, during 1728. Married Jean, daughter of
Rev Archibald Stobo, in 1729. Father of Archibald. Died
in 1780.   (SHR)

BUNKLE GEORGE
Born in Scotland(?) Indentured servant to Joseph Wardrope.
Landed in Georgia on 21 August 1734. Allocated a land grant
in Savannah during 1736. Moved to Carolina in May 1742.(ESG)

BURGES JAMES
27. Merchant. Edinburgh. Margaret Hogg, his wife.
Emigrated from Greenock, Renfrewshire, to North Carolina
on the Ulysses, master James Wilson in May 1775.(PRO/T47.12)

BURGES JAMES
Born in Scotland. Married Janet Hogg. Father of Jane.
Merchant in Cumberland County, NC.   (Pr. 1.1787 NC)

BURGES JAMES
Born in Linlithgow, West Lothian, c1763. Married Mary
Margaret ... Father of James. Settled in Charleston, SC,
during 1788. Died 20 November 1805. Buried in St Michael's,
Charleston, SC.   (St Michael's Gs)

SCOTS IN THE CAROLINAS

BURK ELIZABETH
Emigrated from Scotland or Ireland to South Carolina
on the Pearl, master Walter Buchanan, in December 1767.
Allocated a 100 acre land grant on 12 December 1767.   (OL)

BURNET Dr ANDREW
Emigrated from Aberdeen to America c1752. Settled in South
Carolina. Married Sabina, daughter of Rev John Baxter.
Died on 15 November 1764.   (DP)

BURNS CHARLES D.
Born in Scotland. Nat. 28 May 1824 SC.(Circuit Ct Jl 9.348)

BURNS GEORGE
Born in Scotland. Declaration of intent to naturalise
given in Fairfield, Wayne County, Illinois. Settled in
Granville County, NC, during 1822. Nat. 11 March 1825
Granville County, NC.   (NCA/CRO44.311.4)

BURN JOHN
HM Councillor in Charleston, SC. Died in Musselburgh,
Midlothian, on 12 December 1773.   (SM 36.679)

BURT PATRICK
Son of James Burt, baker in Perth. Settled in St Michael's
parish, SC. Died before August 1775.   (SRO/CC8.8.123)

BUSS MARY
46. Born in Scotland. Stephen 40. Farmer. Born in NC.
Flora 23. Born in NC. Margaret 17. Born in NC. John 14.
Born in NC. Mary 12. Born in NC. Jane 10. Born in NC.
Harriet 8. Born in NC. Cornelius 5. Born in NC. Frances 1.
Born in NC. Richmond County, NC.   (C)

CAIRNS JAMES G.
50. Factory manager. Born in Scotland. ....(f) 38. Born
in Massachusetts. George 14. Born in NC. Mary 13. Born in
NC. ... (f) 10. Born in NC. ... (m) 8. Born in NC.
Isabella 2. Born in NC. John 1 month. Born in NC. Rowan
County, NC.   (C)

CALDER ALEXANDER
Born in Edinburgh during 1773. 'Cabiner' Nat. 25 March 1803
Charleston, SC.   (Nat Arch M.1183.1)

CALDER HENRY
Born in Scotland. Planter. Died on Edisto Island, SC, on
8 June 1820.   (BM 6.1820)(CCG 14.6.1820)

SCOTS IN THE CAROLINAS

CALDER JAMES
Born in Glasgow during 1790. Cabinet-maker in Charleston.
Nat. 1 September 1813 Charleston, SC.
James Calder 60. Cabinet-maker. Born in Scotland. Sarah 49.
Born in SC. Alexander 30. Clerk. Born in SC. Charleston, SC.
(Nat Arch M.1183.1)(C)

CALDER MARY
Daughter of William Calder, MD, Edisto Island, SC, married
James Cruikshanks, surgeon, Edinburgh, in Dean, Bo'ness,
West Lothian, on 19 September 1823.   (S.388.624)

CALDER WILLIAM
Born in Paisley, Renfrewshire, during 1797. Merchant in
Charleston. Nat. 27 July 1831 Charleston, SC.(Nat Arch M1183.1)

CALDER WILLIAM
50. Merchant. Born in Scotland. Agnes 45. Born in SC.
Mary 20. Born in SC. Priscilla 18. Born in SC. George 17.
Clerk. Born in SC. Samuel 16. Student. Born in SC. Agnes
14. Born in SC. Alexander 11. Born in SC. William 9. Born
in SC. Eli G. 6. Born in SC. Charleston, SC.   (C)

CALDCLEUGH ANDREW
Born in Scotland on 7 September 1744. Married Sarah ...
(1754-1814) Father of Alexander (1784-1833) Revolutionary
soldier. Died 10 May 1821. Buried Lexington City Cemetery,
Davidson County, NC.   (Lexington Gs)

CALDWELL DONALD
18 Shoemaker. Kintyre, Argyllshire. Emigrated from Greenock,
Renfrewshire, to Wilmington, North Carolina, on the Ulysses,
master J Chalmers, in August 1774.   (PRO/T47.12)

CALDWELL JOHN W.
55. Wheelwright. Born in Scotland. Colleton County, SC. (C)

CALDWELL JOHN
53. Upholsterer. Born in Scotland. Jane 56. Born in Scotland.
James 29. Clerk. Born in Scotland. John 24. Upholsterer. Born
in Scotland. Elizabeth 17. Born in Maryland. Jane 14. Born in
Maryland. Sarah 23. Born in Scotland. Elizabeth 5. Born in
Maryland. John 3. Born in Maryland. Charleston, SC.   (C)

CALDWELL JOHN
Born in 1780. Emigrated to America during 1801. Merchant
in Morganton County, NC. Nat September 1812.   (1812)

CALDWELL JOHN
51. Farmer. Born in Scotland. Margaret 49. Born in NC.
Samuel S. 24. Born in NC. Margaret I. 20. Born in NC.
John H. 13. Born in NC. Robert I. 10. Born in NC.
Cabarrus County, NC.   (C)

CALDWELL WILLIAM
Born in Scotland during 1792. Emigrated to America in 1793.
Farmer in York District, SC.   (1812)

CALHOUN CATHERINE
Born in Appin, Argyllshire, during 1762, daughter of
Duncan Calhoun. Married Hugh McLaurin(1751-1840)
Emigrated to America during 1790. Died on 20 March 1841.
Buried in Stewartsville Cemetery, Laurinburg, Scotland
County, NC.   (Laurinburg Gs)

CALHOUN CATHERINE
60. Born in Scotland. Mary 45. Born in NC. Catherine 23.
Born in NC. Richmond County, NC.   (C)

CALHOUN DUNCAN
Born in Scotland(?) c1760. Emigrated to America during 1790.
Farmer in Richmond County, NC, with a wife and six children.
                                                              (1812)

CALHOUN DUNCAN
Born in Scotland(?) c1764. Emigrated to America during 1791.
Farmer in Richmond County, NC, with a wife and eight children.
                                                              (1812)

CALHOUN JAMES
Born in Scotland c1684. Moved to Donegal, Ireland.
Emigrated to America. Killed by Indians at Long Cane, SC, on
1 February 1760.   (WM)

CALHOUN MARY
55. Born in Scotland. Hugh Blue 4. Born in NC. Richmond, NC.(C)

CALLAN ALEXANDER
22. Workman. Emigrated from Greenock, Renfrewshire, to
Wilmington, NC, on the Ulysses, master J Chalmers, during
August 1774.   (PRO/T47.12)

CALLUM JAMES
Glover and merchant in Dumfries. Covenanter - possibly at
the Battle of Rullion Green in 1666. Banished to the
Plantations. Died in Carolina.   (HD)

CALLUM ROBERT
Born in Scotland. Merchant in Raleigh, NC. Drowned at
Petersburg in October 1817.   (RM)

CAMERON ALLAN
28. Farmer. Kintyre, Argyllshire. Emigrated from Greenock,
Renfrewshire, to Wilmington, North Carolina, on the Ulysses,
master J Chalmers, in August 1774.   (PRO/T47.12)

CAMERON ALLEN
Born in Auchtermuchty, Fife. Married Mary Stewart. Emigrated
from Scotland to Wilmington, NC. Settled at Baker's Creek,
Bladen County, NC. Father of Archibald, Dougald, James,
Margaret and Nancy. Died in Bladen County, NC, 1800.   (GBF)

CAMERON ALLAN
Emigrated from Scotland to America on the Mary Ann in 1790.
Landed at Cape Fear, NC. Millwright.   (NCA 2.1.13N)

CAMERON ANGUS
18. Farmer. Wife Katrine aged 21. Kintyre, Argyllshire.
Emigrated from Greenock, Renfrewshire, to Wilmington, North
Carolina, on the Ulysses, master J Chalmers, in August 1774.
                                              (PRO/T47.12)

CAMERON DONALD
Jacobite soldier captured after the Siege of Preston,
Lancashire. Transported from Liverpool to South Carolina
on the Susannah, master Thomas Bromhall, 7 May 1716.
                                              (SPC)(CTB)

CAMERON DONALD
Born in Scotland c1752. Emigrated from Scotland to America
in 1811. Farmer in Richmond County, NC, with a wife and two
children in 1812. Nat. Richmond County 20 September 1813.
                                              (RCCR)(1812)

CAMERON DOUGALD
Born in Scotland during 1784. Moore County, NC.   (C)(CCAI)

CAMERON JAMES
Born in Scotland during 1786, son of Allen Cameron and
his wife Mary Stewart. Emigrated to America in 1791.
Married Marion Campbell. Settled in Cumberland County,
NC. Father of Daniel, John, James, Neill, Allen, Mary,
Margaret, Nancy, Sarah(?) and Jeanette.   (PCM)

CAMERON JOHN
Jacobite soldier captured after the Siege of Preston,
Lancashire. Transported from Liverpool to South Carolina
on the Susannah, master Thomas Bromhall, 7 May 1716.
                                                        (SPC)(CTB)

CAMERON JOHN
Emigrated from Scotland to Brunswick, North Carolina,
during September 1739.   (VOS)

CAMERON JOHN
Born in Scotland(?) during 1769. Emigrated to America in
1790. Farmer in Richmond County, NC, with a wife and four
children in 1812.   (1812)

CAMERON JOHN
Born in Dingwall, Ross-shire. Settled in South Carolina
during January 1802. Nat. 3 March 1804 SC.   (Cit Book 49)

CAMERON JOHN
Born in Edinburgh. Nat. 11 November 1830 Craven County, NC.
                                           (Craven Co Ct Rec)

CAMERON NORMAN
Born in Scotland. Married Rachel ..., a Scot. Father of
Angus Bruce, born 1 January 1816 in Cumberland County, NC.
                                                         (CCAI)

CAMERON R.
44. Born in Scotland. Kershaw County, SC.   (C)

CAMPBELL of LOSSETT ALEXANDER
Ballole, Islay, Argyllshire. Merchant in Kingston, Jamaica.
Settled in North Carolina. Father of Polly, Kitty, Jean,
Colin, Donald and Colin. Died in Cumberland County, NC,
during 1779.   (Pr 10.1779 NC)

CAMPBELL ALEXANDER
90. Farmer. Born in Scotland. Isabella 85. Born in Scotland.
Chesterfield County, SC.   (C)

CAMPBELL ALEXANDER
Emigrated from Scotland or Ireland to South Carolina on the
Pearl, master Walter Buchanan, during December 1767.
Allocated a 100 acre land grant on 12 December 1767.   (OL)

CAMPBELL ALEXANDER
Born in Scotland(?) during 1777. Emigrated to America
in 1787. Farmer in Richmond County, NC, with a wife and
three children in 1812.   (1812)

CAMPBELL ALEXANDER
Born in Scotland c1792. Died in North Carolina in 1840.
Buried at Gilchrist Cemetery, NC.   (Gilchrist Gs)

CAMPBELL ALEXANDER
58. Farmer. Born in Scotland. Flora 56. Born in Scotland.
Catherine A. 25. Born in NC. Cumberland County, NC.   (C)

CAMPBELL ALLAN
83. Farmer. Born in Scotland. Elizabeth 55. Born in NC.
Mary 33. Born in NC. Christian 24. Born in NC. Sarah 22.
Born in NC. Alexander 20. Farmer. Born in NC. John 17.
Born in NC. Richmond County, NC.   (C)

CAMPBELL ANGUS
74. Farmer. Born in Scotland. John 34. Born in NC.
Margaret 36. Born in NC. Sarah 22. Born in NC.
Cumberland County, NC. Emigrated to America in 1788.(1812)(C)

CAMPBELL ARCHIBALD
Scots Highlander. Settled in Bladen County, NC.
Allocated a land grant in June 1740.   (HSNC)

CAMPBELL ARCHIBALD
Born in Jura, Argyllshire, during 1750. Married Sarah
(1780-1835). Died on 28 June 1853. Buried at Campbell
Cemetery, Anderson Creek, NC.   (Campbell Gs)

CAMPBELL ARCHIBALD
Son of Alexander Campbell of Kirnan. Physician and
minister of the Scots Church in Jamaica. Married Elizabeth
Mackay, a widow. Father of Alexander, Janet, Katherine, Colin,
Donald, Duncan, John, Elizabeth, Ann, and George. Emigrated
from Tongue, Sutherland, to America. Settled at Crook Creek,
Mecklenburg County, NC, c1770.   (CI)(HGP)

CAMPBELL ARCHIBALD
38. Farmer. Wife - Jean McNeill 32, children Mary 7,
Lachlan 2, and Girzie 6. Kintyre, Argyllshire. Emigrated
from Greenock, Renfrewshire, to Wilmington, North
Carolina, on the Diana, master D Ruthven, in September 1774.
                                          (PRO/T47.12)

CAMPBELL ARCHIBALD
87. Farmer. Born in Scotland. Euphane 52. Born in NC.
Bladen County, NC.   (C)

CAMPBELL CATHERINE
Niece and adopted daughter of the Duke of Argyll, married
William Williamson in Scotland. Died in NC during 1805.
Buried in Philips Cemetery, Raeford, Hoke County, NC.
                                                (Hoke Gs)

CAMPBELL CHRISTIAN
48. Born in Scotland. Duncan M. 20. Born in Scotland.
Marlborough County, SC.   (C)

CAMPBELL COLIN
Born in Scotland c1738. Emigrated from Falmouth, England,
to Carolina during 1774 on the Lady Spencer.   (HGP)

CAMPBELL COLIN
Landowner in Georgia and South Carolina.   (Pr. 5.1783 PCC)

CAMPBELL COLIN
Strachur parish, Argyllshire. Settled in South Carolina.
                                          (Pr. 21.5.1784 SC)

CAMPBELL COLIN
Brother of Hugh Campbell of Lix, Argyllshire. Charleston, SC.
Died pre 1791.   (Pr 6.1794 PCC)(SRO/SH)

CAMPBELL COLIN
Son of John Campbell, tacksman of Benmore. Died in
Charleston, SC, on 17 July 1810.   (EA)

CAMPBELL COLIN
Born in Scotland(?) during 1758. Emigrated to America in
1791. Farmer in Richmond County, NC, with five children.(1812)

CAMPBELL DANIEL
Born in Scotland(?) in 1758. Emigrated to America in 1790.
Farmer in Cumberland County, NC, with a wife and five
children in 1812.   (1812)

CAMPBELL DANIEL
25. Farmer. Kintyre, Argyllshire. Emigrated from Greenock,
Renfrewshire, to Wilmington, NC, on the Ulysses, master
J Chalmers, in August 1774.   (PRO/T47.12)

CAMPBELL DANIEL
Born in Scotland(?) during 1768. Emigrated to America in
1802. Farmer in Richmond County, NC, with a wife and four
children in 1812.   (1812)

CAMPBELL DANIEL
Born in Scotland(?) during 1773. Emigrated to America in
1788. Farmer in Richmond County, NC, with a wife and five
children in 1812.   (1812)

CAMPBELL DANIEL
76. Farmer. Born in Scotland. Chesterfield County, SC.(C)

CAMPBELL DANIEL
Argyllshire(?) Died in Cumberland County, NC, 1800.(NCA.WBA28)

CAMPBELL DAVID
30. Tailor. Perthshire. Emigrated from Greenock, Renfrewshire, to Charleston, SC, on the Countess, master R Eason
in October 1774.   (PRO/T47.12)

CAMPBELL DONALD
50. Farmer. With his wife and son aged 12 emigrated
from Ardahoolish, Sutherland, to Wilmington, NC, on the
Bachelor of Leith in April 1774.   (PRO/T47.12)

CAMPBELL DONALD
Born c1714 in the island of Scalpay, near Skye, Inverness-
shire. Married Katherine McDonald. Emigrated from
Scotland to North Carolina in 1774. Father of John, Isobel,
Christian, Barbara, Margaret and Alexander. Settled at
McLendon's Creek, Cumberland County, NC. Planter. Died on
2 June 1784.   (MRM)(Pr 1.1785 Cumb Co)

CAMPBELL DONALD
Born in Nairn during 1808. Died in NC 11 November 1885.
Buried in Raleigh City Cemetery, NC.   (Raleigh Gs)

CAMPBELL DUGALD
Emigrated from Skye, Invernessshire, to America with his
father, a doctor, and his family. Settled in NC c1771.
                      (Boyd letter 1771, McAllister pp, SHC/UNC)

CAMPBELL of KILDUSKLAND DUNCAN
Emigrated from Argyllshire to Cape Fear, NC, 1739.
(ASCB 19.7.1739)

CAMPBELL DUNCAN
Argyllshire to North Carolina during 1739. Allocated a
land grant of 75 acres in Bladen County, NC, on
4 June 1740. (SHA.105)

CAMPBELL DUNCAN
Argyllshire to North Carolina during 1739. Allocated a
land grant of 140 acres in Bladen County, NC, on
4 June 1740. (SHA.105)

CAMPBELL DUNCAN
Argyllshire to North Carolina during 1739. Allocated a
land grant of 148 acres in Bladen County, NC, on
4 June 1740. (SHA.106)

CAMPBELL DUNCAN
Argyllshire to North Carolina during 1739. Allocated a
land grant of 150 acres in Bladen County, NC, on
4 June 1740. (SHA.105)

CAMPBELL DUNCAN
Argyllshire to North Carolina during 1739. Allocated a
land grant of 300 acres in Bladen County, NC, on
4 June 1740. (SHA.105)

CAMPBELL DUNCAN
Argyllshire to North Carolina during 1739. Allocated a
land grant of 320 acres in Bladen County, NC, on
4 June 1740. (SHA.106)

CAMPBELL DUNCAN
Argyllshire to North Carolina during 1739. Allocated a
land grant of 400 acres in Bladen County, NC, on
4 June 1740. (SHA.106)

CAMPBELL DUNCAN
Argyllshire to North Carolina during 1739. Allocated a
land grant of 640 acres in Bladen County, NC, on
4 June 1740. (SHA.106)

CAMPBELL DUNCAN
60. Shoemaker. Born in Scotland. Chesterfield County, SC.(C)

CAMPBELL DUNCAN
55. Born in Scotland. Christian 50. Born in NC.
Robeson County, NC.   (C)

CAMPBELL DUNCAN
Born c1794 in Kilmartin, Argyllshire, son of Angus
Campbell and his wife Christian McLellan. Emigrated from
Scotland to North Carolina during 1804. Married Christian
McKinnon. Settled in Robeson County, NC. Died on
18 September 1881.   (St Paul's Presb Ch Rec)

CAMPBELL DUNCAN
Born in Islay, Argyllshire, c1790. Emigrated from Scotland
to America during 1802. Settled in Charleston, SC, and
later in Charlotte, Mecklenburg County, NC. Nat. 10 May 1823
Mecklenburg.   (NCA/CR.065.311.1)

CAMPBELL D.
40. Stonecutter. Born in Scotland. J(f) 24. Born in NC.
W(m) 14. Born in NC. C(m) 12. Born in NC. C(f) 6. Born in
NC. H(m) 4. Born in NC. J(f) 2. Born in NC. M(f) 1 month.
Wake County, NC.   (C)

CAMPBELL EFFIE
50. Born in Scotland. Dougald 45. Born in NC. Robeson
County, NC.   (C)

CAMPBELL EDWARD
Emigrated from Scotland to South Carolina c1800, with his
wife Mary McLellan and family. Settled in Hammer, SC. (SHC)

CAMPBELL FARQUHAR
Born in Scotland c1721. Emigrated from Scotland to North
Carolina c1740. Married (1) Isabell McAlister (2) Mrs
Elizabeth Whitfield Smith (3) Rachel Whitfield. Patriot and
politician. Died during 1808. Buried at Old Bluff Church, NC.
                                                       (SFV)

CAMPBELL FLORA
54. Born in Scotland. Mary A. 30. Born in NC. Isabell 27.
Born in NC. Randal 16. Farmer. Born in NC. John A. 15.
Born in NC. William A. 8 months. Born in NC. Moore County, NC.
                                                       (C)

SCOTS IN THE CAROLINAS

CAMPBELL GEORGE
Emigrated from Scotland, with his family, to America.
Settled in North Carolina before 1771.
(McCuaig letter 1771, McAllister pp SHC/UNC)

CAMPBELL HANNAH
Born in Nairn during 1810. Died in NC 14 January 1840.
Buried in Raleigh City Cemetery, NC.   (Raleigh Gs)

CAMPBELL HENRIETTA
Born in Scotland during 1764. Settled in Charleston, SC.
Nat. 3 May 1832 Charleston.   (Nat Arch M.1183.1)

CAMPBELL HUGH
Probably a Scot. Settled on the Cape Fear River, NC, in 1733.
Married Magdalene ... Died in 1736.   (HSNC)

CAMPBELL HUGH
Born in Scotland(?) during 1765. Emigrated to America in 1804.
Farmer in Richmond County, NC, with a wife and four children
in 1812.   (1812)

CAMPBELL ISABEL
65. Born in Scotland. Duncan Kelly 33. Farmer. Born in NC.
Catherine Kelly 28. Born in NC. Anne E. 3. Born in NC.
Mary F. 2. Born in NC. Bladen County, NC.   (C)

CAMPBELL JAMES
Born in Campbelltown, Argyllshire, during 1705. Emigrated
from Scotland to America in 1730. Settled in Philadelphia,
Pennsylvania. Licenced as a preacher in Pennsylvania 1735.
Presbyterian minister on the Conewehoya. Married a Miss
Kennedy. Settled on Cape Fear, NC, 1758. Planter. Died in
1780. Buried Old Bluff Cemetery, Cumberland County, NC.
                              (NCA.2.1.13N)(SHA)(HGP)

CAMPBELL JAMES
Argyllshire. Emigrated from Scotland to North Carolina in
1739. Allocated a 640 acres land grant in Bladen County on
4 June 1740.   (SHA.106)

CAMPBELL Col JAMES
Son of Robert Campbell, Middletoncarse, Clackmannanshire.
Agent for the State Bank of North Carolina. Died in
Leakesville, America, on 2 January 1822.   (BM 12.250)

CAMPBELL JAMES
Born in Argyllshire. Nat. 22 August 1810 SC.
                              (Circuit Ct Jl 10.74)

CAMPBELL JENNET
91. Born in Scotland. Mary Murphy 67. Born in NC.
Ellen McIntyre 60. Born in NC. Cumberland County, NC.(C)

CAMPBELL JOHN
Jacobite soldier captured after the Siege of Preston,
Lancashire. Transported from Liverpool to South Carolina
on the Susannah, master Thomas Bromhall, 7 May 1716.
(CTB)(SPC)

CAMPBELL JOHN
Scottish Highlander in Lt Col Cochrane's Company, who
deserted at Charleston SC, on 12 March 1739.(SCGaz 17.3.1739)

CAMPBELL JOHN
Emigrated from Scotland to America as an indentured
servant to Young, Miller and Company. Storekeeper in
Hillsboro, Orange County, NC, and later in Guilford County,
NC. Landed in America during 1764.   (NCSJ.XI.26)

CAMPBELL JOHN
Emigrated from Jura, Argyllshire, with his wife and son
(probably) on the General Wolfe, master J MacLean, to
America. Landed at Brunswick, NC, in November 1767.
Allocated a land grant of 300 acres and settled in
Cumberland or Mecklenburg Counties, NC.(SCGaz.1671)(SHA.111)

CAMPBELL JOHN
Born in Scotland during 1762. Emigrated to America in 1788.
Farmer in Moore County, NC, with a wife and five children
in 1812.   (1812)

CAMPBELL JOHN
75. Born in Scotland. Nancy 55. Born in Scotland John 27.
Born in Robeson County, NC. James 23. Born in Robeson County,
NC. Sally Ann 21. Born in Robeson County, NC. Robeson County,
NC.   (C)

CAMPBELL JOHN
Born in Scotland. Died in Fayetteville, NC, on
25 October 1815.   (RR 3.11.1815)

CAMPBELL JOHN
65. Born in Scotland. Margaret 70. Born in NC. Robeson
County, NC.   (C)

CAMPBELL JOHN
65. Born in Scotland. Hugh 63. Farmer. Born in
Scotland. Mary 52. Born in Scotland. Moore County, NC.   (C)

CAMPBELL JOHN
Born in Scotland(?) during 1775. Emigrated to America
in 1792. Farmer in Robeson County, NC, with his parents,
wife and five children in 1812.   (1812)

CAMPBELL JOHN
Born in Glasgow. Nat. 1 November 1821 SC.(Circuit Ct J1 9.194)

CAMPBELL JOHN
Born in Scotland. Mariner. Nat. 19 January 1796 Charleston,
SC.   (Nat Arch M.1183.1)

CAMPBELL JOHN
Born in Glasgow during 1792. Merchant in Charleston, SC.
Nat. 17 May 1825 Charleston.   (Nat Arch M.1183.1)

CAMPBELL JOHN
Born in Scotland on 6 May 1803. Apprenticed as a silversmith
in Fayetteville, NC, in 1818. Silversmith in NC and Tenn.(SNC)

CAMPBELL KATY
60. Born in Scotland. Cumberland County, NC.   (C)

CAMPBELL LAURENCE
Glasgow. Died in Charleston, SC, during 1804.   (SM.66.566)

CAMPBELL MALCOLM
70. Farmer. Born in Scotland. Chesterfield County, SC.   (C)

CAMPBELL MALCOLM
53. Born in Scotland. Margaret 56. Born in NC. Margaret 24.
Born in NC. Edward 22. Born in NC. Betsy 20. Born in NC.
Harriet 17. Born in NC. Christian 15. Born in NC.
Robeson County, NC.   (C)

CAMPBELL MARGARET
84. Born in Scotland. Nancy 50. Born in NC. Robeson County,
NC.   (C)

CAMPBELL MARGARET
61. Born in Scotland. Daniel 21. Farmer. Born in
Marion County, SC. John 10. Born in Marion County, SC.
Marion County, SC.   (C)

CAMPBELL MARGARET
60. Born in Scotland. Daniel 28. Born in NC. Robeson
County, NC.   (C)

CAMPBELL MARY
86. Born in Scotland. Jennett 69. Born in NC. Mary 40.
Born in NC. Catherine 30. Born in NC. Robeson County, NC.(C)

CAMPBELL MARY
45. Born in Scotland. Archibald 55. Farmer. Born in NC.
William 16. Born in NC. Flora 14. Born in NC. Mary 12.
Born in NC. Margaret 10. Born in NC. Bladen County, NC. (C)

CAMPBELL NANCY
75. Born in Scotland. Marlborough County, SC.   (C)

CAMPBELL NANCY
68. Born in Scotland. Moore County, NC.   (C)

CAMPBELL Mrs NANCY
Born in Scotland during 1794. Married Alexander Campbell.
Died in North Carolina during 1873. Buried in Gilchrist
Cemetery, NC.   (Gilchrist Gs)

CAMPBELL NANCY
60. Born in Scotland. James 28. Born in NC. Peter 21.
Farmer. Born in NC. Moore County, NC.   (C)

CAMPBELL NEIL
Born in Scotland(?) during 1752. Emigrated to America in
1789. Farmer in Cumberland County, NC, with a wife and
five children in 1812.   (1812)

CAMPBELL NEILL
85. Farmer. Born in Scotland. Sarah 65. Born in Scotland.
Archibald 32. Born in NC. Norman 35. Farmer. Born in NC.
Catherine 25. Born in NC. Cumberland County, NC.   (C)

CAMPBELL PATRICK
Born in Scotland(?) Settled in North Carolina. Died 1775.
(HSNC)

CAMPBELL PETER
Emigrated from Scotland to South Carolina c1800.
Settled near Campbell's Bridge, on the Little Pee Dee
River, Dillon, SC.   (SHC)

CAMPBELL PETER
Born in Glasgow during 1777. Mariner. Nat. 16 June 1809
Charleston, SC.   (Nat Arch M.1183.1)

CAMPBELL PETER
59. Born in Scotland. McDowall County, NC.   (C)

CAMPBELL SARAH
80. Born in Scotland. Duncan 55. Farmer. Born in Scotland.
Catherine 47. Born in Scotland. Mary 25. Born in NC.
.... 22. Blacksmith. Born in NC. Catherine 19. Born in NC.
Richmond County, NC.   (C)

CAMPBELL SARAH
65. Born in Scotland. Robert 16. Labourer. Born in NC.
Richmond County, NC.   (C)

CAMPBELL WILLIAM
Son of Hugh Campbell, tenant farmer in Argyllshire.
Indentured with John McLeod in Edinburgh for service in
Carolina on 31 January 1737.   (SRO/GD170)

CAMPBELL Lord WILLIAM
Son of the Duke of Argyll, married Sarah, daughter of
Ralph Izard, in Charleston, SC, on 17 June 1763. (SM 25.359)

CAMPBELL WILLIAM
Born after 1763, son of William Campbell and his wife
Sarah Izard. Officer in the Royal Navy. Later settled on his
maternal estate in Carolina.   (SP)

CAMPBELL WILLIAM
28. Labourer. With his wife Katherine 32, and children
Robert 2, and Duncan an infant emigrated from Glen Orchy,
Argyllshire, to Wilmington, NC, on the Jupiter of Larne,
master Samuel Brown, in September 1775.   (PRO/T47.12)

CAMPLEY ARCHIBALD
Emigrated (probably) from Argyllshire to North Carolina
during 1739. Allocated a 320 acre land grant in Bladen
County, NC, on 4 June 1740.   (SHA.106)

CAMPBELLY H.
51. Equity commissioner. Born in Scotland. Ann 52. Born
in Scotland. William L. 21. Clerk. Born in SC. John C. 16.
Born in SC. Mary W. 15. Born in SC. Robert 12. Born in SC.
Daniel P. 10. Born in SC. Colleton County, SC.   (C)

CARGILL DAVID
55. Born in Scotland. Elizabeth 27. Born in NC. Georgina
12. Born in NC. David 9. Born in NC. Victoria 5. Born in
NC. ...(f) 1. Born in NC. Granville County, NC.   (C)

CARMiCHAEL ARCHIBALD
Born in Lanark during 1754. Emigrated from Scotland to
America. Married (1) Elizabeth Nix, who had been born in
Scotland c1755 (2) Sally. Settled in Caswell County, NC.
Father of Stirling, Jane, Richard, Sarah, Alexander,
Joseph, Archibald and Elizabeth. Revolutionary soldier.
Died in Stokes County, NC, c1828.
                                          (INC17075)(EF)

CARMICHAEL ARCHIBALD
26. Labourer. With his wife Mary 26 and daughter Catherine
7. Emigrated from Lismore, Argyllshire to Wilmington, NC,
on the Jupiter of Larne, master Samuel Brown, during
September 1775.   (PRO/T47.12)

CARMICHAEL ARCHIBALD
Born in Scotland during 1749. Emigrated to North Carolina
during 1775. Settled in Cumberland County NC, Richmond
County NC, and Marion County SC. Died after 1830.   (SHC)

CARMICHAEL CHRISTIAN
Married Dougal McIntyre, Lismore, Argyllshire. Mother of
Rev Duncan McIntyre and three other sons. Emigrated from
Scotland to South Carolina c1821. Settled in Dillon, SC.(SHC)

CARMICHAEL CHRISTIAN
14. Servant to Kenneth Stewart, Breadalbane, Perthshire.
Emigrated from Scotland to Wilmington, NC, on the
Jupiter of Larne , master Samuel Brown, during September
1775.   (PRO/T47.12)

CARMICHAEL DANIEL
Born in Scotland during 1736. Shepherd in Appin,
Argyllshire. Married (1) ....., parents of Daniel
(2) Sallie McCall parents of Malcolm, John born 1761,
Christian, Mary and Sarah. Emigrated from Scotland to
America c1773. Died in South Carolina in 1822.   (SHC)

CARMICHAEL DANIEL
Born in Scotland during 1746. Emigrated to America in
1790. Settled in Richmond County, NC. Farmer in Richmond
County, NC, with three children in 1812.   (SHC)(1812)

CARMICHAEL DANIEL
Born in Scotland. Emigrated to North Carolina c1792.
Settled in Richmond County, NC, and later moved to Marion
County, SC.   (SHC)

CARMICHAEL DONALD
22. Servant to Lieutenant A Stewart. With Lilly Stewart,
his natural daughter emigrated from Breadalbane, Perthshire,
to Wilmington, NC, on the Jupiter of Larne, master Samuel
Brown, during September 1775.   (PRO/T47.12)

CARMICHAEL DOUGALD
Born in Scotland c1768. Settled in Richmond County, NC,
and later in Marion County, SC.   (SHC)

CARMICHAEL DOUGALD
Born in Scotland. Settled in Cumberland County, later
in Richmond County, NC, and then in Marion County, SC.
Loyalist soldier.   (SHC)

CARMICHAEL DOUGALD
55. Farmer. Emigrated with his wife Mary 55, and her
children Archibald Colquhoun 22 and Ann Colquhoun 20,
from Breadalbane, Perthshire, to Wilmington, NC, on the
Jupiter of Larne, master Samuel Brown, in September 1775.
                                                   (PRO/T47.12)

CARMICHAEL DOUGALD
Blacksmith. Emigrated from Scotland to America during 1773.
Settled in Cumberland County, NC, then Richmond County, NC,
from 1780 to 1790, and later in Marion County, SC, from
1790 to 1800.   (SHC)

CARMICHAEL DOUGALD
Son of Archibald Carmichael. Shipyard craftsman.
Emigrated from Scotland to North Carolina c1794. Settled
in Richmond County, NC.   (SHC)

CARMICHAEL DUNCAN
Born in Scotland(?) during 1746. Emigrated to America
during 1791. Farmer in Richmond County, NC, with one
child in 1812. (1812)

CARMICHAEL DUNCAN
Born in Scotland on 11 May 1755. Emigrated, with his
father and family, to America in 1769. Married Charity
Witt c1774. Settled in North Carolina. Revolutionary
soldier. Father of John, Sarah, Leminah, William, Lemuel,
Mary, Barzillai, Soloman and Richard. Died before
September 1821. (EF)

CARMICHAEL DUNCAN
Born in Scotland. Emigrated to North Carolina c1773.
Settled in Cumberland County, NC, and then Richmond County,
NC. (SHC)

CARMICHAEL EWEN
40. Labourer. Emigrated from Breadalbane, Perthshire, with
his wife Margaret 38, and children Archibald 14, Allan 12,
and Katherine 8, to Wilmington, NC, on the Jupiter of Larne
master Samuel Brown, in September 1775. (PRO/T47.T2)

CARMICHAEL GILBERT
Born in Scotland during 1763. Emigrated from Scotland to
North Carolina c1773. Settled in Cumberland County, NC.(SHC)

CARMICHAEL HUGH
Born in Scotland. Emigrated from Scotland to North Carolina
before 1790. Married Margaret Stewart. Settled in Richmond
County, NC. (SHC)

CARMICHAEL HUGH
Born in Scotland(?) during 1774. Emigrated to America in
1804. Farmer in Robeson County, NC, with a wife and children
in 1812. (1812)

CARMICHAEL JAMES
Emigrated from Appin, Argyllshire, to America c1773.
Settled in Orangeburg County, SC. (SHC)

CARMICHAEL JAMES
Born in Glasgow during 1775. Merchant. Nat. 21 March 1803
Charleston, SC. (Nat Arch M.1183.1)

CARMICHAEL JOHN
Born in Scotland c1650. Emigrated via Kent, England, Ireland, and Barbados to Charleston, SC, on the <u>Carolina</u> in 1669. Indentured servant. Died during 1695. (ESSC)

CARMICHAEL JOHN
Born in Scotland during 1752. Emigrated from Scotland to North Carolina with his wife and children in 1780. Settled in Cumberland County, NC, and later Richmond County, NC. Farmer. (SHC)(1812)

CARMICHAEL JOHN
60. Farmer. Born in Scotland. Catherine 59. Born in Scotland. Margaret 30. Born in NC. Catherine 28. Born in NC. Christian 18. Born in NC. Mary 16. Born in NC. Richmond County, NC.(C)

CARNEGIE JAMES
Second son of Charles Carnegie, Regent of St Leonard's College, St Andrews, Dean of Brechin, Minister of Farnell, and his wife Barbara Martin, who died 1694. Sailor and by February 1721 mate of the sloop Ruby. Married and settled in Charleston, SC. (SP VIII/75)

CARNOCHAN RICHARD
Born in Galloway during 1783. Merchant in Charleston, SC. Nat. 16 November 1813 Charleston. (Nat Arch M.1183.1)

CARTY DANIEL
Born in Greenock, Renfrewshire. Nat. 20 October 1824 SC. (Circuit Ct Jl 9.362)

CARUTH JOHN
Born in Galloway during 1777. Mariner. Nat. 17 July 1805 Charleston, SC. (Nat Arch M.1183.1)

CARUTH PETER
Born in Galloway(?) Scotland. Nat. 30 November 1797 Charleston, SC. (Nat Arch M.1183.1)

CARRUTHERS JOHN
Born in Scotland c1710. Married Content ... Died in Craven County, NC, c1751. (INC 07078)

SCOTS IN THE CAROLINAS

CARSON JAMES
12. Dumfries. Emigrated from Greenock, Renfrewshire, to
Charleston, SC, on the Countess, master R Eason during
October 1774.   (PRO/T47.12)

CARSON WILLIAM
Born in Kirkcudbright during 1793. Merchant in Charleston,
SC. Nat. 6 February 1824 Charleston.   (Nat Arch M.1183.1)

CASSELS ROBERT
Born 5 March 1728, fourth son of James Cassels, merchant
and shipowner in Bo'ness, West Lothian, and his wife Hannah
Spiers. Died during 1750 at sea off Carolina.   (FC)

CATTENACH JOHN
50. Farmer. Emigrated with his wife and four children aged
between 7 and 19 from Scrabster, Rea, Caithness, to
Wilmington, NC, on the Bachelor of Leith in April 1774.
                                                   (PRO/T47.12)

CATHCART WILLIAM
Born c1710 in Genoch, Wigtonshire,(?) Surgeon - educated
in Edinburgh c1726. Physician and merchant in North
Carolina from c1737. Married (1) Penelope Maule in 1742
(2) Prudence West. Father of Gabriel, Peggy and Francis.
Settled on Roanoke River, Northampton County, NC. Died
on 27 February 1773.   (DNCB)(SRO/GD180)

CAW ALEXANDER
Former merchant in Leith. Died in Charleston, SC, on
18 August 1817.   (S 4.2.1817)

CAW THOMAS
Born in Scotland. Gentleman in Charleston, SC.(Pr 5.2.1773 SC)

CEARL JOHN
40. Farmer. Dumfries-shire. Emigrated from Greenock,
Renfrewshire, with his wife aged 50, to Charleston, SC,
on the Countess, master R Eason, during October 1774.
                                                   (PRO/T47.12)

CHALMERS LIONEL
Born in Scotland during 1715. Educated at the University of
St Andrews - graduated MD in 1756. Settled in South
Carolina during 1737. Died in 1777.   (SA)

41

SCOTS IN THE CAROLINAS

CHAMBERS JOSEPH
Jacobite soldier captured after the Siege of Preston,
Lancashire. Transported from Liverpool to South
Carolina on the Susannah, master Thomas Bromhall, on
7 May 1716.   (CTB)(SPC)

CHAMSON ELIZABETH
Emigrated from Scotland or Ireland to South Carolina
on the Pearl, master Walter Buchanan, in December 1767.
Allocated a 100 acre land grant on 12 December 1767.   (OL)

CHAPMAN Mrs BARBARA
Second daughter of James Rutherford of Bowland, and
wife of Alexander Chapman, merchant in Wilmington, NC,
died in Wilmington during November 1763.   (SM 26 55)

CHAPMAN SAMUEL
Born c1779 son of James Chapman (1733/98), farmer in
Ponfeigh, Carmichael, Lanarkshire, and his wife Jane
(1740/1814). Died in Charleston, SC, on 8 September 1806.
                                              (Carmichael Gs)

CHISHOLM ALEXANDER
Son of Archibald Chisholm of Fasnakyle. Emigrated from
Scotland to South Carolina during 1717. Settled on the
Wando River.   (BAF)

CHISHOLM ALEXANDER
26. Indentured servant to Farquhar McGilivery. Emigrated
to Georgia on 20 October 1735. Landed in Georgia on
10 January 1736. Moved to Carolina in August 1742.   (ESG)

CHISHOLM ALEXANDER
Born in Inverness during 1738, son of John Ban Chishom and
Catherine MacRae. Emigrated to South Carolina c1746.
Planter in Charleston, SC, and Chisholm's Island,
St Bartholemew's parish, Georgia. Married Christina
Chisholm on 5 October 1766. Father of Alexander Robert
born 1767, William born 1770, George born 1772, and Robert
Trail born 1773. Died on 10 December 1810. Buried in the
Scots Presbyterian Cemetery, Charleston, SC.   (BAF)

CHISHOLM ALEXANDER
Born in Scotland c1786. Emigrated to America in 1803.
In North Carolina 1812.   (1812)

CHISHOLM ANN
58. Born in Scotland. Marion County, SC.   (C)

42

CHISHOLM CATHERINE
66. Born in Scotland. Catherine 43. Born in NC. Kenneth
37. Born in NC. Alexander 27. Born in NC. Jennett 23.
Born in NC. Robeson County, NC.   (C)

CHISHOLM CATHERINE
Born in Sleat, Inverness-shire, c1783, daughter of
Alexander and Catherine Chisholm. Married John Kelly.
Died on 24 August 1859. Buried in Stewartsville Cemetery,
Laurinburg, Scotland County, NC.   (Laurinburg Gs)

CHISHOLM DANIEL
70. Farmer. Born in Scotland. Murdoch 60. Born in Scotland.
Alexander 58. Farmer. Born in Scotland. Moore County, NC.(C)

CHISHOLM FINDLAY
Born in Scotland. Merchant. Died in Fayetteville, NC, on
13 April 1813.   (RR 23.4.1813)

CHISHOLM GEORGE
Born in Edinburgh during 1783. Mariner. Nat. 20 March 1809
Charleston, SC.   (Nat Arch M.1183.1)

CHISHOLM HUGH
Born in Scotland. Shoemaker. 48. Tyrell County, NC.   (C)

CHISHOLM JAMES
Born in Skye, Inverness-shire, during 1773. Emigrated to
America during 1803. A farmer in Robeson County with
Catherine, his wife, and five children in 1812. Died on
28 January 1833. Buried in Stewartsville Cemetery,
Laurinburg, Scotland County, NC.   (Laurinburg Gs)(SG)(1812)

CHISHOLM JOHN
Balintrade, Scotland. Died in Carolina before March 1801.
                                         (Pr 3.1801 PCC)

CHISHOLM MARY
40. Born in Scotland. Marlborough County, SC.   (C)

CHISHOLM NANCY
80. Born in Scotland. Rachael 60. Born in Scotland.
Montgomery County, NC.   (C)

CHRISTIE ANN ELIZABETH
Daughter of Alexander Christie, Charleston, SC,
married John B Thomson, born in Kilmarnock, a
Member of the Bar in South Carolina, in
Charleston, SC, on 31 May 1827.   (S 787 472)

CHRISTIE EDWARD
Born in Scotland. Merchant in Charleston, SC.(Pr 1.12.1797SC)

CHRISTIE JOHN
56. Born in Scotland. Elizabeth 29. Born in Scotland.
Edgefield County, SC.   (C)

CLARK ALEXANDER
Emigrated from Scotland to Brunswick, North Carolina,
in September 1739.   (VOS)

CLERK ALEXANDER
Emigrated from Jura, Argyllshire, with his family, to
North Carolina before 1764.   (NCA.PC20.1)

CLARK ANDREW
Born in Scotland c1759. Merchant in Fayetteville, NC.
Died 23 September 1796. Buried St James's Cemetery,
Wilmington, NC.   (Wilmington Gs)

CLARK ANDREW
Born in Scotland. Emigrated from Scotland to America
during 1798. Nat. Edgecombe County, NC, September 1813.
                                (Edgecombe Co Ct Rec)

CLARK ARCHIBALD
Emigrated from Scotland to Brunswick, NC, during
September 1739.   (VOS)

CLARK DANIEL
73. Farmer. Born in Scotland. Flora 62. Born in NC.
Isabel 32. Born in NC. Christian 29. Born in NC. Mary 27.
Born in NC. Duncan 19. Born in NC. Bladen County, NC.   (C)

CLARK ELEANOR
61. Born in Scotland. Duncan 18. Farmer. Born in NC.
Bladen County, NC.   (C)

CLARK ELEANOR
57. Born in Scotland. Alexander 22. Farmer. Born in SC.
William 19. Farmer. Born in SC. John 16. Farmer. Born
in SC. Gilbert 13. Born in SC. Chesterfield County, SC. (C)

CLARK FRANCIS
48. Labourer. Born in Scotland. Jeanette 32. Born in NC.
Frances 16. Born in NC. Mary 14. Born in NC. Steele Creek,
Mecklenburg County, NC.   (C)

CLARK HUGH
Jacobite soldier captured after the Siege of Preston,
Lancashire. Transported from Liverpool to South Carolina
on the Susannah, master Thomas Bromhall, on 7 May 1716.
                                                 (CTB)(SPC)

CLARK JAMES
Jacobite soldier captured after the Siege of Preston,
Lancashire. Transported from Liverpool to South Carolina
on the Wakefield, master Thomas Beck, on 21 April 1716.
                                                 (CTB)(SPC)

CLARK JAMES
Born in Scotland. Emigrated to America on 18 June 1798.
Nat. 14 April 1802 Union, SC.   (Union Nat Pet 6)

CLARK JOHN
Emigrated from Argyllshire(?) to North Carolina in 1739.
Allocated a land grant of 320 acres in Bladen County, NC,
on 4 June 1740.   (SHA.105)

CLARKE JOSEPH
51. Agent. Born in Scotland. Elizabeth A. 48. Born in
Connecticut. Jeanette 17. Born in New York. Isabell 12.
Born in New York. Edgefield County, SC.   (C)

CLARK MALCOLM
Emigrated from Scotland to Brunswick, NC, in September 1739.
                                                 (VOS)

CLARK MARY
72. Born in Scotland. John M.N. 43. Farmer. Born in NC.
Margaret 43. Born in NC. Niven 15. Labourer. Born in NC.
Ann C. 13. Born in NC. George M. 12. Born in NC. Mary M.
10. Born in NC. John M. 8. Born in NC. Duncan A. 1. Born in NC.
Montgomery County, NC.   (C)

CLARK MARY
60. Born in Scotland. Catherine 31. Born in NC.
Archibald 34. Born in NC. Christian 28. Born in NC.
Donald 26. Farmer. Born in NC. Moore County, NC.   (C)

CLARK NEILL
Emigrated from Jura, Argyllshire, (probably) on the
General Wolfe, master J MacLean, to America. Landed
at Brunswick, NC, on 4 November 1767. Allocated a
100 acre land grant in Cumberland or Mecklenburg
Counties, NC.   (SHA.111)(SCGaz.1671)

CLARK NEILL
75. Farmer. Born in Scotland. Mary 41. Born in NC.
Flora 20. Born in NC. Bladen County, NC.   (C)

CLARK NEIL
57. Lawyer. Born in Scotland. Mary M. 46. Born in SC.
Robert 10. Born in NC. Elizabeth 6. Born in NC.
Alexander 4. Born in NC. Wilmington, New Hanover County. (C)

CLERK THOMAS
Jacobite soldier captured after the Siege of Preston,
Lancashire. Transported from Liverpool to South Carolina
on the Wakefield, master Thomas Beck, 21 April 1716.
                                            (CTB)(SPC)

CLARK THOMAS
Born in Galloway c1722. Educated at the University of
Glasgow. Physician. Married Elizabeth Nesbitt(1730-1762)
in Ireland. Emigrated to New York during 1764.
Associated Presbyterian minister in New York and in South
Carolina. Father of Ebenezer, Robert, Elizabeth and
Benjamin. Died in Long Cane, Cedar Springs, SC, on
26 December 1792.   (CCMC)

CLARKSON JAMES
Linlithgow, West Lothian. Covenanter. Prisoner in the
Tolbooth of Edinburgh. Banished to the Plantations.
Transported from Leith to Carolina in May 1684 by Robert
Malloch, merchant in Edinburgh.   (PC)

CLATWORTHY JANETTE
38. Born in Scotland. James 45. Carpenter. Born in Ireland.
James T. 17. Student. Born in SC. Margaret 7. Born in SC.
Thompson 14. Born in SC. Ninian 6 months. Born in SC.
Benjamin 3. Born in SC. Abbeville County, SC.   (C)

CLAYTON FRANCIS
Edinburgh. Merchant and planter in Wilmington, New
Hanover, NC. Brother of Thomas Clayton. Died on
4 October 1790. Pr. 1790 NC.   (SRO/CC8/8/128.2)

CLAYTON JOHN
Emigrated from Argyllshire(?) to North Carolina during
1739. Allocated a 100 acre land grant in Bladen County,
NC, on 4 June 1740.   (SHA.106)

CLAYTON THOMAS
Scotland. Settled in New Hanover parish, NC. Died in 1793.
                                                (Pr 23.7.1793 NC)

CLELAND Dr
Brother of Robert Cleland in Fife, Scotland. Physician in
Charleston, SC. Died before 1747.   (SRO/RD2.171.312)

CLUB ALEXANDER
Born in Fraserburgh, Aberdeenshire, during 1767. Merchant.
Nat. 25 September 1802 Charleston, SC.   (Nat Arch M.1183.1)

CLUNIE ALICE
Wife of Dr Daniel McNeil. Died in Wilmington, NC, on
12 November 1791.   (EEC.11510)

COCHRAN JAMES
Possibly from Tranent, East Lothian. Planter in North Carolina.
                                                (Pr 29.3.1798SC)

COCHRAN JAMES GOULD
Born in Scotland. Planter in Horry, SC. Died 15 August 1830.
                                                (WI 15.9.1830)

COLQUHOUN ANGUS
Born in Scotland. Emigrated to America during 1790.
Settled in SC during 1805. Nat. 5.11.1806 Marlborough, SC.
                                                (SCA)

COLQUHOUN ARCHIBALD
Son of James Colquhoun, Provost of Dunbarton. Died in
Washington, NC, on 7 August 1786.   (SM 48 518)

COLQUHOUN ARCHIBALD
Born in Scotland(?) during 1768. Emigrated to America
in 1802. Farmer in Richmond County, NC, with a wife and
two children in 1812.   (1812)

COLQUHOUN ARCHIBALD
Born in Scotland(?) during 1769. Emigrated to America in
1791. Farmer in Richmond County, NC, with a wife and three
children in 1812.   (1812)

COLQUHOUN DUNCAN
Born in Scotland(?) during 1760. Emigrated to America in
1790. A cooper in Richmond County, NC, with a wife and six
children in 1812.   (1812)

COLQUHOUN DUNCAN
Born in Scotland(?) during 1764. Emigrated to America in
1790. Settled in Richmond County, NC, by 1812, with a wife
and eight children.   (1812)

COLVIN ALEXANDER
Emigrated from Scotland to Brunswick, NC, in September 1739.
                                                            (VOS)

CONNOLLY MARY
Emigrated from Scotland or Ireland to South Carolina on the
Pearl, master Walter Buchanan, in December 1767. Allocated
100 acres of land on 12 December 1767.   (OL)

CONNOR EDWARD
Emigrated from Scotland to Brunswick, NC, in September 1739.
                                                            (VOS)

COOK MARIA
50. Midwife. Born in Scotland. Beaufort County, SC.   (C)

COOK ROBERT
52. Miller. Born in Scotland. Keziah D 25. Born in SC.
John L 5 months. Born in SC. Edgefield County, SC.   (C)

COOPER BARBARA
Emigrated from Scotland or Ireland to South Carolina on the
Pearl, master Walter Buchanan, in December 1767. Allocated
a land grant of 100 acres on 12 December 1767.   (OL)

COOPER CHRISTIAN
35. Born in Scotland. MC 16. Born in SC. MK 14. Born in SC.
Georgetown County, SC.   (C)

48

COOPER JAMES
Born in Scotland c1787. Carpenter. Emigrated from Greenock,
Renfrewshire, to Virginia. Settled in Granville County, NC,
during 1802. James Cooper 60. Farmer. Born in Scotland.
Ann 50. Born in NC. Frances 17. Born in NC. Jane E 15.
Born in NC. Ellen 11. Born in NC. Granville County, NC.
(DNCB)(1812)(C)

COOPER PETER
Born in Scotland. Mariner. Nat. 25 March 1797 Charleston, SC.
(Nat Arch M.1183.1)

COOPER WILLIAM
Born in Tarbert, Argyllshire, during 1802. Emigrated from
Greenock, Renfrewshire, to Charleston, SC, in December 1821.
Nat. 9 March 1830 Marlborough, SC. (SCA)

CORBETT EDWARD
20. Merchant. Edinburgh. Emigrated from Greenock, Renfrewshire, to Charleston, SC, on the Countess, master R Eason
during October 1774. (PRO/T47.12)

CORBETT HENRY
Born in Edinburgh during 1795. Settled in Columbia, SC.
Nat. 18 November 1824 Charleston, SC. (Nat Arch M.1183.1)

CORMACK ALEXANDER
"Canteness" (Caithness?) Scotland. Tailor in Charleston, SC.
(Pr 8.10.1773SC)

CORNELL GEORGE
Jacobite soldier captured after the Siege of Preston,
Lancashire. Transported from Liverpool to South Carolina
on the Susannah, master Thomas Bromhall, 7 May 1716.(SPC)(CTB)

CORRIE ALEXANDER
Born in Galloway during 1776. Merchant. Nat. 20.9.1803
Charleston, SC. (Nat Arch M.1183.1)

CORRIE JOHN
Dumfries. Settled in South Carolina. (Pr 17.1.1791 SC)

CORRIE JOHN
Born in Scotland. Nat. 10 May 1803 Charleston, SC.
(inferior City Court W3.474)

CORRIE JOHN
Born in Scotland(?) during 1761. Emigrated to America in
1791. Farmer in Robeson County, NC, with a wife and four
children in 1812. (1812)

CORSTORPHIN JAMES
Born in Scotland. Son of Robert Corstorphin. Emigrated to
America. Settled in Halifax, NC. Married (1) ... Parents
of Nancy, Elizabeth, Owen, Datus, Thomas C., Joseph J.,
and James H. (2) Mary Powell. Parents of Sarah and William D.
Died during 1816.   (Corstorphin pp/G179/SHC/UNC)

CORSTORPHIN ROBERT
Born in Scotland. Son of Robert Corstorphin. Emigrated to
America. Settled in Halifax, NC. Married Drusilla Evans
prior to 1778. Parents of Robert, Joel, John, Marshall,
Elizabeth and Oney.   (Corstorphin pp/G179/SHC/UNC)

COTTERAL CATHERINE
Emigrated from Scotland or Ireland to South Carolina on the
Pearl, master Walter Buchanan in December 1767. Allocated a
land grant of 100 acres on 12 December 1767.   (OL)

COUSINS JOHN
Jacobite soldier captured after the Siege of Preston,
Lancashire. Transported from Liverpool to South Carolina
on the Susannah, master Thomas Bromhall, on 7 May 1716.
                                                    (SPC)(CTB)

COUTY JOHN
State Engineer, married Miss Jean Ewart, late of
Scotland, in Charleston, SC, on 17 March 1821.(RRw 19.3.1821)

COWAN JOHN T
Born c1798 son of John Cowan and his wife Rosanna Thomson,
Blairs, Kirkmabrick, Wigtonshire. Died in Charleston, SC,
on 12 July 1827.   (Wigton Gs)

CRABB ROBERT
Dundee, Angus. Merchant and planter in Amelia, SC.
Died on 4 December 1811.   (SRO/CC8/8/151)

CRAIG ARCHIBALD
Born in Scotland. Emigrated from Scotland to Charleston,
SC, on 15 June 1821 with his children Jane and James.
Nat. 15 April 1822 Laurens, SC.   (Laurens Court Roll 76)

CRAIG Captain DAVID
Born in Scotland during 1732. Married Elinor Johnston.
Parents of Margaret, Mary, William, Johnston, Isabel, John,
Elinor, David and Samuel. Died in NC during 1785.   (LOS)

SCOTS IN THE CAROLINAS

CRAIG ROBERT
Born in Greenock, Renfrewshire, during 1786. Mariner.
Nat. 19 March 1806 Charleston, SC.   (Nat Arch M.1183.1)

CRAIG THOMAS
Son of Archibald Craig, stonemason, Bracksich, Glasgow.
Settled in Charleston, SC.   (Pr 11.10.1799 SC)

COWSON WILLIAM
Jacobite soldier captured after the Siege of Preston,
Lancashire. Transported from Liverpool to South Carolina
on the Wakefield, master Thomas Beck, on 21 April 1716.
                                            (CTB)(SPC)

CRAWFORD DANIEL
Emigrated from Scotland to America. Allocated a 776 acre
land grant in Granville County, SC, on 12 August 1737.
Later settled in Charleston, SC.   (Pr 20.6.1760 SC)

CRAWFORD DAVID
Second son of William Crawford in Scotland. Merchant in
South Carolina c1737.   (Deed of Sale, Book t.381)

CRAWFORD GIDEON
Lanark. Covenanter. Prisoner in the Tolbooth of Edinburgh.
Warded there 20 June 1684. Banished to the Plantations on
2 July 1684. Transported from Leith to Carolina on 1 August
1684 by Robert Malloch, merchant in Edinburgh.   (PC)(ETR)

CRAWFORD JOHN
Born in Frenock(Greenock?) during 1769. Physician.
Nat. 20 September 1809 Charleston, SC.   (Nat Arch M.1183.1)

CRAWFORD ROBERT
50. Miller. Born in Scotland. Elizabeth 48. Born in Scotland.
Margaret 17. Born in SC. John 14. Born in SC. Thompson 12.
Born in SC. Caroline 9. Born in SC. Abbeville County, SC.(C)

CREIGHTON JAMES
Jacobite soldier captured after the Siege of Preston,
Lancashire. Transported from Liverpool to South Carolina
on the Susannah, master Thomas Bromhall, 7 May 1716.(SPC)(CTB)

CRICHTOUN JOHN
Kilpatrick on the Muir. Covenanter. Prisoner in the
Canongate Tolbooth. Banished to Carolina on 19 June 1684.
Transported from Leith to Carolina by Robert Malloch,
merchant burgess of Edinburgh, in August 1684.   (PC)

CRICHTON WILLIAM
Born in Scotland. In Charleston, SC, c1780.
                                        (SRO/RD4.230.876)

CROCKETT JAMES
Son of George Crockett, surgeon in Coupar Angus, Perthshire.
Doctor in South Carolina. Serviced as heir to his father on
18 May 1763. Died in Winyaw on 10 April 1765. George, his
nephew, son of David Wilson, merchant in Coupar Angus,
serviced as his heir on 11 October 1765.
                                        (SM 27 335)(SRO/SH)

CROCKETT JOHN
Jacobite soldier captured after the Siege of Preston,
Lancashire. Transported from Liverpool to South Carolina
on the Susannah, master Thomas Bromhall, on 7 May 1716.
                                        (SPC)(CTB)

CROCKETT JOHN
Son of Daniel Crockett in Scotland. Merchant in
Charleston, SC.   (Pr 23.11.1759 SC)

CROCKET WILLIAM
74. Saddler. Born in Scotland. Edgecombe County, NC.   (C)

CROFT DAVID
Jacobite soldier captured after the Siege of Preston,
Lancashire. Transported from Liverpool to South Carolina
on the Wakefield, master Thomas Beck, 21 April 1716.(CTB)(SPC)

CROMARTIE WILLIAM
Born in South Ronaldsay, Orkney Islands, on 1 May 1731.
Settled on South River, NC, during 1758. Married (1) ...
Stewart. Parents of William. (2) Ruhamah Doane in 1766.
Parents of James, Thankful, Elizabeth, Hannah, Alexander,
John, Margaret, Catherine, Jean, Peter, Ann and Mary.
Died on 21 September 1807. Buried in Cromarty Cemetery,
Garland, Bladen County, NC.   (INC12090)(WCF)(Bladen Gs)

CROW JOHN
Born in Dundee, Angus, c1788. Emigrated to America prior to
1816. Settled in NC during 1819. Nat. 12.1824 Cumberland
County, NC.   (NCA/CR.029.301.16)

CRUICKSHANKS GEORGE
Born in Rhynie, Aberdeenshire, during 1796. Emigrated
from Scotland to Quebec in July 1817. Settled in
Laurens County, SC, during 1818. Nat. 14 April 1819
Laurens County.   (Laurens Court Roll 60)

CRUIKSHANKS JAMES
Surgeon in Edinburgh, married Mary, daughter of William
Calder MD, Edisto Island, SC, in Dean, Bo'ness, West
Lothian, on 19 September 1823.   (S.388.624)

CRUIKSHANKS WILLIAM
Born in Morayshire during 1775. Emigrated from Scotland
to Charleston, SC, in 1793. Shoemaker. Nat. 15 August 1805
Charleston.   (Nat Arch M.1183.1)

CULBRETH ARCHIBALD
Born in Scotland(?) during 1752. Emigrated to America in
1792. Farmer in Robeson County, NC, with two children in
1812.   (1812)

CUMING ....
A trumpeter. Emigrated from Gourock, Renfrewshire, to
Port Royal, South Carolina, on the Carolina Merchant,
master Walter Gibson, on 21 July 1684.   (ECJ)

CUMMING ROBERT
Educated in Scotland. Episcopalian minister in SC from
1749 to 1750. Died in St Joseph's parish, SC, on
26 July 1750.   (CCVC)

CUNNINGHAM GEORGE
Jacobite soldier captured after the Siege of Preston,
Lancashire. Transported from Liverpool to South Carolina
on the Wakefield, master Thomas Beck, 21 April 1716.(SPC)(CTB)

CUNNINGHAM ROBERT
A Scottish soldier in Captain Sand's company - deserted
in Carolina during 1703.   (SPC)

CUNNINGHAM THOMAS
Emigrated from Scotland or Ireland to South Carolina on the
Pearl, master Walter Buchanan, in December 1767. Allocated
a land grant of 100 acres on 12 December 1767.   (OL)

CUPIT JAMES
Born in Scotland c1707. An indentured servant who
absconded from his master James Graeme in Charleston,
SC, during February 1737.   (SCGaz 5.2.1737)

CURRIE ANGUS
Born in Scotland during 1762. Emigrated to America in
1790. A farmer in Moore County, NC, with a wife and eight
children in 1812.   (1812)

CURRIE ANGUS
Born in Colonsay, Argyllshire, on 17 September 1770.
Emigrated from Scotland to America in 1791. A farmer
in Robeson County, NC, with a wife and five children in
1812.   (McEachern Gs)(1812)

CURRIE ARCHIBALD
Born in Scotland(?) during 1762. Emigrated to America
in 1791. A farmer in Moore County, NC, with a wife and
seven children in 1812.   (1812)

CURRY CATHERINE
59. Born in Scotland. Archibald 54. Farmer. Born in NC.
Sarah 52. Born in NC. Iredell County, NC.   (C)

CURRIE FLORAH
80. Born in Scotland. Nancy 60. Born in Scotland.
Robeson County, NC.   (C)

CURRIE Mrs FLORA
Born in Kintyre, Argyllshire, on 20 January 1774.
Emigrated from Scotland to America in 1775. Married
Angus Currie. Died in NC on 19 September 1834. Buried
in McEachern Cemetery, NC.   (McEachern Gs)

CURRIE JOHN
Born in Scotland(?) during 1780. Emigrated to America in
1805. A farmer in Robeson County, NC, with a wife and
three children in 1812.   (1812)

CURRIE JOHN
80. Farmer. Born in Scotland. Margaret 50. Born in NC.
Donald 46. Born in NC. Catherine 43. Born in NC.
Mary A. 39. Born in NC. Elsy 36. Born in NC. Benjamin
Warren 15. Born in NC. Bladen County, NC.   (C)

CURRIE JOHN
70. Born in Scotland. Isabella 80. Born in NC.
Robeson County, NC.   (C)

CURRIE LAUCHLEN
Born in Scotland(?) during 1771. Emigrated to America in
1791. A farmer in Moore County, NC, with a wife and four
children in 1812.   (1812)

CURRIE MALCOLM
Born in Islay, Argyllshire, on 20 August 1790. Died in
NC on 5 March 1866. Buried in Union Presbyterian Church,
Carthage, Moore County, NC.   (Moore Gs)

CURRIE MURDOCH
Born in Colonsay, Argyllshire, c1715, Died in NC during
1775. Buried in McEachern Cemetery, NC.   (McEachern Gs)

CUTHBERT GEORGE
Born in Scotland. Married Mary Grimball in St Helena's
parish church, Beaufort, SC, on 3 February 1754.
                                         (St Helena's OPR)

CUTHBERT JAMES
Born in Inverness during December 1716, son of John
Cuthbert of Castlehill and his wife Jane Hay. Settled
in Prince William's parish, SC. Married Mrs Mary Wigg,
a widow, in St Helena's parish church, Beaufort, SC, on
24 February 1758.   (St Helena's OPR)

CUTHBERT JAMES G
Born in Scotland(?) Nat. June 1814 Craven County, NC.
                                          (Craven Co Ct Rec)

CUTHBERT JOHN
Emigrated from Inverness, Scotland, to Georgia. Moved to
Carolina in August 1742.   (ESG)

CUTHBERT WILLIAM
Born in Scotland(?) Nat. 10 February 1823 Craven County, NC.
                                          (Craven Co Ct Rec)

CUTHILL JOHN
Born in Glasgow on 20 February 1782, son of Thomas Cuthill
and his wife Mary Cameron. Married Margaret McLachlan in
Glasgow during 1808. Emigrated from Glasgow to NC in 1811.
Father of Marion, Thomas, Thomas Hugh and three other sons.
                                                    (CCAI)

SCOTS IN THE CAROLINAS

CUTLAR ELIZABETH
74. Born in Scotland. Mrs AEDavis 52. Born in NC.
Horatio 11. Born in NC. Wilmington, New Hanover County. (C)

CUTTS CATHERINE
55. Born in Scotland. John 23. Labourer. Born in NC.
David 22. Labourer. Born in NC. Cumberland County, NC.   (C)

DABRALL WILSON
25. Jeweller. Scotland. Emigrated from London to
Carolina on the James in October 1774.   (PRO/T47.12)

DALGAIRNE ALEXANDER
Born in Scotland. Died in Wilmington, NC, on
6 October 1808.   (RR 20.10.1808)

DALGETTY ALEXANDER
Jacobite soldier captured after the Siege of Preston,
Lancashire. Transported from Liverpool to South Carolina
on the Susannah, master Thomas Bromhall, on 7 May 1716.
                                                  (CTB)(SPC)

DALLAS ALEXANDER
Born in Argyllshire during 1796. Emigrated from
Scotland to Wilmington, NC, on 10 November 1820.
Settled in Chesterfield, SC. Nat. 8.11.1825 SC. (Cit Bk 109)

DALLAS PETER
Born in Scotland(?) during 1752. Emigrated to America in
1791. A farmer in Robeson County, NC, with a wife and
nine children in 1812.   (1812)

DALRYMPLE ANN
Born in Scotland during 1766. Married Sion Harrington
possibly in Cumberland County, NC. Died in Moore County,
NC.   (INC60176)

DALRYMPLE ELIZABETH
81. Born in Scotland. Janet 49. Born in NC. Margaret 47.
Born in NC. Archibald 37. Farmer. Born in NC. Moore County,
NC.   (C)

DALRYMPLE JOHN
Second son of Sir John Dalrymple of Courland. Married
Martha (Watters?). Planter in Spring Garden, Brunswick
County, NC. A reduced captain in Sir William Pepperal's
Regiment of Foot.   (Pr 8.10.1767 PCC)(NCA)(NCHGR.3)

DALRYMPLE JOHN
49. Farmer. With his wife Margaret Gordon 39, and their
children Mary 19, John 17, Archibald 15, James 11, Ann 9,
Janet 7, Jean 5, and William 2, emigrated from Stranraer,
Wigtonshire, to NC on the Jackie, master J Morris, during
May 1775. Died in Moore County, NC. (INC60176) (PRO/T47.12)

DALRYMPLE WILLIAM
Born in Scotland. 77. Farmer. Moore County, NC.   (C)

DALZIEL JOHN
Brother of the Earl of Darnworth. Jacobite in the 1715
Rebellion. Ordered to be transported to Virginia or
Carolina and to be set at liberty there, 21 June 1716. (SPC)

DALZIEL WILLIAM
Jacobite soldier captured after the Siege of Preston,
Lancashire. Transported from Liverpool to South Carolina
on the Susannah, master Thomas Bromhall, on 7 May 1716.
                                                      (SPC)(CTB)

DALZELL WILLIAM
25. Jeweller. Scotland. Emigrated from London to
Carolina on the James, master I Thompson, during
October 1774.   (PRO/T47.12)

DARRACH JENNY
Emigrated from Jura, Argyllshire, to America (probably)
on the General Wolfe, master J MacLean. Landed at Brunswick,
NC, on 4 November 1767. Allocated a 100 acre land grant in
Cumberland or Mecklenburg Counties, NC.(SCGaz.1671)(SHA.111)

DAVIDSON DONALD
Jacobite soldier captured after the Siege of Preston,
Lancashire. Transported from Liverpool to South Carolina
on the Susannah, master Thomas Bromhall, on 7 May 1716.
                                                      (SPC)(CTB)

DAVIDSON GILBERT
Born in Scotland c1760. Settled in SC before 1783. Nat.
20 March 1786. Died 5 June 1823.(Pendleton Messenger 25.6.1823)

DAVIDSON JOHN
Born in Scotland(?) Settled in Edenton,NC. Test.11.1773(NCA)

DAVIDSON WILLIAM
52. Planter. Born in Scotland. Julia E. 32. Born in SC.
Charleston, SC.   (C)

DAWKINS EFFIE
60. Born in Scotland. Jesse 58. Farmer. Born in NC.
Sarah 27. Born in NC. John 25. Tailor. Born in NC.
Jane 23. Born in NC. Ann 5. Born in NC. Richmond County,
NC.   (C)

DAWSON WILLIAM
Born in East Lothian during 1718. Educated at the
University of St Andrews. Episcopalian minister in SC
from 1765 to 1767. Died on St John's Island, SC, on
19 January 1767.   (CCVC)

DEANE JOHN
Emigrated from Glasgow to South Carolina during 1723.
Minister in James Island, SC. Died in April 1726.   (F)(APC)

DEANS ROBERT
Scottish joiner settled in South Carolina 1750 (Advert)
                                                       (SCGaz 29.1.1750)

DEAS DAVID
Born during 1722 son of David Deas, shipmaster in Leith,
and his wife Catherine Dundas. Emigrated to Carolina on
1 May 1738. Merchant in Charleston, SC. Admitted a
Burgess and Gildsbrother of Edinburgh on 21 November 1764
by right of his father, gratis. Died in Charleston, SC,
on 29 August 1775.   (REB)(HGP)(SM 37.637)

DEAS JOHN
Born in 1735 son of David Deas, shipmaster in Leith, and
his wife Catherine Dundas. Emigrated to South Carolina on
28 January 1749. Admitted a Burgess and Gildsbrother of
Edinburgh on 18 October 1769. Died in Charleston, SC, on
30 September 1790. Pr.26 November 1790 SC.
                                          (REB)(SM 52.517)(HGP)

DEAS JOHN
Son of John Deas. Died in Charleston, SC, on 24 October 1790.
                                                       (SM 52.519)

DEAS WILLIAM
Landscape painter in SC, admitted Burgess and Gildsbrother
of Edinburgh, gratis, 18 October 1769.   (REB)

SCOTS IN THE CAROLINAS

DEMPSTER GEORGE
Born in Scotland. A cooper. An indentured servant who
absconded from his master J Fraser in Charleston, SC,
during June 1734.   (SCGaz 22.6.1734)

DENNISON JAMES
Orkney Islands. Mariner. Nat.12 December 1796
Charleston, SC.   (Nat Arch M.1183.1)

DEWARS ALEXANDER
Prisoner. Transported to America as an indentured servant
on the brigantine John and Robert, master Thomas Clark,
from Glasgow. Landed in SC on 22 July 1730. Bail bond by
Robert Paterson dated 2 October 1728.   (SRO/JC.27)

DICK ALEXANDER
Son of George Dick, Airth, Stirlingshire. Died in SC
before 1742.   (SCHGM 4.287)

DICK JAMES
50. Engineer. Born in Scotland. Horry County, SC.   (C)

DICK JOHN
A runaway from the snow Nancy of Burntisland, master
Alexander Ritchie, during December 1753. (SCGaz 24.12.1753)

DICK MARY
Daughter of George Dick, surgeon in Carolina, Serviced as
Heir to her great grandfather George Campbell of Croonan,
Scotland, on 29 July 1796.   (SRO/SH)

DICKSON JOHN
Probably born in Scotland, son of James Dickson and his
wife Jennett Dixon. Settled in Dobbs County, NC.
Testament dated 16 April 1769.   (NCA)

DICKSON THOMAS
Born in Scotland. Settled in Wilkes County, NC. Died in
Ashe County, NC, c1809.   (INC60187)

DIRKIE MARY
Emigrated from Scotland or Ireland to South Carolina on the
Pearl, master Walter Buchanan, during December 1767.
Allocated a land grant of 100 acres on 12 December 1767.(OL)

DOCTOR DAVID
Jacobite soldier captured after the Siege of Preston,
Lancashire. Transported from Liverpool to South Carolina
on the Susannah, master Thomas Bromhall, on 7 May 1716.
                                              (SPC)(CTB)

DON ALEXANDER
Born in Scotland c1757. Settled in Charleston, SC,
c1814. Died 19 May 1824. Buried in St Michael's
Cemetery, Charleston, SC.   (St Michael's Gs)

DOUGAL MARGARET
Emigrated from Scotland or Ireland to South Carolina on the
Pearl, master Walter Buchanan, during December 1767.
Allocated a 100 acre land grant on 12 December 1767.   (OL)

DOUGALL WILLIAM
Born in Paisley, Renfrewshire, c1796. Merchant in
Wilmington, NC. Died on 9 April 1837. Buried in
St James's Cemetery, Wilmington.   (Wilmington Gs)

DOUGLAS ALEXANDER
22. Husbandman. Born in Scotland. Emigrated from London
to Carolina on the Briton, master A Urquhart, during
November 1774.   (PRO/T47.12)

DOUGLAS ALEXANDER
46. Farmer. Born in Scotland. Catherine 46. Born in NC.
Hugh 14. Born in NC. Mary E 11. Born in NC. Archibald 9.
Born in NC. Sarah 11. Born in NC. Poston Nancy 55. Born
in NC. Chesterfield County, SC.   (C)

DOUGLAS ANGUS
Born in Scotland during 1759. Died in Richmond County, NC,
during 1819.   (INC12019)

DOUGLAS ANTHONY
42. Merchant. Born in Scotland. Kershaw County, SC.   (C)

DOUGLAS ARCHIBALD
Scottish Highlander. Settled in New Hanover and Bladen
Counties, NC. Allocated land grants during June 1740. (HSNC)

DOUGLAS CAMPBELL
Born in Kirkcudbrightshire during 1782. Grocer in
Charleston, NC. Nat. 19 October 1813 Charleston, SC.
                                        (Nat Arch M.1183.1)

DOUGLAS CAMPBELL
69. Accountant. Born in Scotland. Charleston, SC.   (C)

DOUGLAS DANIEL
Born in Scotland c1735. Married Effie McLean. Died in
Richmond County, NC, in 1816.   (INC)

DOUGLAS JAMES
Born in Galloway during 1772. Mariner. Nat. 10 December
1804 Charleston, SC.   (Nat Arch M.1183.1)

DOUGLAS JAMES
Born in the Lothians during 1776. Turner. Nat.16 October
1805 Charleston, SC.   (Nat Arch M.1183.1)

DOUGLAS JAMES KENNEDY
Born in Scotland. Nat.14 May 1804 Charleston, SC.
                                            (Misc Rec U3.48)

DOUGLAS JOHN
60. Carpenter. Born in Scotland. Marion County, SC.   (C)

DOUGLAS JOHN
Born near Edinburgh during 1773. Cabinetmaker. Nat.
24 September 1802 Charleston, SC.   (Nat Arch M.1183.1)

DOUGLAS JOHN
Born in Scotland. Emigrated to America during 1788.
Settled in SC during 1790. Nat.4 November 1806
Marlborough, SC.   (SCA)

DOUGLAS JOHN
Born in Edinburgh. Nat.29 December 1799 SC.(Misc Rec Q3.270)

DOUGLAS JOHN
50. Coachbuilder. Born in Scotland. Rachael 50. Born in NC.
Elizabeth 19. Born in Marion County, SC. Marion County, SC(C)

DOVE CATHERINE
74. Born in Scotland. Darlington County, SC.   (C)

DOW G.
Son of Archibald Dow, Stirling. Emigrated to Charleston, SC,
on the Friendship, Captain Rattray, during 1755. Sought via
an advertisement in 1759.   (SCGaz 24.3.1759)

DOWNES JEREMIAH
Clyde, Scotland. Mariner. Nat.24.3.1796 Charleston, SC.
                                            (Nat Arch M.1183.1)

SCOTS IN THE CAROLINAS

DOWNY CHRISTIAN
25. Spinner. Glen Orchy, Argyllshire. Emigrated from
Scotland to Wilmington, NC, on the Jupiter of Larne,
master Samuel Brown, in September 1775.   (PRO/T47.12)

DOWNIE ROBERT
60. Born in Scotland. Charleston, SC.   (C)

DRUMMOND JOHN
Cooper in Leith. Emigrated from Kirkcaldy, Fife, to
Brunswick, NC, on the Jamaica Packet, Captain Smith
in June 1775.   (PRO/T47.12)

DRUMMOND JOHN
Born in Stirling during 1800. Settled in Charleston, SC.
Nat.17 October 1825 Charleston, SC. A shoemaker in
Charleston in 1850.   (Nat Arch M.1183.1)(C)

DRUMMOND WILLIAM
Born in Scotland. Settled in Virginia. Married Sarah ..
Appointed Governor of Albemarle, NC, in October 1664.
Executed in Virginia during 1677 for his part in
Bacon's Rebellion. Pr. October 1677 PCC.   (HSNC)(HGP)

DUFF DONALD
Jacobite soldier captured after the Siege of Preston,
Lancashire. Transported from Liverpool to South Carolina
on the Susannah, master Thomas Bromhall, on 7 May 1716.
                                                       (SPC)

DUFF JOHN
20. Herdsman. New Luce, Wigtonshire. Emigrated from
Stranraer, Wigtonshire, to North Carolina on the Jackie,
master J Morris, in May 1775.   (PRO/T47.12)

DUFF THOMAS
Jacobite soldier captured after the Siege of Preston,
Lancashire. Transported from Liverpool to South Carolina
on the Susannah, master Thomas Bromhall, on 7 May 1716.
                                                  (SPC)(CTB)

DUFFUS ALEXANDER
Born in Morayshire during 1783. Merchant. Nat.15 November
1806 Charleston, SC.   (Nat Arch M.1183.1)

SCOTS IN THE CAROLINAS

DUNCAN ALEXANDER
Probably from Edinburgh. Merchant in the firm of Duncan,
Schaw and Sutherland, Wilmington, NC. Died in Wilmington
during 1767.   (NCA)(St James OPR)

DUNCAN DAVID
Emigrated from Scotland or Ireland to South Carolina on the
Pearl, master Walter Buchanan, in December 1767. Allocated
a 100 acre land grant on 12 December 1767.   (OL)

DUNCAN GEORGE
Born in Dundee during 1770. Mariner. Nat.17 June 1799
Charleston, SC.   (Nat Arch M1183.1)

DUNCAN JAMES
27. Farmer. Emigrated from Moudlein, Farr, Sutherland,
with his wife and two children to Wilmington, NC, on the
Bachelor of Leith during April 1774.   (PRO/T47.12)

DUNCAN JOHN
Born in Aberdeen. Settled at Duncan's Creek, Laurens
County, SC, during 1752.   (SCHGM.49.225)

DUNCAN JOHN
Son of James Duncan (1736-1786) wright in Perth, and his
wife Anne Simpson (1747-1829) Emigrated to America. Died
in Charleston, SC.   (Perth Greyfriars Gs)

DUNCAN WILLIAM
Born in Scotland c1744. Married (2) Patsy West during 1779
in NC. Resident of Chatham County.   (INC05065)

DUNDEE DAVID
Born in Scotland. An indentured servant who absconded from
his master Charles Shepherd in SC during November 1744.
                                            (SCGaz 30.1.1744)

DUNLOP ALEXANDER
Son of James Dunlop and his wife Eliza Cunningham, Dunlop,
Ayrshire. Covenanter. Married Antonia Brown of Fordell in
1667. Father of John, Mary, Anna, Robert, Margaret and
Francis. Fought at the Battle of Bothwell Bridge in 1679.
Prisoner in 1683. Emigrated to Carolina during 1684.
Sheriff in Carolina in 1686. Died during 1696.
                                            (MdHS/MS316)(DD)

DUNLOP JAMES
Jacobite soldier captured after the Siege of Preston,
Lancashire. Emigrated from Liverpool to South Carolina
on the <u>Wakefield</u>, master Thomas Beck, on 21 April 1716.
(CTB)(SPC)

DUNLOP JESSE sr
Born in Edinburgh c1783. Emigrated, with his sons James
and Douglas, to America during 1805. Settled in NC.
Died in 1875.   (SG)

DUNLOP PATRICK
Born in Scotland. Cordwainer in Charleston, SC.(Pr22.5.1767SC)

DUNN JOHN
74. Farmer. Born in Scotland. Martha 61. Born in SC.
Charlotte 24. Born in SC. Francis 21. Farmer. Born in SC.
John 17. Born in SC. Horry County, SC.   (C)

DUNN MARY
Emigrated from Scotland or Ireland to South Carolina on the
Pearl, master Walter Buchanan, during December 1767.
Allocated a 100 acre land grant on 12 December 1767.   (OL)

DUNN WILLIAM
Born c1794. Brother of Henry Dunn, merchant in Wigton,
Scotland. Died in Halifax, NC, on 1 October 1818.(Wigton Gs)

DYSART GEORGE
Jacobite soldier captured after the Siege of Preston,
Lancashire. Transported from Liverpool to South Carolina
on the <u>Wakefield</u>, master Thomas Beck, on 21 April 1716.
(SPC)(CTB)

EASON ROBERT
Born in Scotland during 1779. Merchant. Nat.11.October
1804 Charleston, SC.   (Nat Arch M1183.1)

EASTERLEY JANE
48. Born in Scotland. Margaret 17. Born in SC. JL 20.
Clerk. Born in SC. Georgetown County, SC.   (C)

ECCLES WILLIAM
40. Shoemaker. Emigrated, with his wife Martha McKenzie 45
and son John 12,from Inch via Stranraer, Wigtonshire, to
NC on the <u>Jackie</u>, master J Morris, during May 1775.
(PRO/T47.12)

EDGAR JAMES
Born in Dumfries during 1782. Mariner. Nat.7 May 1805
Charleston, SC.   (Nat Arch M1183.1)

EDMUND JAMES
Born in Glasgow. Settled in Camden, SC. Nat.20 November
1817 SC.   (Cit. Book 76)

EDMUNSTON CHARLES
Born in Lerwick, Shetland Islands, on 20 June 1782, son
of Laurence Edmunston, surgeon. Emigrated to Charleston,
SC, on 25 August 1799. Married Mary Pratt in 1810. Died
1872. Nat. 26 March 1810 Charleston, SC.
Charles Edmunston 68. Merchant. Born in Scotland. Mary 61.
Born in SC. Laurence 36. Merchant. Born in SC. Charles 34.
Merchant. Born in SC. Jesse 29. Born in SC. Patrick 31.
Born in SC. Elizabeth P. 27. Born in SC. Caroline K. 25.
Born in SC. Thomas 24. Born in SC. Isabella 21. Born in
SC. James 19. Clerk. Born in SC. Robert 18. Clerk. Born
in SC. Henry 17. Clerk. Born in SC. Charleston, SC.
                            (ZFH)(Nat Arch M1183.1)(C)

EDWARD JAMES
Greenock, Renfrewshire. Covenanter. Prisoner in the Tolbooth
of Edinburgh. Warded there on 2 July 1684. Banished to
Carolina on 2 July 1684. Transported to Carolina by Robert
Malloch, merchant in Edinburgh, on 1 August 1684. (PC)(ETR)

EGGOE JOHN
Jacobite soldier captured after the Siege of Preston,
Lancashire. Transported from Liverpool to South Carolina
on the Susannah, master Thomas Bromhall, on 7 May 1716.
                                              (CTB)(SPC)

EGGOE WILLIAM
Jacobite soldier captured after the Siege of Preston,
Lancashire. Transported from Liverpool to South Carolina
on the Susannah, master Thomas Bromhall, on 7 May 1716.
                                              (CTB)(SPC)

ELDER JAMES
Born in West Linton, Peebles-shire, during 1782. Tanner
in Charleston-neck. Nat.6 October 1830 Charleston, SC.
                                     (Nat Arch M1183.1)

ELLIOT CHARLES
Son of Sir Gilbert Elliot of Stobs. Attorney General of NC.
Died in Newham, NC, on 2 October 1756.   (SM 18.627)

65

ELLIOT GEORGE
Born in Dumfries during 1747, son of Henry Elliot of
Peel and his wife Jean. Educated at the University of
Edinburgh. Emigrated to America c1767. Settled at Elderslie,
Little Lower River, Cumberland County, NC. Married Mary
Smith on 4 April 1790. Parents of Henry, Alexander, George
and John. Timber merchant and politician. Died 1 November
1807. (E)(SFV)

ELTON WILLIAM
Born in Scotland. Saddler. 46. Warren County,NC. (C)

EMOND THOMAS
Edinburgh. Silversmith. Presbyterian. Settled in
Petersburg, Virginia, before 1802. Silversmith in
Raleigh, NC, from 1806 to 1821. (SNC)

EVANS MARY
80. Born in Scotland. Angus 56. Born in NC. Margaret 56.
Born in NC. Mary 25. Born in NC. Margaret 21. Born in NC.
Elizabeth 19. Born in NC. John 20. Born in NC. Robeson
County, NC. (C)

EWART Miss JEAN
Late of Scotland, married John Couty, State Engineer, in
Charleston, SC, on 17 March 1821. (RRw 19.3.1821)

EWART THOMAS
Son of David Ewart, Deputy Clerk of Chancery, apprenticed
to Sir Henry Jardine. Admitted to the Society of Writers
to HM Signet on 21 November 1815. Married 16 September
1828 Alicia, daughter of Thomas Yourstoun, Chamberlain to
the Duke of Queensberry. Struck off the Roll 15 February 1830.
Died in Charleston, SC, 6 March 1831. (WS)

EWING DANIEL
Youngest son of Thomas Ewing, Keppoch, Inverness-shire.
Died in Charleston, SC, on 23 August 1807. (SM 69.958)

EWING JOHN
Born in Scotland. Tavern keeper near Charleston, SC.
Advertisement in 1753. (SCGaz 30.4.1753)

FAICHNEY ANN
Perthshire. Wife of John Blair. Died in SC c1797.
(SRO/CC8/8/130.2)

FAIRLY ALEXANDER
Born in Argyllshire during 1753. Died 25 December 1827
in NC. Buried in the Alexander Fairly Cemetery, NC.
(Fairly Gs)

FAIRLY FLORA
49. Born in Scotland. Angus 64. Born in NC. Angus McQueen
70. Farmer. Born in Scotland. Richmond County, NC. (C)

FAIRWEATHER ROBERT
Dundee. Barber in Charleston, SC. (Pr 1.7.1763 SC)

FALCONER ALEXANDER
Born in St Andrews, Fife. Died at The Glebe, Franklin
County, NC, on 17 March 1818. (RR)

FARQUHAR ROBERT
Son of John and Elizabeth Farquhar in Aberdeen. Merchant
in Charleston, SC. Nat. 24 January 1783. (Pr 17.2.1784 SC)

FARQUHAR ROBERT
Born in Scotland. Mariner. Nat.1 September 1795
Charleston, SC. (Nat Arch M1183.1)

FARQUHARSON JAMES
Son of Barbara Farquharson, White House of Cromarty,
Aberdeenshire. Settled in SC. (Pr 1.12.1780 SC)

FERGUS JAMES
Scottish Highlander settled in New Hanover County, NC.
Allocated a land grant in June 1740. (HSNC)

FERGUS JOHN
Born before 1758 in Scotland. Doctor. Settled in NC.
Died during 1802. (SA)

FERGUSON CHARLES
49. Mechanic. Born in Scotland. Barnwell County, SC. (C)

FERGUSON DANIEL
Born in Scotland. Nat.10 October 1826.SC.(Circuit Ct Jl 9.436)

FERGUSON DANIEL
55. Farmer. Born in Scotland. Janet 47. Born in NC.
Murdoch 23. Carpenter. Born in NC. Daniel 19. Farmer.
Born in NC. Mary A. 17. Born in NC. Margaret 14. Born in
NC. Neill 12. Born in NC. John 6. Born in NC. Elizabeth 5.
Born in NC. Moore County, NC. (C)

FERGUSON DUNCAN
Covenanter. Prisoner in Edinburgh Tolbooth. Banished to
the Plantations in Carolina. Transported there by Robert
Malloch, merchant in Edinburgh, on 5 August 1684. (ETR)(PC)

FERGUSON DUNCAN
Born in Dalmany, Glen Orchy, Argyllshire, during 1767.
Married Isabella McNab in Argyllshire. Settled in NC
during 1793. Father of Adam (1796-1862) Died in 1808. (BAF)

FERGUSON FINLAY
Jacobite soldier captured after the Siege of Preston,
Lancashire. Transported from Liverpool to South Carolina
on the Wakefield, master Thomas Beck, on 21 May 1716.
(SPC)(CTB)

FERGUSON HUGH W.
Born in Rogart, Sutherland. Nat.22 February 1822 SC.
(Circuit Ct Jl 9.220)

FERGUSON JAMES
Emigrated from Scotland to America. Settled in SC
during 1700. Married Mrs Skipper, a widow from
Barbados. (AABB)

FERGUSON JOHN
19. Workman. Kintyre, Argyllshire. Emigrated from Greenock,
Renfrewshire, to Wilmington, NC, on the Ulysses, master
J Chalmers, during August 1774. (PRO/T47.12)

FERGUSON JOHN
Born in Sutherland during 1787. Tailor in Charleston, SC.
Nat. 17 November 1813 Charleston. (Nat Arch M1183.1)

FERGUSON JOHN
Born in Perthshire during 1794. Nat.June 1821 Cumberland
County, NC. (Cumb Co Ct Rec)

FERGUSON JOHN
Born in Scotland. Died in Plymouth NC on 8 September 1826.
(RRw 29.9.1826)

FERGUSON JOHN
Born in Scotland during 1793. Died in NC February 1865.
Buried in McDonald Cemetery, NC. (McDonald Gs)

FERGUSON MURDO
Born in Scotland(?) during 1756. Emigrated to America
in 1803. A farmer in Moore County, NC, with a wife and
eight children in 1812.   (1812)

FERGUSON NEILL
49. Farmer. Born in Scotland. Catherine 49. Born in
Scotland. Murdoch 19. Born in NC. Mary 15. Born in NC.
Catherine 14. Born in NC. Flora 12. Born in NC. Daniel
9. Born in NC. Nancy 7. Born in NC. Rachael 3. Born in NC.
Bladen County, NC.   (C)

FERGUSON ROBERT
Born in Scotland c1700. Married Sarah ... Died in NC
during 1794.   (INC28505)

FERGUSON WALTER
Born in Scotland during 1763. Doctor in Edenton, NC.
Serviced as Heir to his brother William Ferguson of
Troston, Scotland, on 31 May 1788. Died in 1789.(SRO/SH)(SA)

FIFE JAMES
35. Merchant. Renfrewshire. Emigrated from Greenock,
Renfrewshire, to Charleston, SC, on the Countess,
master R Eason, during October 1774.   (PRO/T47.12)

FIFE JAMES
Haddington, East Lothian. Died in Charleston, SC, on
18 December 1804.   (SM 67.565)

FINCH Mrs ISABELLA
Probably born in Scotland. Died in Charleston, SC.
                                                 (Pr 28.8.1761 SC)

FINDLATER WILLIAM
Born in Stonehaven, Kincardineshire. Mariner.
Nat.18 November 1796 Charleston, SC.   (Nat Arch M1183.1)

FINDLAY ALEXANDER
Aberdeen. Settled in St Stephen's parish, SC.(Pr 17.1.1784SC)

FINDLAYSON ANGUS
60. Farmer. Born in Scotland. Catherine 58. Born in Scotland.
Christian A. 28. Born in NC. Mary 26. Born in NC. Alexander
24. Farmer. Born in NC. Margaret 22. Born in NC. Malcolm 20.
Labourer. Born in NC. Catherine 16. Born in NC. Cumberland
County, NC.   (C)

SCOTS IN THE CAROLINAS

FINLAYSON MARY
Born in Scotland during 1769. Married James Hogg.
Died in Orange County, NC, during 1817.   (INC28605)

FISHER ARCHIBALD
Born in Hulmechal, Glasreugh, (Glassary?), Argyllshire.
Died in Bladen County, NC, on 25 September 1820.
Buried in Brown Marsh Presbyterian Church Cemetery, NC.
                                              (Brown Marsh Gs)

FISHER DANIEL
Son of Margaret Fisher, Inveraray, Argyllshire. Settled
in St Bartholemew's parish, Colleton County, SC.
                                              (Pr 1.12.1791 SC)

FISHER EBENEZER
Born during 1739, son of Professor James Fisher, University
of Glasgow, and Jean Turpie, Erskine. Emigrated from
Scotland to America. Died in New Berne, NC, in 1767.   (EHG)

FISHER PETER
Glasgow. Merchant. Nat.11.December 1798 SC. (Fed.Ct.L3.321)

FLEMING DAVID
Glasgow. Merchant. Died in Charleston, SC, on 31 August 1809.
                                              (SM 72.77)

FLEMING JOHN
Stenhouse, Stirlingshire. Covenanter. Prisoner in Canongate
or Edinburgh Tolbooths. Banished to the Plantations on
2 July 1684. Transported from Leith to Carolina in August
1684 by Robert Malloch, merchant in Edinburgh.   (PC)

FLEMING JOHN
Born in Glasgow. Nat. 19 February 1810 SC.(Circuit Ct Jl 10.45)

FLETCHER ANGUS
46. Farmer. Glen Orchy, Argyllshire. Emigrated from Greenock,
Renfrewshire, with his wife Katherine McIntyre and children
Euphane 10, Mary 6, and Nancy 3, to Wilmington, NC, on the
Ulysses, master J Chalmers, in August 1774.   (PRO/T47.12)

FLINT JAMES
Jacobite soldier captured after the Siege of Preston,
Lancashire. transported from Liverpool to South Carolina
on the Wakefield, master Thomas Beck, on 21 May 1716.
                                              (SPC)(CTB)

FORBES ALEXANDER
Born in Peterhead, Aberdeenshire, during 1783. Merchant.
Nat. 14 December 1807 Charleston, SC.   (Nat Arch M1183.1)

FORBES GEORGE
Jacobite soldier captured after the Siege of Preston,
Lancashire. Transported from Liverpool to South Carolina
on the Susannah, master Thomas Bromhall, on 7 May 1716.
                                                  (CTB)(SPC)

FORBES GEORGE
Aberdeen. Planter in St Anne's County, Jamaica. Died in
Charleston, SC, during June 1781.   (APB)

FORBES HUGH
Born in Scotland. An indentured servant who absconded from
his master J Fraser in Charleston, SC, in June 1734.
                                             (SCGaz 22.6.1734)

FORBES JEAN
Wife of Ludovick Grant of Culnakyle. Died in Charleston,
SC, during June 1781.   (APB)

FORBES WILLIAM
Born in Scotland. Allocated a land grant on the Cape Fear
River, NC, in 1733.   (SO)(HSNC)

FORDYCE WILLIAM DINGWALL
Born in Aberdeen on 22 September 1798, second son of
William Dingwall Fordyce and his wife Margaret Ritchie.
Merchant. Died in Charleston, SC, on 13 April 1839.   (SAA)

FORREST Rev JOHN
57. Born in Scotland. Jane 40. Born in SC. John 12.
Born in SC. CHarleston, SC.   (C)

FORSTER MARY
55. Born in Scotland. William 50. Born in SC. Marcilla 18.
Born in SC. Delilah 16. Born in NC. MalindaC. 12. Born in
Tennessee. Buncombe County, NC.   (C)

FORSYTH BEZABEER
22. Gentleman. Scotland. Emigrated from London to Carolina
on the James, master I Thompson, in October 1774.(PRO/T47.12)

FORSYTH JOHN A.
Born in Scotland. Nephew of Thomas Reid, lawyer in
Aberdeen. Merchant in Statesville, Iredell County, NC,
from 1818 to 1864. (DU)

FOTHERINGHAM JOHN
Jacobite soldier captured after the Siege of Preston,
Lancashire. Transported from Liverpool to South Carolina
on the Susannah, master Thomas Bromhall, on 7 May 1716.
(SPC)(CTB)

FOWLER JOHN
Born in Scotland. Nat.13 June 1799 Charleston, SC.
(Ct of Common PLeas M3.140)

FRANCIS MICHAEL
48. Farmer. Born in Scotland. Ericana 38. Born in NC.
Furdesia 19. Student. Born in NC. Acaine 15. Born in NC.
Mary 9. Born in NC. Haywood County, NC. (C)

FRANKILL SALLY M.
70. Born in Scotland. Archibald McRae 40. Born in NC.
Mary 35. Born in NC. Malcolm 10. Born in NC. Anny 8.
Born in NC. Sarah 7. Born in NC. Norman 5. Born in NC.
Daniel 2. Born in NC. Robeson County, NC. (C)

FRASER ALEXANDER
Emigrated from Scotland to America. Merchant in
Charleston, SC, and Goose Creek, SC. Father of William.
Late eighteenth century. (SA)

FRASER ALEXANDER
Born in Montrose, Angus, during 1760. Mariner.
Nat. 24 January 1792 Charleston, SC. (Nat Arch M1183.1)

FRAZER DUNCAN
Jacobite soldier captured after the Siege of Preston,
Lancashire. Transported from Liverpool to South Carolina
on the Susannah, master Thomas Bromhall, on 7 May 1716.
(SPC)(CTB)

FRAZER HUGH
Jacobite soldier captured after the Siege of Preston,
Lancashire. Transported from Liverpool to South Carolina
on the Susannah, master Thomas Bromhall, on 7 May 1716.
(CTB)(SPC)

FRASER Rev HUGH
Born in Scotland during 1763. Rector of All Saints,
Waccamaw, SC. Died in November 1838.   (Waccamaw Gs)

FRASER HUGH
Born in Morayshire during 1769. Professor of Divinity
in Georgetown, SC. Nat.21 February 1817 Charleston, SC.
                                         (Nat Arch M1183.1)

FRASER JOHN
Born in Wigton. Emigrated to Carolina in 1700. Indian trader
at Coosawhatchie. Married Judith Warner. Father of
Alexander, Judith, Susan and Ann. Died in Charleston, SC,
on 14 January 1754.   (SCGen.1983)

FRASER JOHN
Jacobite soldier captured after the Siege of Preston,
Lancashire. Transported from Liverpool to South Carolina
on the Wakefield, master Thomas Beck, on 21 May 1716.
                                         (CTB)(SPC)

FRASER JOHN
Born in Inverness during 1769. Merchant. Nat. 16 March
1807 Charleston, SC.   (Nat Arch M1183.1)

FRASER JOHN
Born in Inverness during 1785. Merchant. Nat.26 February
1810 Charleston, SC.   (Nat Arch M1183.1)

FRASER JOHN
70. Merchant. Born in Scotland. Clara 17. Born in SC.
Charleston, SC.   (C)

FRASER JOSEPH
Born in Stirling. Nat.17 August 1838 Craven County, NC.
                                         (Craven Co Rec)

FRASER MALCOLM
66. Farmer. Born in Scotland. Isabel 64. Born in Scotland.
Daniel 35. Farmer. Born in Scotland. Lydia 34. Born in NC.
Alexander 30. Physician. Born in NC. Moore County, NC. (C)

FRAZER WILLIAM
Jacobite soldier captured after the Siege of Preston,
Lancashire. Transported from Liverpool to South Carolina
on the Susannah, master Thomas Bromhall, on 7 May 1716.
                                         (SPC)

SCOTS IN THE CAROLINAS

FRASHIER CATHERINE
75. Born in Scotland. William 44. Born in Scotland.
Angus 42. Born in Scotland. Robeson County, NC.   (C)

FULLARTON ALEXANDER
Born in Scotland during 1806. Emigrated to Philadelphia,
Pennsylvania, during 1823. Settled in Charleston, SC,
in 1827. Nat.9 October 1832 Charleston, SC.   (SCA)

FULLARTON Miss C
Daughter of Alexander Fullarton, land surveyor in Perth,
married Robert Bowden, SC, in Ellisbank, Glasgow, on
1 February 1802.   (SM 64.181)

FULLARTON GEORGE
Ayrshire. Merchant in Charleston, SC.(Pr 3.1.1709 SC)
                    (Pr 9.1709 PCC)(Admin Act Book 1691f91)

FULLARTON JAMES
Born in Rothesay, Bute, during 1774. Mariner. Nat. 14 June 1799
Charleston, SC.   (Nat Arch M1183.1)

FYFFE ALEXANDER
Dron, by Dundee, Angus. Emigrated from Scotland to America.
Settled in South Carolina during the 1750s. Merchant and
Planter.   (SA)

FYFFE DAVID
Dron, by Dundee, Angus. Emigrated from Scotland to America.
Settled in SC during 1750s. Merchant and planter.   (SA)

FYFFE WILLIAM
Dron, by Dundee, Angus. Emigrated from Scotland to America.
Settled in SC during 1750s. Planter and merchant.   (SA)

GAIRDNER JOHN
Servant to James Ralston in Wester Harieburn. Covenanter.
Prisoner in the Tolbooth of Edinburgh. Warded there on
2 July 1684. Banished to the Plantations 2 July 1684.
Transported from Leith to Carolina by Robert Malloch,
merchant in Edinburgh, on 1 August 1684.   (PC)(ETR)

GAIRNS JOHN
Carpenter in Dundee. Indentured for four years service with
John Rutherford and Company, merchants at Cape Fear, NC, at
their shipyards there, at Leith on 1 November 1752.
Possibly emigrated on the snow Grenadier from Leith to NC.
                                           (SRO/RD4.178.2)

GALBREATH ALEXANDER
50. Born in Scotland. Margaret 30. Born in NC.
Archibald J. 10. Born in NC. Florah 8. Born in NC.
Margaret J. 5. Born in NC. Alexander 2. Born in NC.
Robeson County, NC.   (C)

GALBREATH ANGUS
30. Workman. Glen Orchy, Argyllshire. Emigrated, with his
wife Katherine Brown 26, from Greenock, Renfrewshire, to
Wilmington, NC, on the Ulysses, master J Chalmers, in
August 1774.   (PRO/T47.12)

GALLOWAY CHARLES
Born in Scotland c1728. Emigrated to America. Married
Mary Spraggins, Halifax County, Virginia, on 15 May 1770.
Settled in Guilford County, NC. Merchant. Patriot.
Father of Mary Spraggins Galloway. Died in Rockingham
County, NC, in 1795.   (EF)

GALLOWAY JAMES
Born in Scotland c1742. Emigrated to America. Married
Elizabeth Spraggins. Settled in Guilford County, NC.
Father of James, Thomas S., and a daughter. Patriot and
politician. Died at Spring Garden, Rockingham County,
NC, during 1799.   (EF)

GALLOWAY ROBERT
Born in Scotland on 23 September 1750. Emigrated to
America in 1783. Married Mary Spraggins Galloway. Father
of Charles, Robert, Marian, Thomas S., Mary S., Rowlay
and Elizabeth. Merchant and tavern-owner in Wentworth,
Rockingham County, NC. Died on 9 July 1852 in Rockingham
County, NC.   (EF)

GAMBELL ADAM
Glasgow. Died in North Carolina pre 1709.
                                    (Albemarle Co ppCR2/501)

GANDY ...
73. Farmer. Born in Scotland. Darlington County, SC.   (C)

GARDEN ALEXANDER
Born in Edinburgh during 1685. Emigrated from Scotland to
America. Rector of the Episcopal Church of St Philip in
Charleston, SC, from 1719 to 1753. Bishop's Commissary in
SC from 1726 to 1748. Died on 21 September 1756. (SO)(CCVC)

GARDEN ALEXANDER
Son of Rev Garden, minister of Birse, Aberdeenshire.
Aberdeen Alumnus 1726. Educated in Aberdeen and Edinburgh.
Graduated MD in Aberdeen 2 November 1753. Physician in
Charleston, SC.   (MCA)

SCOTS IN THE CAROLINAS

GARDEN Dr FRANCIS
Physician. Graduated MD from the University of Edinburgh
in 1768. Died in Charleston, SC, during October 1770.
(SA)(SM 33.53)

GARDNER PATRICK
Jacobite soldier captured after the Siege of Preston,
Lancashire. Transported from Liverpool to South Carolina
on the Hockenhill, master H. Short, on 25 June 1716.   (SPC)

GARDNER WILLIAM
57. Mechanic. Born in Scotland. Isabel 50. Born in Scotland.
Mary 17. Born in SC. Alexander 13. Born in SC. Grace 10.
Born in SC. Kershaw County, SC.   (C)

GARDINER Mrs
Wife of John Gardiner, former tenant farmer in Pitcaithly,
Perthshire. Died in Charleston, SC, during December 1806.
(SM 69.638)

GARDYNE SAMUEL
Charleston, South Carolina, admitted a Burgess of Banff
during 1785.   (AOB)

GEDDIE JAMES DONALD
Born in Scotland c1755. Farmer and cooper. Emigrated to
Cape Fear, NC, during 1772. Married Catherine Isabella
McPhaill in NC. Died in Cumberland County, NC.(INC60061)(GMG)

GIBBONS ....
Merchant in Charleston, SC, admitted a Burgess and Gildsbrother of Glasgow, gratis, on 7 August 1724.   (GBG)

GIBSON ALEXANDER
68. Merchant. Born in Scotland. Adam 32. Born in SC.
Antonia 31. Born in SC. Annie 20. Born in SC. Weston 8.
Born in SC. Walter 5. Born in SC. Bentley 2. Born in SC.
Alexander Gibson. Born in Ayrshire during 1781. Emigrated
to America in 1805. Merchant in Charleston, SC, in 1812.
Nat.20 December 1821 Charleston, SC.(1812)(NatArch M1183.1)(C)

GIBSON DAVID
57. Farmer. Born in Scotland. Ann. Born in Marion County,
SC. Jesse 21. Farmer. Born in Marion County, SC. James 17.
Farmer. Born in Marion County, SC. Allen 14. Born in Marion
County, SC. Albert 11. Born in Marion County, SC. Robert 9.
Born in Marion County, SC. David 7. Born in Marion County,
SC. Oscar 6. Born in Marion County, SC. John 4. Born in
Marion County, SC. Marion County, SC.   (C)

GIBSON WILLIAM
Born in Moffat, Dumfriesshire. Merchant. Nat.2 January 1798
Charleston, SC.   (Nat Arch M1183.1)

GIEKIE JAMES
Born in Scotland during 1774. Doctor. Settled in NC.
Died in 1793.   (SA)

GILBERT ANN
Emigrated from Scotland or Ireland to South Carolina on the
Pearl, master Walter Buchanan in December 1767. Allocated
a 100 acre land grant on 12 December 1767.   (OL)

GILBERT JUNIAN
Emigrated from Scotland or Ireland to South Carolina on the
Pearl, master Walter Buchanan during December 1767. Allocated
a 100 acre land grant on 12 December 1767.   (OL)

GILCHRIST ANGUS
25. Kintyre, Argyllshire. Emigrated from Greenock, Renfrewshire, to Wilmington, NC, on the Ulysses, master J Chalmers,
during August 1774.   (PRO/T47.12)

GILCHRIST ISABELLA
60. Born in Scotland. Mary 50. Born in Scotland. Nancy
Campbell 59. Born in Scotland. Alexander Campbell 21. Born
in NC. Mary Campbell 20. Born in NC. George Campbell 10.
Born in NC. Moore County, NC.   (C)

GILCHRIST JAMES
60. Farmer. Born in Scotland. George 32. Farmer. Born in
Scotland. Catherine 30. Born in Scotland. Elizabeth 26.
Born in NC. Duncan Shaw 8. Born in NC. Moore County, NC. (C)

GILCHRIST JOHN
25. Cooper. Kintyre, Argyllshire. Emigrated, with his wife
Marion Taylor 21, from Greenock, Renfrewshire, to
Wilmington, NC, on the Ulysses, master J Chalmers, during
August 1774.   (PRO/T47.12)

GILCHRIST JOHN
Born in Kintyre, Argyllshire, during 1740. Married Effie
McMillan (1748-1794). Settled in Robeson County, NC, in
1770. Died during 1802.   (LRS)

GILCHRIST MARGARET
55. Born in Scotland. Moore County, NC.   (C)

GILCHRIST WILLIAM
Born in Scotland during 1802. Settled in Charleston, SC, on
5 June 1821. Nat.19 April 1825 SC.   (Laurens Court Roll 97)

GILL HENRY
Jacobite soldier captured after the Siege of Preston,
Lancashire. Transported from Liverpool to South Carolina
on the Susannah, master Thomas Bromhall on 7 May 1716. (SPC)

GILLIS ALEXANDER
Born in Scotland(?) during 1769. Emigrated to America in
1802. A farmer in Cumberland County, NC, with a wife and
four children in 1812.   (1812)

GILLIS ARCHIBALD
Born in Scotland(?) during 1749. Emigrated to America in
1788. A farmer in Moore County, NC, with a wife in 1812.
                                                          (1812)

GILLIS ARCHIBALD
Born in Scotland(?) during 1767. Emigrated to America in
1788. A farmer in Richmond County, NC, with a wife and
five children in 1812.   (1812)

GILLIES CHRISTIAN
85. Born in Scotland. Daniel 45. Farmer. Born in NC.
Mary 35. Born in NC. Mary 2. Born in NC. William 6 months.
Born in NC. Richmond County, NC.   (C)

GILLIES DONALD
Eldest son of Duncan Gillies and his wife Nancy McCaskill.
Married Florence Stewart in Scotland on 21 December 1803.
Emigrated to America c1810. Settled in Moore County, NC.
Moved to Kershaw District, SC, c1819. Died before 1822.(STK)

GILLIES DUNCAN
Born in Skye(?), Inverness-shire, c1750. Married Nancy
McCaskill. Emigrated to America c1810. Died in NC or
Kershaw, SC.   (STK)

GILLIS HECTOR
Born in Scotland c1764. Emigrated to America c1811. A
farmer in Richmond County, NC, with a wife and two
children in 1812. Nat.20 September 1813 Richmond County,
NC.   (RCCR)(1812)

GILLIS JOHN
Born in Scotland during 1752. Emigrated to America in
1788. A farmer in Cumberland County, NC, with a wife and
seven children in 1812.   (1812)

GILLIS JOHN
45. Carpenter. Born in Scotland. Malcolm 27. Carpenter.
Born in NC. Nancy 21. Born in NC. John 4 months. Born in
NC. Lauchlin McLaurin 7. Born in NC. Richmond County, NC.(C)

GILLES K.
61. Farmer. Born in Scotland. Sally 50. Born in NC.
Daniel 29. Farmer. Born in NC. William 21. Farmer. Born
in NC. Cynthia 23. Born in NC. John O. 19. Farmer. Born
in NC. Sally P. 17. Born in NC. Mary A. 13. Born in NC.
MJ(m) 11. Born in NC. Granville County, NC.   (C)

GILLIS KENNETH EDWARD
Born in Skye(?) Inverness-shire, son of Duncan Gillis
and his wife Nancy McCaskill. Emigrated to America c1810.
Settled in Person County, NC.   (STK)

GILLIS MALCOLM
Born in Scotland(?) during 1745. Emigrated to America in
1789. A farmer in Cumberland County, NC, with a wife and
three children in 1812.   (1812)

GILLIS MALCOLM
Born in Scotland(?) during 1762. Emigrated to America in
1802. A farmer in Richmond County, NC, with a wife and
six children in 1812.   (1812)

GILLIS MALCOLM
Born in Scotland during 1776. Married Alice .... in
Scotland. Died in Montgomery County, NC, during 1862.
                                                  (INC28259)

GILLIS MALCOLM
Born in Scotland. Farmer. 85. Mary 65. Born in Scotland.
Margaret 40. Born in NC. Richmond County, NC.   (C)

GILLIS MARY
Born in Scotland. 60. Malcolm 65. Born in NC. David M.
29. Farmer. Born in NC. Harriet 25. Born in NC.
Cumberland County, NC.   (C)

GILLIS NANCY
Born in Scotland. 67. Daniel 40. Born in Scotland.
Ann 30. Born in NC. Richmond County, NC.   (C)

GILLIS NEILL
Born in Scotland c1762. Emigrated to America c1811.
A farmer in Richmond County, NC, with a wife and five
children in 1812. Nat.20 September 1813 Richmond County,
NC.   (1812)(RCCR)

GILLIS NORMAN
Born in Scotland(?) during 1767. Emigrated to America in
1788. A farmer in Robeson County, NC, with a wife and five
children in 1812.   (1812)

GILLIES ROBERT
Born in Scotland. Merchant in Cross Creek, NC, pre 1776.
                                                       (HSNC)

GILLIS RODERICK
Born in Scotland(?) during 1774. Emigrated to America in
1789. A farmer in Cumberland County, NC, with a wife and
four children in 1812.   (1812)

GILLIS SWAIN
Born in Scotland(?) during 1784. Emigrated to America in
1788. A farmer in Cumberland County, NC, in 1812.   (1812)

GILLESPIE Rev GEORGE
Born in Scotland. Emigrated to America c1700. Father of
George Gillespie, born 1751, Rowan County, NC.   (BAF)

GILLESPIE THOMAS
Born in Stirlingshire. Emigrated to America in 1817.
Nat.12 October 1830 Charleston, SC.   (SCA)

GLEN JAMES
Born in Linlithgow, West Lothian, during 1701. Educated at
the University of Leyden, the Netherlands. Emigrated to
SC in 1743. Governor of South Carolina.   (ANY)

GLENDINNING WILLIAM
Born in Scotland. Merchant. Died in Raleigh, NC, on
24 June 1816.   (RR)

GLOVER CHRISTIANA
Born in Scotland. 60. Joseph 60. Born in Robeson County, NC.
John 25. Born in Robeson County, NC. Mary A. 22. Born in
Robeson County, NC. Susan A. 18. Born in Robeson County, NC.
William J. 4. Born in Robeson County, NC. Watts McK. 7 months.
Born in Robeson County, NC. Robeson County, NC.   (C)

SCOTS IN THE CAROLINAS

GOLDIE WALTER
Born in Nithsdale, Dumfries-shire, during 1777.
Nat.11 December 1797 Charleston, SC.   (Nat Arch M1183.1)

GOLDIE WILLIAM
Scotland. HMS Rose. Died in Carolina c1736. (Pr 12.1736 PCC)

GOODLATT ALEXANDER
Younger son of Goodlatt of Abbotshaugh, Stirlingshire.
Merchant in NC. Married Elizabeth ... Died pre August 1813.
                                                          (NCA)

GORDON ALEXANDER
Born in Aberdeen during 1692. Educated at Marischal College,
Aberdeen, from 1704 to 1708. Graduated M.A. Died in SC 1754.
                                                          (VI)

GORDON ALEXANDER
50. Merchant. Born in Scotland. Jane 40. Born in SC.
Euphemia 17. Born in SC. Jesse 12. Born in SC. Robert 9.
Born in SC. Alexander Gordon, born in Kirkcudbright,
merchant in Charleston, SC, nat.20 September 1824
Charleston, SC.   (Nat Arch M1183.1)(C)

GORDON CHARLES
Emigrated from Scotland to South Carolina. Presbyterian
minister in SC from 1759.   (CCVC)

GORDON GEORGE
Born in Edinburgh during 1806. Baker. Emigrated from
Scotland to Philadelphia, Pennsylvania, during November 1828.
Settled in Charleston, SC, in 1829. Nat.10 October 1834
Charleston, SC.   (NCA)

GORDON JAMES
Son of Alexander Gordon of Craichlaw, Wigtonshire, and his
wife Anna Stroyen. Settled in Charleston, SC. Died before
19 June 1817.   (GL)

GORDON ROBERT
Prisoner in Edinburgh or the Canongate Tolbooths. Banished
to the Plantations in Carolina. Transported there by
Robert Malloch, merchant burgess of Edinburgh in August 1684.
                                                          (PC)

GORDON WILLIAM
60. Farmer. Wynmore, Clyne, Sutherland. Emigrated from
Scotland to Wilmington, NC, on the Bachelor of Leith
with six of his children (one a weaver and another a
shoemaker) and the wives and children of his sons
Alexander and John, in April 1774.   (PRO/T47.12)

GORDON WILLIAM
Born in Scotland during 1765. Died on 26 October 1817
in Charleston, SC.   (CCG 28.11.1817)

GORDON ....
With forty Highlanders, settled in 'one of the
northern townships' of South Carolina during 1734.   (SPC)

GORRIE DAVID
Born in Perth. Died in Camden(?), SC, on 23 March 1821.
                                        (Camden Gaz 29.3.1821)

GORIE JOHN
Born in Scotland(?) c1778. Merchant and trader.
Nat.3 November 1813 Cumberland County, NC.
                                (Cumb Co Min Docket Sup Ct)

GORRIE JOHN
Born in Scotland(?) c1782. Settled in America during 1807.
Merchant in Wilmington, NC. Nat.April 1817 New Hanover
County, NC.   (1812)(NH Sup Ct Mins)

GORRIE JOSEPH
Perthshire. Settled in Wilmington, NC. Died c1830.
                                (Williams pp/787/SHC/UNC)

GOURLAY JAMES
Born in Tillicoutry, Clackmannanshire, during 1720s.
Presbyterian minister in SC from 1774 to 1782.   (CCVC)

GOW ANDREW
Glasgow. Merchant in Charleston, SC, c1798.   (VMHB/1898/6)
Died in Gambia during January 1804.   (SM 66.726)

GOWAN PETER
58. Watchmaker. Born in Scotland. Sarah 43. Born in SC.
Alexander HG 21. Watchmaker. Born in SC. Eliza G. 19.
Born in SC. Emma 12. Born in SC. Peter 6. Born in SC.
Charleston, SC. Peter Gowan, born in Galloway 1797,
nat.5 July 1848 Charleston, SC.   (C)(Nat Arch M1183.1)

GRAHAM ALEXANDER
Emigrated from Scotland to North Carolina before 1771.
                    (Letter 10.1771,McAllister pp/SHC/UNC)

GRAHAM ALEXANDER
69. Born in Scotland. Margaret 50. Born in NC. John 19.
Born in NC. Alexander 9. Born in NC. Robeson County, NC. (C)

GRAHAM ALEXANDER
62. Farmer. Born in Scotland. Sarah 43. Born in NC.
Flora A. 6. Born in NC. Moore County, NC. (C)

GRAHAM ALEXANDER
50. Merchant. Born in Scotland. Mary 40. Born in NC.
Harriet 19. Born in NC. JM 18. Clerk. Born in NC.
Isabel 15. Born in NC. Rufus 12.Born in NC. Deborah 9.
Born in NC. Julia 7. Born in NC. Josephine 3. Born in NC.
Margaret 5. Born in NC. William 1 month. Born in NC.
Catherine 74. Born in Scotland. Charlotte, Mecklenburg
County, NC. (C)

GRAHAM ANN
89. Born in Scotland. Dugald 45. Farmer. Born in NC.
Nancy 47. Born in NC. Sarah 16. Born in NC. Moore County,
NC. (C)

GRAHAM ARCHIBALD
Born in Scotland(?) during 1775. Emigrated to America in
1804. A farmer in Richmond County, NC, with a wife and four
children in 1812. (1812)

GRAHAME ARCHIBALD
Born in Glasgow. Nat.26 December 1809 SC.(Circuit Ct Jl 10.26)

GRAHAM ARCHIBALD
65. Farmer. Born in Scotland. Elizabeth 28. Born in NC.
Duncan 26. Farmer. Born in NC. Mary 24. Born in NC.
Margaret 4. Born in NC. Moore County, NC. (C)

GRAHAM ARCHIBALD
60. Farmer. Born in Scotland. Mary M. 56. Born in NC.
Lucy A. 27. Born in NC. Mary 21. Born in NC. Sarah 18.
Born in NC. Thomas 15. Labourer. Born in NC.
Montgomery County, NC. (C)

GRAHAM ARCHIBALD
45. Schoolmaster. Born in Scotland. Cumberland County, NC.(C)

GRAHAM DANIEL
Born in Scotland(?) during 1736. Emigrated to America in
1788. A farmer in Richmond County, NC, with a wife and
four children in 1812. (1812)

SCOTS IN THE CAROLINAS

GRAHAM DANIEL
90. Born in Scotland. Cumberland County, NC.   (C)

GRAHAM DANIEL
65. Born in Scotland. Jennett 50. Born in NC. John 24.
Born in NC. Archibald 22. Born in NC. Catherine 20. Born
in NC. Rebecca 18. Born in NC. Elizabeth 16. Born in NC.
Daniel Graham, born in Scotland(?) c1787, emigrated to
America in 1803, a farmer in Robeson County, NC, with
a wife in 1812.   (1812)(C)

GRAEME DAVID
Emigrated from Scotland to South Carolina on 14 October
1753.   (SCGaz 15.10.1753)(Pr 4.1778 PCC)

GRAHAM DAVID
76. Farmer. Born in Scotland. Moore County, NC.   (C)

GRAHAM DUGALD
Born in Scotland(?) during 1737. Emigrated to America in
1803. A farmer in Robeson County, NC, with three children
in 1812.   (1812)

GRAHAM DUNCAN
55. Born in Scotland. Betsy 35. Born in NC. Isabel 20.
Born in NC. Sally 18. Born in NC. Mary 14. Born in NC.
Robert 22. Born in NC. Hugh 17. Born in NC. Duncan 4.
Born in NC. Florah 9 months. Born in NC. Robeson County,
NC.   (C)

GRAHAM GEORGE
Born in Scotland(?) during 1789. Emigrated to America in
1804. Tailor in Robeson County, NC, in 1812.   (1812)

GRAHAM JAMES
Formerly of the 64th Regiment. Died in Charleston, SC,
during 1802.   (SM 64.708)

GRAHAM JAMES
Born in Scotland during 1772. Emigrated to America in 1803.
A farmer in Richmond County, NC, with a wife and six
children in 1812. Nat. 20 September 1813 Richmond County,
NC.   (RCCR)(1812)

GRAHAM JANE
Wife of WJImries. Died in Charleston, SC, 7 August 1817.
                                                    (S 40.17)

GRAHAM JOHN
Born in Scotland. Farmer and tanner. Indentured servant.
Emigrated to Georgia on 15 June 1733. Landed 29 August
1733. Allocated a land grant in Savannah, Georgia. Moved
to Carolina in December 1739.   (ESG)

GRAHAM JOHN
Born in Greenock, Renfrewshire. Nat.29 January 1797
Charleston, SC.   (Nat Arch M1183.1)

GRAHAM JOHN
Born in Glasgow. Died 3 March 1817 Charleston, SC.
                                                (CCG 6.11.1817)

GRAHAM JOHN
Born in Scotland. Settled in NC during 1769. Died on
2 April 1825. Buried in Graham Nicolson Cemetery,
Hoke County, NC.   (LOS)(Hoke Gs)

GRAHAM JOHN
Born in Scotland(?) during 1766. Emigrated to America in
1803. A farmer in Richmond County, NC, with a wife and
eight children in 1812.   (1812)

GRAHAM JOHN
Born in Scotland(?) during 1781. Emigrated to America in
1803. A farmer in Robeson County, NC, with a wife and
two children in 1812.   (1812)

GRAHAM JOHN
77. Farmer. Born in Scotland. Mary 59. Born in NC.
Neal 27. Born in SC. Susannah 22. Born in SC.
Chestefield County, SC.   (C)

GRAHAM NEIL
66. Mechanic. Born in Scotland. Margaret 62. Born in NC.
Isabel 21. Born in NC. William 30. Deputy Sheriff. Born
in NC. Ann 25. Born in NC. James 31. Mechanic. Born in NC.
Richmond County, NC.   (C)

GRAHAM NEILL
Born in Scotland(?) during 1745. Emigrated to America in
1804. A farmer in Robeson County, NC, in 1812.   (1812)

SCOTS IN THE CAROLINAS

GRANT ALEXANDER
Born in Banffshire during 1776. Merchant.
Nat.2 November 1807 Charleston, SC.   (Nat Arch M1183.1)

GRANT ALEXANDER
Elgin, Morayshire. Died (in SC) 19 August 1827.(ChO 1 9 1827)

GRANT GEORGE
20. Farmer. Aschog, Kildonan, Sutherland. Emigrated to
Wilmington, NC, on the Bachelor of Leith in April 1774.
                                              (PRO/T47.12)

GRANT HARRY
Son of Robert Grant in Leith. Merchant in Charleston,
SC, c1792.   (SRO/RD4.252.1272)

GRANT JAMES
Born in 1726, seventh son of John Grant, 6th laird of
Glenmoriston. Emigrated to America during 1746. Settled
in Norfolk, Virginia, and later in Raleigh, NC. Married
Martha Bustin in 1767. Father of James, 1775-1818.
Died during 1786.   (BAF)

GRANT JAMES
Born c1783, son of John Grant, 1737-1792, farmer, Croft,
Cromdale, Morayshire, and his wife Jean Fraser, 1743-1820.
Wright. Died in NC during 1828.   (SG)

GRANT JOHN
Born in Scotland during 1742. Emigrated to America in 1802.
A blacksmith in Richmond County, NC,with a wife and three
children in 1812.   (1812)

GRANT JOHN
Born in Scotland(?) during 1742. Emigrated to America in
1802. A farmer in Richmond County, NC, with a wife and
three children in 1812.   (1812)

GRANT LUDOVICK
Jacobite soldier captured after the Siege of Preston,
Lancashire. Transported from Liverpool to South Carolina
on the Susannah, master Thomas Bromhall, on 7 May 1716.(SPC)

GRAY JAMES
Covenanter. Prisoner in Edinburgh Tolbooth. Banished to
the Plantations in Carolina on 6 August 1684. To be
transported by Robert Malloch, merchant in Edinburgh.
Later - to be transported to the foreign Plantations by
John Ewing (therefore Jamaica?) 11 August 1685.   (ETR)(PC)

GRAY JOHN
Born in Scotland during 1690. Married Ann Bryan in
Chowan County, NC, during 1717. Died in Bertie
County, NC, during 1756.   (INC28605)

GRAY WILLIAM
Born in Glasgow during 1780. Merchant in Charleston,
SC. Nat.23 October 1813 Charleston, SC.   (Nat Arch M1833.1)

GREENLEES JOHN
25. Farmer. Kintyre, Argyllshire. Emigrated, with his
wife Mary Howie 25, from Greenock, Renfrewshire, to
Wilmington, NC, on the Ulysses, master J Chalmers, in
August 1774.   (PRO/T47.12)

GREGG ALEXANDER
Born in Scotland. Emigrated to America in 1820.
Nat.13 October 1834 Charleston, SC.   (SCA)

GREGORY or McGREGOR ALEXANDER
Born in Glasgow. Married Catherine McAlister, who died in
1796. Planter in Cumberland County, NC. Died during 1793.
                              (NCA.WB.B18)(Pr.10.1793)

GREGORIE JAMES
Born in Glasgow. Merchant. Nat.19 October 1803
Charleston, SC.   (Nat Arch M1183.1)

GRIEVE WILLIAM
Linlithgow, West Lothian. Covenanter. Prisoner in the
Canongate Tolbooth. Banished to the Plantations in
America on 27 May 1684. Transported from Leith to
Carolina in June 1684 by Robert Malloch, merchant
burgess of Edinburgh.   (PC)

GRINDLAY JAMES
Born in Scotland. Attorney in Charleston, SC.
                              (Pr 12.7.1765 SC)

GUDGER WILLIAM
Born in Scotland during 1752. Married Martha Patsy Young
in Maryland during 1775. Settled in Surry County, NC.
Died in Buncombe County, NC, during 1833.   (INC04195)

GUILD THOMAS
Jacobite soldier captured after the Siege of Preston,
Lancashire. Transported from Liverpool to South Carolina
on the Susannah, master Thomas Bromhall, on 7 May 1716.
                                    (CTB)(SPC)

GUILD THOMAS
Possibly from Glamis, Angus. Planter in St Paul's parish,
Colleton County, SC.   (Pr 22.9.1737SC)

GUNN DONALD
33. Tailor. Achinnaris, Halkirk, Caithness.
Emigrated from Scotland to Wilmington, NC, on the
Bachelor of Leith in April 1774.   (PRO/T47.12)

GUTHRIE JOHN
Jacobite soldier captured after the Siege of Preston,
Lancashire. Transported from Liverpool to South Carolina
on the Susannah, master Thomas Bromhall, on 7 May 1716.
                                                    (SPC)(CTB)

GUTHRIE ROBERT
Jacobite soldier captured after the Siege of Preston,
Lancashire. Transported from Liverpool to South Carolina
on the Wakefield, master Thomas Beck, on 21 April 1716.
                                                    (SPC)(CTB)

HAIG Mrs
Wife of David Haig. Died in Charleston, SC, during
August 1805.   (SM 68.78)

HAIG Mrs AGNES
Daughter of Alexander Ritchie in Glasgow, wife of
Dr MH Haig. Died in Charleston, SC, 23 November 1817.
                                                    (DPCA.809)

HAIG LILLIA
Berkeley County, SC. Cousin of John Fullarton,
Montrose, Angus.   (Pr 8.11.1742 SC)

HALL GEORGE
Born in Roxburghshire during 1780. Merchant in
Charleston, SC. Nat.15 June 1812 Charleston, SC.
                                            (Nat Arch M1183.1)

HALL JOHN
Born in Roslin, Midlothian, on 19 August 1785. Married
Susannah ..., born in Edinburgh during 1791. Parents of
Janet, John, Jemima, Margaret and Jane. Nat. 23 April 1824
SC.   (SCA Misc Rec W4.405)

HALL JOHN sr
68. Farmer. Born in NC. Mary 66. Born in Scotland. Nancy 38.
Born in SC. Daniel 14. Born in SC. Janet 10. Born in SC.
Chesterfield County, SC.   (C)

HALL JOHN A.
Born in Scotland c1803. Married Eliza Young in
Rutherford County, NC, during 1828. Died in
Cherokee County, NC, c1880.   (INC08015)

HALL WILLIAM
Born in Kelso, Roxburghshire, during 1775. Merchant.
Nat. 23 January 1804 Charleston, SC. Died at Sandy River,
Chester District, SC, on 29 April 1828. Buried in
Columbia Presbyterian Cemetery.(PM 14.5.1828)(SCGaz3.5.1828)
                                        (Nat Arch M1183.1)

HALLIBURTON DAVID
Born in Scotland c1727. Emigrated to America in 1746.
Married Amy Humphreys (1735-1790) in Virginia during 1752.
Parents of David, John, Charles, William, Thomas, Margaret.
Settled in Little Stone Creek, Mecklenburg, Virginia, and
in 1760 moved to Orange County, NC, where he died in 1767.
                              (HHF)(Pr 8.1767 Orange Co)

HAMILTON ALEXANDER
Born in Scotland(?) during 1787. Settled in NC before 1803.
Merchant in Granville County, NC. Nat. 6 March 1813
Granville County, NC.   (NCA/CR 044.311.2)

HAMILTON ARCHIBALD
Glasgow. Partner in the firm of John Hamilton and Company.
Merchant in Suffolk, Nansedmond County, NC, pre 1776. (SRA)

HAMILTON JAMES
Prisoner in Canongate Tolbooth. Transported to Carolina
by Walter Gibson, merchant in Glasgow, on 19 August 1684(PC)

HAMILTON JAMES
Born in Arran, Bute. Mariner. Nat. 24 July 1797
Charleston, SC.   (Nat Arch M1183.1)

HAMILTON PATRICK
Born in Scotland(?) during 1790. Emigrated to America
during 1807. Merchant in Granville County, NC, in 1812.
                              (1812)(NCA/CR 044.311.2)

HAMILTON P.
61. Farmer. Born in Scotland. William B. 37. Merchant.
Born in Virginia. Mary 35. Born in NC. William P. 13.
Born in NC. Mary 9. Born in NC. Rebecca 6. Born in NC.
Granville County, NC.   (C)

HAMILTON PAUL
Merchant in SC. Admitted a Burgess and Gildsbrother of
Glasgow, gratis, 9 March 1723.   (GBG)

HAMILTON ROBERT
Born in Lanarkshire c1782. Clerk. To settle in
Granville County, NC, 1799.
                    (VSA List of Aliens,City Point, Va,1799)

HAMILTON ROBERT
Born in Scotland(?) Emigrated to America in 1798.
Nat. 1813 Franklin County, NC.   (Franklin Co Ct Rec)

HAMILTON WILLIAM
Born in Lanarkshire c1780. Clerk. To settle in
Granville County, NC, 1799.
                    (VSA List of Aliens, City Point,Va,1799)

HAMMOND GEORGE
Jacobite soldier captured after the Siege of Preston,
Lancashire. Transported from Liverpool to South Carolina
on the Susannah, master Thomas Bromhall, 7 May 1716.   (SPC)

HANBY JOHN
Born in Dumfries-shire during 1780. Mariner.
Nat.11 October 1804 Charleston, SC.   (Nat Arch M1183.1)

HANNAH ANDREW
Born in Galloway during 1779. Merchant.
Nat. 9 November 1807 Charleston, NC.   (Nat Arch M1183.1)

HARDIE MARIAN
56. Born in Scotland. Henry 26. Born in NC. George D. 20.
Born in NC. Packney 18. Born in NC. Anna 16. Born in NC.
Wake County, NC.   (C)

HARRIS CHARLES
Born in Ayrshire c1789. Emigrated to Wilmington, NC,
during 1817. Nat. 12.1824 Cumberland County, NC.
                              (NCA/CR 029.301.16)

HARRIS CHARLES
62. Farmer. Born in Scotland. Rosa 47. Born in Scotland.
Cumberland County, NC.   (C)

SCOTS IN THE CAROLINAS

HARRIS Mrs CHRISTINA
Born c1750, daughter of Rev Thomas Boston, Jedburgh,
Roxburghshire, and granddaughter of Rev Thomas Boston,
Ettrick, Selkirkshire, wife of Tucker Harris MD. Died
in Charleston, SC, on 10 March 1818.   (BM 3.364)

HARRIS Col ROBERT
Born in Scotland during 1714. Revolutionary soldier.
Married Frances Cunningham. Father of Robert, William,
Elizabeth, Martha and Margaret. Died in NC during 1798.(LOS)

HART ANDREW
Born in Scotland. Nat. September 1830 Carteret County,
NC.   (Carteret Co Rec)

HARVIE ALEXANDER
Born in Aberdeen. Mariner. Married Elizabeth ..., born
in Aberdeen. Died in Wilmington, NC, during 1763.
                                    (NCA/CR 070.801)

HATTRIDGE ALEXANDER
Born in Glasgow on 15 September 1781. Married Ann Blount,
who died in 1817. Emigrated to America in 1804. Merchant
in Wilmington, NC. Died in Wilmington on 2 February 1823(?)
Died on 29 November 1841(?) Buried in St James's Cemetery,
Wilmington, NC.   (1812)(RR 21.2.1823)(Wilmington Gs)

HATTRIDGE WILLIAM
Born in Glasgow c1781. Merchant. Died in Fayetteville,
NC, in September 1809.   (SM 71.958)(HGP)

HAY ALEXANDER
Born in Scotland. Emigrated to America before 18 June 1798.
Nat. 12 March 1810 Union, SC.   (Union Nat Pet 13)

HAY ALEXANDER
Born in Auldearn, Nairn, during 1807. Emigrated to America
in June 1828. Nat. 25 July 1838 Union, SC.(Union Nat Pet 19)

HAY JAMES
Son of John Hay, farmer, Duncan Law, Gifford, East Lothian.
Shipwright in Wilmington, NC. Died in 1775. (NCA/CR 070.801)

HAY JOHN
Born in Scotland. Merchant in SC.   (Pr 25.9.1733 SC)

SCOTS IN THE CAROLINAS

HAY JOHN
Born in Scotland c1700. Married Mary Stafford in Beaufort,
NC, c1735. Died in Pitt County, NC, during 1764. (INC13264)

HAY ROBERT
Born in Scotland(?) Nat. June 1814 Craven County, NC.
(Craven Co Ct Rec)

HAY ROBERT sr
96. Chairmaker. Born in Scotland. Nancy 67. Born in NC.
Frances 30. Born in NC. Mary 16. Born in NC. Elizabeth
Lewis 6. Born in NC. Newberne, Craven County, NC.   (C)

HAZEL W
Born in Scotland during 1717. An indentured servant who
ranaway from the brig Dorothy.   (SCGaz 26.2.1737)

HEARD ANTHONY
Born in Scotland c1790. Nat. April 1817 New Hanover County,
NC.   (New Han Co Ct Mins)

HEASTIE JOHN
30. Shoemaker. Perthshire. Emigrated from Greenock,
Renfrewshire, to Charleston, SC, on the Countess,
master R Eason, in October 1774.   (PRO/T47.12)

HENDERSON DAVID
Bertie, NC. On 16 August 1737 David, Isobel, John, Thomas
and Mary, children of Andrew Thomson in Baad, his nieces
and nephews, were Serviced as his Heirs.
(SRO/SH)(pr 9.3.1735 Bertie)

HENDERSON JAMES
Born in Scotland(?) during 1780. Emigrated to America
in 1803. Merchant in Fayetteville, NC, in 1812.   (1812)

HENDERSON JOHN
Born in Scotland c1741. Died in Pittsburgh, Chatham County,
NC, 4 May 1825.   (WC 31.5.1825)

HENDERSON THOMAS
Born in Scotland. Chaplain to the Royal Scots Regiment at
St Augustine, Florida. Presbyterian minister in SC from
1775 to 1780.   (CCVC)

92

HENDERSON WILLIAM
Jacobite soldier captured after the Siege of Preston,
Lancashire. Transported from Liverpool to South Carolina
on the Wakefield, master Thomas Beck, on 21 April 1716.(SPC)

HENDRICK ALEXANDER
Emigrated from Scotland or Ireland to South Carolina on the
Pearl, master Walter Buchanan, in December 1767. Allocated
a 100 acre land grant on 12 December 1767.   (OL)

HENDRIE ANDREW
Born in Scotland. Planter in St Peter's parish, SC.
                                        (Pr 6.6.1766 SC)

HENRY Mrs CATHERINE
Born in Scotland during 1735. Died in Fayetteville, NC,
on 13 November 1811.   (RR 18.11.1811)

HENDRY NEIL
27. Tailor. Kintyre, Argyllshire. Emigrated from Greenock,
Renfrewshire, to Wilmington, NC, on the Diana, master
D Ruthven, during September 1774.   (PRO/T47.12)

HENRY WILLIAM
Born in Scotland c1759. Settled in NC c1783. Died at
Colvin's Creek, New Hanover County, NC, on 29 April 1833.
                                        (PP 22.5.1833)

HEPBURN CHARLES
Glasgow. Merchant at Cape Fear, NC. Died in July 1741.
                                        (SRO/CC8/8/107)

HERD JOHN
Jacobite soldier captured after the Siege of Preston,
Lancashire. Transported from Liverpool to South Carolina
on the Susannah, master Thomas Bromhall, 7 May 1716.(SPC)(CTB)

HERIOT ALEXANDER
Covenanter. Prisoner in Edinburgh Tolbooth. Banished to
Carolina on 6 August 1684. Transported from Leith to
Carolina by Robert Malloch, merchant burgess in Edinburgh.(PC)

HERON SAMUEL
Born in Galloway during 1781. Merchant. Nat. 4 August 1803
Charleston, SC.   (Nat Arch M1183.1)

HEWSON DAVID
Emigrated from Scotland or Ireland to South Carolina on the
Pearl, master Walter Buchanan, during December 1767.
Allocated a 100 acre land grant on 12 December 1767.   (OL)

HEYNS JAMES
Born in Lanark during 1778. Mariner in Charleston.
Nat. 23 August 1813 Charleston, SC.   (Nat Arch M1183.1)

HIGGINS GEORGE
Linlithgow, West Lothian. Covenanter. Prisoner in the
Canongate Tolbooth. Banished to the Plantations in
America on 27 May 1684. Transported from Leith to Carolina
by Robert Malloch, merchant burgess in Edinburgh, on
29 May 1684.   (PC)

HILL DUNCAN
Probably from Greenock, Renfrewshire. Died in Charleston, SC.
                                              (Pr 3.5.1799 SC)

HILL NATHANIEL
Born in Scotland during 1769. Emigrated from Scotland to
America. Settled in NC. Died during 1842.   (SA)

HILL THOMAS
Dundee, Angus. Joiner. Emigrated from Kirkcaldy, Fife, to
South Carolina on the Jamaica Packet, master Thomas Smith,
in June 1775.   (PRO/T47.12)

HOCKETT PHILIP
Born in Scotland c1687. Married Mary Glendinning. Died in
Guilford County, NC, during 1783.   (INCO2175)

HOGG ELIZABETH
Born in Scotland c1764. Married John Huske in 1784.
Died in New Hanover County, NC, 1788.   (INC28723)

HOGG HELEN
Born in Scotland c1768. Married (1)William Hooper in
Orange County, NC (2)Joseph Caldwell in Orange County, NC.
Died in Orange County, NC, during 1846.   (INC28723)

HOGG JAMES
Born in East Lothian c1730. Tacksman of Borlum, Thurson,
Caithness. Married Alves McDowell in Scotland during
1762. Emigrated to NC on the Bachelor of Leith in 1774.
Merchant. Militiaman. Father of Walter, Gavin, Helen,
Elizabeth and Robina. Settled at Cross Creek, Orange
County, NC. Died on 9 November 1805 in Orange County.
Buried in the Hillsborough Presbyterian Cemetery.
(INC28723)(SM.67)(Hoggpp/241/SHC/UNC)

HOGG JAMES
Born in Scotland(?) c1765. Emigrated to America in 1798.
A lawyer in Orange County, NC, with a wife and eight children
in 1812.   (1812)

HOGG ROBINA
Born in Scotland during 1772. Emigrated from Scotland to
America. Married William Norwood in Orange County, NC,
prior to 1800. Settled in Hillsborough, NC. Died in
Orange County, NC, during 1860.
(Hogg-Norwood pp,SHC/UNC)(INC28723)

HOGGATT or HOCKETT PHILIP
Born in Scotland c1687. Married Mary Glendinning. Died
in Guilford County, NC, during 1783.   (INC02175)

HOLIDAY WILLIAM
Ecclesfechan, Dumfries-shire. Planter in Goose Creek
parish, SC.   (Pr 5.1810PCC)(Pr 13.7.1781 SC)

HOLMES SAMUEL
Born in Scotland(?) Allocated a 200 acre land grant in
Georgia on 18 April 1733. A debtor - fled to Carolina in
January 1739. Died in Charleston, SC, September 1739. (ESG)

HORN ALEXANDER
Son of Alexander Horn, Forgue, Aberdeenshire(?)
Emigrated to America c1763. Died in SC c1777.   (APB)

HORSBURGH WILLIAM
Born in Scotland. Physician in Carolina.   (Pr 24.8.1761 SC)

HOUSTON GEORGE
42. Merchant. Born in Scotland. Mary I 34. Born in NC.
Mary F. 13. Born in NC. Robert M. 12. Born in NC.
Washington Town, Beaufort County, NC.   (C)

HOUSTON WILLIAM
Born in Scotland. Emigrated to America and settled in NC
during C18. A doctor.   (SA)

HOW ROBERT
Son of Job How, planter in NC. Serviced as Heir to his
grandfather Alexander, son of James Goodlet of
Abbotshaugh, Scotland, on 28 December 1743.   (SRO/SH)

HOW ROBERT NESBIT
Born in Berwick during 1799. Settled in Georgetown
District, SC. Nat. 8.12.1821 Charleston, SC.(Nat Arch M1183.1)

HOW THOMAS
Born in Scotland. Nat.21 October 1822 SC.(Circuit Ct J1 9.266)

HOWIE ROBERT
18. Workman. Glen Orchy, Argyllshire. Emigrated from
Greenock, Renfrewshire, to Wilmington, NC, on the Ulysses,
master J Chalmers, in August 1774.   (PRO/T47.12)

HUCKABY NANCY
79. Born in Scotland. Thomas W. 38. Schoolmaster. Born in
SC. Marlborough County, SC.   (C)

HUGHES JOHN
Born in Scotland. Customs controller in Charleston, SC.
Died on 20 March 1772.   (SCGaz 26.3.1772)

HUME PETER
Probably born in Scotland, son of Robert Hume. Planter.
Allocated a 900 acre land grant in Craven County, SC, on
1 June 1738. Died in Berkeley County, SC, on 3 October 1746.
                                                        (DP)

HUNT JOHN
Born in Dunfermline, Fife. Settled in Charleston, Sc, in
November 1803. Nat.7 January 1808 SC.(Ct Common Pleas Z3.150)

HUNTER ABRAM
28. Shipmaster. Greenock. Emigrated from Greenock,
Renfrewshire, to Wilmington, NC, on the Ulysses, master
J Chalmers, in August 1774.   (PRO/T47.12)

HUNTER GEORGE
Ayrshire. Landowner and planter in Charleston, SC.
Surveyor General of SC. Died in Charleston on 10 July 1755.
                        (SM 17.316)(SC Deeds 3.286)

SCOTS IN THE CAROLINAS

HUNTER JAMES
Born in Montrose, Angus, during 1782. Merchant in
Charleston. Nat. 22 August 1810 Charleston, SC.
(Nat Arch M1183.1)

HUNTER JOHN
Third son of Charles Hunter of Burnside, Angus(?)
Died on Horseshoe Plantation, SC, in 1825. (BM 17.254)

HUNTER PETER
Carpenter in Leith. Indentured at Leith on 1 November 1752
for three years service with John Rutherford and Company,
merchants at Cape Fear, NC, at their shipyards there.
Possibly emigrated on the snow Grenadier from Leith to NC.
(SRO/RD4.178.2)

HUNTER THOMAS
Born in Glasgow during 1790. Blacksmith in Charleston, SC.
Nat. 8 October 1813 Charleston. (Nat Arch M1183.1)

HUNTER WILLIAM
48. Brickmason. Born in Scotland. Spartanburg County, SC.(C)

HURST GEORGE
Born in Scotland in 1758. Married ... Henderson. Settled
in Surry County, NC. Died in Buncombe County, NC, 1844.
(INC60752)

HUTCHINSON GEORGE
Born in Scotland during 1772. Emigrated to America during
1803. A steam sawmiller with three children in 1812. Later
a merchant in Wilmington, NC. Died in Wilmington 24 September
1829. Buried at St James Church, Wilmington.
(CFR 30.9.1829)(1812)(St James OPR)

HUTCHISON JOHN
63. Farmer. Born in Scotland. Isabel 60. Born in SC.
Elizabeth 29. Born in SC. Nancy 22. Born in SC.
Margaret 20. Born in SC. William 17. Farmer. Born in SC.
Chesterfield County, SC. (C)

HUTTON JAMES
Born in Fife during 1747. Factor. Nat.20 April 1796
Charleston, SC. (Nat Arch M1183.1)

SCOTS IN THE CAROLINAS

HUTCHINGSTON ANDREW
57. Tanner. Born in Scotland. Jenny 62. Born in York
County, SC. William A. 22. Labourer. Born in York
County, SC. George R. 20. Brickmaker. Born in York
County, SC. Samuel 18. Labourer. Born in York County,
SC. John 15. Born in York County, SC. Sarah A. 12.
Born in York County, SC. York County, SC.   (C)

HYNDMAN ANDREW
46. Farmer. Kintyre, Argyllshire. Emigrated, with his
wife Catherine Campbell 46, and their children Mary 18,
and Margaret 14, from Greenock, Renfrewshire, to
Wilmington, NC, on the Ulysses, master J Chalmers,
during August 1774.   (PRO/T47.12)

IMBRIE W.
Emigrated from Scotland to America, with his wife.
Settled in Charleston, SC, during 1816. Died there
on 7 August 1817.   (CCGaz 12.8.1817)

IMRIE W.J.
Husband of Jane Graham, died in Charleston, SC, on
6 August 1817.   (S 40.17)

INGLIS Captain JOHN
Born in Scotland. Emigrated to America during 1773.
Revolutionary War officer. Settled in Edgecombe County,
NC. Militia Colonel. Died in Raleigh, NC, on
11 October 1816.   (RR 18.10.1816)

INGRAM ANDREW
Born in Eyemouth, Berwickshire, during 1773. Shipscarpenter.
Nat.12 December 1803 Charleston, SC.   (Nat Arch M1183.1)

INNES DANIEL
Born in Argyllshire. Mariner. Nat.10 August 1797
Charleston, SC.   (Nat Arch M1183.1)

INNES JAMES
Born c1700 possibly in Canisby, Caithness. Settled on
Cape Fear, NC, during 1732. Colonel of the NC Regiment
and Commander of the Expedition to the Ohio in 1754.
Married Jean ...   (SHA.103)(NCA)

IRVIN GEORGE
52. Farmer. Born in Scotland. Jane 43. Born in Scotland.
John 15. Born in NC. Georgina 13. Born in NC. Richard 11.
Born in NC. Washington 8. Born in NC. Lilly 7. Born in NC.
Scott 1. Born in NC. Rockingham County, NC.   (C)

IRVING THOMAS
Born in the Shetland Islands. Nat. 17 February 1825
Craven County, NC.   (Craven Co Ct Rec)

IRVING WINIFRED
Daughter of William Irving of Gribton. Widow of
Archibald Baird, Georgetown, SC, c1779.(RS Dumfries22.154)

IZARD SARAH
Daughter of Ralph Izard, married Lord William Campbell,
son of the Duke of Argyll, in Charleston, SC, on
17 June 1763.   (SM 25.359)

Izat John
Ships carpenter in Alloa, Clackmannanshire. Later a
merchant in Charleston, SC. Died in 1800.   (SRO/CC8/8/135)

JAFFREY EDWARD
Born in Glasgow. Merchant. Died in Charleston(?),SC,
on 15 October 1795.   (CCG 17.10.1795)

JAMIESON DAVID
Linlithgow, West Lothian. Covenanter. Prisoner in the
Canongate Tolbooth. Banished to the Plantations in
America on 27 May 1684. Transported from Leith to
Carolina by Robert Malloch, merchant in Edinburgh, on
29 May 1684.   (C)

JAMIESON JAMES
Shetland Islands. Farmer and fisherman. Emigrated, with
his wife and four children, from Kirkcaldy, Fife, to
Brunswick, NC, on the Jamaica Packet, master Thomas
Smith, in June 1775.   (PRO/T47.12)

JEFFREY JAMES
Born in Scotland. Emigrated to America in 1808. Merchant
in Warrenton, NC. Died in Warrenton on 6 April 1815.
                                  (RR 14.4.1815)(1812)

JEFFREY JANE
Emigrated from Scotland or Ireland to South Carolina on the
Pearl, master Walter Buchanan, in December 1767. Allocated
a 100 acre land grant on 12 December 1767.   (OL)

JENKINS JAMES
45. Carpenter. Born in Scotland. Fairfield County, SC.   (C)

JERVEY THOMAS
Son of Allan Jervey and Alice Graham his wife. Born in
Scotland. Married Isabella Simpson. Emigrated via
England to America in 1705. Settled in SC. Father of
David J., 1711-1771.   (BAF)

SCOTS IN THE CAROLINAS

JOHNSON ALEXANDER
Born in Scotland(?) Emigrated to America in 1804.
A farmer in Robeson County, NC, with a wife and five
children in 1812.   (1812)

JOHNSON ALEXANDER
Born in Scotland. Nat. 6 October 1830 SC. (Circuit Ct Jl 8.80)

JOHNSON CATHERINE
64. Born in Scotland. Richmond County, NC.   (C)

JOHNSON DUNCAN
Born in Scotland during 1770. Emigrated to America in
1802. A farmer in Robeson County, NC, with a wife and
children in 1812. Died in Robeson County, NC, in June 1823.
                              (RaNCSw 27.6.1823)(1812)

JOHNSON ISABELLA
68. Born in Scotland. Jane 40. Born in Scotland. Janett
38. Born in NC. Nancy 36. Born in NC. Archibald 34.
Born in NC. Hugh 30. Born in NC. Robeson County, NC.   (C)

JOHNSON NANCY
80. Born in Scotland. Catherine Baxter 55. Born in NC.
Duncan Baxter 19. Born in NC. Mary Baxter 18. Born in NC.
Robeson County, NC.   (C)

JOHNSON PETER
52. Born in Scotland. Margaret 52. Born in Scotland.
Mary 18. Born in NC. Margaret 17. Born in NC. Isabel 16.
Born in NC. Daniel 14. Born in NC. Harriet 13. Born in
NC. Eliza 9. Born in NC. Effie 8. Born in NC. James 6.
Born in NC. Benjamin 4. Born in NC. Robeson County, NC.   (C)

JOHNSTON ALEXANDER
Born in Scotland during 1799. Shoemaker in Charleston.
Nat.5 October 1832 Charleston, NC.   (Nat Arch M1183.1)

JOHNSTON ANDREW
30. Farmer. Dumfries-shire. Emigrated from Greenock,
Renfrewshire, to Charleston, SC, on the Countess,master
R Eason, during October 1774.   (PRO/T47.12)

JOHNSTON ARCHIBALD
Glasgow. Died in Charleston, SC, on 28 December 1807.
                                              (SM 70.317)

SCOTS IN THE CAROLINAS

JOHNSTON ARCHIBALD SIMPSON
Born in Port Glasgow during 1784, eldest son of Adam
Johnston, Customs Collector in Greenock, Renfrewshire.
Planter in SC. Nat. 23 August 1813 Charleston, SC.
Died in Roslin, SC, on 15 September 1819.
(Nat Arch M1183.1)(S 149.19)

JOHNSTON ARCHIBALD
Born in Dumfries-shire during 1798. Settled in Charleston.
Nat.12 December 1825 Charleston, SC.   (Nat Arch M1183.1)

JOHNSTON DONALD
Emigrated from Scotland to North Carolina before 1771.
(McAlister pp/3774/SHC/UNC)

JOHNSTONE ELIZABETH
Sister of Governor Gabriel Johnstone of North Carolina.
Born in Scotland, daughter of John Johnstone and his wife
Elizabeth Belchier. Married Thomas Kenan in Armagh,
Ireland. Emigrated, via Ireland, to Wilmington, NC, in
1733. Mother of Kenneth, born 1740 - Receiver General.
(NC Gravestone & Bible Records, 1961)

JOHNSTON GABRIEL
Born in Dundee, Angus. Educated at the University of
St Andrews and Leyden University in the Netherlands.
Professor of Hebrew at St Andrews c1724. Married Frances
... Father of Penelope. Appointed Governor of NC in 1733.
Emigrated to NC in 1734. Died 17 January 1752.
(Haye pp(324) SHC/UNC)(NCA)(HGP)(Pr 3.1795 PCC)

JOHNSTON Mrs
Widow of the late Governor of NC, married John Rutherford,
formerly in Bowland, in NC during 1754.   (SM 16.204)

JOHNSTON GILBERT
Born in Scotland, third son of John Johnston of Stapleton
and his wife Elizabeth Belcher. Father of Gilbert(1725-1794)
Henry and Robert. Jacobite in 1745. Emigrated to Cape Fear,
NC, in 1746. Died in 1775.   (HOJ)

JOHNSTON JOHN
Jacobite soldier captured after the Siege of Preston,
Lancashire. Transported from Liverpool to South Carolina
on the Susannah, master Thomas Bromhall, on 7 May 1716.(CTB)

JOHNSTON JOHN
Aberdeen. Patroon in New Windsor, SC.   (Pr 23.7.1744 SC)

JOHNSTON JOHN
Tailor. Emigrated from Scotland to NC before 1771.
(McAlister pp(3774),SHC/UNC)

JOHNSTONE MARY
65. Born in Scotland. Nancy 44. Born in Scotland.
Alexander 40. Schoolmaster. Born in Scotland. Mary 38.
Born in Scotland. John 36. Farmer. Born in Scotland.
Margaret 30. Born in Scotland. Steele Creek,
Mecklenburg County, NC.   (C)

JOHNSTON NEIL
Born in Scotland(?) during 1776. Emigrated to America
in 1802. A farmer in Richmond County, NC, with a wife
and five children in 1812.   (1812)

JOHNSTON PETER
Born in Duns, Berwickshire, during 1794. Emigrated from
Scotland to Savannah, Georgia, in November 1819.
Nat. 18 October 1836 Chester, SC.   (Chester Nats. B.60)

JOHNSTON SAMUEL
Born in Scotland during 1702. Emigrated to NC in Spring 1735.
Married Helen Scrimgeour in Scotland. Father of Jean,
Hannah, Isabella, Samuel, John, etc. Settled Onslow
County, NC. Surveyor General of NC. Died during 1757.
                              (Haye pp(324)SHC/UNC)(HOJ)

JOHNSTON SAMUEL
Born in Dundee, Angus, c1733, son of Samuel Johnston and
his wife Helen Scrimgeour. Emigrated to NC in 1735.
Planter in Edenton, NC. Educated at Newhaven, Connecticut,
and at Yale. Lawyer, revolutionary and politician.
Died in Edenton during 1816.   (Haye pp(324)SHC/UNC)

JOHNSTON WILLIAM
Son of Robert and Isabella Johnston, Harthwood,
Lochmaben, Annandale, Dumfries-shire. Merchant in Orange
County, NC. His family was buried on his plantation on the
Little River, Orange County, NC, according to his will
dated 1780.   (NCA)

JONES CATHERINE MUNRO or
Born in Fife during 1778. Settled in Charleston, SC.
Nat. 21 March 1828 Charleston, SC.   (Nat Arch M1183.1)

KAY JAMES
Born in Kirkcaldy, Fife. Emigrated to NC during 1817.
Nat. 15 August 1827 Craven County, NC.   (NCA CR 028.311.1)

KAY ROBERT
Born in Scotland(?) Nat.1827 NC.   (NCA CR 028.301.27)

KEDDIE WILLIAM
Born in Scotland during 1756. Died in Wilmington, NC,
on 10 October 1809. Buried St James's Cemetery,
Wilmington, NC.   (Wilmington Gs)

KEITH ALEXANDER
New Machar, Aberdeenshire. Clerk to the minister of
St Stephen's parish, SC.   (Pr 4.12.1772 SC)

KEITH DUNCAN
Born in Argyllshire on 12 December 1814. Died in
Keyser, NC, on 19 April 1893. Buried in Bethesda
Cemetery, Aberdeen, Moore County, NC.   (Moore Gs)

KEITH HUGH
74. Farmer. Born in Scotland. Catherine 59. Born in
Scotland. Duncan 38. Farmer. Born in NC. Elizabeth 36.
Born in NC. Mary 34. Born in NC. Margaret 32. Born in
NC. Effy 24. Born in NC. Hugh 22. Farmer. Born in NC.
John 20. Farmer. Born in NC. Moore County, NC.   (C)

KEITH JOHN
Born in Islay, Argyllshire, c1812. Died in Keyser, NC,
10 November 1882. Buried in Bethesda Cemetery, Aberdeen,
Moore County, NC.   (Moore Gs)

KEITH MARY
Born in Scotland(?) Settled in Georgetown, SC.(Pr 8.1807 PCC)

KEITH WILLIAM
Eldest son of Dr William Keith, SC, married Miss Jean,
daughter of James Moodie, Jamaica, both in New Kirk
parish. Married in Edinburgh on 12 March 1769.   (EMR)

KEITH WILLIAM
Son of William Keith, surgeon in South Carolina.
Admitted as a Burgess of Banff in 1764.   (AOB)

KEITH WILLIAM
Son of Dr Keith. Landed in Charleston, SC, from Scotland
in September 1769.   (SCGaz 28.9.1769)

KELLO JOHN
Prisoner in Edinburgh or Canongate Tolbooth. Banished to
the Plantations. Transported from Leith to Carolina by
Robert Malloch, merchant burgess in Edinburgh, during
August 1684.   (PC)

KELLY CATHERINE
70. Born in Scotland. Margaret 27. Born in NC. Iver 33.
Farmer. Born in NC. Eliza 42. Born in NC. Eliza 8. Born
in NC. Elizabeth 5. Born in NC. Evander 3. Born in NC.
Daniel 8 months. Born in NC. Moore County, NC.   (C)

KELLY CATHERINE
65. Born in Scotland. Margaret 29. Born in Marion County,
SC. John 26. Farmer. Born in Marion County, SC. Daniel
24. Farmer. Born in Marion County, SC. Marion County,SC.(C)

KELLY Mrs CATHERINE
Born in Skye, Inverness-shire, c1780. Married Daniel
Kelly. Died on 3 April 1864. Buried in Union Presbyterian
Cemetery, Carthage, Moore County, NC.   (Moore Gs)

KELLY DANIEL
Born in Scotland(?) during 1760. Emigrated to America in
1786. A farmer in Robeson County, NC, with a wife and four
children in 1812.   (1812)

KELLY DONALD
72. Farmer. Born in Scotland. Donald 21. Farmer. Born in
NC. Mary 19. Born in NC. James 18. Farmer. Born in NC.
Angus 15. Born in NC. John 13. Born in NC. Cornelius 11.
Born in NC. Moore County, NC.   (C)

KELLY DONALD
Born in Skye, Inverness-shire, during 1773. Died on
26 February 1855. Buried in Union Cemetery, Carthage,
Moore County, NC.   (Moore Gs)

KELLY HUGH
Born in Scotland on 3 August 1784. Died in NC on
17 April 1851. Buried in Kelly Cemetery, Moore County, NC.
          (Moore Gs)

KELLY JOHN
Born in Dumfries c1769. Director of the Salisbury branch of
the State Bank of NC. Died on his Salisbury plantation on
25 January 1813.   (RM)

KELLY JOHN
Born in Sleat, Inverness-shire, c1788. Married Catherine
Chisholm. Died on 25 August 1836. Buried in Stewartsville
Cemetery, Laurinburg, Scotland County, NC. (Laurinburg Gs)

KELLY JOHN
Born in Scotland during 1789. Died in NC on 9 February
1847. Buried in Union Presbyterian Cemetery, Moore County,
NC.   (Moore Gs)

KELLY NANCY
Born in Scotland on 15 February 1784. Died in NC on
17 December 1858. Buried in Kelly Cemetery, Moore
County, NC.   (Moore Gs)

KELLY PETER
70. Farmer. Born in Scotland. Christian 29. Born in NC.
Daniel 26. Born in NC. Flora 23. Born in NC. Moore
County, NC. Died in NC on 30 June 1853. Buried in   (C)
Union Presbyterian Cemetery, Carthage, Moore County, NC.
                                                       (Moore Gs)

KELSO MATHEW
Born in Greenock, Renfrewshire. Nat. 22 February 1821,SC.
                                           (Circuit Ct Jl 9.137)

KEMP ARCHIBALD
56. Farmer. Born in Scotland. Elizabeth 60. Born in SC.
Edgefield County, SC.   (C)

KENNEDY CHARLES
Born in Edinburgh during 1787. Mariner. Nat.24 January
1805 Charleston, SC.   (Nat Arch M1183.1)

KENNEDY Mrs JOAN
Born in Edinburgh during 1800. Married Dr AJ Kennedy.
Emigrated to America c1818. Died during November 1823 in
Camden, SC.   (SC 26.11.1823)

KENNEDY JOHN
68. Farmer. Born in Scotland. Margery 63. Born in NC.
Duncan 30. Constable. Born in NC. Margery 1. Born in NC.
Moore County, NC.   (C)

KENNEDY MALCOLM
Jacobite soldier captured after the Siege of Preston,
Lancashire. Transported from Liverpool to South Carolina
on the Wakefield, master Thomas Beck, 21 April 1716.   (SPC)

KENNEDY MARY
21. Spinner. Scotland. Indentured servant. Emigrated from
London to NC in May 1774 on the Friendship, master J Smith.
                                                       (HGP)

KENNEDY WILLIAM
22. Tailor. Indentured servant to John Cuthbert of
Draikes, Inverness. Embarked for Georgia on
20 October 1735 - landed January 1736. Moved from
Georgia with his family to Carolina in August 1742.   (ESG)

KENNEDY WILLIAM
Born in Dunbartonshire. Nat.18 April 1827 Kershaw, SC.
(Cit Bk 116)

KENNEDY WILLIAM
46. Farmer. Born in Scotland. Mary 38. Born in SC.
William 17. Student. Born in SC. Ronald 13. Born in SC.
Walter 9. Born in SC. Edward 5. Born in SC. Caroline 11.
Born in SC. Janet 10. Born in SC. Helen 8. Born in SC.
PMS 2. Born in SC. Kershaw County, SC.   (C)

KENNIBURGH JOHN
24. Labourer. Glasgow. Emigrated from Greenock, Renfrewshire,
to NC on the Ulysses, master J Wilson, in May 1775.
(PRO/T47.12)

KERR ALEXANDER
Born in Scotland during 1726. Married Mary Elizabeth Rice.
Died in Caswell County, NC, in 1810.   (INC27375)

KERR ANN BLAIR
Born in Edinburgh during 1789. Settled in Charleston.
Nat.31 October 1810 Charleston, SC.   (Nat Arch M1183.1)

KERR ISABELLA
Second daughter of William MacWhinnie, merchant, married
John Paul, Charleston, SC, in Kirkcudbright on 27 July 1829.
(BM 26.841)

KERR JOHN CESSFORD
Born in Inverness-shire during 1779. Merchant.
Nat.11 February 1820 Charleston, SC.   (Nat Arch M1183.1)

KETCHEN THOMAS
Howgate, Midlothian. Theology student in 1810.
Emigrated from Scotland to America. Minister in SC.   (UPC)

KEWANS WILLIAM
Born in Scotland. Nat.11 February 1796 Charleston, SC.
(SCA Misc Rec)

KIMSEY BENJAMIN
Born in Scotland c1725. Married in Scotland to Agnes Lamb.
Settled in Buncombe County, NC. Died in Burke County, NC,
1827.   (INC)

SCOTS IN THE CAROLINAS

KING AGNES
Paisley, Renfrewshire. Settled in SC. Serviced as Heir to
her uncle John King in New York, 7 February 1820.   (SRO/SH)

KING DUNCAN
Born in Scotland c1729. Married Lydia Fosque. Died in
Bladen County, NC, in 1793.   (INC28141)

KING MITCHELL
Born in Crail, Fife, during 1783. Emigrated from Scotland
to America during 1805. Teacher and judge in Charleston,
SC. Nat. 17 November 1810 Charleston, SC. Died in
Flatwick, NC, in 1862.   (Nat Arch M1183.1)(TSA)
Mitchell King, born in Scotland, 66, attorney. Margaret 49.
Born in SC. McMillan 37. Planter. Born in SC. Mitchell 34.
Physician. Born in SC. Kirkwood 29. Physician. Born in SC.
Susan 21. Born in SC. John G 18. Student. Born in SC.
Louisa 16. Born in SC. Ellen 14. Born in SC. Elizabeth 24.
Born in SC. Alexander 13. Born in SC. Frances 11. Born in SC.
Margaret 10. Born in SC. Mitchell 9. Born in SC. McMillan 7.
Born in SC. Mary 4. Born in SC. Kirkwood 3. Born in SC.
Henrietta 1. Born in SC. Charleston, SC.   (C)

KINLOCH ALEXANDER
Born in Scotland, son of Sir Francis Kinloch of Gilmerton.
Emigrated to Carolina in 1703. Merchant.   (SCGen)
Storekeeper at Red Bank, SC.   (SRO/GD237)

KINLOCH CLELAND
SC. Admitted a Burgess and Gildsbrother of Glasgow on
30 June 1779.   (GBG)

KINLOCH FRANCIS
Scotland. Settled in SC.   (Pr 7.11.1767 SC)

KINLOCH JAMES
Born in Scotland c1685, second son of Sir Francis Kinloch of
Gilmerton. Emigrated from Scotland to Port Royal, SC, in
1703. Settled in Waccamaw, SC, in 1703 - later moved to
Grove Hall, St James's parish, Santee, SC. Allocated 5449
acres in Craven County, SC, 1737, and 4200 acres in Craven
County, Sc, in 1738. Married (1) Mrs Susannah Strode (2) Mrs
Marie E Paget or Gaillard. Father of James and Francis.
Politician and planter. Died during 1757.   (SCGen)

KINLOCH JAMES
Charleston, SC. Admitted a Burgess and Gildsbrother of
Glasgow, gratis, on 18 October 1723. Brother of ... Kinloch,
merchant in SC - sons of Mary Lesly, Edinburgh, in SC 1728.
                                            (SRO/GD345)(GBG)

KIRK ALEXANDER
Born in Airth, Stirlingshire, during 1782.
Merchant. Nat. 2 January 1806 Charleston, SC.
(Nat Arch M1183.1)

KIRKLAND WILLIAM
Born in Ayrshire c1767. Settled in Hillsborough, NC,
during 1790. Married Margaret Blain Scott on
24 December 1792. Father of fourteen children. Died
at Ayr Mount, Hillsborough, NC, on 21 June 1836.   (RSA)

KIRKPATRICK JOHN
Born in Galloway during 1779. Merchant.
Nat. 8 August 1805 Charleston, SC.   (Nat Arch M1183.1)

KNOWLES JOHN
Born in Scotland. Inspector of Revenue for the Port
of New Bern, NC. Died on 17 June 1811.   (RR 5.7.1811)

KNOX JAMES
Born in Scotland c1708. Married Jean Gracy in Ireland,
who died in 1772. Emigrated from Ireland to America
c1740. Settled in Rowan County, NC. Father of William,
Samuel, James, Absalom, John, Benjamin, Mary and
Joseph. Died on 25 October 1758. Buried in Thyatira
Cemetery, Rowan County, NC.   (Hist of Rowan Co)

KNOX WALTER
Born in Glasgow during 1770. House carpenter.
Nat. 14 October 1806 Charleston, SC.   (Nat Arch M1183.1)

LAIRD PATRICK
Son of James Laird of Mugil (Muthill?), Perthshire.
Settled in Charleston, SC.   (Pr 20.11.1761 SC)

LAMB JOHN
Born in Scotland. Mariner. Nat. 25.3.1797 Charleston, SC.
(Nat Arch M1183.1)

LAMB JOHN
Born in Findhorn, Morayshire. Mariner.
Nat. 19 March 1804 Charleston, SC.   (Nat Arch M1183.1)

LAMOND DANIEL
47. Born in Scotland. Ann 34. Born in Robeson County,NC.
Sarah M 10. Born in Robeson County, NC. Elizabeth A 8.
Born in Robeson County, NC. Isabel 6. Born in Robeson
County, NC. John C 4. Born in Robeson County, NC.
Elizabeth 6 months. Born in Robeson County, NC.
Robeson County, NC.   (C)

LAMONT FLORA
55. Born in Scotland. Mary 31. Born in Scotland.
Malcolm 28. Constable. Born in NC. Cumberland County,
NC.   (C)

LAMONT HENRY
60. Born in Scotland. Christian 60. Born in Scotland.
Robeson County, NC.   (C)

LAMOND ROBERT
Son of John Lamond in Edinburgh. Surgeon in
Charleston, SC.   (Pr 25.3.1763 SC)

LAUDER ALEXANDER
100. Born in Scotland. Cumberland County, NC.   (C)

LAUGHTON WILLIAM
Orkney Islands. Mariner. Nat. 18 January 1796
Charleston, SC.   (Nat Arch M1183.1)

LAW JOHN
32. Born in Scotland. Indentured as a servant to John Smith,
merchant in London, on the 11th April 1684 for four years
service in Carolina. Transported from London to
Carolina on the Joseph and Ashton, Captain John Jones.
                                                           (NWI)

LAWSON JOHN
Born in Aberdeen c1658. Surveyor General of NC in 1690.
Author. Killed by the Tuscarora Indians during 1712.   (TSA)

LEACH ALEXANDER
66. Farmer. Born in Scotland. Christian 55. Born in NC.
Mary 26. Born in NC. Angus 20. Farmer. Born in NC.
Alexander 17. Born in NC. Jane M. 10. Born in NC.
Moore County, NC.   (C)

LEACH ALEXANDER
Born in Scotland on 15 May 1784. Died in NC on
26 November 1886. Buried in Leach Cemetery, NC.   (Leach Gs)

LEACH ANGUS
Born in Scotland. Married Mary ..., who died in 1844.
Died in NC on 22 March 1846. Buried in Union
Presbyterian Cemetery, Carthage, Moore County, NC.(Moore Gs)

LEACH ARCHIBALD
Born in Scotland(?) Emigrated to America during 1804.
A farmer in Richmond County, NC, in 1812.   (1812)

LEACH ARCHIBALD
55. Farmer. Born in Scotland. Catherine 48. Born
in NC. Alexander 20. Farmer. Born in NC. Daniel 18.
Farmer. Born in NC. Mary 19. Born in NC. Angus 16.
Farmer. Born in NC. John 14. Born in NC. Neill 12.
Born in NC. Ann 10. Born in NC. Sarah 8. Born in NC.
Moore County, NC.   (C)

LEACH DANIEL
60. Blacksmith. Born in Scotland. Elizabeth 60.
Born in NC. Chesterfield County, SC.   (C)

LEACH DONALD
74. Farmer. Born in Scotland. Daniel 31. Farmer.
Born in NC. Mary 70. Born in Scotland. Archibald 38.
Farmer. Born in NC. Neil 21. Farmer. Born in NC.
Richmond County, NC.   (C)

LEACH DUGALD
Born in Scotland(?) during 1766. Emigrated to America
in 1803. A farmer in Robeson County, NC, with a wife
and six children in 1812.   (1812)

LEACH DUGALD
Born in Scotland(?) during 1782. Emigrated to America
in 1803. A farmer in Richmond County, NC, with a wife
and two children in 1812.   (1812)

LEACH JOHN
68. Farmer. Born in Scotland. Mary 60. Born in NC.
Chesterfield County, SC.   (C)

LEACH JOHN
67. Farmer. Born in Scotland. Catherine 58. Born in
Scotland. Elizabeth 22. Born in NC. Mary 20. Born in
NC. James 18. Born in NC. Catherine 15. Born in NC.
Martin 10. Born in NC. Randolph County, NC.   (C)

LEACH JOHN
Born in Scotland(?) during 1753. Emigrated to America
in 1804. A farmer in Robeson County, NC, with a wife
and three children in 1812.   (1812)

LEACH JOHN
Born in Scotland(?) during 1785. Emigrated to America
in 1804. A farmer in Richmond County, NC, with his
mother and sister in 1812.   (1812)

LEACH JOHN
Born in Scotland(?) during 1762. Emigrated to America
in 1804. A farmer in Richmond County, NC, with a wife
and six children in 1812.   (1812)

LEACH JOHN
60. Born in Scotland. Mary 22. Born in NC. John 2.
Born in NC. Robeson County, NC.   (C)

LEACH MALCOLM
Born in Scotland during 1755. Emigrated from
Scotland to America during 1804. Died in NC
during 1822. Buried in Leach Cemetery, NC.   (Leach Gs)

LEACH Mrs MARY
Born in Scotland. Married Angus Leach. Died in NC on
3 May 1844. Buried in Union Presbyterian Church
Cemetery, Moore County, NC.   (Union Gs)

LEACH MARY
55. Born in Scotland. Cumberland County, NC.   (C)

LEACH NEILL
57. Born in Scotland. Christian 50. Born in Scotland.
Nancy 60. Born in Scotland. Sallie 50. Born in
Scotland. Fanny 28. Born in NC. Dougald 23. Born in
NC. James 1. Born in NC. John 21. Born in NC.
Catherine 19. Born in NC. Mary A 14. Born in NC.
Sarah B 13. Born in NC. Effie J 10. Born in NC.
Robeson County, NC.   (C)

LEACH NEILL
52. Farmer. Born in Scotland. Duncan 55. Farmer.
Born in Scotland. Flora McLauchlin 85. Born in
Scotland. Catherine McLauchlin 28. Born in NC.
Richmond County, NC.   (C)

LEARMONTH ALEXANDER
Edinburgh. Tanner and merchant in Charleston, SC.
Died before 1800.   (NRAS.0063)

LEMON JOHN
Jacobite soldier captured after the Siege of Preston,
Lancashire. Transported from Liverpool to South
Carolina on the Susannah, master Thomas Bromhall,
7 May 1716.   (SPC)(CTB)

LENNOX JAMES
Born in Scotland. Merchant in Charleston, SC, c1765.
                                       (SRO/RD3.224/1.627)

111

LENNOX JOHN
Cousin of John and William Lennox in Glasgow.
Merchant in Edenton, NC, c1802.   (SRA/T-LX3.24)

LENNOX ROBERT
Born in Scotland. Doctor. Settled in Edenton, NC,
c1755.   (SA)

LESLIE ALEXANDER
Jacobite soldier captured after the Siege of Preston,
Lancashire. Transported from Liverpool to South
Carolina on the Susannah, master Thomas Bromhall,
7 May 1716.   (SPC)(CTB)

LESLIE GEORGE
Born in Scotland. Merchant in Campbelltown, SC.
Died on 27 September 1798.   (GG 4.10.1798)

LETHAM ROBERT
Born in Scotland. Died in Halifax County, NC, on
14 October 1813.   (RM)

LEWIS ADAM
Born in Kirkconnelll's land, Fraquaire parish,
Dunfairs. (Kirkconnel, Sanquhar, Dumfries?). Son of
Gavin Lewis and his wife Agnes Greenlaw, Galloway.
Pedlar in SC.   (Pr 4.12.1745 SC)

LEWIS RICHARD
Emigrated from Scotland or Ireland to South Carolina
on the ship Pearl, master Walter Buchanan, during
December 1767. Allocated a 100 acre land grant on
12 December 1767.   (OL)

LINDSAY ARCHIBALD C.
Born in Scotland(?) Nat. 21 October 1809 New Hanover
County, NC.   (NH Sup Ct Mins)

LINDSAY Rev COLIN
Born in Scotland during 1744. Emigrated to America
in 1761. Settled in New Hanover County, NC. Pastor
of Black River Church, NC, from 1788 to 1791.
Minister in Robeson County, NC, from 1800 to 1812
Minister of Smyrna Presbyterian Church, Scotland
County, NC. Died on 1 December 1817. Buried in
Stewartsville, Richmond County, NC.
          (PCM)(St Paul's Pres Ch Rec)(Laurinburg Gs)

LINDSAY EUPHEMIA
Born in Scotland during 1797. Died in NC during 1883.
Buried in Piney Forest Cemetery, Chadbourn,
Columbus County, NC.   (Chadbourn Gs)

LINDSAY THOMAS
Born in Scotland. Settled in Columbia, SC.
Nat. 30 November 1803 Charleston, SC.   (Nat Arch M1183.1)

LINDSAY WILLIAM
Corsock, Colvend parish, Kirkcudbrightshire.
Merchant in Charleston, SC.   (Pr 3.7.1786 SC)

LINDSAY WILLIAM
51. Tailor. Born in Scotland. Mary 50. Born in SC.
Helen 12. Born in SC. Robert 3. Born in SC.
Laurens County, SC.   (C)

LINN WILLIAM
Born in Scotland. Settled in Charleston, SC. (Pr 2.1735 PCC)

LINNING ELIZABETH
Kidnapped and transported from Greenock, Renfrewshire,
to Carolina on the Carolina Merchant, Walter and James
Gibson, in the summer of 1684.   (TC)

LINING JOHN
Born in Dundee, Angus, during 1708. Physician -
educated in Edinburgh. Emigrated from Scotland to
America in 1730. Married Sarah Hill in 1739. Doctor
in Charleston, SC. Died on 21 September 1760.   (WA)(SA)

LISTON ANDREW
Born in Perthshire during 1777. Millwright. Settled
in St John's parish, Colleton County, SC.
Nat. 16 November 1813 Charleston, SC.   (Nat Arch M1183.1)

LITHGOW ROBERT
Born in Scotland during 1758. Settled in Glynn County,
SC, during 1775. Died there 11 October 1802. (CM 22.10.1802)

LITTLEJOHN WILLIAM
Born in Inverness during 1740. Emigrated to America
prior to 1760. Settled in Edenton, Chowan County,
NC. Shipping merchant for forty years. Married
Sarah Blount on 21 November 1771. Father of Sarah,
Thomas B, Jane, Joseph, Ann B, William A, John,
John L, John W, Helen F, Mary PB, Elizabeth M,
Francis L, and Lemuel E. Episcopalian. Died on
3 April 1817.   (NCHGR,I.2)(RR)

LIVINGSTON HUGH
Born in Argyllshire during 1779. Mariner in
Charleston. Nat. 12 May 1819 Charleston, NC(Nat Arch M1183.1)

LIVINGSTON JOHN
Possibly from Port Glasgow. Died in Wilmington, NC,
during 1800.   (NCA/CR 070.801)

LIVINGSTON JOHN W.
54. Clerk. Born in Scotland. Bladen County, NC.   (C)

LIVINGSTON PETER
Born in Scotland(?) during 1764. Emigrated to America
in 1804. A farmer in Robeson County, NC, with a wife
and three children in 1812.   (1812)

LIVINGSTON PETER
59. Born in Scotland. Isabella 50. Born in NC. John 28.
Born in NC. Sarah 26. Born in NC. Hugh 24. Born in NC.
Catherine 20. Born in NC. Isabella 18. Born in NC.
Archibald 16. Born in NC. Duncan 13. Born in NC.
Elizabeth 11. Born in NC. Mary 9. Born in NC. Susan 7.
Born in NC. Robeson County, NC.   (C)

LOGAN JOHN
Son of Isabella Logan, widow of William Lennox,
Glasgow. Tailor in Charleston, SC.   (Pr 11.2.1761)

LOUDEN JOHN
Wilmington, NC. Admitted as a Burgess and Gildsbrother
of Glasgow on 3 October 1776.   (GBG)

LOWE THOMAS
Emigrated from Scotland or Ireland to South Carolina
on the ship Pearl, master Walter Buchanan, during
December 1767. Allocated a 100 acre land grant on
12 December 1767.   (OL)

SCOTS IN THE CAROLINAS

LOWNDES JOHN
Born in Stirling during 1780. Mariner.
Nat. 16 October 1805 Charleston, NC.   (Nat Arch M1183.1)

LUMSDEN JAMES
38. Minister. Born in Scotland. Eleanor 38. Born in
NC. Jane B 16. Born in NC. Victor N 14. Born in NC.
Susan 9. Born in NC. Isabella 5. Born in NC. William
4. Born in NC. Charles F 2. Born in NC.
Guilford County, NC.   (C)

LYON GEORGE
Born in Scotland. Formerly of Cape Fear, NC. Former
Colonel of the Royal North Carolina Regiment.(Pr 8.1790 PCC)

LYON Captain JAMES
Born in Scotland(?) Allocated a land grant in NC 1734.(HSNC)

LYON JOHN
Brother of James Lyon, (Dundee). 'A botanist who
travelled the Southern wilds of North America'.
Died in Nashville, NC, on 14 August 1814.   (Dundee Gs)

LYON MATTHEW
49 Weaver. Wife Mary 50. Son James 21, weaver.
Glasgow. Emigrated from Greenock, Renfrewshire, to
NC on the Ulysses, master J Wilson, in May 1775.(PRO/T47.12)

LYON PHILIP
Jacobite soldier captured after the Siege of Preston,
Lancashire. Transported from Liverpool to South
Carolina on the Wakefield, master Thomas Beck,
on 21 April 1716.   (SPC)

LYTLE Col Archibald
Born in Scotland during 1730. Married Margaret Johnson.
Father of Kate, Margaret and Mary. Revolutionary
soldier. Died during 1790 in NC.   (LOS)

MABEN ROBERT
62. Farmer. Born in Scotland. Susan 35. Born in NC.
Mary H 12. Born in NC. Susanna 10. Born in NC.
Jonathan 9. Born in NC. Granville County, NC.   (C)

MacADAM JAMES
Born in Drymen, Stirlingshire, during 1769.
Merchant. Nat. 17 June 1799 Charleston, SC(Nat Arch M1183.1)

115

MacADAM JOHN
Son of Peter MacAdam, Easterhouse. Died on
Sullivan's Island, Charleston, SC, on
15 July 1823.   (BM 14.374)

McALLISTER ALEXANDER
Loup, Islay, Argyllshire. Emigrated from Argyllshire
to Wilmington, NC, in 1736. Returned to Scotland 1739
and then came back to NC in 1740. Settled on the
Cape Fear River,near Fayetteville. Colonel of the
Cumberland County Militia. Member of the Provincial
Congress and State Senate. Married Mary McNeil, who
died at sea in 1740 (2) Flora McNeill - mother of
four children (3) Jean Colvin - mother of eleven
children.   (McAllister pp(3774)SHC/UNC)

McALISTER ALEXANDER
Emigrated from Scotland to NC pre 1771.
                        (Letter of Jas McAlister,3774/SHC/UNC)

McALISTER ALEXANDRA
Allocated a 75 acre land grant in NC during 1771.   (HSNC)

McALISTER ANGUS
Emigrated from Scotland to New York in 1738.
By 1763 he had settled in South Carolina.   (NWI)

McALISTER ANGUS
Settled in NC before 1771.
                        (Letter of Jas McAlister,3774/SHC/UNC)

McALESTER ANGUS
Tarbert, Argyllshire. Emigrated from Scotland, with his
wife, two sons and a daughter, to Carolina in 1774.
                        (Letter of Hector McAlister,3774/SHC)

McALISTER COLL
Argyllshire. Emigrated from Scotland to America.
Settled at Cross Creek, NC, in 1739.   (SO)

McALESTER COLL
24. Tailor. Kintyre, Argyllshire. Emigrated from
Greenock, Renfrewshire, to Wilmington, NC, on the
Diana, master D Ruthven, in September 1774.   (PRO/T47.12)

McALESTER HECTOR
Emigrated from Scotland to Brunswick, NC, in
September 1739.   (VOS)

McALLISTER HECTOR
Cousin of Alexander McAllister, settled in NC pre 1771.
(Boyd letter, McAllister pp,SHC/UNC)

McALISTER JAMES
Argyllshire(?) Emigrated to NC during 1739. Settled
in Bladen County, NC. Allocated a 640 acre land grant
on 4 June 1740.   (SHA.105)

McALESTER JOHN
Emigrated from Scotland to Brunswick, NC, in
September 1739.   (VOS)

McALESTER MARY
31. Kintyre, Argyllshire. Emigrated from Greenock,
Renfrewshire, to Wilmington, NC, on the Diana,
master D Ruthven, in September 1774.   (PRO/T47.12)

McAlister Sarah
74. Born in Scotland. John 64. Born in NC. Janet 59.
Born in NC. Richmond County, NC.   (C)

McALLUM ARCHIBALD
Probably from Glendruar, Argyllshire. Settled in NC.
Father of Hector, John and Mary. Died during 1800.
Will dated 1800 Cumberland County, NC.   (NCA)

McALLUM DUNCAN
22. Shoemaker. Wife Catherine McAlester, 30. Kintyre,
Argyllshire. Emigrated from Greenock, Renfrewshire,
to Wilmington, NC, on the Ulysses, master J Chalmers,
during August 1774.   (PRO/T47.12)

McALPIN ARCHIBALD
Born in Glasgow during 1772. Settled Georgia and SC.
Died at Sister's Ferry, SC, on 24 September 1822.
(CCG 2.10.1822)

McALPINE COLIN
Edinburgh. Settled in SC.   (Pr 28.3.1772 SC)

McALPINE JOHN
Born in Scotland c1777. Married Susanna P Anderson in
Robeson County, NC, c1807. Settled in Cumberland
County, NC. Died in Richmond County, NC, in 1827. (INC)

McALPINE MALCOLM
Born in Scotland c1755. Married Mary Smith in Scotland
c1775. Settled in Cumberland County, NC. Died in
Robeson County, NC, c1825.   (INC60177)

McAREE SARAH
60. Born in Scotland. Nancy McBay 35. Born in NC.
William McBay 30. Farmer. Born in NC. Catherine
McAree 17. Born in NC. Washington McAree 14. Born in
NC. Paula 3. Born in NC. Richmond County, NC.   (C)

McARN JOHN
49. Farmer. Born in SC. Margaret 51. Born in
Scotland. Marlborough County, SC.   (C)

McARTHUR CATHERINE
84. Born in Scotland. Samuel 50. Farmer. Born in NC.
Evander 23. Farmer. Born in NC. Daniel 2. Born in NC.
Rachel 7. Born in NC. Richmond County, NC.   (C)

McARTHUR DANIEL
Born in Islay, Argyllshire, c1745. Died in NC on
9 August 1819. Buried in Longstreet Presbyterian
Cemetery, Hoke County, NC.   (Hoke Gs)

McARTHUR JANET
Born in Islay, Argyllshire, c1764. Died in NC on
16 June 1852. Buried in Antioch Cemetery, Red Springs,
Hoke County, NC.   (Hoke Gs)

McARTHUR NEIL
Scottish merchant. Settled in Cross Creek, NC,
during 1764.   (HSNC)

McARTHUR PETER
58. Farmer. Kintyre, Argyllshire. Emigrated from
Greenock, Renfrewshire, with his wife Christian
Bride 52, and children John 28, Ann 38, Joan 20
and John 16, to Wilmington, NC, during August 1774
on the Ulysses, master J Chalmers.   (PRO/T47.12)

McARTHUR PETER
80. Born in Scotland. Margaret 50. Born in NC.
Neill 35. Born in NC. Sally 30. Born in NC.
Robeson County, NC.   (C)

SCOTS IN THE CAROLINAS

McAULAY ANGUS
Uig, Inverness-shire. Emigrated from Stornaway, Ross
and Cromarty, with his wife Margaret McLeod, to
Wilmington, NC, in 1773, on the ship ....., master
Malcolm McMillen.   (Montgomery Co Rec 7.11.1837)

McAULAY FARQUHAR
Son of Daniel McAulay, Uig, Lewis, Inverness.
Emigrated from Stornaway, Isle of Lewis, Ross and
Cromarty, to Wilmington, NC, in 1773.
                                   (Montgomery Co Rec 7.11.1837)

McAULAY NANCY
49. Born in Scotland. John 69. Farmer. Born in NC.
Christian 25. Born in NC. Jane 22. Born in NC.
William 21. Labourer. Born in NC. John 18. Labourer.
Born in NC. Mary A 15. Born in NC. Hugh W 12. Born
in NC. Aulay 9. Born in NC. Montgomery County, NC.   (C)

MacAUSLAN Mrs JANE
Born in Scotland. Died in Fayetteville, NC, on
14 February 1814.   (RR 25.2.1814)

McAUSLIN JOHN
Born in Dunbartonshire during 1761. Died in
Wilmington, NC, on 23 February 1836.
                                        (Wilm Adv 26.2.1836)

McBANE DANIEL
Born in Scotland. Revolutionary soldier. Settled in
Chatham County, NC. Father of William, 1789-1875.
Buried at Snow Camp, Alamanco County, NC.   (Alamanco Gs)

McBEAN LACHLAN
Jacobite soldier captured after the Siege of Preston,
Lancashire. Transported from Liverpool to South
Carolina on the Wakefield, master Thomas Beck,
21 April 1716.   (CTB)

McBEATH JOHN
37. Farmer and shoemaker. Mault, Kildonan, Sutherland.
Emigrated from Lerwick, Shetland Islands, with his wife
and five children aged from 13 years to 9 months, to
Wilmington, NC, on the Bachelor of Leith, April 1774.
                                             (PRO/T47.12)

119

McBRAINE MURDOCH
Emigrated from Argyllshire(?), Scotland, to NC in
1739. Allocated a 320 acre land grant in Bladen
County, NC, on 4 June 1740.   (SHA.105)

McBRYDE ALEXANDER
22. Labourer. New Luce, Wigtonshire. Emigrated from
Stranraer, Wigtonshire, to NC on the Jackie, master
J Morris in May 1775. Settled in Moore County, NC,
during 1775.   (MRM)(PRO/T47.12)

McBRYDE ALEXANDER
Born in Scotland(?) during 1785. Emigrated to
America during 1804. A farmer in Robeson County, NC,
with a wife and children in 1812.   (1812)
Alexander McBryde, born in Scotland, 63. Mary, born in
NC, 60. Robeson County, NC.   (C)

McBRYDE ARCHIBALD
Born in Wigtonshire on 28 September 1766.
Emigrated from Scotland, with his parents, to
America. Settled in Carbonton, NC. Politician.
Died on 15 February 1816(1836?) at The Grange, NC.
Buried in Farrar Cemetery.   (Farrar Gs)(WA)

McBRYDE JAMES
38. Farmer. New Luce, Wigtonshire. Emigrated from
Stranraer, Wigtonshire, with his wife Janet McMiken 39,
and children Archibald 7, Elizabeth 5, and Jenny 4, to
NC on the Jackie, master J Morris, 31 May 1775.
                                      (MRM)(PRO/T47.12)

McBRYDE JOHN
Born in Stranraer, Wigtonshire, during 1801, third son of
John McBryde and his wife Margaret Donnan. Emigrated to
Augusta, Georgia, in 1819. Later settled in Abbeville,
SC. Married Susan Henrietta McLaren in 1836. Father of
John McLaren McBryde, 1841-1923. Died 12 August 1865. (BAF)

McBRYDE MARGARET
66. Born in Scotland. Hugh Clerk 34. Born in NC.
Jennett 26. Born in NC. Mary 1 month. Born in NC.
Robeson County, NC.   (C)

McBRYDE MARY
45. Born in Scotland. Edgefield County, SC.   (C)

McBRIDE THOMAS
Son of Edward McBride and his wife Margaret Gordon, Old
Luce, Wigtonshire. Storekeeper in Charleston, SC. Died
on passage from London to America. Power of attorney
to his brother James on 5 March 1795.   (Pr 9.1795 PCC)
                                  (SC Misc Rec Bk FFF.140/1)

McCALLUM ARCHIBALD
Born in Scotland(?) during 1786. Emigrated to America
in 1804. A farmer in Robeson County, NC, with a wife
in 1812.   (1812)

McCALLUM DUNCAN
30. Labourer. Breadalbane, Perthshire. Emigrated from
Scotland to Wilmington, NC, on the Jupiter of Larne,
master S Brown, in September 1775.   (PRO/T47.12)

McCALLUM DUNCAN
Born in Scotland. Revolutionary soldier. Died in 1824.
Buried in McCallum Cemetery, NC.   (McCallum Gs)

McCALLUM DUNCAN
Born in Scotland(?) during 1762. Emigrated to America
in 1792. A farmer in Cumberland County,NC , with a wife
and three children in 1812.   (1812)

McCALLUM DUNCAN
66. Farmer. Born in Scotland. Janette Williams 37.
Born in Scotland. Amelia 21. Born in York County, SC.
James A 11. Born in York County, SC. William LK 9.
Born in York County, SC. York County, SC.   (C)

McCALLUM FLORA
80. Born in Scotland. Daniel 53. Farmer. Born in
NC. Effy 40. Born in NC. Moore County, NC.   (C)

McCOLLUM JOHN
Born in Scotland. Emigrated to America in 1750.
Settled near Guilford Court House, NC. Father of
John and Thomas.   (NCGS.IV.3)

McCALLUM DONALD
Jacobite soldier captured after the Siege of Preston,
Lancashire. Transported from Liverpool to South
Carolina on the Susannah, master Thomas Bromhall,
on 7 May 1716.   (CTB)(SPC)

McCALLUM DUNCAN
Jacobite soldier captured after the Siege of Preston,
Lancashire. Transported from Liverpool to South
Carolina on the Susannah, master Thomas Bromhall.
7 May 1716.   (CTB)(SPC)

McCALLUM JOHN
Jacobite soldier captured after the Siege of Preston,
Lancashire. Transported from Liverpool to South
Carolina on the <u>Susannah</u>, master Thomas Bromhall,
7 May 1716.   (CTB)(SPC)

McCALLUM JOHN
58. Tailor. Born in Scotland. Susan 33. Born in NC.
Iver 17. Born in NC. Margaret 5. Born in NC.
Bladen County, NC.   (C)

McCALLUM MARGARET
70. Born in Scotland. Moore County, NC.   (C)

McCALLUM MARY
84. Born in Scotland. Archibald 48. Farmer. Born in NC.
Mary 32. Born in NC. John R 11. Born in NC. Mary P 9.
Born in NC. Catherine 7. Born in NC. Duncan 5. Born in
NC. Murdoch 2. Born in NC. Cumberland County, NC.   (C)

McCARTHY DANIEL
60. Farmer. Born in Scotland. Sarah 60. Born in NC.
Martha A. 31. Born in NC. James 20. Labourer.Born
in NC. Pitt County, NC.   (C)

McCARTNEY SAMUEL
Born in Kirkcudbright during 1780. Merchant.
Nat. 24 June 1805 Charleston, SC.   (Nat Arch M1183.1)

McCASKIE DONALD
Born in Scotland during 1773. Emigrated to America in
1791. A farmer in Richmond County, NC, with a wife and
five children in 1812.   (1812)

McCASKIE JOHN
Born in Scotland during 1755. Emigrated to America in
1802. A farmer in Richmond County, NC, with a wife
and five children in 1812.   (1812)

McCASKIE MALCOLM
50. Born in Scotland. Mary W 37. Born in SC. Elizabeth A
17. Born in SC. Henrietta C 15. Born in SC. Laura M 13.
Born in SC. Ann W 11. Born in SC. Sarah A 9. Born in SC.
Mary F 7. Born in SC. John A 5. Born in SC. Esther C 3.
Born in SC. Chesterfield County, SC.   (C)

McCASKIE MARGARET
48. Born in Scotland. Chesterfield County, SC.   (C)

McCASKILL ALEXANDER
Born in Scotland during 1767. Emigrated to America
c1802. Nat. 20 September 1813 Richmond County, NC.   (RCCR)

McCASKILL ALEXANDER
55. Farmer. Born in Scotland. Margaret 52. Born in
Scotland. Richmond County, NC.   (C)

McCASKILL ALLAN
Son of Finaly McCaskill. Born in Skye, Inverness-shire,
during 1727. Married Margaret Morrison. Emigrated to
NC before 1775. Father of Finlay, Allen, Peter,
Christian, Sarah, Margaret, Elizabeth, and Mary. Died
in Richmond County, NC, during 1788.   (MCF)

McCASKILL ALLEN
Born in Scotland during 1767. Emigrated to America
in 1811. A tailor in Robeson County, NC, in 1812.   (1812)

McCASKILL ALLAN
Probably son of Allan McCaskill and his wife Margaret
Morrison. Born in Skye, Inverness-shire, c1760.
Settled in NC. Married Effie... Father of Daniel,
Allen, Norman, Peter, John, Rhoda, Sarah, Nancy and
Roderick. Died during 1850 in Cumberland County, NC.   (MCF)

McCASKILL ALLEN
Born in Skye, Inverness-shire, during 1765. Died in
Stewartsville, NC, during 1847. Buried in
Stewartsville Cemetery, Laurinburg, Scotland County,
NC.   (Laurinburg Gs)

McCASKILL ALLEN
Born in Skye, Inverness-shire, during 1768. Probably a
son of Daniel McCaskill and his wife Christian McLean.
Settled in NC. Father of Daniel, Allen, and Kenneth.
Died in Richmond(?) County, NC.   (MCF)

McCASKILL ANGUS
Son of Finaly McCaskill. Born c1737 in Skye, Inver-
ness-shire. Settled in Moore County, NC. Father of
Angus Alexander, Kenneth, John Alexander. Died in
Moore County, NC.   (MCF)

McCASKILL ANGUS ALEXANDER
Born in Skye, Inverness-shire, c1769. Son of Angus
McCaskill. Settled in NC. Hatmaker. Father of Angus
and Alexander. Died in Moore County, NC, on 4 March
1807. Buried in Old Scotch Cemetery, Moore County.   (MCF)

McCASKILL ANN
Born in Skye, Inverness-shire, c1747. Died in 1819.
Buried in Stewartsville Cemetery, Laurinburg,
Scotland County, NC.   (Laurinburg Gs)

McCASKILL CHRISTIAN
Born in Skye, Inverness-shire, c1750. Daughter of
Allen McCaskill and his wife Margaret Morrison.
Married Peter Campbell. Settled in Richmond
County, NC.   (MCF)

McCASKILL DANIEL
Born in Skye, Inverness-shir, c1732. Married (1)
Christine McLean (2) Sarah ... Settled in NC.
during 1775. Father of Daniel, Dodd, McLean, Allen,
John and Malcolm. Died in Richmond County, NC,c1798. (MCF)

McCASKILL DANIEL D M
Born in Skye, Inverness-shire, c1760. Son of
Daniel McCaskill and his wife Christine McLean.
Settled in NC c1775. Married (2) Catherine Campbell.
Moved to SC c1806. Father of Randall, Angus, Donald,
Peter, Jenny, Kenneth, Christiana, Allen, Donald,
Sarah, Nancy, Mary and Charles. Died in Kershaw
County, Sc, c1838.   (MCF)

McCASKILL DANIEL
Born in Scotland during 1762. Emigrated to America
in 1811. A farmer in Robeson County, NC, with a wife
and five children in 1812.   (1812)

McCASKILL DANIEL
Born in Skye, Inverness-shire, c1769. Son of John
McCaskill and his wife Catherine Campbell.
Married Sarah ... Settled in Richmond County, NC.
Father of Alexander, William, Christian, Daniel,
Norman and Hugh. Died in Montgomery County, NC,
on 5 February 1853.   (MCF)

McCASKILL DANIEL
81. Farmer. Born in Scotland. Hugh 37. Farmer. Born in
NC. Norman 39. Carpenter. Born in NC. Ann 26. Born in
NC. Montgomery County, NC.   (C)

McCASKILL DANIEL
Born in Scotland during 1779. Emigrated to America
during 1811. A farmer in Robeson County, NC, 1812. (1812)

McCASKILL DANIEL
Born in Skye, Inverness-shire, on 15 July 1792.
Married Mary ....,1795-1882. Died in NC on
9 May 1882. Buried in Sandy Grove Cemetery,
Raeford, Hoke County, NC.   (Hoke Gs)

McCASKILL DANIEL
Born in Skye, Inverness-shire, during 1793. Died
during 1821 in Stewartsville, Laurinburg,
Scotland County, NC. Buried in Stewartsville
Cemetery.   (Stewartsville Gs)

McCASKILL DANIEL
56. Farmer. Born in Scotland. Mary 57. Born in
NC. Sarah 25. Born in NC. Mary A 23. Born in NC.
Neill 22. Born in NC. Roderick 20. Born in NC.
John 18. Born in NC. David 14. Born in NC. Nancy
13. Born in NC. Rhoda 45. Born in Scotland.
Cumberland County, NC.   (C)

McCASKILL EFFIE
Born in Skye, Inverness-shire, during 1745. Died
during 1819 in Stewartsville, Laurinburg,
Scotland County, NC. Buried in Stewartsville
Cemetery.   (Stewartsville Gs)

McCASKILL ELIZABETH
Born in Skye, Inverness-shire, c1750. Daughter of
Allen McCaskill and Margaret Morrison. Settled in
Richmond County, NC. Married Robert McKinnon.
Mother of Allen.   (MCF)

McCASKILL FINLEY
Born in Skye, Inverness-shire, c1730. Son of Finley
McCaskill. Settled in NC before 1774. Moved to
Kershaw County, SC, during 1790s.   (MCF)

McCASKILL FINLAY
Born in Skye, Inverness-shire, during 1754. Son of
Finlay McCaskill and his wife Margaret Morrison.
Married Margaret McCaskill in 1774. Settled in NC.
Revolutionary soldier. Father of Finlay, Alexander,
Elizabeth, Angus, Catherine, Sarah, Daniel, Allen
and Margaret.   (MCF)

McCASKILL FLORA
Born in Skye, Inverness-shire, c1750. Daughter of
Malcolm McCaskill and his wife Margaret Morrison.
Emigrated to America. Married John McCaskill.
Mother of Murdoch, Catherine, Daniel and
Alexander. Died in Kershaw County, SC.   (MCF)

McCASKILL HECTOR
60. Farmer. Born in Scotland. Christian 56. Born
in Scotland. Ann 26. Born in NC. Sarah 24. Born in
NC. Jennet 20. Born in NC. Effie 18. Born in NC.
Murdoch 16. Labourer. Born in NC. Catherine 13.
Born in NC. Montgomery County, NC.   (C)

McCASKILL JOHN
Son of Finlay McCaskill. Born in Skye, Inverness-
shire, during 1742. Married Rachael McLeod in
Richmond County, NC. Father of Alexander and
Daniel. Died 11 August 1811. Buried in the Old
Scotch Cemetery, Montgomery County, NC.   (MCF)

McCASKILL JOHN
Born in Skye, Inverness-shire, in 1742. Died in
Stewartsville, Laurinburg, Scotland County, NC,
during 1818. Buried in Stewartsville Cemetery.
                                          (Stewartsville Gs)

McCASKILL JOHN
Born in Skye, Inverness-shire, c1750. Son of Malcolm
McCaskill and his wife Margaret Morrison. Emigrated
to America in 1770. Married Catherine Campbell.
Settled in Richmond County, NC. Father of Daniel,
Margaret and Sarah. Died in Richmond County, NC,
during 1845.   (MCF)

McCASKILL JOHN
Born in Scotland c1756. Emigrated to America c1802.
Nat. 20 September 1813 Richmond County, NC.   (RCCR)

McCASKILL KENNETH
Born in Scotland c1740. Son of Finlay McCaskill.
Married Ann Findlay(?) Emigrated to America.
Settled in Richmond County, NC, in 1790.   (MCF)

McASKILL KENNETH
Married Nancy McKinnon in Scotland, she died in 1825.
Father of Margaret. Founder members of Bensalem
Church, NC.   (NCA/Ro68.08001)

McASKILL KENNETH
Married Mary Campbell in Scotland. Father of Jane,
born in Scotland. Settled in NC. Founder members
of Bensalem Church, NC. Died in 1834.   (NCA/R068.08001)

McCASKILL K.
Born in Scotland(?) during 1762. Emigrated to
America during 1811. A farmer in Moore County, NC,
with one child in 1812.   (1812)

McCASKILL KENNETH
50. Farmer. Born in Scotland. Mary 45. Born in
Scotland. Alexander 21. Born in SC. Mary 19.
Born in SC. Allan 18. Born in SC. Sarah 16. Born
in SC. Catherine 12. Born in SC. John 8. Born in
SC. Christian 14. Born in SC. Kershaw County, SC.   (C)

McCASKILL MALCOLM
Born in Skye, Inverness-shire, during 1730. Son of
Finlay McCaskill. Married Kate Morrison. Settled
in Richmond County, NC. Moved to Kershaw County,
SC, c1793. Father of Margaret, Taskill, Flora,
Katherine and John. Died in Richmond County, NC.   (MCF)

McCASKILL MARGARET
Born in Scotland during 1756. Daughter of Malcolm
McCaskill and his wife Kate Morrison. Married
Finlay McCaskill. Settled in NC. Died in 1817.   (MCF)

McCASKILL MARY
Born in Skye, Inverness-shire, c1750. Daughter of
Allen McCaskill and his wife Margaret Morrison.
Settled in NC. Married Hugh McCaskill. Mother of
John, Charles and William.   (MCF)

McCASKILL MURDOCH
Born in Skye, Inverness-shire, c1738. Settled in
NC before 1770. Loyalist. Planter in Anson County,
NC. Father of Daniel.   (MCF)

McCASKILL NANCY
74. Born in Scotland. Angus 47. Farmer. Born in
Scotland. Catherine 30. Born in SC. Alexander 31.
Farmer. Born in SC. Julia 22. Born in SC. Nancy 3.
Born in SC. Kershaw County, SC.   (C)

McCASKILL NANCY
65. Born in Scotland. Sarah 40. Born in Scotland.
Flora 32. Born in SC. Peter 30. Farmer. Born in
SC. Esther 22. Born in SC. Chesterfield County, SC.   (C)

McCASKILL NORMAN
50. Farmer. Born in Scotland. Effie 58. Born in
Scotland. Sarah 52. Born in Scotland. Nancy 46.
Born in Scotland. Cumberland County, NC.   (C)

McCASKILL PETER
Born in Skye, Inverness-shire, during 1770. Son of
Allen McCaskill and his wife Margaret Morrison.
Settled in NC. Married Sarah... Moved to SC.
Father of Allen, Mary, Sarah and Finlay. Died in
Kershaw County, SC, during 1861.   (MCF)

McCASKILL PETER
Born in Scotland(?) during 1787. Emigrated to
America during 1811. A farmer in Robeson County,
NC, during 1812.   (1812)

McCASKILL PETER
Born in 1793. Emigrated to America in 1802. A
farmer in Kershaw County, SC, in 1812.   (1812)

McCASKILL SALLIE
Born in Skye, Inverness-shire, c1769. Died 2 April
1859. Buried in Stewartsville, Laurinburg, Scotland
County, NC.   (Laurinburg Gs)

McCASKILL SARAH
Born in Skye, Inverness-shire, c1750. Daughter of
Allen McCaskill and his wife Margaret Morrison.
Married Peter McLeod. Settled in Richmond County,
NC. Mother of Daniel, Roderick, Farquhar, Norman,
Benjamin, Peter, Allen, Kenneth, Sweyne, Nancy,
Archibald and Catherine.   (MCF)

McCASKILL TASKILL
Born in Skye, Inverness-shire, c1750. Son of
Malcolm McCaskill and Margaret Morrison.
Emigrated to NC. Settled in Kershaw County, SC,
before 1806. Militiaman. Died in Kershaw County
during 1850.   (MCF)

McCAULAY WHITE
43. Moulder. Born in Scotland. Margaret 39. Born
in Scotland. Helena 19. Born in SC. Charlotte 14.
Born in SC. Charleston, SC.   (C)

McCHISHOLM JOHN
Spittal. Covenanter. Prisoner in the Canongate
Tolbooth. Banished to Carolina on 19 June 1684.
Transported from Leith by Robert Malloch,
merchant burgess of Edinburgh, on
19 October 1684.   (PC)

McCLENNEGHAN HORATIO
48. Farmer. Born in Scotland. Emily 54. Born in
Marion County, SC. John 17. Born in Marion County,
SC. Horatio 14. Born in Marion County, SC.
Constantine 15. Born in Marion County, SC.
George 8. Born in Marion County, SC. Tracy 5. Born
in Marion County, SC. Walter 2. Born in Marion
County, SC. Marion County, SC.   (C)

McCLURE ALEXANDER
Born in Scotland. Nat. 24 May 1796 Charleston, SC.
                          (Ct of Common Pleas H3.54)

McCOLE DAVID
30. Labourer. Breadalbane, Perthshire. Emigrated
from Scotland to Wilmington, NC, on the Jupiter of
Larne, master Samuel Brown, in September 1775.
                                              (PRO/T47.12)

McCOLE DONALD
34. Labourer. Breadalbane, Perthshire. Emigrated
from Scotland, with his wife Katherine 40, and
son Ewan 6, to Wilmington, NC, on the Jupiter of
Larne, master Samuel Brown, in September 1775. (PRO/T47.12)

McCOLE DUGAL
38. Labourer. Glen Orchy, Argyllshire. Emigrated
from Scotland with his wife Ann 38, and children
Margaret 10, Mary 8, Sarah 2, and an infant, to
Wilmington, NC, on the Jupiter of Larne, master
Samuel Brown, in September 1775.   (PRO/T47.12)

McCOLE DUNCAN
45. Farmer. Breadalbane, Perthshire. Emigrated
from Scotland with his wife Christine 40, and
children Duncan 21, Mary 18, Sarah 15, Christian
10, Mildred 6, and Ann 3, to Wilmington, NC, on
the Jupiter of Larne, master Samuel Brown, in
September 1775.   (PRO/T47.12)

McCOLE DUNCAN
35. Farmer. Breadalbane, Perthshire. Emigrated
from Scotland with his wife Christian 35, and
children Dugald 20, Christian 2, and Katherine 3,
to Wilmington, NC, on the Jupiter of Larne,
master Samuel Brown, in September 1775.   (PRO/T47.12)

McCOLE JOHN
49. Labourer. Breadalbane, Perthshire. Emigrated
from Scotland with his wife Mildred 40, and children
John 16, Samuel 15, Donald 12, Douglas 8,
Alexander 4, Katherine 2, to Wilmington, NC, on the
Jupiter of Larne, master Samuel Brown, in September
1775.   (PRO/T47.12)

McCALL DANIEL
Born in Scotland(?) during 1785. Emigrated to
America during 1793. A tailor in Fayetteville,
NC, with a wife and child during 1812.   (1812)

McCALL DANIEL
55. Farmer. Born in Scotland. Mary 57. Born in
NC. Archibald 25. Farmer. Born in NC.
Catherine 21. Born in NC. Hugh 19. Born in NC.
Duncan 17. Born in NC. Daniel 15. Born in NC.
Cumberland County, NC.   (C)

McCALL DANIEL
62. Farmer. Born in Scotland. Mary 58. Born in
Marion County, SC. Flora 34. Born in Marion
County, SC. Anna 24. Born in Marion County, SC.
Margaret 21. Born in Marion County, SC.
Marion County, SC.   (C)

McCOLL DUGALD
48. Born in Scotland. Margaret 43. Born in NC.
Catherine 11. Born in NC. Mary 9. Born in NC.
Mary 9. Born in NC. Margaret A 8. Born in NC.
Christian 6. Born in NC. Amanda 5. Born in NC.
Peter 4. Born in SC. Duncan 2. Born in SC.
Marlborough County, SC.   (C)

McCOLL DANIEL
Born in Scotland(?) during 1742. Emigrated to
America during 1787. A farmer in Richmond County,
NC, with a wife and two children in 1812.   (1812)

McCOLL D.
Born in Scotland(?) during 1762. Emigrated to
America in 1792. A farmer in Cumberland County,
NC, with a wife and seven children in 1812.   (1812)

McCOLL DUNCAN
Son of James McColl, farmer in Glasdrum.
Emigrated from Scotland to SC in 1803. Died in 1850.   (HGP)

McCOLL DUNCAN
Born in Scotland(?) during 1754. Emigrated to
America in 1791. A farmer in Richmond County,
NC, with a wife and five children in 1812.   (1812)

McCOLL DUNCAN
Born in Appin, Argyllshire, during June 1774.
Died in Stewartsville, Laurinburg, NC, on
15 July 1850.   (Stewartsville Gs)

McCALL DUNCAN
74. Born in Scotland. Catherine 79. Born in
Scotland. Christian 35. Born in Scotland.
Marlborough County, SC.   (C)

McCOLL HUGH
Born in Scotland. Settled in America before
1790. Planter in Darlington County, SC.
Nat. 5 November 1806 Marlborough, SC.   (SCA)

McCOLL HUGH
Born in Scotland(?) during 1745. Emigrated to
America in 1791. A farmer in Richmond County, NC,
with a wife and children in 1812.   (1812)

McCOLL H.
Born in Scotland(?) during 1780. Emigrated to
America in 1803. A merchant in Fayetteville,
NC, in 1812.   (1812)

McCALL JOHN
Emigrated from Scotland, with his wife Margaret
and children, to Wilmington, NC, in 1775.   (HGP)

McCOLL JOHN
Inverfolla, Appin, Argyllshire. Emigrated from
Scotland to SC on the _Mary Currie_ during 1790. (HGP)

McCOLL JOHN
Born in Scotland(?) during 1758. Tailor.
Emigrated to America during 1803. Nat. March 1814
Richmond County, NC.   (RCCR)

McCOLL JOHN
77. Born in Scotland. Marlborough County, SC.   (C)

McCOLL JOHN
Born in Scotland(?) during 1757. Emigrated to
America during 1803. A farmer in Richmond County,
NC, with a wife and seven children in 1812.   (1812)

131

SCOTS IN THE CAROLINAS

McCOLL JOHN
Born in Scotland(?) during 1745. Emigrated to
America in 1792. A farmer in Cumberland
County, NC, with a wife and five children
in 1812.   (1812)

McCOLL JOHN
Born in Scotland during 1742. Emigrated to
America during 1792. A farmer in Richmond
County, NC, with a child in 1812.   (1812)

McCOLL JOHN
Born in Scotland(?) during 1774. Emigrated to
America in 1792. A farmer in Richmond County, NC,
with a wife and four children in 1812.   (1812)

McCOLL JOHN
Born in Scotland. Emigrated to America before
14 April 1802. Nat. March 1814 Richmond County, NC.   (RCCR)

McCALL JOHN
Born in Argyllshire during 1780. Grocer.
Nat. 19 September 1808 Charleston, SC.   (Nat Arch M1183.1)

McCOLL JOHN
Born at Loch Etive, Argyllshire, c1761. Died
in Stewartsville, Laurinburg, Scotland County,
NC, on 20 June 1815.   (Laurinburg Gs)

McCOLL JOHN
75. Farmer. Born in Scotland. Dolly 72. Born in
Scotland. Marion County, SC.   (C)

McCOLL LAUCHLEN
Emigrated from Scotland to America c1790.
Settled at Beaverdam Creek, NC. Nat 20 March 1806.   (HGP)

McCOLL MARY
28. Born in Scotland. John 29. Farmer. Born in
NC. Cumberland County, NC.   (C)

McCALL NANCY
Born in Scotland. Marlborough County, SC.   (C)

McCOLL SOLOMAN
Born at Inverfalla, Appin, Argyllshire, in 1746.
Emigrated from Scotland to SC c1790. Merchant
and schoolmaster. Nat. 1809. Died 1814. Buried
Stewartsville, SC.   (HGP)

McCAUL WILLIAM
Born in Scotland. Nat.1 April 1796 Charleston, SC.
                                   (Nat Arch M1183.1)

SCOTS IN THE CAROLINAS

McCAW PETER
Born in Galloway. Mariner. Nat. 14 November 1797
Charleston, SC.   (Nat Arch M1183.1)

McCOLMAN MALCOLM
65. Farmer. Born in Scotland. Catherine 45.
Born in NC. Malcolm 28. Student. Born in NC.
Mary 4. Born in NC. Cumberland County, NC.   (C)

McCOMAY DUNCAN
Born in 1772. Emigrated to America in 1792.
A farmer in Richmond County, NC, with a wife
and ten children in 1812.   (1812)

McCONCHIE SAMUEL
Born in Galloway during 1781. Merchant. Nat.
2 March 1807 Charleston, SC.   (Nat Arch M1183.1)

McCORKIE ALEXANDER
Born in Scotland during 1722. Married (1) Agnes
Montgomery in Pennsylvania during 1745 (2) Mrs
Rebecca Brandin in Rowan County, NC, during 1791.
Died in Iredell County, NC, 25 December 1800.   (INC20450)

McCORKLE FRANCIS sr
Born in Scotland or England in May 1745. Married
Elizabeth Brandon on 13 April 1780. Father of ten
children. Revolutionary soldier. Died in Rowan
County, NC, on 9 October 1802.   (RTRA)

McCORMICK DUNCAN
Born in Appin, Argyllshire, on 18 December 1758.
Married Katherine Carmichael in Glasgow.
Emigrated from Scotland to Wilmington, NC, on
10 August 1791. Settled in Richmond County, NC.
Father of Katherine, Archibald, Daniel, John C,
Christian, Duncan C, Nancy, Mary and Margaret.
Died on 18 June 1845. Buried in Stewartsville
Cemetery, Laurinburg, Scotland County, NC.   (OCM)

McCORMAC FLORA
80. Born in Scotland. Jane 49. Born in NC.
Richmond County, NC.   (C)

McCORMICK JOHN
Born in Kintyre, Argyllshire, on 20 March 1738.
Married Barbara McEachern, born Kintyre on
22 October 1747 and died NC 1 October 1851.
Emigrated to America in 1768. Revolutionary
soldier. Father of Archibald, Barbara, Flora,
Mary, Katherine, John, Neill, Margaret,
Elizabeth, Sarah and Malcolm. Died in Robeson
County, NC, 8 February 1814. Buried in
McCormick Cenetery, Rowan County, NC.   (MOK)(RTRA)

McCORMACK JOHN
Born in Appin, Argyllshire, during 1756. Married
Mary ... Emigrated from Scotland to Wilmington,
NC, on 10 September 1791. Landed at Fort Jackson,
Brunswick County, on 11 November 1791. Settled
in Richmond County, NC. Farmer. Father of John,
Archibald M, Daniel, William, Barbara and
Catherine. Died on 19 September 1831. Buried in
Stewartsville Cemetery, Laurinburg, Scotland
County, NC.   (Laurinburg Gs)(OCM)

McCORMACK MARY
Born in Knapdale, Argyllshire, c1751. Married
Alexander Graham. Died in NC on 2 October 1826.
Buried in Longstreet Presbyterian Cemetery,
Hoke County, NC.   (Hoke Gs)

McCORMAIG MARY
64. Born in Scotland. Mary 40. Born in Robeson
County, NC. James 25. Born in Robeson County, NC.
Robeson County, NC.   (C)

McCORMACK WILLIAM
Merchant in North Carolina. Testament
registered 28 June 1821.   (SRO/CC8/8)

McCORMICK WILLIAM
Born in Galloway during 1796. Nat. 6 March 1822
Charleston, SC.   (Nat Arch M1183.1)

McCORQUDALE JOHN
80. Born in Scotland. Robeson County, NC.   (C)

McCOUGAN ANGUS
53. Farmer. Born in Scotland. Margaret M 35.
Born in SC. John C 21. Born in NC. Donald 51.
Born in Scotland. William 19. Born in NC.
Harriet G 17. Born in NC. ? (m) 13. Born in
NC. Charles F 7. Born in NC. Edward F 5.
Born in NC. Anson County, NC.   (C)

McCOY ALEXANDER
Born in Scotland c1754. Revolutionary soldier.
Died in Iredell County, NC, on 29 August 1830.
                        (WC 14.9.1830)(RR 23.9.1830)

McCOY DONALD
Jacobite soldier captured after the Siege of
Preston, Lancashire. Transported from
Liverpool to South Carolina on the Susannah,
master Thomas Bromhall, 7 May 1716.   (SPC)(CTB)

McCOY DONALD
Jacobite soldier captured after the Siege of
Preston, Lancashire. Transported from
Liverpool to South Carolina on the Wakefield,
master Thomas Beck, 21 April 1716.   (CTB)

McCOY JOHN
Jacobite soldier captured after the Siege of
Preston, Lancashire. Transported from
Liverpool to South Carolina on the Wakefield,
master Thomas Beck, 21 April 1716.   (CTB)

McCRACKEN JOHN
Born in Scotland. Married Jean Rebecca Lythe
in Pennsylvania c1768. Died in Rowan County,
NC, c1810.   (INC 27301)

McCRAINE HUGH
Born in Argyllshire(?) Emigrated to NC in 1739.
Allocated a 500 acre land grant in Bladen
County, NC, 4 June 1740.   (SHA.105)

McCRAINE MURDOCH
Emigrated from Scotland to Brunswick, NC,
in September 1739.   (VOS)

McCRAIN KENNETH
Born in Scotland during 1782. Emigrated to
America during 1787. A farmer in Richmond
County, NC, with a wife and four children
in 1812.   (1812)

McCRAINE ....
Emigrated from Jura, Argyllshire, to NC pre 1764.
                                                   (NCA.PC20.1)

McCRAINEY KENNETH
Born in 1772. Emigrated to America in 1788.
A farmer in Richmond County, NC, with a wife
and four children in 1812.   (1812)

McCRAINEY MALCOLM
Born in 1748. Emigrated to America in 1802.
A farmer in Robeson County, NC, with a wife
in 1812.   (1812)

McCRAINEY NEILL
56. Farmer. Born in Scotland. Catherine 27.
Born in NC. Cumberland County, NC.
Emigrated to America in 1788. A farmer in
Cumberland County with a wife and four
children in 1812.   (C)(1812)

McCRIMMON MALCOLM
Born in Skye, Inverness-shire, on 7 March 1776.
Died 9 July 1858. Buried in Bethesda Cemetery,
Aberdeen, Moore County, NC.
75. Born in Scotland. Catherine 83. Born in
Scotland. Christian 59. Born in NC. Sarah M 46.
Born in NC. Charles C. 39. Newspaper Agent. Born
in NC. Norman 37. Born in NC. Eliza 31. Born in
NC. Isabella 29. Born in NC. Ann 25. Born in NC.
Malcolm 22. Born in NC. Brenda(?) 21. Born in NC.
John 19. Born in NC. Catherine 55. Born in NC.
Moore County, NC.   (Moore Gs)(C)

McCRIMMON MALCOLM
Born in Scotland(?) during 1742. Emigrated to
America in 1787. A farmer in Moore County, NC,
with a wife and seven children in 1812.   (1812)

McCRIMMON RODRIC
74. Born in Scotland. Isabella 74. Born in
Scotland. Norman 30. Born in NC. Robeson
County, NC.   (C)

McCRIMMON RODERICK
Born in Scotland c1774. Died on 28 August
1856. Buried in McCrimmon Cemetery, Hoke
County, NC.   (Hoke Gs)

McCRORIE WILLIAM
Tailor in Warrenton, NC. Serviced as Heir to
his sister Grizel McCrorie in Glasgow, on
21 November 1827.   (SRO/SH)

McCUISTON JAMES
Possibly from Paisley, Renfrewshire.
Emigrated to Newcastle, Delaware, on
6 August 1735. Settled in NC.   (H 21.5)

McCUISTON THOMAS
Possibly from Paisley, Renfrewshire.
Emigrated to Newcastle, Deleware, on
6 August 1735. Settled in NC.   (H 21.5)

McCULLOCH CHARLES
Born in Scotland. Emigrated from Scotland
to New York in October 1818. Settled in
SC before November 1823. Nat.28 October
1828 Chester, SC.   (Chester Nats A.233)

McDANIEL ASA
Born in Scotland on 5 September 1776.
Emigrated to America. Married Sarah
McCollum in Randolph County, NC, on
16 December 1802. Father of William,
Harriet and Samuel. Died 30 May 1854,
in Hendricks County, Indiana.   (SG)

McDANIEL MALCOLM
65. Farmer. Born in Scotland. Mary 49.
Born in Marion County, SC. Ann 28. Born in
Marion County, SC. Alexander 26. Born in
Marion County, SC. Jane 24. Born in
Marion County, SC. Catherine 22. Born in
Marion County, SC. Neal 20. Born in
Marion County, SC. Christina 18. Born in
Marion County, SC. Daniel 18. Born in
Marion County, SC. Marion County, SC.   (C)

McDIARMID Rev ANGUS
Born in Islay, Argyllshire, c1757. Married
Ann .. (1773-1853). Died 1 April 1827.
Buried in Longstreet Cemetery, Fort Bragg,
Hoke County, NC.   (Hoke Gs)

McDIARMID DIARMID
Born in Islay, Argyllshire, c1799. Died in
NC on 30 January 1874. Buried in Longstreet
Presbyterian Cemetery, Fort Bragg, Hoke
County, NC.   (Hoke Gs)

McDIARMID MARY
60. Born in Scotland. Margaret 34. Born in NC.
Mary 27. Born in NC. Catherine 25. Born in NC.
Daniel 23. Farmer. Born in NC. Angus 22.
Farmer. Born in NC. Flora 18. Born in NC.
Martin 14. Farmer. Born in NC. Anson County, NC.   (C)

McDEARMID WILLIAM
47. Farmer. Born in Scotland. Elizabeth
37. Born in NC. Effie 22. Born in NC.
Hector 20. Tanner. Born in NC. Christian
16. Born in NC. John C 14. Born in NC.
Whitfield 12. Born in NC. David A 8.
Born in NC. Harriet. Born in NC.
Cumberland County, NC.   (C)

McDONALD ALEXANDER
Born in Scotland(?) during 1756. Emigrated
to America in 1802. A farmer in Moore
County, NC, with a wife and four children in 1812.   (1812)

McDONALD ALEXANDER
Born in Scotland. Died in Fayetteville,
NC, in January 1830.   (RR 4.2.1830)

McDONALD ALEXANDRA
Born in Scotland c1776. Died in NC on
25 February 1827. Buried in Union
Presbyterian Cemetery, Carthage, Moore
County, NC.   (Moore Gs)

McDONALD ALLAN
Emigrated from Scotland to NC. Settled
in Anson County, NC, C18.   (HSNC)

McDONALD ANGUS
Born in Scotland during 1767. Emigrated
to America in 1791. A farmer in Richmond
County, NC, with a wife and seven
children in 1812.   (1812)

McDONALD ANGUS
Born in Scotland(?) during 1767. Emigrated
to America in 1802. A farmer in Moore County,
NC, with a wife and seven children in 1812.   (1812)

McDONALD ANGUS
82. Farmer. Born in Scotland. Dugald 50.
Tailor. Born in Scotland. Catherine 45.
Born in NC. Mary 43. Born in NC.
Moore County, NC.   (C)

McDONALD ANGUS
Born in Scotland. Emigrated to America
before 14 April 1802. Nat. March 1814
Richmond County, NC.   (RCCR)

McDONALD ANGUS
81. Farmer. Born in Scotland. Sarah 78. Born
in Scotland. Allen 36. Farmer. Born in NC.
Malvina(?) 18. Born in NC. Nelly 38. Born
in NC. William 2. Born in NC. Moore County, NC.   (C)

McDONALD ANGUS
70. Farmer. Born in Scotland. Margaret 72.
Born in Scotland. Cumberland County, NC.   (C)

McDONALD ARCHIBALD
Born in Scotland c1740. Died in Bladen
County, NC, c1830.   (INC60568)

McDONALD ARCHIBALD
Born in Argyllshire on 4 July 1776.
Emigrated to America with his parents
during 1777. Settled at Big Swamp,
Maysville, NC, and later on Cape Fear,
NC. Married (1) Catherine McDonald
(2)Sarah McDonald. Died 2 June 1855.
                    (St Paul's OPR, Robeson)

McDONALD ARCHIBALD
Born in Scotland(?) during 1777. Emigrated
to America in 1803. A farmer in Robeson
County, NC, with a wife and children in 1812.   (1812)

McDONALD ARCHIBALD
74. Farmer. Born in Scotland. Sarah 41.
Born in NC. Harriet 20. Born in NC. John W
16. Born in NC. Samuel 14. Born in NC.
James D 12. Born in NC. Mary 10. Born in
NC. Malcolm 7. Born in NC. Margaret 5. Born
in NC. Barbary 3. Born in NC. Bladen County, NC.   (C)

McDONALD ARCHIBALD
72. Born in Scotland. John McIntyre 30. Born
in NC. Sally McIntyre 30. Born in NC. John
McIntyre 3. Born in NC. Margaret 2. Born in
NC. Milton 5 months. Born in NC. Robeson County, NC.   (C)

McDONALD CATHERINE
64. Born in Scotland. Mary 35. Born in NC.
Christian 33. Born in NC. Flora 25. Born in
NC. Ronald 23. Farmer. Born in NC.
Moore County, NC.   (C)

McDONALD CHRISTY
25. Seamstress. Breadalbane, Perthshire.
Emigrated from Scotland to Wilmington, NC,
on the Jupiter of Larne, master Samuel Brown,
in September 1775.   (PRO/T47.12)

McDONALD CHRISTIAN
61. Born in Scotland. John B 27. Farmer.
Born in NC. Caroline 19. Born in NC.
Archibald 1. Born in NC. Ann 24. Born
in NC. Mary 24. Born in NC. Cumberland County, NC.   (C)

McDONALD CHRISTIAN
50. Born in Scotland. Donald 28. Farmer.
Born in NC. Catherine 26. Born in NC.
Archibald 24. Farmer. Born in NC.
Catherine 8. Born in NC. Moore County, NC.   (C)

McDONALD DANIEL
Born in Scotland during 1760.
Emigrated to America during 1802. A
farmer in Moore County, NC, with a wife
and three children in 1812.   (1812)

McDONALD DANIEL
Born in Scotland during 1763.
Continental soldier from 1780 to 1782.
Died in Richmond County, NC, in 1842.
Buried in McDonald Chapel Cemetery,
Moore County, NC.   (McDonald Chapel Gs)

McDONALD DANIEL
Born in Scotland in 1762. Emigrated to
America during 1787. A farmer in Robeson
County, NC, with a wife and seven children
in 1812.   (1812)

McDONALD DANIEL
Born in Scotland during 1766. Emigrated to
America in 1792. A farmer in Robeson County,
NC, with awife and four children in 1812.   (1812)

McDONALD DANIEL
Born in Scotland during 1769. Emigrated to
America in 1792. A farmer in Richmond County,
NC, with a wife and nine children in 1812.   (1812)

McDONALD DANIEL
75. Born in Scotland. Christian 73. Born in
NC. Archibald 33. Born in NC. Mary 31. Born
in NC. Alexander 27. Born in NC. Robeson County, NC.   (C)

McDONALD DANIEL
Born in Scotland c1781. Died in Winyaw,
SC, during November 1819.   (WI 10.11.1819)

McDONALD DANIEL
Born in Scotland during 1786. Emigrated
to America in 1805. A farmer in Richmond
County, NC, with a wife in 1812.   (1812)

McDONALD DANIEL
Born in Scotland c1793. Died in NC on
28 September 1831. Buried in Brown Marsh
Presbyterian Cemetery, NC.   (Brown Marsh Gs)

McDONALD DANIEL
43. Farmer. Born in Scotland. Catherine 33.
Born in NC. Sarah 13. Born in NC. Christian
10. Born in NC. Mary 18. Born in NC. John 6.
Born in NC. Daniel 4. Born in NC. Richmond County, NC.   (C)

McDONALD DANIEL
Born in Scotland on 28 September 1813.
Died 28 September 1851. Buried Brown Marsh,
Bladen County, NC.   (Brown Marsh Gs)

MacDONALD DONALD
Former Lieutenant of the 105th Regiment.
Former merchant in Edinburgh. Died at
Cross Creek, NC, in January 1773.   (SM 35.223)

McDONALD DONALD
29. Farmer and tailor. Reay, Caithness.
Emigrated from Scotland, with his wife
and six year old child, to Wilmington, NC,
on the Bachelor of Leith, in April 1774.   (PRO/T47.12)

McDONALD DONALD
85. Farmer. Born in Scotland. Flora 65.
Born in Scotland. Mary 35. Born in SC.
Kershaw County, SC.   (C)

McDONALD ELIZABETH
29. Unmarried servant. Farr, Sutherland.
Emigrated from Scotland to Wilmington, NC,
on the Bachelor of Leith in April 1774.   (PRO/T47.12)

McDONALD FLORA
80. Born in Scotland. Daniel 47. Born in
Scotland. Farmer. Bladen County, NC.   (C)

McDONALD FLORA
60. Born in Scotland. Lauchlin Cameron
40. Millwright. Born in NC. Ann Cameron
41. Born in NC. Cumberland County, NC.   (C)

McDONALD HECTOR
75. Farmer. Langwell, Rogart, Sutherland.
Emigrated from Scotland, with his sons
John, Alexander and George aged 27 to 22,
also his grandsons Hector Campbell 16 and
Alexander Campbell 12 who were going to
join their mother, to Wilmington, NC, on
the Bachelor of Leith in April 1774.   (PRO/T47.12)

McDONALD HUGH
Third son of Somerled McDonald and his wife
Mary McLeod. French Army officer. Tacksman
of Armadale, Sleat, Inverness-shire, 1745.
Militiaman in 1746. Emigrated to NC in 1772.
Married Marion McDonald. Father of James,
Florence and Annabella. Died in NC during 1780.   (TML)

McDONALD HUGH
Born in Scotland during 1758. Emigrated to
America in 1804. A farmer in Richmond County,
NC, with a wife and two children in 1812.
Nat. 20 September 1813 Richmond County.   (RCCR)(1812)

McDONALD HUGH
Born in Inverness-shire during 1806.
Emigrated from Greenock, Renfrewshire, to
New York in December 1826. Nat. 13 March
1833 Marlborough County, SC.   (SCA)

McDONALD HUGH
79. Farmer. Born in Scotland. Mary 70.
Born in Scotland. Moore County, NC.   (C)

McDONALD ISABELLA
50. Born in Scotland. Angus 55. Born in NC.
Duncan 19. Born in NC. Archibald 17. Born
in NC. Elizabeth 15. Born in NC. Sarah 13.
Born in NC. Isabella 11. Born in NC.
Robeson County, NC.   (C)

McDONALD JAMES
Jacobite soldier captured after the Siege of
Preston, Lancashire. Transported from
Liverpool to South Carolina on the
Susannah, master Thomas Bromhall, on
7 May 1716.   (SPC)(CTB)

McDONALD JANE
55. Born in Scotland. Rockingham County,NC.   (C)

McDONALD JOHN
Jacobite soldier captured after the Siege
of Preston, Lancashire. Transported from
Liverpool to South Carolina on the
Susannah, master Thomas Bromhall, on
7 May 1716.   (SPC)(CTB)

McDONALD JOHN
Jacobite soldier captured after the Siege
of Preston, Lancashire. Transported from
Liverpool to South Carolina on the
Wakefield, master Thomas Beck, on
21 April 1716.   (CTB)

McDONALD JOHN
Born in Inverness during 1747. Emigrated
from Scotland to America in 1766.
Merchant in Charleston, SC. Married
Annie Shorey.   (SG)

McDONALD JOHN
Born in Scotland c1770. Emigrated to America
in 1803. A farmer in Richmond County, 1812.
John McDonald. 80. Farmer. Born in Scotland.
Christian 80. Born in Scotland. Nancy 41.
Born in NC. Mary 35. Born in NC. Richmond County, NC.
                                              (1812)(C)

McDONALD JOHN
Born in Scotland during 1752. Emigrated to
America in 1804. A farmer in Cumberland
County, NC, with a wife and four children
in 1812.   (1812)

McDONALD JOHN
Born in Scotland during 1777. Emigrated
to America in 1803. A farmer in
Richmond County, NC, in 1812.   (1812)

McDONALD JOHN
Born in Scotland during 1787. Emigrated
to America in 1811. A farmer in
Richmond County, NC, in 1812.   (1812)

McDONALD JOHN
65. Farmer. Born in Scotland. Mary 60. Born
in Scotland. Sarah 27. Born in NC. Angus 25.
Born in NC. Neill 24. Born in NC. Farmer.
Cumberland County, NC.   (C)

McDONALD KENNETH
Born in Scotland(?) during 1793. Emigrated
to America in 1811. A farmer in Richmond
County, NC, in 1812.   (1812)

McDONALD LAUCHLAN
Born in Scotland c1764. Emigrated to
America c1804. A farmer in Richmond
County, NC, with a wife and four
children in 1812. Nat. 20 September 1813
Richmond County, NC.   (1812)(RCCR)

McDONALD LAUCHLAN
Born in Scotland during 1785. Emigrated
to America in 1790. A farmer in
Richmond County, NC, in 1812.   (1812)

McDONALD MALCOLM
53. Farmer. Born in Scotland. Nancy 40.
Born in NC. Kenneth 18. Labourer. Born in
NC. Donald 16. Labourer. Born in NC.
Archibald 14. Born in NC. Mary Ann 13.
Born in NC. Christian 11. Born in NC.
Malcolm 8. Born in NC. Christian 4. Born
in NC. John 2. Born in NC. Cumberland County, NC.   (C)

McDONALD MARGARET
70. Born in Scotland. John 30. Cabinet-
maker. Born in Scotland. Charleston, SC.   (C)

McDONALD MARGARET
67. Born in Scotland. Angus 58. Cooper.
Born in Scotland. Jane Campbell 78. Born
in Scotland. Cumberland County, NC.   (C)

McDONALD MARY
70. Born in Scotland. Alexander 35. Farmer.
Born in Scotland. Sarah 25. Born in
Scotland. John 14. Born in NC. Moore County, NC.   (C)

144

McDONALD MARY
70. Born in Scotland. John A 28.
Cooper. Born in NC. Flora 38.
Born in NC. Bladen County, NC.   (C)

McDONALD NANCY
67. Born in Scotland. John 28.
Born in NC. Cumberland County, NC.   (C)

McDONALD NANCY
62. Born in Scotland. Flora 30. Born
in NC. Nancy 26. Born in NC.
Catherine 24. Born in NC. Mary 18.
Born in NC. Isabel 16. Born in NC.
Randolph County, NC.   (C)

MacDONALD NEIL
Emigrated from Skye, Inverness-shire,
with his wife ... Finlayson and three
sons, to America in 1802. Settled in
Cumberland County, NC.   (NCA)

McDONALD NORMAN
Born in Scotland(?) during 1795.
Emigrated to America in 1811. A
farmer in Richmond County, NC, 1812.   (1812)

McDONALD ROBERT
50. Agent. Born in Scotland. Edgefield County, SC.   (C)

McDONALD RODERICK
Born in Scotland(?) during 1756.
Emigrated to America during 1790.
A farmer in Cumberland County, NC,
with a wife and two children in 1812.   (1812)

McDONALD RODERICK
Born in Scotland. Emigrated to
America during 1789. Nat. 16 November
1813 Fairfield, SC.   (SCA)

McDONALD RONALD
Born in Scotland c1784. Married Jane,
born 1786, in Scotland during 1816.
Emigrated to Norfolk, Virginia, in 1818.
Nat. May 1826 Rockingham County, NC.
                          (McDonald-Ivory pp(2803)SHC/UNC)

McDONALD RORY
Jacobite soldier captured after the Siege
of Preston, Lancashire. Transported from
Liverpool to South Carolina on the
Susannah, master Thomas Bromhall
7 May 1716.   (SPC)(CTB)

McDONALD SALLY
60. Born in Scotland. Angus 44. Born in
NC. Mary 41. Born in NC. Sarah 19. Born
in NC. John 17. Born in NC. Archibald 15.
Born in NC. Margaret C 13. Born in NC.
Mary V 11. Born in NC. James A 8. Born in
NC. Catherine 6. Born in NC. Angeline 4.
Born in NC. Elizabeth 2. Born in NC.
Robeson County, NC.   (C)

McDONALD SAMUEL
66. Farmer. Born in Scotland. Margaret 68.
Born in Scotland. Flora 71. Born in
Scotland. Moore County, NC.   (C)

McDONALD WILLIAM
Jacobite soldier captured after the Siege
of Preston, Lancashire. Transported from
Liverpool to South Carolina on the
Susannah, master Thomas Bromhall, on
7 May 1716.   (SPC)(CTB)

McDONALD WILLIAM
71. Farmer. Little Savall, Lairg,
Sutherland. Emigrated from Scotland, with
three children aged from 7 to 3 years, to
Wilmington, NC, on the Bachelor of Leith,
in April 1774.   (PRO/T47.12)

McDONALD WILLIAM
40. Farmer. Kintyre, Argyllshire.
Emigrated from Greenock, Renfrewshire,
with his wife Isobel Wright 36, and
children Mary 4, and Jessy 2, to
Wilmington, NC, on the Diana, master
Dugald Ruthven, in September 1774.   (PRO/T47.12)

McDOUGALD ALEXANDER
Emigrated from Jura, Argyllshire, to
America (probably) on the General Wolfe,
master J MacLean. Landed at Brunswick,
NC, on 4 November 1767. Allocated a 100
acre land grant in Cumberland or
Mecklenburg Counties, NC.   (SHA.111)(SCGaz.1671)

McDOUGALD ALEXANDER
Emigrated from Jura, Argyllshire, with
his wife and daughter, to America
(probably) on the General Wolfe, master
J MacLean. Landed at Brunswick, NC, on
4 November 1767. Allocated a 300 acre
land grant in Cumberland or
Mecklenburg Counties, NC.   (SHA.111)(SCGaz.1671)

McDUGAL ALEXANDER
Born in Scotland during 1761. Emigrated
to America in 1792. A farmer in Robeson
County, NC, with a wife and nine children
in 1812.   (1812)

McDUGALD ALEXANDER
45. Farmer. Born in Scotland. Nancy 35.
Born in NC. Mary A 7. Born in NC.
Isabel 5. Born in NC. David 3. Born in
NC. Hugh 1. Born in NC. Cumberland County, NC.   (C)

McDUGALD ALLAN
60. Farmer. Born in Scotland. Janet 40.
Born in NC. John 21. Farmer. Born in Scotland.
Mary 15. Born in Scotland. Flora 5. Born
in NC. Cumberland County, NC.   (C)

McDOUGALD ANGUS
Emigrated from Jura, Argyllshire, with his
wife, to America (probably) on the General
Wolfe, master J MacLean. Landed at
Brunswick, NC, on 4 November 1767.
Allocated a 200 acre land grant in
Cumberland or Mecklenburg Counties, NC. (SHA.111)(SCGaz.1671)

McDOUGALD ANGUS
Emigrated from Jura, Argyllshire, to
America (probably) on the General Wolfe,
master J MacLean. Landed at Brunswick, NC,
on 4 November 1767. Allocated a 100 acres
land grant in Cumberland or Mecklenburg
Counties, NC.   (SHA.111)(SCGaz.1671)

McDUGALD ANGUS
66. Farmer. Born in Scotland. Moore County, NC.   (C)

McDOUGAL ARCHIBALD
47. Farmer. Born in Scotland. Mary 51.
Born in NC. Anson County, NC.   (C)

147

McDOUGAL DANIEL
Emigrated from Scotland to Brunswick,
NC, in September 1739.   (VOS)

McDOUGALD DONALD
Emigrated from Jura, Argyllshire, to
America (probably) on the General Wolfe,
master J MacLean. Landed at Brunswick, NC,
on 4 November 1767. Allocated a 100 acre
land grant in Cumberland or Mecklenburg
Counties.   (SCGaz.1671)(SHA.111)

McDOUGALD DONALD
Emigrated from Jura, Argyllshire, to
America (probably) on the General Wolfe,
master J MacLean. Landed at Brunswick, NC,
on 4 November 1767. Allocated a 100 acre
land grant in Cumberland or Mecklenburg
Counties, NC.   (SCGaz.1671)(SHA.111)

McDOUGALD DOUGALD
Emigrated from Jura, Argyllshire, to
America (probably) on the General Wolfe,
master J MacLean. Landed at Brunswick, NC,
on 4 November 1767. Allocated a 640 acre
land grant in Cumberland or Mecklenburg
Counties, NC. Accompanied by his wife,
three sons and a daughter.   (SCGaz.1671)(SHA.111)

McDOUGALD DOUGALD
Emigrated from Jura, Argyllshire, with his
wife and two sons to America (probably) on
the General Wolfe, master J MacLean.
Allocated a 400 acre land grant in
Cumberland or Mecklenburg Counties, NC.(SCGaz1671)(SHA111)

McDUGALD DUGALD
62. Farmer. Born in Scotland. Margaret 50.
Born in NC. Flora 24. Born in NC. John 22.
Born in NC. Margaret 14. Born in NC.
Dugald A. 13. Born in NC. Cumberland County, NC.   (C)

McDUGALD DUNCAN
Born in Scotland during 1755. Emigrated
to America during 1795. A farmer in
Richmond County, NC, with a wife and
four children in 1812.   (1812)

McDOUGALL HUGH
Emigrated from Scotland or Ireland to South
Carolina on the ship Pearl, master Walter
Buchanan, in December 1767. Allocated a
100 acre land grant on 12 December 1767.   (OL)

McDOUGALD HUGH
Born in Jura, Argyllshire, c1753. Died in
NC on 27 February 1827. Buried in Longstreet
Cemetery, Fort Bragg, Hoke County, NC.   (Hoke GS)

McDUGALD JAMES
Emigrated from Argyllshire(?) to NC during
1739. Allocated a 640 acre land grant in
Bladen County, NC, on 4 June 1740.   (SHA.105)

McDOUGALD JOHN
80. Farmer. Born in Scotland. Margaret 81.
Born in Scotland. Moore County, NC.   (C)

McDOUGALD JOHN
60. Born in Scotland. Florah 56. Born in NC.
Martha 24. Born in NC. Mary 22. Born in NC.
Neill M 20. Born in NC. CMD 18. Born in NC.
Jennett 16. Born in NC. Caroline 11. Born
in NC. Robeson County, NC.   (C)

McDOUGALD JOHN
52. Farmer. Born in Scotland. Isabel 57.
Born in Scotland. Catherine 18. Born in NC.
Cumberland County, NC.   (C)

McDOUGALD MALCOLM
Emigrated from Jura, Argyllshire, with his
wife and daughter, to America (probably) on
the General Wolfe, master J MacLean.
Landed in Brunswick, NC, on 4 November 1767.
Allocated a 300 acre land grant in
Cumberland or Mecklenburg Counties,NC. (SCGaz.1671)(SHA.111)

McDOUGALD MARGARET
66. Born in Scotland. John G 27. Lawyer.
Born in NC. Bladen County, NC.   (C)

McDOUGALD PEGGY
Emigrated from Jura, Argyllshire, to
America (probably) on the General Wolfe,
master J MacLean. Landed at Brunswick,
NC, on 4 November 1767. Allocated a 100
acre land grant in Cumberland or
Mecklenburg Counties, NC.   (SCGaz.1671)(SHA.111)

McDUGALD SAMUEL
Born in Scotland during 1756. Emigrated
to America in 1793. A farmer in
Robeson County, NC, with a wife and
three children in 1812.   (1812)

McDOWALL ANDREW
Born in Galloway. Merchant in Charleston,
SC. Nat.3 January 1816 Charleston, SC.
Andrew McDowall. 60. Merchant. Born in
Scotland. Camilla 50. Born in SC. C 26.
Born in SC. Charleston, SC.   (Nat Arch M1183.1)(C)

McDOWALL DANIEL
51. Farmer. Born in Scotland. Hannah A 48.
Born in Chester County, SC. Robert R 14.
Born in York County, SC. James M 11. Born
in York County, SC. John K 8. Born in
York County, SC. Mary K 6. Born in York
County, SC. York County, SC.   (C)

McDOUALL JAMES
Born in Wigtonshire during 1752.
Merchant. Nat.21 September 1807
Charleston, SC.   (Nat Arch M1183.1)

McDOWALL JOHN
Born in Galloway during 1807. Settled in
Charleston, SC. Nat. 29 July 1830
Charleston, SC.   (Nat Arch M1183.1)

McDUFFIE ABIGAIL
Born in Scotland. 75. Mary 45. Born in NC.
John 18. Farmer. Born in NC.Richmond County, NC.   (C)

McDUFFIE ALEXANDER
63. Born in Scotland. Catherine 55. Born
in Robeson County, NC. Daniel 38. Born in
Robeson County, NC. Duncan 32. Born in
Robeson County, NC. Robeson County, NC.   (C)

McDUFFIE ANGUS
Born in Scotland during 1782. Emigrated
to America in 1803. A farmer in Richmond
County, NC, with a wife and two children
in 1812.   (1812)

McDUFFIE CATHERINE.
61. Born in Scotland. John McIntyre 55.
Born 'at sea'. Robeson County, NC.   (C)

McDUFFIE CATHERINE
68. Born in Scotland. John 70. Farmer.
Born in NC. Dugald 35. Born in NC.
Gilbert 33. Born in NC. Alexander 23.
Born in NC. Cumberland County, NC.   (C)

McDUFFIE DANIEL
Emigrated from Scotland to Brunswick,
NC, in September 1739.   (VOS)

McDUFFIE MARGARET
90. Born in Scotland. Gilbert McInnis
35. Tailor. Born in NC. Catherine 36.
Born in NC. Mary 5. Born in NC.
Alexander 4. Born in NC. Nicholson
1 month. Born in NC. Ann Nicholson 39.
Born in NC. Richmond County, NC.   (C)

McDUFFIE MURDO
Born in Scotland during 1788.
Emigrated to America in 1802. A farmer
in Robeson County, NC, in 1812.   (1812)

McDUFFIE MURDOCH
58. Farmer. Born in Scotland. Catherine
54. Born in NC. Alexander 20. Born in NC.
David 14. Born in NC. Catherine A 13. Born
in NC. Duncan 11. Born in NC.
Cumberland County, NC.   (C)

McDUFFIE NEIL
Born in Scotland during 1779. Emigrated
to America in 1802. A farmer in Robeson
County, NC, with a wife and two children
in 1812.   (1812)

McDUFFIE SALLY
70. Born in Scotland. Robeson County, NC.   (C)

McEACHIN ALEXANDER
Born in Scotland during 1790. Settled
in Richmond County, NC. Died in 1881.   (INC27335)

McEACHERN ANGUS
Born in Argyllshire during 1768.
Mariner. Nat. 24 May 1811 Charleston, SC. (Nat Arch M1183.1)

McEACHEN DANIEL
Born in Scotland in 1767. Emigrated to
America in 1804. A farmer in Cumberland
County, NC, with a wife and eight
children in 1812.   (1812)

McEACHEN EFFY
46. Born in Scotland. John 21. Born in
SC. Marlborough County, SC.   (C)

McEACHEN MALCOLM
66. Born in Scotland. Mary C 30. Born in
Robeson County, NC. Isabella 26. Born in
Robeson County, NC. Elizabeth 23. Born in
Robeson County, NC. John C 21. Born in
Robeson County, NC. Margaret 1. Born in
Robeson County, NC. Robeson County, NC.   (C)

McEACHERN MARY
Born in Scotland during 1740. Died in NC
on 26 July 1837. Buried in McNeill
Cemetery, Wagram, Scotland County, NC.   (Wagram Gs)

McEACHEN MARY
50. Born in Scotland. Jane 17. Born in
Marion County, SC. Evander 14. Born in
Marion County, SC. John 12. Born in
Marion County, SC. Marion County, SC.   (C)

McEACHIN PATRICK
Born in Argyllshire c1750. Married Mary
... , who died in 1834. Died in NC on
25 September 1828. Buried in Old Centre
Cemetery, Maxton, NC.   (Maxton Gs)

McEACHIN PATRICK
Born in Scotland. Blacksmith. Settled
in NC before 1776.   (NCA.2.1.13N)(HSNC)

McEWAN JAMES
71. Merchant. Born in Scotland. Dinah 61.
Born in Scotland. Dinah 35. Born in
Scotland. Kershaw County, SC.   (C)

McEWING JOHN
Born in Glasgow during 1774. Mariner.
Nat. 9 February 1804 Charleston, SC.   (Nat Arch M1183.1)

McFADYEN ARCHIBALD
Born in Islay, Argyllshire, during 1754.
Died in 1830. Buried in Longstreet,
Cemetery, Fort Bragg, Hoke County, NC.   (Hoke Gs)

McFADYEN ARCHIBALD
Born in Scotland(?) during 1760.
Emigrated to America in 1785. A
fuller in Cumberland County, NC,
in 1812 with a wife and seven children.   (1812)

McFADYEN JOHN
Born in Scotland. Farmer. 53. Barbara 42.
Born in NC. Archibald 18. Born in NC.
Richmond County, NC.   (C)

McFADYEN MARGARET
61. Born in Scotland. Jenett 21. Born in
NC. Daniel 19. Born in NC. Robeson County, NC.   (C)

McFARLAND ARCHIBALD
65. Farmer. Born in Scotland. Catherine 45.
Born in NC. Chesterfield County, SC.   (C)

McFARLANE ALLEN
30. Farmer. Born in Scotland. Janet 67.
Born in Scotland. Catherine 28. Born in
Scotland. Janet 32. Born in Scotland.
Marjory 25. Born in Scotland.
Chesterfield County, SC.   (C)

McFARLANE DONALD
26. Farmer. Glen Orchy, Argyllshire.
Emigrated from Greenock, Renfrewshire,
with his son Donald 6, to Wilmington,
NC, on the Ulysses, master J Chalmers
in August 1774.   (PRO/T47.12)

McFARLANE FLORA
60. Born in Scotland. Cumberland County, NC.   (C)

McFARLAND JOHN
Emigrated from Scotland to NC. Died in 1767.   (HSNC)

McFARLANE MALCOLM
Born in Perthshire during 1786. Merchant
in Charleston. Nat. 23 October 1813
Charleston, SC.   (Nat Arch M1183.1)

McFARLANE SARAH
Born in Scotland. Christian. Born in Scotland.
Richmond County, NC.   (C)

McFARLAND WALTER
20. Gentleman or merchant. Emigrated from
Greenock, Renfrewshire, to NC on the Ajax,
master R Cunningham, in May 1775.   (PRO/T47.12)

McFEELY JAMES
52. Planter. Born in Scotland. Eliza 46.
Born in Scotland. Timothy 24. Carpenter.
Born in SC. Anna 21. Born in SC.
Charleston, SC.   (C)

MacFIE DUGALD
Born in Greenock, Renfrewshire, during 1770.
Merchant in Charleston. Nat.25 June 1812
Charleston, SC.   (Nat Arch M1183.1)

McGACHIN JAMES
Dalry, Kirkcudbrightshire. Covenanter. Prisoner
in the Canongate Tolbooth. Banished to Carolina
on 19 June 1684. Transported from Leith by
Robert Malloch, merchant burgess in Edinburgh,
during August 1684.   (PC)

McGAW SAMUEL
Emigrated from Scotland to Brunswick, NC,
in September 1739.   (VOS)

McGEACHY ALEXANDER
Kintyre, Argyllshire. Emigrated to America
after 1783. Married Catherine McCoulskey.
Settled in Robeson County, NC. Father of
Neil, Ronald, Peter, Alexander, and Janet.
Died on 24 March 1844.   (St Paul's Pres Ch Rec)

McGIBBON HUGH
Emigrated from Scotland or Ireland to SC
on the ship Pearl, master Walter Buchanan,
in December 1767. Allocated a 100 acre land
grant on 12 December 1767.   (OL)

McGILBRAY DONALD
Born in Scotland during 1758. Emigrated to
America c1803. Nat. 20 September 1813
Richmond County, NC.   (RCCR)

McGILBRAY DANIEL
Born in Scotland during 1758. Emigrated to
America during 1805. A farmer in Richmond
County, NC, with a wife and five children
in 1812. Nat. 20 September 1813 Richmond
County, NC.   (RCCR)(1812)

McGILBRAY DANIEL
Born in Scotland during 1765. Emigrated to
America in 1803. A farmer in Richmond County,
NC, with a wife and three children in 1812.   (1812)

McGILBRAY JAMES
Born in Scotland during 1789. Emigrated to
America c1803. Nat.20 September 1813
Richmond County, NC.   (RCCR)

McGILBRAY MALCOLM
Born in Scotland during 1787. Emigrated to
America c1803. In NC during 1812.
Nat. 20 September 1813 Richmond County, NC.   (RCCR)(1812)

McGILCHRIST MALCOLM
Settled in NC pre 1771.   (Jas McAlister letter(3774)SHC/UNC)

McGILCHRIST WILLIAM
Son of James McGilchrist, Inchinnan,
Renfrewshire. Episcopalian minister.
Emigrated from England to SC on
2 October 1741.   (EMA)

McGILL A C
49. Farmer. Born in Scotland. Catherine 47.
Born in NC. Smiley 20. Schoolmaster. Born
in SC. Joseph 18. Farmer. Born in SC.
Alexander 15. Born in SC. John 13. Born in
SC. MC 11. Born in SC   ? 6. Born in SC.
Marlborough County, SC.   (C)

McGILL ANGUS
Born in Kintyre, Argyllshire, c1749.
Died in NC on 22 December 1827.   (RaNCSw 24.1.1828)

McGILL ARCHIBALD
Emigrated from Argyllshire(?) to NC in 1739.
Allocated a 500 acre land grant in Bladen
County, NC, on 4 June 1740.   (SHA.106)

155

McGILL DONALD
Born in Scotland(?) c1782. Emigrated to
America in 1804. A farmer in Richmond
County, NC, with six people in his
family in 1812.   (1812)

McGILL EFFIE
79. Born in Scotland. Daniel 50. Farmer.
Born in Scotland. Archibald 34. Farmer.
Born in Scotland. Cumberland County, NC.   (C)

McGILL FLORA
65. Born in Scotland. Angus 36. Farmer.
Born in NC. Catherine 45. Born in NC.
Mary 43. Born in NC. Anna 25. Born in
NC. Daniel 28. Farmer. Born in NC.
Cumberland County, NC.   (C)

McGILL ISABEL
60. Born in Scotland. Duncan 30. Farmer.
Born in Scotland. Daniel 20. Born in
Scotland. Cumberland County, NC.   (C)

McGILL JOHN
65. Farmer. Born in Scotland. Mary 50.
Born in Scotland. Richmond County, NC.   (C)

McGILL MALCOLM
Settled in NC pre 1771. (Jas McAlister letter(3774)SHC/UNC)

McGILL MARY
89. Born in Scotland. Torquil Stewart 55.
Born in NC. Annabella Stewart 28. Born in NC.
John Stewart 24. Born in NC. Caroline Stewart
19. Born in NC. Robeson County, NC.   (C)

McGILL NEILL
Emigrated from Scotland to Brunswick, NC, in
September 1739.   (VOS)

McGILVERY A
Born in Scotland during 1788. Emigrated to
America in 1792. A clerk in Fayetteville,
NC, in 1812.   (1812)

McGILVERY ALEXANDER
Born in Scotland during 1785. Emigrated to
America in 1805. A farmer in Richmond County,
NC, with a wife and two children in 1812.   (1812)

McGILLIVERAY DONALD
Jacobite soldier captured after the Siege
of Preston, Lancashire. Transported from
Liverpool to South Carolina on the
Susannah, master Thomas Bromhall, on
7 May 1716.   (CTB)(SPC)

McGILLIVRAY FERGUS
Jacobite soldier captured after the Siege
of Preston, Lancashire. Transported from
Liverpool to South Carolina on the
Susannah, master Thomas Bromhall, on
7 May 1716.   (SPC)(CTB)

McGILLIVRAY JAMES
Jacobite soldier captured after the Siege
of Preston, Lancashire, Transported from
Liverpool to South Carolina on the
Wakefield, master Thomas Beck, 21 April 1716.   (CTB)

McGILLIVRAY JOHN
Jacobite soldier captured after the Siege
of Preston, Lancashire. Transported from
Liverpool to South Carolina on the
Wakefield, master Thomas Beck, 21 April 1716.   (CTB)

McGILLIVRAY LOUGHLAN
Jacobite soldier captured after the Siege
of Preston, Lancashire. Transported from
Liverpool to South Carolina on the
Wakefield, master Thomas Beck, 21 April 1716.   (CTB)

McGILLIVRAY OWEN
Jacobite soldier captured after the Siege
of Preston, Lancashire. Transported from
Liverpool to South Carolina on the
Wakefield, master Thomas Beck, 21 April 1716.   (CTB)

McGILROY ANGUS
87. Born in Scotland. Moore County, NC.   (C)

McGILROY ARCHIBALD
87. Farmer. Born in Scotland. Alexander 38.
Farmer. Born in NC. Moore County, NC.   (C)

157

McGILRAY JANE
47. Born in Scotland. John 18. Born in NC.
Janet 16. Born in NC. Richmond County, NC.   (C)

McGILRAY MARY
48. Born in Scotland. Richmond County, NC.   (C)

McGILVRAY DANIEL
77. Farmer. Born in Scotland. Ann 76.
Born in Scotland. Cumberland County, NC.   (C)

McGINNIS JOSEPH
87. Born in Scotland. Charleston, SC.   (C)

McGOOGAN DANIEL
72. Born in Scotland. Mary 65. Born in
Scotland. Isabella 35. Born in NC.
Jennett 29. Born in NC. Duncan 27.
Born in NC. Margaret 7. Born in NC.
Daniel 5. Born in NC. Robeson County, NC.
Daniel McGoogan, born in Scotland,
emigrated to America in 1804, a farmer
in Robeson County, Nc, with a wife and
seven children in 1812.   (1812)(C)

McGOOGAN DUNCAN
51. Born in Scotland. Anny 41. Born in SC.
John 19. Born in NC. Catherine 17. Born in
NC. Margaret 15. Born in NC. Duncan 12.
Born in NC. Mary 10. Born in NC. Rebecca
8. Born in NC. James 6. Born in NC. Jane
3. Born in NC. Charles 7 months. Born in
NC. Robeson County, NC.   (c)

McGOWAN ANDREW
Shipmaster in NC. Uncle of John McGowan
in Garlieston, Scotland, who was
Serviced as his Heir on 10 October 1811.   (SRO/SH)

McGRATH HONOR
Emigrated from Scotland or Ireland on the
ship Pearl, master Walter Buchanan, in
December 1767. Allocated a 100 acre land
grant 12 December 1767.   (OL)

McGREGOR ALEXANDER
Born in Denny, Stirlingshire, during 1797.
Merchant in Charleston. Nat 29 September
1827 Charleston, SC.   (Nat Arch M1183.1)

McGREGOR ARCHIBALD
70. Farmer. Born in Scotland. Effie 65.
Born in Scotland. Flora 40. Born in
Scotland. Hugh 30. Millwright. Born in
NC. Garry 26. Farmer. Born in NC.
Archibald McGregor, born in Scotland,
emigrated to America during 1804, a
farmer in Cumberland County, NC, with
a wife and five children in 1812.   (C)(1812)

McGREGOR DUNCAN
Jacobite soldier captured after the Siege
of Preston, Lancashire. Transported from
Liverpool to South Carolina on the
Susannah, master Thomas Bromhall, 7 May 1716.   (SPC)(CTB)

McGREGOR MALCOLM
Jacobite soldier captured after the Siege
of Preston, Lancashire. Transported from
Liverpool to South Carolina on the
Susannah, master Thomas Bromhall, 7 May 1716.   (CTB)(SPC)

McGREGOR MALCOLM
Son of Duncan McGregor, Lismore, Argyllshire.
Mariner in Charleston, SC.   (Pr 1.10.1793 SC)

McGREGOR MALCOLM
58. Farmer. Born in Scotland. Mary 56. Born
in NC. Gregor 25. Doctor. Born in NC.
Christopher 23. Student. Born in NC. Mary 21.
Born in NC. Sarah 18. Born in NC. Dugald 16.
Farmer. Born in NC. Malcolm 14. Born in NC.
John 12. Born in NC. Cumberland County, NC.   (C)

McGREGOR NEIL
Born in Perthshire during 1773. Gardener in
Charleston. Nat. 23 August 1813 Charleston, SC.
                (Nat Arch M1183.1)

McGUGGAN DUNCAN
Born in North Knapdale, Argyllshire, in May 1794.
Emigrated to America in 1801. Died 15 January 1862.
Buried McGugan Cemetery, Shannon, Hoke County, NC. (Hoke Gs)

McGUGGAN JOHN
67. Farmer. Born in Scotland. Mary 55.
Born in Scotland. Duncan 35. Born in SC.
Catherine 32. Born in SC. Margaret 30.
Born in SC. Mary 28. Born in SC. Daniel
26. Born in SC. Christian 24. Born in SC.
John 22. Born in SC. Angus 20. Born in SC.
Archibald 18. Born in SC. Isabel 15. Born
in SC. William 12. Born in SC. Sarah 12.
Born in SC. Kershaw County, SC.   (C)

McILBRIDE ARCHIBALD
Settled in NC before 1771.(Jas McAlister letter(3774)SHC/UNC)

McILVAY DUNCAN
Prisoner in the Canongate Tolbooth.
Transported from Leith to Carolina by
Robert Malloch, merchant burgess in
Edinburgh, in August 1684.   (PC)

McINNIS ANGUS
Born in Scotland during 1780. Emigrated
to America in 1802. A farmer in Richmond
County, NC, with a wife, sister and three
children in 1812.   (1812)

McINNIS ANGUS
Born in Jura, Argyllshire, on 15 February
1785. Died in NC on 21 October 1849.
Buried in Longstreet Cemetery, Fort
Bragg, Hoke County, NC.   (Hoke Gs)

McINNIS A
65. Land-surveyor. Born in Scotland.
Orangeburg County, SC.   (C)

McINNIS ANGUS
60. Born in Scotland. Christian 62. Born
in Scotland. Miles 30. Born in NC. Effie
27. Born in NC. Anny 25. Born in NC.
Hugh 23. Born in NC. Robeson County, NC.   (C)

McINNIS CATHERINE
96. Born in Scotland. Daniel McLeod 48.
Born in NC. Catherine 48. Born in NC.
Margaret 12. Born in NC. Mary 15.
Born in NC. Robeson County, NC.   (C)

McINNIS CATHERINE
65. Born in Scotland. Archibald Buie 43.
Born in Robeson County, NC. Flora 35.
Born in Robeson County, NC. Daniel 15.
Born in Robeson County, NC. Duncan 15.
Born in Robeson County, NC. Catherine
13. Born in Robeson County, NC. John 11.
Born in Robeson County, NC. Annabella 8.
Born in Robeson County, NC. Mary 5. Born
in Robeson County, NC. Malcolm 2. Born in
Robeson County, NC. Robeson County, NC.   (C)

McINNIS DANIEL
Born in Scotland(?) during 1752. Emigrated
to America in 1792. A farmer in Moore County,
NC, with a wife and four children in 1812.   (1812)

McINNIS DUNCAN
Born in Scotland during 1764. Emigrated to
America in 1802. A farmer in Cumberland
County in 1812.   (1812)

McINNIS DUNCAN
Born in Scotland during 1775. Emigrated to
America during 1792. A farmer in Moore
County, NC, with a wife and four children
in 1812.   (1812)

MacINNISH DONALD
Born in Scotland on 16 August 1772.
Landed at Wilmington, NC, on
2 October 1792. Settled in Fayetteville,
Cumberland County. Merchant on Hay Street,
Fayetteville. Died in 1811.   (NCA.WBA.171/2)(Pr 12.1811 NC)

McINNIS JAMES
Born in Scotland during 1766. Emigrated to
America in 1792. A farmer in Richmond
County, NC, with a wife and five children
in 1812.   (1812)

McINNES JOHN
Jacobite soldier captured after the Siege
of Preston, Lancashire. Transported from
Liverpool to South Carolina on the
Susannah, master Thomas Bromhall,
7 May 1716.   (SPC)(CTB)

MCINNIS JOHN
Born in Scotland during 1783. Emigrated
to America in 1792. A farmer in Moore
County, NC, with a wife and four
children in 1812.   (1812)

McINNES MALCOLM
40. Labourer. Breadalbane, Perthshire.
Emigrated from Scotland, with his wife
Janet 36, and children John 20, Ann 15,
Catherine 11, Donald 8 and Archibald 4,
to Wilmington, NC, on the Jupiter of
Larne, master Samuel Brown, during
September 1775.   (PRO/T47.12)

McINNIS MURDOCH
Married Sally Bethune. Emigrated from
Scotland to NC c1790. Father of Angus,
Flora, Neil, Elizabeth, Alexander, John,
Duncan, Miles, Sally, Mary, Jennie and
Daniel. Buried in Mount Carmel Cemetery,
NC.   (NCA/GVF)

McINTAGART DANIEL
Born in Scotland during 1757. Emigrated
to America in 1792. A farmer in Robeson
County, NC, with a child in 1812.   (1812)

McINTAGART GILBERT
Born in Scotland during 1756. Emigrated
to America in 1791. A farmer in Robeson
County, NC, with a wife and six
children in 1812.   (1812)

McINTOSH DANIEL
86. Farmer. Born in Scotland. John A
Phillips 52. Carpenter. Born in NC.
Isabel Phillips.48. Born in NC.
Elizabeth A Phillips 9. Born in NC.
John H Phillips 7. Born in NC.
Moore County, NC.   (C)

McINTOSH DONALD
Born in Inverness-shire during 1809.
Settled in Charleston. Nat. 12 October
1830 Charleston, SC.   (Nat Arch M1183.1)

McINTOSH DUNCAN
Jacobite soldier captured after the Siege
of Preston, Lancashire. Transported from
Liverpool to South Carolina on the
Susannah, master Thomas Bromhall, on
7 May 1716.   (CTB)(SPC)

MCINTOSH DUNCAN
Jacobite soldier captured after the Siege
of Preston, Lancashire. Transported from
Liverpool to South Carolina on the
Wakefield, master Thomas Beck, 21 April 1716.   (CTB)

McINTOSH EWAN
Jacobite soldier captured after the Siege
of Preston, Lancashire. Transported from
Liverpool to South Carolina on the
Susannah, master Thomas Bromhall, 7 May 1716.   (CTB)(SPC)

McINTOSH JAMES
Jacobite soldier captured after the Siege
of Preston, Lancashire. Transported from
Liverpool to South Carolina on the
Susannah, master Thomas Bromhall, 7 May 1716.   (SPC)(CTB)

McINTOSH JAMES
Jacobite soldier captured after the Siege
of Preston, Lancashire. Transported from
Liverpool to South Carolina on the
Wakefield, master Thomas Beck, 21 April 1716.   (CTB)

McINTOSH JOHN
Jacobite soldier captured after the Siege
of Preston, Lancashire. Transported from
Liverpool to South Carolina on the
Susannah, master Thomas Bromhall, 7 May 1716.   (CTB)(SPC)

McINTOSH JOHN
Jacobite soldier captured after the Siege
of Preston, Lancashire. Transported from
Liverpool to South Carolina on the
Susannah, master Thomas Bromhall, 7 May 1716.   (CTB)(SPC)

McINTOSH JOHN
Jacobite soldier captured after the Siege
of Preston, Lancashire. Transported from
Liverpool to South Carolina on the
Susannah, master Thomas Bromhall, 7 May 1716.   (CTB)(SPC)

McINTOSH JOHN
Jacobite soldier captured after the Siege
of Preston, Lancashire. Transported from
Liverpool to South Carolina on the
Wakefield, master Thomas Beck, 21 April 1716.   (CTB)

MACKINTOSH JOHN
21. Farmer. Probably from Dores, Inverness.
Embarked for Georgia on 20 October 1735.
Landed in Georgia on 10 January 1736.
Moved to Carolina in December 1740.   (ESG)

McINTOSH JOHN
Born in Edinburgh during 1771.
A cabinetmaker in Charleston, SC.
Nat. 24 August 1813 Charleston, SC.   (Nat Arch M1183.1)

McINTOSH JOHN
Born in Edinburgh during 1785.
Mariner. Nat 11 April 1810 Charleston, SC.(Nat Arch M1183.1)

McINTOSH LAUCHLIN
Born in Scotland. Emigrated from
Scotland to Nova Scotia in 1800. Moved from
Nova Scotia to New York in 1804. Settled in
Fairfield County, SC, during 1807.
Nat. 20. April 1816 SC.   (Cit Book 73)

McINTOSH LUCY
82. Born in Scotland. James McKay 54. Born
in NC. Margaret McKay 59. Jane A McKay 27.
Born in NC. George A McKay 22. Born in NC.
Archibald McKay 16. Born in NC. James A
McKay 8. Born in NC. Sarah C McKay 7.
Born in NC. Iredell County, NC.   (C)

MACKINTOSH MILES.
Inverness-shire. Settled in Charleston, SC.(Pr 26.3.1729 SC)

McINTOSH WALTER
Born in Scotland(?) on 17 July 1808. Died
12 May 1850. Buried Raleigh City Cemetery, NC. (Raleigh Gs)

McINTOSH WILLIAM
Jacobite soldier captured after the Siege
of Preston, Lancashire. Transported from
Liverpool to South Carolina on the
Wakefield, master Thomas Beck, 21 April 1716.   (CTB)

McINTOSH WILLIAM
Jacobite soldier captured after the Siege
of Preston, Lancashire. Transported from
Liverpool to South Carolina on the
Susannah, master Thomas Bromhall, 7 May 1716.   (CTB)(SPC)

McINTOSH WILLIAM
Born in Scotland. Nat.21 October 1822 SC.(Circuit Ct J19.266)

McINTIRE ALEXANDER
Born in Scotland during 1776. Emigrated
to America in 1802. Merchant in
Fayetteville, NC, during 1812.   (1812)

McINTYRE ANGUS
Born in Morvern, Argyllshire, during 1791.
Settled in Charleston, SC, in October 1822.
Nat. 1 January 1827 Marlborough, SC.   (SCA)

McINTIRE ANN
60. Spinner. Glen Orchy, Argyllshire.
Emigrated from Scotland to Wilmington,
NC, on the Jupiter of Larne, master
Samuel Brown, September 1775.   (PRO/T47.12)

McINTYRE ARCHIBALD
Born in Scotland. Farmer. 79. Mary 68.
Born in NC. Chatham County, NC.   (C)

McINTYRE CATHERINE
63. Born in Scotland. Duncan 26. Farmer.
Born in NC. Margaret 32. Born in NC.
Richmond County, NC.   (C)

McINTYRE DONALD
28. Farmer. Glen Orchy, Argyllshire.
Emigrated from Greenock, Renfrewshire,
with his wife Mary 25, to Wilmington, NC,
on the Ulysses, J Chalmers, in August 1774.   (PRO/T47.12)

MacINTIRE DONALD
54. Labourer. Glen Orchy, Argyllshire.
Emigrated from Scotland, with his wife
Katherine 41, and children Mary 12,
Margaret 9, John 6, and Duncan 5, to
Wilmington, NC, on the Jupiter of Larne,
master Samuel Brown, in September 1775.   (PRO/T47.12)

McINTYRE DANIEL
50. Farmer. Born in Scotland. Mary 48.
Born in Marion County, SC. John 17.
Farmer. Born in Marion County, SC.
Duncan 10. Born in Marion County, SC.
Marion County, SC.   (C)

165

McINTYRE DOUGALD
Married Lilly Campbell in Lismore,
Argyllshire, c1820. Emigrated from
Scotland to SC c1820.   (SHC)

McINTYRE DOUGAL
52. Farmer. Born in Scotland. Lilly 48.
Born in Scotland. Elizabeth 27. Born in
Scotland. Jane 21. Born in Marion County,
SC. Anne 18. Born in Marion County, SC.
Joseph 14. Born in Marion County, SC.
James 12. Born in Marion County, SC.
William 10. Born in Marion County, SC.
Lilly 7. Born in Marion County, SC.
Margaret 2. Born in Marion County, SC.
Mary 4. Born in Marion County, SC.   (C)
Marion County, SC.

McINTYRE DUNCAN
40. Farmer. Glen Orchy, Argyllshire.
Emigrated from Greenock, Renfrewshire,
with his wife Katherine 28, to
Wilmington, NC, on the Ulysses,
master J Chalmers, in August 1774.   (PRO/T47.12)

McINTYRE DUNCAN
55. Labourer. Breadalbane, Perthshire.
Emigrated from Scotland, with his wife
Katherine 55, and children Mary 24,
Katherine 17 and Elizabeth 14, to
Wilmington, NC, on the Jupiter of Larne,
master Samuel Brown, in September 1775.   (PRO/T47.12)

McINTYRE GILBERT
34. Tailor. Breadalbane, Perthshire.
Emigrated from Scotland, with his wife
Ann 36, and children Charles 11, Margaret
9, Ewan 5, and Malcolm 1, to Wilmington, NC,
on the Jupiter of Larne, master Samuel
Brown, in September 1775.   (PRO/T47.12)

McINTYRE JOHN
45. Farmer. Glen Orchy, Argyllshire.
Emigrated from Greenock, Renfrewshire,
with his wife Mary Downie 35, to
Wilmington, NC, on the Ulysses,
master J Chalmers, in August 1774.   (PRO/T47.12)

McINTYRE JOHN
35. Farmer. Glen Orchy, Argyllshire.
Emigrated from Greenock, Renfrewshire,
with his wife Margaret 30, to
Wilmington, NC, on the Ulysses, master
J Chalmers, in August 1774.   (PRO/T47.12)

McINTYRE JOHN
35. Labourer. Glen Orchy, Argyllshire.
Emigrated from Scotland, with his wife
Ann 32, and children Margaret 6,
Archibald 4 and John - an infant, to
Wilmington, NC, on the Jupiter of Larne
master Samuel Brown, in September 1775.   (PRO/T47.12)

McINTYRE JOHN
32. Tailor. Breadalbane, Perthshire.
Emigrated from Scotland, with his wife
Katherine 30, and children Donald 3 and
John1, to Wilmington, NC, on the
Jupiter of Larne, master Samuel Brown,
in September 1775.   (PRO/T47.12)

McINTYRE JOHN
Born in Kinlochlaish, Lismore, Argyllshire,
on 21 August 1750, son of John Donald
McIntyre and his wife Catherine Ann Stuart.
Married (1) Catherine Ann McCallum on
15 December 1789. Emigrated from Appin,
Argyllshire, to Wilmington, NC, on
10 August 1791. Landed at Fort Johnston,
Brunswick County, NC, on 11 November 1791.
Married (2) Mary Wright in 1795 (2) Jane
McColman in 1801 (4)Mary McNeil or
Graham on 10 December 1812. Father of nine
children. Presbyterian minister in
Robeson County, NC, from 1820 to 1837.
Died in Hoke County, NC, on 17 November 1853.
Buried at Antioch, NC.   (St Paul's OPR)(LRS)(Hoke Gs)

McINTYRE JOHN
Born in Argyllshire on 7 March 1767. Died in
NC on 9 March 1854. Buried in Carmichael -
McIntyre Cemetery, Laurinburg, NC.   (Laurinburg Gs)

McINTYRE JOHN
Born in Scotland c1764. Died in
Fayetteville, Cumberland County, NC,
on 10 September 1829.   (RRw 17.10.1829)

McINTYRE JOHN
83. Farmer. Born in Scotland. Nancy 37.
Born in NC. Sarah 25. Born in NC. Lilly
23. Born in NC. Archibald 21. Born in NC.
Margaret 19. Born in NC. Richmond County, NC.   (C)

167

McINTYRE JOHN R
28. Born in Scotland. Elizabeth 23. Born in
NC. Robeson County, NC.   (C)

McINTYRE JOHN
100. Born in Scotland. Robeson County, NC.   (C)

McINTYRE NICHOLAS
Born in Scotland during 1757. Emigrated
to America in 1792. A farmer in
Cumberland County, NC, with a wife and
children in 1812.   (1812)

McIVER Rev COLIN
Born in Stornaway, Lewis, Ross and
Cromarty, on 9 March 1781.
Settled in Fayetteville, NC, as a
teacher in 1809. Presbyterian.
Married Sarah Barge. Died during
1850 in Fayetteville, NC.   (SFV)

McIVER DOROTHY
Born in Skye, Inverness-shire during
October 1802. Died on 1 December 1857
in NC. Buried in Union Presbyterian
Cemetery, Carthage, Moore County, NC.   (Moore Gs)

McIVER EVANDER
Born in Scotland during 1712, son of
Kenneth McIver. Father of Duncan, born
in Skye, Inverness-shire, during 1744.
Died in Chatham, NC.   (SG)

McIVOR EVANDER
56. Farmer. Born in Scotland. Margaret 48.
Born in NC. Flora A. 23. Born in NC.
Duncan R. 21. Born in NC. Donald 16. Born
in NC. Matthew 16. Born in NC. Elizabeth 12.
Born in NC. Chatham County, NC.   (C)

McIVER FLORA
61. Born in Scotland. Catherine 30. Born in
NC. Isabella 25. Born in NC. Kenneth 23.
Born in NC. Moore County, NC.   (C)

McIVER JANE
60. Born in Scotland. Mary 24. Born in NC.
John 22. Farmer. Born in NC. Andrew 20.
Born in NC. Farmer. William 14. Born in NC.
Moore County, NC.   (C)

McIVER JOHN
Merchant in Columbia, SC. Serviced as Heir
to his granduncle Thomas Agnew, tenant in
Clanny, Scotland, on 6 March 1829.   (SRO/SH)

McIVER JOHN
78. Farmer. Born in Scotland. Neill 51.
Tailor. Born in Scotland. Kenneth 45.
Farmer. Born in NC. Catherine 12.
Born in NC. Neill 8. Born in NC.
Moore County, NC.   (C)

McIVER MARY
Born in Skye, Inverness-shire, during
October 1802. Died in NC on 13 August
1856. Buried in Union Presbyterian
Cemetery,Carthage, Moore County, NC.   (Moore Gs)

MacKAY AENEAS
20. Teacher or clerk. Tongue, Sutherland.
Emigrated from Scotland, on the
Bachelor of Leith, to Wilmington, NC,
during April 1774.   (PRO/T47.12)

McKAY ALEXANDER
Emigrated from Scotland to Brunswick,
NC, during September 1739.   (VOS)

McKAY ALEXANDER
Born in Scotland(?) during 1782.
Emigrated to America in 1802. A
farmer in Robeson County, NC,
with a wife and three children in 1812.   (1812)

McKAY ALEXANDER
49. Farmer. Born in Scotland. Eliza 30.
Born in NC. Daniel 11. Born in NC.
Martin 9. Born in NC. Martha A. 7.
Born in NC. John 3. Born in NC.
Margaret M. 5 months. Montgomery County, NC.   (C)

McKAY CATHERINE
Born in Scotland. 71. Daniel 39. Farmer.
Born in NC. Sarah 37. Born in NC. Flora
35. Isabella 44. Born in NC. Catherine
9. Philip 7. Born in NC. Margaret 5.
Born in NC. Richmond County, NC.   (C)

McKAY CATHERINE
Born in Scotland. 60. Malcolm 23.
Farmer. Born in NC. Margaret 28. Born
in NC. Christian 26. Born in NC. John
22. Born in NC. Richmond County, NC.   (C)

McKAY CATHERINE
Born in Scotland. 50. Daniel 27. Farmer.
Born in NC. Isabella 22. Born in NC.
Sarah 19. Born in NC. Mary 18. Born
in NC. Richmond County, NC.   (C)

McKAY CHRISTIAN
60. Born in Scotland. Jennett 55. Born
in Scotland. Mary B. 50. Born in NC.
Robeson County, NC.   (C)

McKAY DONALD
Born in Scotland during 1773. Emigrated
to America during 1803. Nat. 20 September
1813 Richmond County, NC.   (RCCR)

McKAY DANIEL
Born in Scotland(?) Emigrated to America
during 1792. A farmer in Robeson County,
NC, in 1812.   (1812)

McKAY DONALD
20. Tailor. Kintyre, Argyllshire.
Emigrated from Greenock, Renfrewshire,
to Wilmington, NC, on the Ulysses,
master J Chalmers, in August 1774.   (PRO/T47.12)

McKAY DUNCAN
Born in Knapdale, Argyllshire, c1744.
Settled in Cumberland County, NC.
Nat. 19 October 1803 Cape Fear, NC.   (D McKay clln.PC1305)

McKAY DUNCAN sr
Born in Scotland during 1747. Emigrated
to America in 1802. A farmer in
Richmond County, NC, with two children
in 1812.   (1812)

McKAY ELIZABETH
80. Born in Scotland. Alexander 50.
Carriagemaker. Born in SC. Anson County, NC.   (C)

McKAY GEORGE
40. Farmer and tailor. Strathoolie, Kildonan,
Sutherland. Emigrated from Scotland, with his
wife and child, to Wilmington, NC, on the
Bachelor of Leith in April 1774.   (PRO/T47.12)

McKAY HUGH
Born in Scotland during 1780. Emigrated
to America in 1792. A farmer in Robeson
County, NC, in 1812.   (1812)

McKAY JAMES
60. Shoemaker. Strathnavaar, Sutherland.
Emigrated from Scotland, with his wife
and child, to Wilmington, NC, on the
Bachelor of Leith in April 1774.   (PRO/T47.12)

McKAY JOHN
Born in Scotland. Buried in St Helen's,
SC, on 31 August 1768.   (St Helen's OPR)

McKAY MALCOLM
Born in Argyllshire during 1769. Nat.
8 August 1805 Charleston, SC.   (Nat Arch M1183.1)

McKAY MARY
73. Born in Scotland. Gilbert 37. Born
in NC. Robeson County, NC.   (C)

McKAY MUNGO CAMPBELL
Born in Stirling. Merchant. Nat. 31 May
1798 Charleston, SC.   (Nat Arch M1183.1)

McKAY NEIL
Born in Scotland(?) Nat.22 December 1813
Richmond County, NC.   (D McKay clln.PC1305)

McKAY WILLIAM
37. Farmer. Strathaledale, Reay, Caithness.
Emigrated from Scotland, with his wife and
four children aged between 8 and 1½, to
Wilmington, NC, on the Bachelor of Leith,
in April 1774.   (PRO/T47.12)

McKAY WILLIAM
30. Farmer. Farr, Strathnavaar, Sutherland.
Emigrated from Scotland, with his wife and
three children aged between 8 and 2, to
Wilmington, NC, on the Bachelor of Leith,
in April 1774.   (PRO/T47.12)

McKAY WILLIAM
26. Farmer. Craigie, Reay, Caithness.
Emigrated from Scotland to Wilmington, NC,
on the Bachelor of Leith in April 1774.   (PRO/T47.12)

McKEELS DANIEL
Jacobite soldier captured after the Siege
of Preston, Lancashire. Transported from
Liverpool to South Carolina on the
Susannah, master Thomas Bromhall, 7 May 1716.   (CTB)(SPC)

McKEITHAN NEILL
Born in Scotland c1752. Married Loveday
McLaughlin in Moore County, NC, 1785.
Died in Moore County, NC, in 1835.   (INC60040)

McKELLAR DUGALD
Born in Argyllshire. Settled in Abbeville,
SC, during 1816. Nat.21 March 1818 SC.   (Cit. Book 78)

McKELLAR JOHN
Born in Argyllshire c1771. Partner in the
firm McKellar and Ainsley, Augusta, Georgia.
Resident of Cambridge, SC. Died on
23 November 1812.   (Augusta Chron.22.2.1817)

McKELLAR MARY
49. Born in Scotland. Abbeville County, SC.   (C)

McKELLAR PETER
40. Farmer. Born in Scotland. John T. 13.
Born in SC. Elizabeth 11. Born in SC. Ann
9. Born in SC. Leonard 7. Born in SC.
Benjamin 5. Born in SC. Abbeville County, SC.   (C)

SCOTS IN THE CAROLINAS

McKENZIE ALEXANDER
Edinburgh. Tailor in Charleston, SC.
Died in 1793. Alexander Lambert, sailor,
his grandson was Serviced as his Heir on
27 October 1818.   (SRO/SH)(SRO/CC8/8/138)(Pr 17.5.1793SC)

McKENZIE ANDREW
Born in Argyllshire. Grocer. Nat.
17 January 1792 Charleston, SC.   (Nat Arch M1183.1)

MacKENZIE ANNE
Third daughter of the Earl of Cromartie
and his wife Isabella Gordon. Married (1)
Hon Edmond Atkin, Superintendant of
Indian Affairs in Southern America, and
President of the Council of SC, died 1761.
(2) John Murray MD, in Charleston, SC, on
16 February 1764. Died in Charleston, SC,
on 18 January 1768.   (TML)(NHP)(SP.3.81)

McKENZIE CHRISTOPHER
Born in Scotland c1740. Married Christian
..... in Scotland. Died in Chatham County,
NC, during 1773.   (INC28255)

McKENZIE DANIEL
54. Farmer. Born in Scotland. Mary 48.
Born in Scotland. Catherine 20. Born in SC.
Robert 16. Born in SC. Effy 12. Born in SC.
Isabella 12. Born in SC. Joseph 10. Born in
SC. Sara 4. Born in SC. Mary 3. Born in SC.
Daniel 14. Born in SC. Marlborough County, SC.   (C)

McKENZIE DUNCAN
Born in Scotland during 1755. Emigrated to
America in 1790. A farmer in Cumberland
County, NC, with a wife and four children
in 1812.   (1812)

McKENZIE GILBERT
34. Farmer. Kintyre, Argyllshire. Emigrated
from Greenock, Renfrewshire, with his wife
Margaret 27, to Wilmington, NC, on the
Diana, master D Ruthven, in September 1774.   (PRO/T47.12)

McKENZIE JAMES
76. Farmer. Born in Scotland. E. 45.
Born in Scotland. Ezrael 21. Born in
SC. Joseph 17. Born in SC. Wallace 13.
Born in SC. Laura 9. Born in SC.
Alexander 7. Born in SC. Julia 19.
Born in SC. Darlington County, SC.   (C)

McKENZIE JAMES
Born in Scotland c1791. Died in
Charleston, SC, on 26 August 1827.   (Ch O 1.9.1827)

McKENZIE JAMES
Born in Roxburghshire(?) during 1793.
A plasterer in Charleston, SC. Nat.
26 September 1826 Charleston, SC.   (Nat Arch M1183.1)

MacKENZIE JANE
Born in Scotland c1731. A runaway
indentured servant of Same Carne in 1753. (SCGaz 17.12.1753)

McKENZIE JOHN
Born in Scotland during 1757. Emigrated
to America in 1791. A farmer in
Richmond County, NC, with a wife and
seven children during 1812.   (1812)

MacKENZIE JOHN
16. Clerk and book-keeper. Born in
Scotland. Emigrated from London to
Carolina on the Briton, master
Alexander Urquhart, November 1774.   (PRO/T47.12)

McKENZIE JOHN
Born in Argyllshire during 1785.
Merchant. Nat. 11 January 1808
Charleston, SC.   (Nat Arcg M1183.1)

McKENZIE JOHN
58. Cabinetmaker. Born in Scotland.
Mary 58. Born in Scotland. John 32.
Born in Scotland. Clerk. Charleston, SC.   (C)

McKENZIE MARGERY
82. Born in Scotland. Moore County, NC.   (C)

MacKENZIE MARY
22. Spinner. Banff. Indentured servant.
Emigrated from London to NC July 1736.   (LGR)

MACKENZIE Lady MARY
Second daughter of George, third Earl of
Cromartie, and Isobel Gordon. Married
(1) Captain Clark in London on 23 June
1750 (2) Hon Thomas Drayton, member of
HM Council in SC in August 1757 (3)
John ainslie, in Charleston, SC, on
17 June 1762 (4) ... Middleton.(TML)(NHP)(SM 24.451)(SP 3.81)

McKENZIE MARY ANN
60. Born in Scotland. Charleston, SC.   (C)

McKENZIE MURDOCH
Born in Scotland during 1769. Married Rebecca
Tyson. Senator from Moore County, NC.
Will dated 25 October 1821 Chatham County, NC.
                                  (NCSJ 4.1)(INC28255)

McKENZIE MURDOCH
78. Farmer. Born in Scotland. Sarah 50.
Born in NC. Elizabeth 35. Born in NC.
Jane 30. Born in NC. Sarah 25. Born in
NC. Emeline. Born in NC. Moore County, NC.   (C)

McKENZIE ROBERT
Born in Scotland. Died in Charleston, SC. (Pr 29.5.1789 SC)

MACKENZIE THOMAS
Born in Scotland during 1798. Merchant in the
firm of Mackenzie and Hernandez. Settled in
Savannah, Georgia, during 1817. Died in
Purrysburg, SC, on 21 September 1823.   (GaR 11.9.1823)

McKENZIE WILLIAM
Jacobite soldier captured after the Siege
of Preston, Lancashire. Transported from
Liverpool to South Carolina on the
Wakefield, master Thomas Beck, 21 April 1716.   (CTB)(SPC)

McKENZIE WILLIAM
Born in Scotland. Planter in SC.   (Pr 1.12.1738 SC)

MACKENZIE WILLIAM
Merchant in Charleston, SC. Died before 1739.   (SM.1.44)

McKENZIE WILLIAM
Born in Perthshire during 1771. A farmer
in Georgetown, SC. Nat. 27 May 1807 Charleston, SC.
                                  (Nat Arch M1183.1)

McKENZIE WILLIAM
Born in Scotland c1775. Merchant in
Winyaw, SC. Died in October 1825.   (WI 15.10.1825)

McKENZIE WILLIAM
Born in Edinburgh. Settled in Charleston, SC.
Nat. 5 October 1831 Charleston, SC.   (Nat Arch M1183.1)

McKEWN WILLIAM
Emigrated from Scotland or Ireland to SC on
the ship Pearl, master Walter Buchanan in
December 1767. Allocated a 100 acre land
grant on 12 December 1767.   (OL)

McKEICHAN NANCY
Born on 2 September 1765, daughter of John
McKeichen, Maderloch, Scotland. Married
John Carmichael, 1775-1837. Died on 4
August 1838. Buried in Carmichael-McIntyre
Cemetery, Laurinburg, NC.   (Laurinburg Gs)

McKEITHEN NEILL
Born in North Uist, Inverness-shire, c1752.
Settled in Cumberland County, NC, before 1785.
Married Loveday McLauchlan, 1749-1823, in 1785.
Father of Dougald, John, Neill, Daniel and Mary.
Died during 1835.   (SG)

McKIEHAN ROBERT
32. Farmer. Kintyre, Argyllshire. Emigrated from
Greenock, Renfrewshire, with his wife Janet
McKendrick 24, and son Neil 5, to
Wilmington, NC, on the Ulysses, master
J Chalmers, in August 1774.   (PRO/T47.12)

McKEY ALEXANDER
Emigrated from Argyllshire to NC in 1739.
Allocated a 320 acre land grant in
Bladen County, NC, on 4 June 1740.   (SHA.106)

MACKEY JAMES W.
Born in Scotland. Merchantin Plymouth, NC.
Died in Plymouth, NC, on 10 September 1821.   (RR 28.9.1821)

McKIMMEY WILLIAM
Died on May River Plantation, SC. in April 1799.(EA 3708.31)

McKINISH MARY
57. Born in Scotland. Jane 47.
Born in Scotland. Cumberland County, NC.   (C)

MacKINLAY AGNES
Glasgow. Educated at University of
Glasgow. Midwife in Wilmington, NC,
from 1798.   (Hall's Wilm Gaz 8.3.1798)

McKINLAY DUNCAN
Born in Argyllshire. Emigrated to
Charleston, SC, in December 1819.
Resident in NC and in SC.
Nat. 26 September 1840 Union, SC.   (Union Nats 46)

McKINLAY JAMES
Born in Scotland c1751. Married Mary ...,
1756-1840. Merchant in Newbern, NC, for
40 years. Died on 4 February 1819.
Buried at Cedar Grove, Craven County, NC.   (Cedar Grove Gs)

McKINLAY PETER
Born in Greenock, Renfrewshire, during
1803. A carpenter in Charleston, SC.
Nat. 6 October 1830 Charleston, SC.   (Nat Arch M1183.1)

McKINNON ALEXANDER
Born in Scotland during 1765. Emigrated
to America in 1802. A farmer in Richmond
County, NC, with a wife in 1812.   (1812)

McKINNON ALEXANDER
Born in Scotland c1767. Emigrated to
America c1802. Nat. 20 September 1813.   (RCCR)

McKINNON ALEXANDER
68. Farmer. Born in Scotland. Margaret 71.
Born in NC. Murdoch 36. Born in NC.
Roderick 26. Labourer. Born in NC.
Jane 27. Born in NC. John L. 1. Born in NC.
Montgomery County, NC.   (C)

McKINNON ALEXANDER
64. Farmer. Born in Scotland. Janet 42.
Born in NC. Mary 19. Born in NC. Rachel 17.
Born in NC. Angus 16. Born in NC. Abigail
15. Born in NC. Margaret 18. Born in NC.
Lucy 12. Born in NC. Mary 9. Born in NC.
Catherine 8. Born in NC. Lauchlin 6.
Born in NC. Richmond County, NC.   (C)

McKINNON Miss CATHERINE
Born in Kintyre, Argyllshire, c1766.
Died in Fayetteville, Cumberland County,
NC, on 13 July 1826.   (RRw 4.8.1826)

McKINNON CATHERINE
Born in Scotland. 51. Daniel 22. Farmer.
Born in NC. William 18. Student. Born in
NC. Nicholas 14. Born in NC. Richmond County, NC.   (C)

McKINNON CHARLES
Born Sleat, Skye, Inverness-shire, c1778.
Died in NC on 7 May 1816. Buried in
Murchison Cemetery, NC.   (Murchison Gs)

McKINNON CHRISTIAN
Born in Bracadale, Skye, Inverness-shire,
on 21 December 1745. Died 14 February 1824
in NC. Buried in McKinnon Cemetery, NC.   (McKinnon Gs)

MacKINNON DANIEL
Born in Kintyre, Argyllshire, during 1756.
Emigrated to America in 1788. Died in NC
during 1821. Buried in McKinnon Cemetery,
Laurinburg, Scotland County, NC.   (McKinnon Gs)

McKINNON DANIEL
Born in Scotland during 1764. Emigrated
to America in 1787. A farmer in Moore
County, NC, with a wife in 1812.   (1812)

McKINNON DONALD
North Uist, Inverness-shire. Died in
NC before 1803.   (Pr 3.1803 PCC)

McKINNON GILBERT
Born in Galloway during 1782. Died in
Wilmington, NC, on 26 October 1819.   (RR 5.11.1819)

McKINNON JOHN
Born in Scotland on 29 June 1750. Died in
NC on 29 December 1819. Buried in McKinnon
Cemetery, Laurinburg, Scotland County, NC.   (McKinnon Gs)

McKINNON JOHN
Born in Scotland during 1768. A farmer in
Robeson County, NC, with two children in 1812.   (1812)

McKINNON JOHN sr
62. Farmer. Born in Scotland. Celia 53.
Born in SC. Hannah 21. Born in SC.
Alexander 17. Labourer. Born in SC.
Martha 14. Born in NC. Catherine 12.
Born in NC. Mauchlin 11. Born in NC.
Montgomery County, NC.   (C)

McKINNON MARGARET
80. Born in Scotland. John McRae 40.
Born in NC. Isabella McRae 41. Born in
NC. Sarah McRae 13. Born in NC. Florah
12. Born in NC. Margaret 7, Born in NC.
Henrietta 5. Born in NC. Rodric 10. Born
in NC. Alexander Bradford 16. Born in NC.
Robeson County, NC.   (C)

McKINNON MURDOCH
Born in Scotland c1767. Emigrated to
America c1802. A farmer in Richmond County,
NC, with a wife and four children in 1812.
Nat. 20 September 1813 Richmond County, NC.   (RCCR)(1812)

McKINNON NEILL
Born in Scotland c1743. Emigrated to
America during 1803. A farmer in Richmond
County, NC, with a wife and two children
in 1812. Nat. 20 September 1813 Richmond County, NC.
                                              (RCCR)(1812)

McKINNON NEIL
Born in Scotland during 1757. Emigrated to
America in 1791. A farmer in Richmond
County, NC, with a wife and seven
children in 1812.   (1812)

McKINNON RODERICK
60. Farmer. Born in Scotland. Effie 58.
Born in Scotland. Mary 34. Born in NC.
Chesterfield County, SC.   (C)

McKINNON ROY
Born in Scotland c1789. Emigrated to
America c1802. Nat.20 September 1813
Richmond County, NC.   (RCCR)

McKNIGHT SAMUEL
Born in Galloway during 1801. An accountant
in Charleston, SC. Nat.20 April 1825
Charleston, SC.   (Nat Arch M1183.1)

SCOTS IN THE CAROLINAS

McLAUGHLIN HUGH
Emigrated from Scotland to Brunswick,
NC, during September 1739.   (VOS)

McLACHLEN JAMES
Emigrated from Argyllshire(?) to NC
during 1739. Allocated a 320 acre
land grant in Bladen County, NC,
on 4 June 1740.   (SHA.106)

McLACHLEN JAMES
Emigrated from Argyllshire(?) to NC
during 1739. Allocated a 320 acre
land grant in Bladen County, NC,
on 4 June 1740.   (SHA.106)

McLACHLAN PETER
Born in Scotland c1784. Settled in
Robeson County, NC, c1823. Married
(2) Sarah McLean during 1834.
Father of Sarah, Neil and John.   (CLM.1980)

McLACHLAN ROBERT
Born in Scotland c1765. Married
Isabella Campbell c1791 in
Tayvallich, North Knapdale, Argyllshire.
Emigrated to NC(?) during 1814. Father
of Duncan, Peter, Catherine, Isobel,
Christian and Lovedy.   (CLM.1980)

McLAGGAN ARCHIBALD
Settled in NC before 1771.(Jas McAlister letter,3774,SHC/UNC)

MacLAINE ARCHIBALD
Emigrated from Scotland via Ireland to
NC before 1750. Attorney in Wilmington,
NC. Married Elizabeth, daughter of
Jerome Rowan. Revolutionary politician.
Died after 1788.   (WTB)

McLAINE JOHN
Nat. September 1814 Richmond County, NC.   (RCCR)

McLAREN .....
79. Born in Scotland. Janet 76. Born in
Scotland. John 36. Postmaster. Born in SC.
Abbeville County, SC.   (C)

180

McLAURIN ANGUS
Born in Scotland during 1778. Emigrated
to America in 1792. A farmer in Richmond
County, NC, with a wife and four
children in 1812.   (1812)

McLAURIN ANGUS
Born in Scotland during 1779. Emigrated
to America in 1790. A blacksmith in
Richmond County, NC, with a wife and
four children in 1812.   (1812)

McLERAN ARCHIBALD
Born in Glasgow during 1771. Mill-
wright. Nat. 9 November 1814
Charleston, SC.   (Nat Arch M1183.1)

McLAURIN CATHERINE
Born in Appin, Argyllshire, c1762,
daughter of Duncan Colquhoun. Died
on 22 March 1841. Buried in
Stewartsville Cemetery, Laurinburg,
Scotland County, NC.   (Laurinburg Gs)

McLAURIN CATHERINE
84. Born in Scotland. Janet 54. Born in
NC. John 47. Farmer. Born in NC. Mary
36. Born in NC. Margaret 32. Born in
NC. Daniel 18. Farmer. Born in NC. Mary
13. Born in NC. John 12. Born in NC.
Catherine 11. Born in NC. William 10.
Born in NC. Margaret 8. Born in NC.
Janet 3. Born in NC. Lauchlin 1.
Born in NC. Richmond County, NC.   (C)

McLAURIN CATHERINE
65. Born in Scotland. Mary 35. Born
in NC. Nancy 30. Born in NC. Effie
28. Born in NC. Penelope 26. Born
in NC. Hugh 24. Farmer. Born in NC.
Richmond County, NC.   (C)

McLAUREN CHRISTIAN
63. Born in Scotland. Hugh 52.
Farmer. Born in NC. Sarah A. 23.
Born in NC. Anson County, NC.   (C)

McLAREN DANIEL
Born in Scotland c1713. Died in
Rockingham County, NC.   (INC27356)

McLAURIN DANIEL
Born in Scotland during 1772. Emigrated
to America in 1790. A wheelwright in
Richmond County, NC, with a wife and
six children in 1812.   (1812)

McLAREN DONALD
12. Labourer. Breadalbane, Perthshire.
Emigrated from Scotland to Wilmington,
NC, on the Jupiter of Larne, master
Samuel Brown, in September 1775.   (PRO/T47.12)

McLAUREN DONALD
Born in 1772. Emigrated to America
during 1792. A farmer in Richmond
County, NC, with a wife and six
children in 1812.   (1812)

McLAURIN DUNCAN
Born in Glenshiel, Argyllshire, c1741.
Died in NC on 18 July 1828. Buried
in Stewartsville Cemetery, Laurinburg,
Scotland County, NC.   (Laurinburg Gs)

McLAREN DUNCAN
30. Labourer. Breadalbane, Perthshire.
Emigrated from Scotland to Wilmington,
NC, on the Jupiter of Larne, master
Samuel Brown, in September 1775.   (PRO/T47.12)

McLAURIN HUGH
Born in Ballachulish, Appin, Argyllshire,
c1751. Emigrated to NC during 1790.
Married Effy .. Father of Effy,1797-1864.
A farmer in Richmond County, NC, in 1812.
Died on 12 January 1846. Buried in
Stewartsville Cemetery, Laurinburg,
Scotland County, NC.   (Laurinburg Gs)

McLERAN HUGH
Born in Scotland. Planter. Settled in
America during 1791. Nat. 4 November
1806 Marlborough County, SC.   (SCA)

McLAURIN HUGH
Born in Scotland. Emigrated to America
before 14 April 1802. Nat. March 1814
Richmond County, NC.   (RCCR)(1812)

McLAURIN HUGH
62. Farmer. Born in Scotland. Nancy 52.
Born in NC. Daniel 19. Farmer. Born in
NC. Christian 17. Born in NC. Duncan
14. Born in NC. John 12. Born in NC.
Richmond County, NC.   (C)

McLAURIN JAMES
43. Miller. Born in Scotland. Carabell 47.
Born in Scotland. James 17. Miller. Born
in SC. Sarah 14. Born in SC. Henry 11.
Born in SC. Harriet 8. Born in SC.
Isabel 5. Born in SC. Charleston, SC.   (C)

McLAREN JOHN
Jacobite soldier captured after the Siege
of Preston, Lancashire. Transported from
Liverpool to South Carolina on the
Susannah, master Thomas Bromhall, 7 May 1716.   (SPC)(CTB)

McLAURIN JOHN
59. Farmer. Born in Scotland. Effie 39.
Born in Scotland. Niven 7. Born in NC.
Elizabeth 4. Born in NC. Catherine 2.
Born in NC. Richmond County, NC.   (C)

McLAREN LACHLEN
25. Labourer. Breadalbane, Perthshire.
Emigrated from Scotland to Wilmington,
NC, on the Jupiter of Larne, master
Samuel Brown, in September 1775.   (PRO/T47.12)

McLAURIN LAURIN
Born in Scotland. Partner in the firm of
L and D McLaurin, merchants in
Fayetteville, Cumberland County, NC.
Died in Fayetteville on 1 March 1817.   (RR 3.1817)

McLAREN LAWRENCE
20. Joiner. Breadalbane, Perthshire.
Emigrated from Scotland to Wilmington,
NC, on the Jupiter of Larne, master
Samuel Browm, in September 1775.   (PRO/T47.12)

MacLARAN LOWRY
A Scottish soldier who deserted from
Lt Col Cochrane's Company in April 1739.   (SCGaz 4.1739)

McLAURIN MARY
Born in Glenshiel, Argyllshire, c1745,
daughter of Hugh McLaurin. Married
Duncan McLaurin. Died 25 October 1827.
Buried in Stewartsville Cemetery,
Laurinburg, Scotland County, NC.   (Laurinburg Gs)

McLAURIN MARY
73. Born in Scotland. Malcom Calhoun 23.
Farmer. Born in NC. Mary 21. Born in NC.
Richmond County, NC.   (C)

McLAURIN MAURICE
Born in Scotland during 1752. Emigrated
to America in 1790. A farmer in Richmond
County, NC, with a wife and four
children in 1812.   (1812)

McLAURIN NANCY
69. Born in Scotland. Lauchlin 28.
Farmer. Born in NC. Nancy 25. Born in
NC. James 4. Born in NC. Joseph 1.
Born in NC. Richmond County, NC.   (C)

McLAURIN NANCY
58. Born in Scotland. Hugh 30. Farmer.
Born in NC. John 28. Born in NC.
Lauchlin 27. Born in NC. Ann 26.
Born in NC. Catherine 23. Born in NC.
Daniel 20. Farmer. Born in NC. Neal 19.
Farmer. Born in NC. Margaret 17. Born
in NC. Isabel 14. Born in NC. Anson County, NC.   (C)

McLAURIN NANCY
Born in Appin, Argyllshire, c1780,
daughter of Duncan McLaurin. Died in NC
on 23 November 1860. Buried in
Stewartsville Cemetery, Laurinburg,
Scotland County, NC.   (Laurinburg Gs)

McLAURIN NEILL
Born in Appin, Argyllshire, c1772. Died
in NC on 16 October 1827. Buried in
Stewartsville Cemetery, Laurinburg,
Scotland County, NC.   (Laurinburg Gs)

McLAURIN NEIL
Born in Glen Appin, Argyllshire, in
September 1775. Died in Wilmington,
NC, during June 1853. Buried in
Stewartsville Cemetery, Laurinburg,
Scotland County, NC.   (Laurinburg Gs)

McLAURIN NEILL
Born in Glen Etive, Argyllshire,
during September 1778. Died in
June 1853. Buried in Stewartsville
Cemetery, Laurinsburg, Scotland
County, NC.   (Laurinsburg Gs)

McLAURIN NEILL
Born in Appin, Argyllshire, on
14 November 1779. Died in NC on
15 February 1840. Buried in
Stewartsville Cemetery, Laurinburg,
Scotland County, NC.   (Laurinburg Gs)

McLAREN PATRICK
Jacobite soldier captured after the Siege
of Preston, Lancashire. Transported from
Liverpool to South Carolina on the
Susannah, master Thomas Bromhall, 7 May 1716.   (SPC)(CTB)

McLARTY ALEXANDER
Born in Scotland during 1747, son of
John McLarty. Emigrated to America in
1773. Married Barbara McNaught.
Settled in NC.   (NCA/McLarty family pp)

McLARTY ALEXANDER
Born in Scotland during 1757. Married
Jenny Morrison in 1776. Died in
Mecklenburg County, NC, in 1824.   (NCGen XXI.3068)

McLARTY ARCHIBALD
Born in Scotland during 1756. Married
Agnes White in 1787. Died in Cabarrus
County, NC, in 1814.   (NCGen XXI.3068)

McLAUGHLIN ALEXANDER
46. Blacksmith. Born in Scotland.
Cumberland County, NC.   (C)

McLAUGHLIN ARCHIBALD
Born in Scotland during 1732. Emigrated
to America in 1804. A farmer in
Richmond County, NC, with a wife and
four children in 1812.   (1812)

McLAUCHLIN ARCHIBALD
Born in Scotland during 1791, son of
Neil McLauchlin. Settled in
Cumberland County, NC, in 1805.
Married Sarah Blocker during 1814.
A farmer near Fayetteville,
Cumberland County, NC. Father of
Harriet, John, Sarah A., Margaret and
Mary. Died in Cumberland County 1869.   (INC60136)(CLM)

McLAUCHLIN DUGALD
Born in Scotland during 1757. Married
Nancy McIntyre. Settled in Moore County,
NC. Father of Duncan, Neil, Daniel,
Nancy and Kate. Died in 1830. Buried
in Union Presbyterian Cemetery,
Moore County, NC.   (CLM)

McLAUCHLIN DUNCAN
Born in Scotland, son of Neil McLauchlin.
Settled in Cumberland County, NC, in 1805.
Married Catherine McLauchlin during 1831
in Fayetteville. Father of Neil D., John C.,
Sarah J., William A., Benjamin and
Catherine A.   (CLM)

McLAUCHLIN DUNCAN
Born in Argyllshire during 1796, son of
Dugald McLauchlin. Settled in Moore County,
NC. Blacksmith and farmer. Married
Catherine McLeod in Cumberland County
during 1822. Father of John, Sarah, Martha,
Dugald, Robert Alexander, Neil, Mary
Catherine and Nancy C. Died during 1852.
Buried in Moore County Presbyterian Church.   (CLM)

McLAUCHLIN JENNETT
66. Born in Scotland. Robeson County, NC.   (C)

McLAUCHLAN JOHN
Born in Scotland during 1765. Emigrated
to America in 1791. A farmer in
Richmond County, NC, in 1812. (1812)

McLAUCHLAN JOHN
Born in Scotland during 1765. Emigrated
to America in 1811. A tailor in
Richmond County, with a wife and five
children in 1812. (1812)

McLAUCHLEN JOHN
Born in Scotland during 1769. Emigrated
to America in 1803. A farmer in Robeson
County, NC, with a wife and five
children in 1812. (1812)

McLAUCHLAN LAUCHLAN
Born in Scotland during 1784. Emigrated
to America in 1805. A farmer in Robeson
County, with his mother, brother and
two sisters in 1812. (1812)

McLAUGHLIN NANCY
52. Born in Scotland. John 50. Farmer.
Born in NC. Archibald 22. Student.
Born in NC. Neill 20. Born in NC.
Mary A. 18. Born in NC. Sarah C. 12.
Born in NC. Cumberland County, NC. (C)

McLAUCHLIN NEIL
Born in Scotland during 1754. Married
Sarah Leitch in Glassary, Argyllshire,
during 1785. Settled in Cumberland
County, NC, during 1805. Father of
Archibald, Duncan, Alexander, Neil,
Margaret, Mary and Nanse(?) A farmer
in Cumberland County, NC, in 1812. (1812)(CLM)

McLAUCHLIN PETER
66. Born in Scotland. Sally 50. Born in NC.
Sarah 28. Born in Scotland. Neill 25. Born
in NC. John 8. Born in NC. Robeson County, NC. (C)

McLAUCHLAN ROBERT
Born in Scotland during 1764. Emigrated
to America in 1802. A farmer in Moore
County, NC, with a wife and seven children
in 1812. (1812)

McLAUCHLIN SARAH
85. Born in Scotland. Duncan 53. Farmer.
Born in Scotland. Catherine 46. Born in
NC. Neill 18. Student. Born in NC.
John C. 16. Born in NC. Sarah 12. Born
in NC. William A. 9. Born in NC.
Benjamin 6. Born in NC. Catherine 3.
Born in NC. Cumberland County, NC.   (C)

McLEAN ALEXANDER
Jacobite soldier captured after the Siege
of Preston, Lancashire. Transported from
Liverpool to South Carolina on the
Wakefield, master Thomas Beck, 21 April 1716.   (SPC)(CTB)

McLEAN ALEXANDER
Born in Mull(?), Argyllshire, during 1709.
Emigrated via Larne, Ireland, to
Philadelphia, Pennsylvania, in the late
1720s. Presbyterian. Married Elizabeth
Ratchford in Pennsylvania during 1739.
Settled in Rowan County, NC. Father of
eight children. Buried in Old Smith
Graveyard, Lincoln County, NC.   (R L Adams Colln PC261.1)

McLEAN ANGUS
66. Farmer. Born in Scotland. Nancy 60.
Born in Scotland. Christian 23. Born in
NC. Anna 21. Born in NC. Kenneth 19.
Born in NC. Emigrated to America in 1804.
A farmer in Moore County, NC, in 1812.   (1812)(C)

McLEAN ARCHIBALD
Born in Scotland during 1741. Died in
Cumberland County, NC, on 4 May 1822.   (RR 24.5.1822)

McLEAN ARCHIBALD
Born in Scotland during 1769. Emigrated
to America in 1802. A farmer in
Robeson County, NC, with a wife and
three children in 1812.   (1812)

McLEAN CHARLES
Born in Scotland during 1730, son of
John McLean and Mary Moor. Emigrated
to America in 1750. Settled in NC.   (McLean pp/NCA)

McLEAN CHARLES
55. Planter. Born in NC. Sarah 55. Born
in Scotland. Paul 25. Labourer. Born in
SC. Nancy 22. Born in SC. Mary 20.
Born in SC. Alexander 18. Born in SC.
Mary C. 15. Born in SC. Elizabeth 32.
Born in SC. Sumter County, SC.   (C)

McLEAN CHRISTIAN
82. Born in Scotland. Dorothy 48.
Born in NC. John 19. Born in NC.
Sarah 48. Born in Scotland.
Richmond County, NC.   (C)

McLEAN DANIEL
80. Born in Scotland. Catherine 78.
Born in Scotland. William 50. Born
in NC. Florah 30. Born in NC.
Robeson County, NC.   (C)

McLAIN DANIEL
Born in Scotland during 1777. Emigrated
to America in 1802. A carpenter in
Richmond County, NC, with a wife and
four children in 1812.   (1812)

McLEAN DANIEL
61. Farmer. Born in Scotland. Isabel 69.
Born in NC. Archibald 38. Born in NC.
Farmer. John K. 31. Merchant. Born in
NC. Catherine 27. Born in NC. Moore County, NC.   (C)

McLEAN DONALD
Emigrated from Jura, Argyllshire, to
America (probably) on the General Wolfe,
master J MacLean. Landed at Brunswick,
NC, on 4 November 1767. Allocated a 100
acre land grant in Cumberland or
Mecklenburg Counties, NC.   (SCGaz.1671) (SHA.111)

McLEAN DONALD
Born in Scotland during 1773. Emigrated
to America during 1803. A farmer in
Richmond County, NC, with a wife in 1812.   (1812)

McLEAN DUNCAN
Emigrated from Jura, Argyllshire, with
his wife, to America (probably) on the
General Wolfe, master J MacLean.
Landed at Brunswick, NC, on 4 November
1767. Allocated a 200 acre land grant
in Cumberland or Mecklenburg Counties. (SCGaz.1671)(SHA.111)

McLEAN DUNCAN
Born in Scotland(?) during 1742. Emigrated
to America in 1790. A farmer in Richmond
County, NC, with two children in 1812.   (1812)

McLEAN DUNCAN
69. Farmer. Born in Scotland. Sarah 75.
Born in Scotland. Anne Jackson 45. Born
in NC. Cumberland County, NC.   (C)

McLEAN EFFIE
74. Born in Scotland. John C. 48. Born
in Scotland. Alexander 40. Born in NC.
Effie 27. Born in NC. Mary 4. Born in
NC. Archibald 2. Born in NC. Margaret
2 months. Born in NC. Robeson County, NC.   (C)

McLEAN EPHRAIM
Born in Scotland during 1730, son of
John McLean and his wife Mary Moor.
Married Elizabeth Davidson in 1761.
Emigrated to America in 1750. Father
of John, George, Ephraim, Charles,
Samuel, Olney, William and James D.
Revolutionary soldier. Settled in NC.   (McLean pp/NCA)(LOS)

McLEAN FLORA
Born in Jura, Argyllshire, c1823.
Died in NC on 23 April 1867. Buried
in Union Cemetery, Carthage, Moore
County, NC.   (Moore Gs)

McLEAN HECTOR
Born in Scotland during 1777. Emigrated
to America in 1802. A farmer in Robeson
County, NC, with a wife and two children
in 1812.   (1812)

McLEAN HUGH
Emigrated from Jura, Argyllshire, with
his family, to NC before 1764.   (NCA.PC20.1/Shaw pp)

McLEAN HUGH
Nat. 6 May 1806 Cumberland County, NC.   (NCA/CR.029)

McLEAN HUGH
Nat. 7 May 1806 Cumberland County, NC.   (NCA/CR 029.311.1)

McLEAN HUGH
49. Mechanic. Born in Scotland.
Richmond County, NC.   (C)

McLEAN JAMES
Born in Perthshire during 1801.
Settled in Charleston, SC.
Nat. 6 October 1824 Charleston, SC.   (Nat Arch M1183.1)

McLEAN JOHN
Jacobite soldier captured after the Siege
of Preston, Lancashire. Transported from
Liverpool to South Carolina on the
Wakefield, master Thomas Beck, 21 April 1716.   (SPC)(CTB)

McLEAN JOHN
Born in Scotland c1723. Died in
Cumberland County, NC, 4 November 1825. (RaNCSw 25.11.1825)

McLEAN JOHN
Emigrated from Jura, Argyllshire, to
America (probably) on the General Wolfe,
master J MacLean. Landed at Brunswick,
NC, on 4 November 1767. Allocated a
100 acre land grant in Cumberland or
Mecklenburg Counties, NC.   (SCGaz.1671)(SHA.111)

McLEAN JOHN
Born in Scotland during 1767. Emigrated
to America in 1791. A farmer in Robeson
County, NC, with a wife and three
children in 1812.   (1812)

McLEAN JOHN
Born in Mull, Argyllshire, c1771.
Emigrated from Greenock, Renfrewshire,
to Wilmington, NC, on the brig Molly
on 1 September 1792. Landed 16 October
1792. Married Effie McLean,1781-1849.
Settled in upper Robeson County, NC.
Father of Hector, Neil, Allan, Angus,
Duart, Christian, Alexander and Janet.
Died on 15 May 1846.   (LRS)

McLEAN JOHN
Born in Scotland during 1772. Emigrated
to America in 1802. A farmer in Richmond
County, NC, with a wife and four
children in 1812.   (1812)

McLEAN JOHN
Born in Scotland during 1774. Emigrated
to America in 1792. A schoolmaster in
Robeson County, NC, with a wife and
eight children in 1812.   (1812)

MacLEAN JOHN
Born in Islay, Argyllshire. Mariner.
Nat.20 April 1796 Charleston, SC.   (Nat Arch M1183.1)

McLEAN JOHN
65. Born in Scotland. Betsy 50. Born
in NC. Mary 11. Born in NC. Hector 9.
Born in NC. Sandy 8. Born in NC.
Robeson County, NC.
John McLean, emigrated to America in
1803, a farmer in Robeson County in 1812.   (C)(1812)

McLEAN JOHN
62. Farmer. Born in Scotland. Christian
45. Born in NC. Mary 24. Born in NC.
Roderick 21. Schoolteacher. Born in NC.
Richmond County, NC.   (C)

McLAIN JOHN
Born in Scotland during 1788. Emigrated
to America in 1802. A farmer in Richmond
County, NC, with a wife and child in 1812.   (1812)

McLEAN LAUCHLIN
Born in Skye, Inverness-shire. Settled
in Lillington, NC, c1770. Married Mary
McLean. Father of Duncan, Rachel, Mary,
Margaret and John Allen. Loyalist.
Buried in Murchison Cemetery,
Lillington, NC.   (NCSJ.XI.26)

McLEAN MALCOLM
Born in Jura, Argyllshire, c1797. Died
in NC on 1 November 1862. Buried in
Union Cemetery, Carthage, Moore County, NC.   (Moore Gs)

McLEAN NANCY
Emigrated from Jura, Argyllshire, to
America (probably) on the General Wolfe,
master J MacLean. Landed at Brunswick,
NC, on 4 November 1767. Allocated a 100
acre land grant in Cumberland or
Mecklenburg Counties, NC.   (SCGaz.1671)(SHA.111)

McLEAN NEILL
70. Born in Scotland. Nancy 64. Born in
Scotland. Archibald 34. Born in NC.
Robeson County, NC.   (C)

McLEAN NORMAN
Born in Scotland during 1752. Emigrated
to America in 1790. A farmer in Richmond
County, NC, with a wife and three
children in 1812.   (1812)

McLEAN NORMAN
78. Farmer. Born in Scotland. Mary 60.
Born in Scotland. Donald 26. Tailor.
Born in NC. Archibald 25. Farmer. Born
in NC. Norman 21. Farmer. Born in NC.
Nancy 17. Born in NC. Sarah 16. Born
in NC. James 20. Farmer. Born in NC.
Richmond County, NC.   (C)

McLEAN PETER
Emigrated from Jura, Argyllshire, to
America (probably) on the General Wolfe,
master J MacLean. Landed at Brunswick,
NC, on 4 November 1767. Allocated a 100
acre land grant in Cumberland or
Mecklenburg Counties, NC.   (SCGaz.1671)(SHA.111)

McLEARIN NEIL
72. Born in Scotland. Wilmington, NC.   (C)

McLEHOSE JOHN
Brother of Malcolm McLehose. Emigrated
from Scotland to America in June 1770.
Settled on Cape Fear, NC. (Boyd letter, McAlister pp,SHC/UNC)

McLEHOSE MALCOLM
Brother of John McLehose. Emigrated
from Scotland to America in June 1770.
Settled on Cape Fear, NC. (Boyd letter, McAlister pp,SHC/UNC)

McLEISH DANIEL
Born in Scotland during 1778. Emigrated
to America in 1803. A farmer in Robeson
County, NC, with a wife in 1812.   (1812)

McLELLAN ALEXANDER
Emigrated from Scotland, with his family,
to SC c1800. Settled in Hammer, SC.   (SHC)

McLELLAN DANIEL
Born in Scotland during 1761. Emigrated
to America in 1793. A farmer in Richmond
County, NC, with a wife and six children
in 1812.   (1812)

McLENNAN ALEXANDER
Born in Scotland on 5 May 1785.
Emigrated to America during 1833.
Died on 12 April 1856. Buried in
St James's Cemetery, Wilmington, NC.   (Wilmington Gs)

McLENNAN ALEXANDER
65. Shoemaker. Born in Scotland. M.A.(f)
45. Born in NC. Wilmington, New Hanover County, NC.   (C)

McLENNAN JOHN
45. Born in Scotland. Abbeville County, SC.   (C)

McLENNAN MURDOCH
Born in Stirlingshire in 1798. Emigrated
from Greenock, Renfrewshire, to SC on the
Roger Stewart, 25 April 1818.
Nat. 3 August 1820 Marlborough, SC.   (SCA)

McLENNAN NEIL
Born in Scotland. Nat.14 April 1812
New Hanover County, NC.   (New Hanover Sup Ct Mins)

McLEOD ALEXANDER
65. Farmer. Born in Scotland. Anna 45.
Born in NC. Margaret 19. Born in NC.
Anna 17. Born in NC. Mary 15. Born in
NC. Elizabeth 13. Born in NC. C. 9.
Born in NC. Cumberland County, NC.   (C)

McLEOD ALEXANDER
49. Farmer. Born in Scotland. Flora 44.
Born in Scotland. Archibald 19.
Labourer. Born in NC. John F. 18.
Born in NC. Labourer. Elizabeth 13.
Born in NC. Cumberland County, NC.   (C)

McLEOD ANDREW
Born in Inverness-shire c1739. Soldier
in the Revolution. Died 1 March 1816.
Buried on the James Thomas farm,
Raeford, Hoke County, NC.   (Hoke Gs)(LOS)

McLEOD CATHERINE
75. Born in Scotland. John J Currie
40. Born in NC. Catherine Currie 36.
Born in NC. Alexander Currie 17.
Born in NC. Elizabeth 15. Born in NC.
Daniel Currie 13. Born in NC. Nelly
Currie 11. Born in NC. Catherine
Currie 9. Born in NC. Sarah Currie 7.
Born in NC. Mary Currie 5. Born in NC.
Randal Currie 2. Born in NC. Robeson County, NC.   (C)

McLEOD CATHERINE
60. Born in Scotland. Mary 30. Born in
SC. Alexander 28. Born in SC. Robeson County, NC.   (C)

McLEOD DANIEL
Possibly from Ayr. A merchant tailor in
Wilmington, NC. Married Rachael ...
Died in 1791.   (NCA/CR 070.801)

MacLEOD DANIEL
Son of John MacLeod of Glendale, and his
wife Jane Hunter. Emigrated, with his
parents, to NC in 1770. Settled at
Hunts Bluff, Marlborough County, SC,
after 1775. Married Catherine Evans.
Father of John, William, Alexander,
Daniel, Donald, Elizabeth, Mary
Catherine, Isabella and Ellen.   (TML)

McLEOD DANIEL
Born in Scotland c1783. Emigrated
to America in 1803. A farmer in
Richmond County, NC, with a wife
and four children in 1812. Nat.
20 September 1813 Richmond County, NC.   (1812)(RCCR)

McLEOD DANIEL
Born in Scotland c1798. Died in NC
on 3 November 1829. Buried in Union
Presbyterian Church Cemetery,
Moore County, NC.   (Moore Gs)

McLEOD DUNCAN
Born in Scotland during 1787.
Emigrated to America in 1790.
A farmer in Cumberland County, NC, 1812.   (1812)

195

McLEOD DUNCAN
Born in Scotland. Farmer. 76. Sarah 70.
Born in NC. Richmond County, NC.   (C)

McLEOD GEORGE
Born in Sutherland during 1796. A tailor
in Columbia, SC. Nat. 13 April 1830
Charleston, SC.   (Nat Arch M1183.1)

McLEOD HECTOR CHISHOLM
Born in Sutherland during 1790. a clerk
in Charleston, SC. Nat. 19 October 1813
Charleston, SC.   (Nat Arch M1183.1)

McLEOD JOHN
Jacobite soldier captured after the Siege
of Preston, Lancashire. Transported from
Liverpool to South Carolina on the
Wakefield, master Thomas Beck, 21 April 1716.   (SPC)(CTB)

MACLEOD JOHN
Born during 1715, son of Alexander MacLeod
of Glendale and his wife Christina.
A Jacobite in 1745. Married (1) Margaret
McQueen of Totaroam (2)Jane Hunter of Long
Calderwood c1760. Settled in Wilmington,
NC. Father of Angus, William, Kenneth,
John, Daniel, Died at sea off Madagascar
during 1775.   (TML)

McLEOD JOHN
79. Farmer. Born in Scotland. Janet 41.
Born in NC. Christian 39. Born in NC.
Cumberland County, NC.   (C)

MacLEOD JOHN
Son of John MacLeod of Glendale and Jane
Hunter his wife. Emigrated with his
parents to NC during 1770. Died at
Hunt's Bluff, Marlborough County, SC.   (TML)

McLEOD JOHN
Born in Scotland c1770. Married Nancy..
Died in NC on 21 March 1863. Buried at
Markham Clark Cemetery, NC.   (Markham Clark Gs)

196

SCOTS IN THE CAROLINAS

McLEOD JOHN
Born in Skye, Inverness-shire, during
1787. Emigrated to America in 1802.
Married Nancy McIver. Died on 24
October 1877. Buried in Union
Presbyterian Church Cemetery,
Moore County, NC.   (Moore Gs)

McLEOD JOHN
82. Farmer. Born in Scotland. Neill 52.
Physician. Born in NC. Moore County, NC.   (C)

McLEOD JOHN
Born in Scotland. 76. Farmer. Jane 60.
Born in Iredell County, NC. Mary 19.
Born in Burke County, NC. Caldwell County, NC.   (C)

McLEOD JOHN
Born in 1789. Emigrated to America in
1802. A farmer in Richmond County, NC,
with a wife and two children in 1812.   (1812)

McLEOD JOHN
Born in Sutherland on 1 January 1773.
Died in NC on 10 March 1862. Buried
in Union Baptist Cemetery, Lenoir,
Caldwell County, NC.   (Caldwell Gs)

McLEOD JOHN
Born in Skye, Inverness-shire.
Ordained by the Presbytry of Edinburgh
on 13 October 1735. Emigrated from
Scotland to Georgia. Minister at
Darien, Georgia, from 1736 to 1741.
Missionary of the Society in Scotland
for the Propagation of Christian
Knowledge. Presbyterian minister in
Georgia and South Carolina. Settled in
Edisto Island, SC, during 1742.
Chaplain to a Highland Regiment.   (F)(SHA)(CCMC)

McLEOD Rev JOHN
Emigrated from Scotland to NC in 1770.
Presbyterian minister in NC 1770-1773.   (CCVC)

197

MacLEOD KENNETH
Son of John MacLeod of Glendale and
his wife Margaret MacQueen. Jacobite
officer in 1745. Settled in NC.
Killed in the American Revolution.   (TML)

McLEOD MARGARET
65. Born in Scotland. Jennett 33.
Born in Scotland. Daniel 32. Born
in NC. Robeson County, NC.   (C)

McLEOD MARGARET
65. Born in Scotland. Cumberland County, NC.   (C)

McLEOD MURDOCH
Born in Scotland. Settled in Cross
Creek, NC. Surgeon and apothecary, pre 1776.   (HSNC)

McLEOD MURDO
Born in 1752. Emigrated to America in 1804.
A farmer in Richmond County, NC, with a
wife and three children in 1812.   (1812)

McLEOD MURDOCH
Born in 1748. Emigrated to America in 1802.
Settled in Richmond County, NC, with his
wife and three children by 1812.   (1812)

McLEOD NANCY McIVER
Born in Skye, Inverness-shire, c1787.
Emigrated to America in 1802. Died on 24
October 1877. Buried in Union Cemetery,
Carthage, Moore County, NC.   (Moore Gs)

McLEOD NEILL
Born in Scotland. Died on his plantation
in Moore County, NC, 12 April 1814.   (RM)

McLEOD NEILL
56. Farmer. Born in Scotland. Catherine 56.
Born in NC. Mary 27. Born in NC. William 19.
Farmer. Born in NC. Nancy 16. Born in NC.
Jane 14. Born in NC. Isabella 11. Born in
NC. ......(f) 8. Born in NC. Duncan 7.
Born in NC. Sarah 4. Born in NC. Lydia
4 months. Born in NC. Moore County, NC.   (C)

McLEOD NORMAN
85. Farmer. Born in Scotland. John 59.
Born in NC. Montgomery County, NC.   (C)

McLEOD RODERICK
69. Born in Scotland. Margaret 60. Born
in Scotland. Nancy 28. Born in NC.
Cumberland County, NC.   (C)

McLEOD SARRY
Born in Sleat, Skye, Inverness-shire,
c1780. Died in NC during September
1812. Buried in Union Cemetery,
Carthage, Moore County, NC.   (Moore Gs)

McLEOD WILLIAM
26. Farmer. Ardrachoolish, Sutherland.
Emigrated from Scotland, with his wife
and son aged 2, to Wilmington, NC, on
the Bachelor of Leith in April 1774.   (PRO/T47.12)

MacLEOD WILLIAM
Born in Skye, Inverness-shire c1770, son
of William MacLeod of Millivaig. A seaman
and later a farmer and hatter. Married (1)
Effie McInnis in Skye (2) Flora Johnston
in NC during 1831. Emigrated to NC on the
Duke of Kent, Captain Thompson, in 1802.
Settled in Moore County, NC. Father of
John, born in Skye 1801, Kent born in
1802 - died at sea, Archibald, Nancy,
Daniel, Mary, Norman, William J.,
Duncan J., Daniel, Alexander, Evander,
Samuel, Emeline, Sarah A., Flora A,
Effie J and Mary. Died 25 January 1864.
Buried at Bethesda, NC.   (TML)

McLUCAS JOHN
Born in Scotland. Emigrated to America in
1791. Settled in SC during 1805. Planter.
Nat. 4 November 1806 Marlborough, SC.   (SCA)

McLUCAS JOHN L.
79. Farmer. Born in SC. Mary 80. Born in
Scotland. Marlborough County, SC.   (C)

McLURE JOHN
Scottish settler in Carolina c1685.   (ECJ)

McLURE JOHN
Born during 1760. Emigrated to America
in 1788. A farmer in Cumberland County,
NC, with a wife and nine children in 1812.   (1812)

McLURE NORMAN
Born during 1762. Emigrated to America
in 1791. A farmer in Robeson County, NC,
with a wifeand eight children in 1812.   (1812)

McMASTER ANDREW
Son of William McMaster of Myrack,
Kirkmaiden, Wigtonshire. A planter in
St George's parish, Santee, Craven
County, SC.   (Pr 3.8.1764 SC)

McMASTER JANE
68. Born in Scotland. Charleston, SC.   (C)

McMASTERS THOMAS
Born in Scotland. Partner in firm of
McRae and McGill, merchants in
Alexandria. Died in Halifax, NC, on
11 September 1809.   (RR 28.9.1809)

McMILLAN ALEXANDER
Born in Campbelltown, Argyllshire,
during 1766. Mariner. Nat.26 July 1798
Charleston, SC.   (Nat Arch M1183.1)

McMILLAN ALEXANDER
Born in Scotland c1775. Emigrated to
America c1803. Nat.20 September 1813
Richmond County, NC.
Alexander McMillan, 74, born in Scotland,
Farmer. Christian 72. Born in NC.
Joseph 38. Farmer. Born in NC. Margaret
38. Born in NC. Catherine 31. Born in NC.
Richmond County, NC.   (C)(RCCR)

McMILLAN ALEXANDER
Born in Scotland during 1778. Emigrated
to America 14 April 1802. A farmer in
Richmond County, NC, with a wife and
four children in 1812. Nat. September
1815 Richmond County, NC.   (RCCR)(1812)

McMILLAN ALEXANDER
70. Born in Scotland. Margaret 58.
Born in Robeson County, NC. James 33.
Born in Robeson County, NC.
Archibald 25. Born in Robeson County,
NC. Catherine 20. Born in Robeson
County, NC. Caroline 20. Born in
Robeson County, NC. Alexander 18.
Born in Robeson County, NC. Robert 28.
Born in Robeson County, NC. Robeson County, NC.   (C)

McMILLAN ALLAN
Born in 1778. Emigrated to America in
1809. Settled in Richmond County, NC,
with a wife and four children in 1812.   (1812)

McMILLAN ANGUS
50. Born in Scotland. Florah 35. Born
in NC. Margaret 15. Born in NC. Daniel
13. Born in NC. Elizabeth 10. Born in
NC. Malcolm 9. Born in NC. Mary 7.
Born in NC. Sarah 5. Born in NC.
Florah 2. Born in NC. Robeson County, NC.   (C)

McMILLAN ANGUS
48. Born in Scotland. Margaret 35.
Born in NC. Robeson County, NC.   (C)

McMILLAN ARCHIBALD
58. Farmer. Glen Orchy, Argyllshire.
Emigrated from Greenock, Renfrewshire,
with his wife Barbara Taylor 40, and
daughter Barbara 20, to Wilmington,
NC, on the Ulysses, master J Chalmers,
in August 1774.   (PRO/T47.12)

McMILLAN ARCHIBALD
Farmer. Kintyre, Argyllshire.
Emigrated from Greenock, Renfrewshire,
to Wilmington, NC, on the Diana,
master D Ruthven, in September 1774.   (PRO/T47.12)

McMILLAN ARCHIBALD
55. Born in Scotland. Fanny C. 46.
Born in Pitt County, NC. Dougald C. 9.
Born in Robeson County, NC.
Archibald A. 7. Born in Robeson
County, NC. Dougald 48. Born in
Scotland. Robeson County, NC.   (C)

McMILLAN DANIEL
Son of Duncan McMillan and Mary McPhatter,
Kintyre, Argyllshire, married Christina
McLean. Father of Duncan. Settled in
Robeson County, NC, before 1800.   (CMM)

McMILLAN DANIEL
66. Farmer. Born in Scotland.
Columbia County, SC.   (C)

McMILLAN DAVID sr
Born in Scotland. Died in NC on
13 October 1792. Buried in Phillips
Cemetery, Raeford, Hoke County, NC.   (Hoke Gs)

McMILLAN DONALD
Born in 1762. Emigrated to America in
1803. A farmer in Robeson County, NC,
with a wife and seven children in 1812.   (1812)

McMILLAN EDWARD
Born in 1783. Emigrated to America in
1803. A farmer in Richmond County, NC,
with a wife and three children in 1812.   (1812)

MacMILLAN GILBERT
Emigrated from Scotland, with his wife
Christian, to NC in 1770. Settled in
Robeson County, NC. Died in 1772.   (NCA 2.1.13N)

McMILLAN GILBERT
Born in Scotland during 1722. Married
Christian McBryde in Scotland 1747.
Died in Bladen County, NC, in 1772.   (INC27566)

McMILLAN ISABELL
70. Born in Scotland. Angus D McLean 32.
Born in NC. Mary McLean 28. Born in NC.
Dickson McLean 8. Born in NC. Archibald
6. Born in NC. Sally 2. Born in NC.
Robeson County, NC.   (C)

McMILLAN ISABEL
Born in Islay, Argyllshire, c1788. Died
in NC 1 July 1850. Buried in Phillips
Cemetery, Raeford, Hoke County, NC.   (Hoke Gs)

McMILLAN JOANNA
60. Born in Scotland. Charles 30.
Merchant. Born in NC. Cumberland County, NC.   (C)

McMILLAN JOHN
Born in Scotland. Died in NC during 1804.
Buried in Phillips Cemetery, Raeford,
Hoke County, NC.   (Hoke Gs)

McMILLAN JOHN
Born in 1769, son of Robert McMillan, 1749-
1799, and his wife Margaret Donaldson, Dumfries.
Died in Fayetteville, NC, 7 October 1820.   (Dumfries Gs)

McMILLAN JOHN
26. Farmer. Kintyre, Argyllshire.
Emigrated from Greenock, Renfrewshire,
with his wife Jean Huie 23, to
Wilmington, NC, on the Ulysses, master
J Chalmers, in August 1774.   (PRO/T47.12)

McMILLAN JOHN
Emigrated from Knapdale, Argyllshire,
with his wife Sarah McGilp, to Cape
Fear, NC, c1805.   (CMM)

McMILLAN JOHN
Born in Scotland during November 1762.
Married Margaret ..., 1765-1812.
Father of John, Iver, Ann and Margaret.
Died on 29 November 1820 in NC. Buried
in Brown Marsh Presbyterian Church
Cemetery, Bladen County, NC.   (Bladen Gs)

McMILLAN JOHN
Born in Newton Stewart, Galloway, in 1783.
Merchant. Nat. 11 May 1810 Charleston, SC.(Nat Arch M1183.1)

McMILLAN JOHN
Son of Alexander McMillan, merchant in
Campbelltown, Argyllshire. Merchant in
Cheraw, SC. Died on 16 September 1827.   (S 822 768)

McMILLAN JOHN
Born in Scotland on 13 November 1756.
Died in NC on 23 February 1844. Buried
in Polly McMillan Cemetery, Stratford,
Alleghany County, NC.   (Alleghany Gs)

McMILLAN JOHN
60. Postmaster. Born in Scotland.
Sarah 55. Born in Marion County, SC.
Sarah 21. Born in Marion County, SC.
Sidney 19. Clerk. Born in Marion County,SC.
Elizabeth 16. Born in Marion County, SC.
Cicero 14. Born in Marion County, SC.
Marion County, SC.   (C)

McMILLAN JOHN
Emigrated to America in 1803.
A farmer in Robeson County, NC,
with a wife and eight children in 1812.   (1812)

McMILLAN JOHN L.
54. Born in Scotland. Catherine 35.
Born in NC. Elizabeth 12. Born in NC.
Sarah 10. Born in NC. Margaret 4.Born
in NC. Catherine 8. Born in NC.
Daniel 10 months. Born in NC.
Robeson County, NC.   (C)

McMILLAN JOHN
46. Farmer. Born in Scotland. Mary 46.
Born in Scotland. Catherine 12.Born
in NC. Margaret 10. Born in NC.
Duncan 8. Born in NC. Richmond County, NC.   (C)

McMILLAN MALCOLM
58. Farmer. Kintyre, Argyllshire.
Emigrated from Greenock, Renfrewshire,
with his wife Catherine McAlester and
children Daniel 24, Archibald 16, and
Gilbert 8, to Wilmington, NC, on the
Ulysses, master J Chalmers, August 1774.   (PRO/T47.12)

McMILLAN MALCOLM
Born in 1769. Emigrated to America in
1803. A farmer in Richmond County, NC,
with a wife and six children in 1812.   (1812)

McMILLAN MALCOLM
78. Born in Scotland. Flora 75. Born in
Scotland. Robeson County, NC.   (C)

McMILLAN MALCOLM
Born in 1762. Emigrated to America in 1790.
A farmer in Moore County, NC, with a wife
and six children in 1812.   (1812)

McMILLAN MALCOLM
Born in 1752. Emigrated to America
during 1802. A farmer in Robeson
County, NC, with a wife and five
children in 1812.   (1812)

McMILLAN MARIAN
Born in Scotland c1763. Died in NC
on 15 April 1839. Buried in Polly
McMillan Cemetery, Stratford,
Alleghany County, NC.   (Alleghany Gs)

MacMILLAN Mrs MARY
Born in Argyllshire c1753. Died in
NC on 19 September 1825.   (RaNCSw 30.9.1825)

McMILLAN MARY
66. Born in Scotland. James 25. Born
in Robeson County, NC. Robeson County, NC.   (C)

McMILLAN RONALD
Born in Scotland during 1780. Married
Mary ... Died in Columbus County, NC.   (INC12144)

McMILLAN SAMUEL
Possibly son of John McMillan. Born in
Scotland during 1754. Emigrated to
America. Died in SC during 1844.
Buried in Martin Aiken Cemetery,
Winnsboro, Fairfield County, SC.   (H 21.5)

McMILLAN THOMAS
50. Baker. Born in Scotland. Agnes 50.
Born in Scotland. Agnes 25. Born in
SC. Anne 22. Born in SC. James 12.
Born in SC. Beaufort County, SC.   (C)

McMURCHIE FINLAY
45. Farmer. Kintyre, Argyllshire.
Emigrated from Greenock, Renfrewshire,
with his wife Catherine Hendry 35, and
children Archibald 10, Elizabeth 8,
Charles 5, Neil 3, and Barbara 6 months,
to Wilmington, NC, on the Diana, master
D Ruthven, in September 1774.   (PRO/T47.12)

SCOTS IN THE CAROLINAS

McMURCHIE HUGH
46. Farmer. Kintyre, Argyllshire.
Emigrated from Greenock, Renfrewshire,
with his wife Elizabeth Kelso 50, and
children Archibald 21, Patrick 17,
Mary 17, Elizabeth 14, and Robert 9,
to Wilmington, NC, on the Diana,
master D Ruthven, in September 1774.   (PRO/T47.12)

McMURCHY IVOR
Emigrated from Scotland, with his wife
..... McLehose, to America in June 1770.
Settled on Cape Fear, NC. (Boyd letter, McAlister pp,SHC/UNC)

McMURPHY BARBARA
65. Born in Scotland.Wilmington, New Hanover, NC.   (C)

McMURRAY DONALD
83. Born in Scotland. Elizabeth 41.
Born in NC. Sarah 27. Born in NC.
Alexander County, NC.   (C)

McNABB DUNCAN
Born in Islay, Argyllshire, 1798.
Emigrated from Greenock, Renfrewshire,
to Charleston, SC. Nat. 11 March 1830
Marlborough County, SC.   (SCA)

McNABB JOHN
24. Labourer. Argyllshire. Emigrated
from Greenock, Renfrewshire, with his
wife Jean 19, to NC in May 1775 on the
Ulysses, master J Wilson.   (PRO/T47.12)

McNAB ROBERT
45. Baptist clergyman. Born in Scotland.
Elizabeth 39. Born in NC. Edwin 1. Born
in NC. Moore County, NC.   (C)

McNABB TIBBY
20. Argyllshire. Emigrated from Greenock,
Renfrewshire, to NC on the Ulysses,
master J Wilson, in May 1775.   (PRO/T47.12)

206

McNAIR BERNARD
Born in 1745. Emigrated to America
during 1786. A farmer in Robeson
County, NC, with a wife in 1812.   (1812)

McNAIR BETSY
52. Born in Scotland. Edward 25.
Farmer. Born in NC. Mary 23.
Born in NC. Jane 20. Born in NC.
Janet 18. Born in NC. Elizabeth
15. Born in NC. Neal 14. Born in
NC. James 12. Born in NC.
Richmond County, NC.   (C)

McNAIR DANIEL sr
Born in Kintyre, Argyllshire, c1731.
Died in NC during October 1800.
Buried in Old Centre Cemetery.
Maxton, NC.   (Maxton Gs)

McNAIR DUNCAN
Emigrated from Kintyre, Argyllshire,
with his wife Katie McCallum, to NC
during C18. Settled in Robeson
County, NC.   (St Paul's OPR)

McNAIR EDWARD
45. Farmer. Born in Scotland. Richmond County, NC.   (C)

McNAIR Mrs JANET
Born in Greenock, Renfrewshire, c1781.
Died in Fayetteville, NC, 11 October 1826.   (RR 20.10.1826)

McNAIR JOHN
Born in Kilkenny, Argyllshire, c1735,
youngest son of Neill McNair and his
wife Sallie McGill. Emigrated, with
his son Roderick and a daughter, from
Scotland to America in 1770. Settled
in Robeson County, NC. Married (1)
Janet Smyllie, died 1769 (2)Catherine
Buie McFarland,1733-1833, in 1772.
Died on 30 June 1819. Buried in
Richmond County, NC.   (DP)(INC27697)

McNAIR JOHN
63. Born in Scotland. Mary 62. Born
in NC. Isabel 25. Born in NC. Sarah
23. Born in NC. John G. 21. Born in
NC. Richmond County, NC.   (C)

McNAIR Mrs MARY
Wife of Daniel McNair sr. Born
in Gigha, Argyllshire, during 1745.
Died in NC on 15 November 1807.
Buried in Old Centre Cemetery,
Maxton, NC.   (Maxton Gs)

McNAIR RODERICK
Born in Argyllshire in October 1764, son
of John and Catherine McNair. Died in
NC on 6 April 1839. Buried in Old
Laurel Hill Church, Rockingham,
Richmond County, NC.   (Rockingham Gs)

McNARIN JOSEPH
Colmonell parish, Ayrshire. Planter
in St George's parish, Berkeley County,
SC.   (Pr 24.7.1794 SC)

McNAUGHTON DUNCAN
Jacobite soldier captured after the Siege
of Preston, Lancashire. Transported from
Liverpool to South Carolina on the
Susannah, master Thomas Bromhall, 7 May 1716.   (CTB)(SPC)

McNEIL Mrs ALICE
Wife of Dr Daniel McNeil. Died in
Wilmington, NC, on 12 November 1791.   (EEC 11510)

McNEILL ANGUS
Born in North Knapdale, Argyllshire,
during 1762. Died in NC 13 September
1835. Buried in McNeill Cemetery,
Wagram, Scotland County, NC.   (Wagram Gs)

McNEILL ARCHIBALD
Emigrated from Scotland to Brunswick,
NC, in September 1739.   (VOS)

McNEILL ARCHIBALD
Probably from Argyllshire. St George's
parish, Dorchester, SC.   (Pr 23.6.1772 SC)

McNEILL CHRISTIAN
59. Born in Scotland. John 30.
Labourer. Born in NC. Archibald
26. Farmer. Born in NC. Daniel
19. Labourer. Born in NC.
Duncan 14. Born in NC. Ann 12.
Born in NC. Mary 7. Born in NC.
Richmond County, NC.   (C)

McNEIL DANIEL
Emigrated from Argyllshire(?) to
NC during 1739. Allocated a 400
acre land grant in Bladen County,
NC, on 4 June 1740.   (SHA.106)

McNEIL DANIEL
Emigrated from Argyllshire(?) to
NC during 1739. Allocated a 320
acre land grant in Bladen County,
NC, on 4 June 1740.   (SHA.106)

McNEIL DANIEL
Emigrated from Argyllshire(?) to
NC during 1739. Allocated a 105
acre land grant in Bladen County,
NC, on 4 June 1740.   (SHA.106)

McNEIL DANIEL
Son of Archibald McNeil, died 1746.
Jura, Argyllshire. Emigrated to NC
c1760. Probably settled in Hoke
County.   (CMN)

McNEILL DANIEL
Born in Scotland c1770. Married (1)
Rachel Smith in Moore County, NC.
(2) Prately Britt in Moore County.
Died in Moore County(?), NC.   (INC)

McNEILL DANIEL
Born in Scotland during 1792, son
of Hector and Gensie McNeill.
Emigrated to America c1797.
Died in NC during 1869. Buried
in McNeill Cemetery, Moore County, NC.   (Moore Gs)

McNEILL DANIEL
72. Farmer. Born in Scotland. Margaret 65.
Born in NC. Mary 42. Born in NC.
Catherine 31. Born in NC. Mary McKinnon
62. Born in Scotland. Moore County, NC.   (C)

MacNEIL DONALD
Emigrated from Scotland to America.
Settled in Tweedside, Cape Fear
River, NC, during 1746.   (CMN)

McNEILL DUNCAN
Son of Neill McNeill. Born in
Kintyre, Argyllshire, during 1728.
Died in NC on 2 October 1791.
Buried at Bluff Church, Wade County, NC.   (Wade Gs)

McNEILL Miss GRISELL
Emigrated from Scotland to America.
Settled in NC before 1771.(McCuaig letter,McAlister pp,SHC/UNC)

McNEIL HECTOR
Emigrated from Argyllshire(?) to NC
during 1739. Allocated a 300 acre land
grant in Bladen County, NC, on
4 June 1740.   (SHA.105)

McNEILL HECTOR
Emigrated from Scotland to America
after 1746. Settled in Robeson
County, NC. Father of Angus, and
grandfather of Rev Hector H McNeill(Hector McNeill pp(Cab46)DU)

McNEILL HECTOR
Born in Scotland c1750. Married
Sally ... in Scotland. Died in
Moore County, NC.   (INC19183)

McNEILL JOHN
Born in Scotland c1747. Died in
Cumberland County, NC, 4 April 1810.   (RR 3.5.1810)

McNEILL JOHN
Born during 1756. Emigrated to
America in 1788. A farmer in Moore
County, NC, with a wife and five
children in 1812.   (1812)

210

McNEILL JOHN
74. Born in Scotland. Margaret 65.
Born in NC. Henry 25. Born in NC.
Christian 21. Born in NC. Sallie
12. Born in NC. Robeson County, NC.   (C)

McNEIL JOHN
Born in 1780. Emigrated to America
in 1792. A farmer in Robeson County,
NC, with a wife and four children in 1812.   (1812)

McNEILL JOHN
54. Farmer. Born in Scotland. Neill 22.
Born in NC. Duncan 19. Born in NC.Farmer.
Margaret 16. Born in NC. Anne 14. Born
in NC. Catherine 11. Born in NC. Mary
6. Born in NC. Richmond County, NC.   (C)

McNEILL LACHLAN
Emigrated from Scotland to Brunswick,
NC, in September 1739.   (VOS)

McNEIL MALCOLM
Emigrated from Argyllshire to NC in
1739. Allocated a 320 acre land
grant in Bladen County, NC, on
4 June 1740.   (SHA.105)

McNEILL MARGARET
Born in Islay, Argyllshire, c1759.
Married Daniel Ray,1763-1826. Mother
of Catherine,1803-1847, Mary,1800-1826,
Margaret,1818-1897. Died in NC on
8 October 1849. Buried in Longstreet
Presbyterian Church Cemetery, NC.   (Longstreet Gs)

McNEILL MARY
76. Born in Scotland. Mary 29. Born in
NC. Sarah 27. Born in NC. Richmond County, NC.   (C)

McNEIL NEIL
Emigrated from Argyllshire(?) to NC in
1739. Allocated a 321 acre land grant
in Bladen County, NC, 4 June 1740.   (SHA.106)

McNEIL NEIL
Emigrated from Argyllshire(?) to NC
during 1739. Allocated a 400 acre
land grant in Bladen County, NC,
on 4 June 1740.   (SHA.105)

McNEIL NEIL
Emigrated from Argyllshire(?) to NC
during 1739. Allocated a 150 acre
land grant in Bladen County, NC,
on 4 June 1740.   (SHA.105)

McNEILL NEILL
Emigrated from Argyllshire to Cape
Fear, NC, during 1747. Presbyterian
minister in Fayetteville,
Cumberland County, NC, 1747 -   (CCVC)

McNEIL NEIL
64. Farmer. Kintyre, Argyllshire.
Emigrated from Greenock, Renfrewshire,
with his wife Isobel Simpson 64, and
children Daniel 28, Hector 24, Peter
22, Neil 18, William 15, and Mary 9,
to Wilmington, NC, on the Ulysses,
master J Chalmers, in August 1774.   (PRO/T47.12)

MacNEIL NEIL
Born in 1768. Emigrated to America in
1792. A farmer in Richmond County, NC,
with a wife and seven children in 1812.   (1812)

McNEIL NEIL
Born in Jura, Argyllshire, c1770.
Emigrated from Jura to NC in 1792.
Settled on Little River, and later in
Cumberland County, NC. Married Sarah
or Sallie Graham in Bluff c1798.
Settled in Robeson County, NC.
Father of Hector, Neill, Janet,
Christian, Flora, Margaret and
Alexander. Died on 1 June 1858.(NCA/WBC.384.7)(St Paul'sOPR)

McNEILL NEILL
Born in Buchanan, Stirlingshire, c1781.
Grocer. Nat.14 October 1806 Charleston,
SC. Died on 28 March 1851. Buried in
St Michael's, Charleston, SC.(Nat Arch M1183.1)(StMichael's Gs)

McNEIL NEIL
70. Customs House Inspector. Born in
Scotland. Charleston, SC.   (C)

McNEILL NEILL
68. Farmer. Born in Scotland. Sarah 65.
Born in Scotland. Margaret 31. Born in
Scotland. John 28. Born in NC. Anna 25.
Born in NC. Cumberland County, NC.   (C)

McNEILL NEILL
Born in Jura, Argyllshire, in 1784.
Married Sarah, 1784-1860.Emigrated
to America. Died in NC on
17 September 1857. Buried in
Phillips Cemetery, Raeford,
Hoke County, NC.   (Hoke Gs)

McNEILL NEILL
65. Farmer. Born in Scotland. Nancy 37.
Born in NC. Daniel C. 17. Born in NC.
Moore County, NC.   (C)

McNEIL SAMUEL
Born in Whithorn, Galloway, during 1784.
A merchant in Charleston, SC. Nat 25 June
1812 Charleston, SC.   (Nat Arch M1183.1)

McNEILL SARAH
51. Born in Scotland. Daniel 59. Farmer.
Born in NC. John 21. Labourer. Born in
NC. James 19. Labourer. Born in NC.
Mary 16. Born in NC. Nancy 14. Born in
NC. Daniel 11. Born in NC. Richmond County, NC.   (C)

McNEILL SUSAN
58. Born in Scotland. Charleston, SC.   (C)

McNEILL THOMAS
Emigrated from Scotland, with his wife
Ann Talbot, to America. Settled in
Caswell County, NC, before 1777. Died 1787.   (RSA)

McNEILL TORQUIL
Emigrated from Scotland to Brunswick,
NC, in September 1739.   (VOS)

McNEIL WILLIAM
Planter in Bolladino, NC. Father of
Daniel, physician in Wilmington, NC, c1792.(SRO.RD3.258.193)

McNEILL Mrs
Emigrated from Scotland, with her
family, to America before 1771.
Settled in NC.   (McCuaig letter, McAlister pp,SHC/UNC)

McNEISH NANCY
77. Born in Scotland. Cumberland County, NC.   (C)

McNICOL ANGUS
30. Labourer. Glen Orchy, Argyllshire.
Emigrated from Scotland, with his wife
Ann 20, to Wilmington, NC, on the
Jupiter of Larne, master Samuel Brown,
in September 1775.   (PRO/T47.12)

McNICOL DANIEL
Born in Scotland. Nat.22 February 1825 SC.(Circuit Ct J19.378)

MacNICOL DONALD
40. Labourer. Glen Orchy, Argyllshire.
Emigrated from Scotland, with his wife
Katherine 33, and children John 6½,
Nicol 4, Archibald 2, and Mary, an
infant, to Wilmington, NC, on the
Jupiter of Larne, master Samuel Brown,
in September 1775.   (PRO/T47.12)

McNICOL Captain DUNCAN
Emigrated from Argyllshire, with his
wife and children Patrick, Annabell,
Elizabeth and two others, to America.
Settled in Anson County, NC, in 1774.
Died during 1780.   (SG)

McNICOL JOHN
24. Workman. Glen Orchy, Argyllshire.
Emigrated from Greenock, Renfrewshire,
to Wilmington, NC, on the Ulysses,
master J Chalmers, in August 1774.   (PRO/T47.12)

McNICOL ROBERT
30. Gentleman. Glen Orchy, Argyllshire.
Emigrated from Greenock, Renfrewshire,
with his wife Jean Campbell 24, and
daughter Annabel, to Wilmington, NC, on
the Ulysses, master J Chalmers, August 1774.   (PRO/T47.12)

214

McPHAIL FLORA
67. Born in Scotland. Angus 33. Born in
Robeson County, NC. John 30. Born in
Robeson County, NC. Mary 29. Born in
Cumberland County, NC. Flora A. 3. Born
in Robeson County, NC. Daniel 3 months.
Born in Robeson County, NC. Mary
McEachern 74. Born in Scotland.
Robeson County, NC.   (C)

McPHAILL JOHN
Born in Scotland c1770. Married
Barbara Malloy. Settled in Robeson
County, NC. Died in Arkansas 1852.   (INC60516)

McPHAIL JOHN
62. Farmer. Born in Scotland.
Maranetta 56. Born in Scotland.
Jane A. 25. Born in SC. James W
23. Born in SC. Anderson County, SC.   (C)

McPHAIL JOHN
72. Farmer. Born in Scotland. Mary 60.
Born in Scotland. Neill 30. Cooper.
Born in Scotland. Mary 28. Born in
Scotland. Hugh 23. Farmer. Born in
Scotland. Elizabeth 20. Born in
Scotland. Nancy Campbell 72. Born in
Scotland. Cumberland County, NC.   (C)

McPHAIL MALCOLM
Born in Scotland during 1741.
Emigrated to America before 1769.
Died in Cumberland County, NC, on
14 July 1828.   (RRsw 22.7.1828)

McPHAIL MALCOLM
78. Farmer. Born in Scotland. Cumberland County, NC.   (C)

McPHAIL MARY
70. Born in Scotland. Angus 36.
Blacksmith. Born in NC. Cumberland County, NC.   (C)

McPHAIL PETER
38. Farmer. Born in Scotland.
Malvina 27. Born in SC. Lewis 3.
Born in SC. John W. 2. Born in SC.
Mary B. 1. Born in SC. Anderson County, SC.   (C)

McPHATTER MARY
75. Born in Scotland. Robeson County, NC.   (C)

McPHEE ANGUS
Born during 1778. Emigrated to America
in 1802. A farmer in Richmond County, NC,
with a wife and two children in 1812.   (1812)

McPHERSON ALEXANDER
Jacobite soldier captured after the Siege
of Preston, Lancashire. Transported from
Liverpool to South Carolina on the
Wakefield, master Thomas Beck, 21 April 1716.   (CTB)(SPC)

McPHERSON ALEXANDER
50. Farmer. Born in Scotland. Nancy 50.
Born in Scotland. Rebecca 19. Born in
SC. Nancy 17. Born in SC. Nathan 15.
Born in SC. .... 12. Born in SC.
Spartanburg County, SC.   (C)

McPHERSON ANGUS
Jacobite soldier captured after the Siege
of Preston, Lancashire. Transported from
Liverpool to South Carolina on the
Susannah, master Thomas Bromhall, 7 May 1716   (SPC)(CTB)

McPHERSON ARCHIBALD
78. Farmer. Born in Scotland. Nancy 78.
Born in NC. Alexander 47. Farmer. Born
in NC. Margaret 45. Born in NC. Sarah 40.
Born in NC. Catherine 37. Born in NC.
Mary 24. Born in NC. Sarah J. 21. Born
in NC. Flora 8. Born in NC. Anson County, NC.   (C)

McPHERSON ARCHIBALD
78. Farmer. Born in Scotland. Sarah 75.
Born in Scotland. Catherine 30. Born in
NC. Flora Campbell 8. Born in NC. Moore County,NC.   (C)

McPHERSON CATHERINE
42. Born in Scotland. Mary 45. Born in
Scotland. Laughlin 19. Farmer. Born in SC.
Chesterfield County, SC.   (C)

McPHERSON CHRISTIAN
60. Born in Scotland. Anson County, NC.   (C)

McPHERSON DONALD
Jacobite soldier captured after the Siege
of Preston, Lancashire. Transported from
Liverpool to South Carolina on the
Wakefield, master Thomas Beck, 21 April 1716.   (SPC)(CTB)

McPHERSON DONALD
Jacobite soldier captured after the Siege
of Preston, Lancashire. Transported from
Liverpool to South Carolina on the
Susannah, master Thomas Bromhall, 7 May 1716.   (CTB)(SPC)

McPHERSON DONALD
Born in Scotland c1756. Emigrated to
America c1811. Nat.20 September 1813
Richmond County, NC.   (RCCR)

McPHERSON DUGALD
60. Farmer. Born in Scotland. Catharine 60.
Born in Scotland. Catharine 18. Born in SC.
Malcolm 16. Farmer. Born in SC. Angus 14.
Born in SC. Marlborough County, SC.   (C)

McPHERSON DUNCAN
Jacobite soldier captured after the Siege
of Preston, Lancashire. Transported from
Liverpool to South Carolina on the
Susannah, master Thomas Bromhall, 7 May 1716.   (CTB)(SPC)

McPHERSON DUNCAN
Born in Scotland during 1758. Emigrated
to America in 1803. A farmer in Richmond
County, NC, with a wife and three
children in 1812. Nat.20 September 1813
Richmond County, NC.   (RCCR)(1812)

McPHERSON HUGH
50. Farmer. Born in Scotland. Nancy 52.
Born in Scotland. John 20. Born in
Florida. James 18. Born in Florida.
Farmer. Murdoch 16. Born in NC. Farmer.
Margaret 22. Born in NC. Cumberland County, NC.   (C)

McPHERSON JAMES
37. Baker. Born in Scotland. Greenville County, SC.   (C)

McPHERSON JANET
39. Born in Scotland. James 49.
Born in NC. Richmond County, NC.   (C)

McPHERSON JOHN
Jacobite soldier captured after the Siege
of Preston, Lancashire. Transported from
Liverpool to South Carolina on the
Susannah, master Thomas Bromhall, 7 May 1716.   (CTB)(SPC)

McPHERSON JOHN
Emigrated from Argyllshire(?) to NC in
1739. Allocated a 320 acre land grant
in Bladen County, NC, 4 June 1740.   (SHA.105)

McPHERSON MALCOLM
40. Farmer. Glen Orchy, Argyllshire.
Emigrated from Greenock, Renfrewshire,
with his wife Christian Downie 30, and
children Janet 10, and William 9, to
Wilmington, NC, on the Ulysses, master
J Chalmers, in August 1774.   (PRO/T47.12)

McPHERSON M.
Born in Scotland c1790. Emigrated to
America in 1803. A clerk in Fayetteville,
NC, in 1812.   (1812)

McPHERSON NANCY
75. Born in Scotland. Catharine 24. Born
in NC. Anson County, NC.   (C)

McPHERSON NANCY
70. Born in Scotland. Isabel 35. Born in
NC. Catharine 33. Born in NC. Nancy 30.
Born in NC. Richmond County, NC.   (C)

McPHERSON NEIL
Born in 1759. Emigrated to America in
1788. A farmer in Richmond County, NC,
with a wife in 1812.   (1812)

McPHERSON PETER
Born in Greenock, Renfrewshire, 1779.
Tallow chandler. Nat.5 July 1811 SC.(Inferior City Ct.C4.569)

McQUEEN ALEXANDER
Jacobite soldier captured after the Siege
of Preston, Lancashire. Transported from
Liverpool to South Carolina on the
Wakefield, master Thomas Beck, 21 April 1716.   (CTB)(SPC)

McQUEEN ALEXANDER
Jacobite soldier captured after the Siege
of Preston, Lancashire. Transported from
Liverpool to South Carolina on the
Wakefield, master Thomas Beck, 21 April 1716.   (CTB)(SPC)

McQUEEN Dr ALEXANDER
Born in Scotland c1771. Educated at the
Universities of Aberdeen and Edinburgh.
Died in Cheraw, SC, 6 October 1828.   (CJ 18.10.1828)

McQUEEN ANGUS
Born in Skye, Inverness-shire, on 27
May 1764. Died in NC 27 Janaury 1848.
Buried in Stewartsville Cemetery,
Laurinburg, Scotland County, NC.   (Laurinburg Gs)

McQUEEN ANNY
80. Born in Scotland. Duncan McCallum
32. Born in NC. Charity McCallum 36.
Born in NC. Ann McCallum 5. Born in
NC. Angus 3. Born in NC. Annabella 1.
Born in NC. Robeson County, NC.   (C)

McQUEEN DAVID
Jacobite soldier captured after the Siege
of Preston, Lancashire. Transported from
Liverpool to South Carolina on the
Wakefield, master Thomas Beck, 21 April 1716.   (CTB)(SPC)

McQUEEN Col DONALD
Born in Skye, Inverness-shire, 1783.
Emigrated to America during 1802.
Died on 23 July 1867. Buried in
Stewartsville Cemetery, Laurinburg,
Scotland County, NC.   (Laurinburg Gs)

McQUEEN DONALD
67. Born in Scotland. Margaret 31.
Born in NC. Florah 29. Born in NC.
John 21. Born in NC. Effie 20. Born
in NC. Archibald 18. Born in NC.
Edmond 14. Born in NC. Catherine
12. Born in NC. Robeson County, NC.   (C)

McQUEEN DONALD
63. Farmer. Born in Scotland. Susan
60. Born in NC. Mary 16. Born in NC.
Cumberland County, NC.   (C)

McQUEEN DUNCAN
Jacobite soldier captured after the Siege
of Preston, Lancashire. Transported from
Liverpool to South Carolina on the
Wakefield, master Thomas Beck, 21 April 1716.   (CTB)(SPC)

McQUEEN ELIZABETH
53. Born in Scotland. Montgomery County, NC.   (C)

McQUEEN JAMES
Born in Skye, Inverness-shire, c1760,
son of Archibald McQueen and his wife
Flora McDonald. Emigrated from Greenock,
Renfrewshire, to Wilmington, NC, in 1772.
Married Ann (Nancy) McRae c1790. Settled
in Robeson County, NC. Father of twelve
children. Member of the Legislature and
a teacher. Buried in Stewartsville, NC.   (MQQ)

McQUEEN JOHN
Jacobite soldier captured after the Siege
of Preston, Lancashire. Transported from
Liverpool to South Carolina on the
Wakefield, master Thomas Beck, 21 April 1716.   (SPC)(CTB)

MacQUEEN Mrs MARGARET MARTIN
Widow. Skye, Inverness-shire.
Emigrated from Scotland, with
daughter Flora and sons Alexander,
Donald and Angus, to Wilmington,
NC, during 1802. Settled in Moore
County, NC.   (PMQ)

McQUEEN MARY
80. Born in Scotland. Alexander 57.
Farmer. Born in NC. Sarah 42. Born
in NC. Daniel 22. Labourer. Born in
NC. Alexander M. 15. Born in NC.
William P. 12. Born in NC. Sarah A.
10. Born in NC. Neill N. 2. Born in
NC. Montgomery County, NC.   (C)

McQUEEN Mrs MARGARET
Born in Skye, Inverness-shire, c1757.
Married Alexander McQueen. Died on
5 September 1837. Buried in
Stewartsville Cemetery, Laurinburg,
Scotland County, NC.   (Laurinburg Gs)

McQUEEN MURDOCH
Emigrated from Greenock, Renfrewshire,
to Wilmington, NC, in 1772. Settled
in Moore County, NC.   (MQQ)

MacQUEEN MURDOCH
Possibly from Skye, Inverness-shire.
Emigrated from Scotland to America
in 1772. Settled in Cumberland
County, NC.   (PMQ)

McQUEEN MURDO
Born in Skye, Inverness-shire, c1743.
Died in Chatham County, NC, on
21 July 1828.   (RaNCSw 7.8.1828)

McQUEEN NANCY
42. Born in Scotland. Malcom 41.
Labourer. Born in NC. Margaret J. 8.
Born in NC. Montgomery County, NC.   (C)

McQUEEN NEILL
50. Born in Scotland. Eliza 35.
Born in NC. Sarah 18. Born in NC.
Peter 14. Born in NC. Isabel 14.
Born in NC. Neill 12. Born in NC.
Paul 10. Born in NC. Archibald 8.
Born in NC. William 6. Born in NC.
Cumberland County, NC.   (C)

McQUEEN PETER
Born in Skye, Inverness-shire, 1763,
son of Rev William McQueen and his
wife Alice McAulay. Married Nancy
Isabella Campbell in 1799. Father of
Neill, Catherine and William.
Emigrated from Scotland to Wilmington,
NC, during 1802. Settled in Moore
County, NC.   (PMQ)

McQUIN ALEXANDER
Jacobite soldier captured after the Siege
of Preston, Lancashire. Transported from
Liverpool to South Carolina on the
Wakefield, master Thomas Beck, 21 April 1716.   (CTB)(SPC)

McQUIN JOHN
Jacobite soldier captured after the Siege
of Preston, Lancashire. Transported from
Liverpool to South Carolina on the
Susannah, master Thomas Bromhill, 7 May 1716.   (CTB)(SPC)

McQUISTON JOHN
46. Labourer. Inch, Wigtonshire.
Emigrated from Stranraer, Wigtonshire,to
NC on the Jackie, master J Morris, on
31 May 1775.   (PRO/T47.12)

McRACKEN Mrs MARGARET
Born in Scotland c1744. Died in
Fayetteville, Cumberland County, NC,
on 24 September 1829.   (RaNCSw 8.10.1829)

McRAE ANN
Born in Kintyre, Argyllshire, c1770.
Emigrated to Charleston, Sc, in 1772.
Married James MacQueen c1790. Settled in
Robeson County, NC. Died 14 August 1855.
Buried Stewartsville, NC.   (MQQ)

McRAE CHRISTIAN
82. Born in Scotland. John C. 53.
Farmer. Born in SC. Catharine 51.
Born in SC. Marlborough County, SC.   (C)

MacRAE DUNCAN
Strathglass, Inverness-shire.
Emigrated from Scotland, with his
wife Ann Cameron, to Norfolk,
Virginia, in 1773. Settled in
Wilmington, NC, then in Moore
County and later in Fayetteville,
NC. Father of Duncan, Christian,
Farquhar, Alexander, Margaret and
Nancy. Died 23 December 1781.   (DAM)

MacRAE DUNCAN
Born in Conchra, Lochalsh, Wester
Ross, during 1754. Emigrated from
Scotland to SC before 1776.
Settled in Camden, SC. Officer
in the Revolution. Married (1)
Sarah Powell (2)Mary Chesnut.
Died during November 1824.   (FKC)

McRAE DUNCAN
Born in Skye, Inverness-shire.
Married Margaret McQueen. Emigrated
from Scotland to Carolina before 1780.   (McRae pp/NCA)

McRAE FINLAY
Skye, Inverness-shire. Emigrated from
Scotland, with his wife, to
Wilmington, NC, c1780. Father of
Christian, Murdoch, John A.,Alexander,
Duncan, Colin, Roderick, Donald,
Malcolm, Christopher and Mary. Died
at sea off Wilmington, NC.   (McRae pp/NCA)

MacRAE FINLAY PHILIP
Possibly son of Hugh MacRae.
Jacobite in 1745. Emigrated from
Kintail, Wester Ross, to
Wilmington, NC, during 1770.   (CMR)

McRAE FLORA
75. Born in Scotland. Catherine 45.
Born in NC. Montgomery County, NC.   (C)

McRAE JANET
Born in Scotland during 1799. Died
in NC during 1888. Buried in
Euphronia Presbyterian Cemetery,
Glendon, Lee County, NC.   (Lee Gs)

MacRAE JOHN
Emigrated from Kintail, Wester Ross,
with his wife .... Chisholm, to NC
during 1774. Father of John. Died
in 1775(?)   (CMR)

McRAE JOHN
Kintyre, Argyllshire. Emigrated from
Scotland, with his wife Mary ... to
America. Settled in Queensdale,
Robeson County, NC, C18.   (MQQ)

MacRAE JOHN
Born c1809, son of Colin MacRae and
his wife Isabella MacRa, Kintail,
Wester Ross. Emigrated to SC c1828.
Married his cousin Isabella Scota
MacRae.   (CMR)

McRAE Mrs KATHERINE
Born in Scotland c1765. Married
Peter McRae. Died 13 October 1847.
Buried in Stewartsville Cemetery,
Laurinburg, Scotland County, NC.   (Laurinburg Gs)

McRAE MALCOLM
Born in 1756. Emigrated to America
in 1791. A farmer in Robeson County,
NC, with a wife and eight children
in 1812.   (1812)

McRAE Mrs MARGARET
Born in Argyllshire during 1787.
Married Norman McRae,1782-1850.
Died on 11 January 1856. Buried in
Stewartsville Cemetery, Laurinburg,
Scotland County, NC.   (Laurinburg Gs)

MacRAE MARY
Daughter of Hugh MacRae. Emigrated
from Kintail, Wester Ross, to
Wilmington, NC, during 1770.
Settled in Moore County, NC.   (CMR)

MacRAE MURDOCH
Son of Donald MacRae and Anne MacKenzie,
Kintail, Wester Ross. Emigrated to NC
c1773. Loyalist - killed at Moore's
Bridge, NC, in February 1776.   (CMR)

McRAE MURDOCH
84. Farmer. Born in Scotland. Nancy 30.
Born in NC. James 28. Farmer. Born in
NC. Moore County, NC.   (C)

McRAE NORMAN
Born in Skye, Inverness-shire. Married
Margaret ...., died 1856. Died on 7
December 1850 at Stewartsville, NC.
Buried in Richmond County, NC.   (Richmond Gs)

McRAE PETER
Born in Scotland during 1761.
Emigrated to America in 1788. A
farmer in Richmond County, NC, with
a wife and four children in 1812.
Died 24 September 1824. Buried in
Stewartsville Cemetery, Laurinburg,
Scotland County, NC.   (Laurinburg Gs)

McRAE PHILIP
Born in Scotland. Married Margaret
McQueen. Died in NC during 1785.   (INC13105)

McRAE ROBERT
Born in Scotland. Farmer. 54. Mary Ann
20. Born in SC. Christian 55. Born in
Scotland. Catherine Jane 18. Born in SC.
Alexander C. 16. Born in SC. James C. 14.
Born in SC. Margaret 12. Born in SC.
Marlborough County, SC.   (C)

MacRAE RODERICK
Son of Hugh MacRae. Emigrated from Kintail.
Wester Ross, to Wilmington, NC, in 1770.
Settled in Cumberland County. Married (1)
Mrs Catherine Burke. Father of Colin and
John (2)Christian Murchison. Father of John.   (CMR)

McRAE SARAH
65. Born in Scotland. William 31.
Born in NC. Florah 29. Born in NC.
Daniel 7. Born in NC. Mary 5. Born in
NC. Angus 3. Born in NC. Sarah 1. Born
in NC. Robeson County, NC.   (C)

McRAINEY MALCOLM
66. Born in Scotland. John 24. Born in
NC. Florah 19. Born in NC. Robeson County, NC.   (C)

McROB DUNCAN
26. Tailor. Kintyre, Argyllshire.
Emigrated from Greenock, Renfrewshire,
to Wilmington, NC, on the Diana,
master D Ruthven, in September 1774.   (PRO/T47.12)

MacSUINE DONALD
Probably from Skye, Inverness-shire.
Died in Cumberland County, NC, 1809.(Pr12.1809)(NCA.WBA.144)

McSWEEN ANGUS
Born in Scotland c1740. Emigrated to
America c1802. A farmer in Richmond
County, NC, with a wife and two
children in 1812. Nat. 20 September
1813 Richmond County, NC.   (1812)(RCCR)

McSWEEN ANGUS
Born in Scotland during 1776.
Emigrated to America c1802.
Nat. 20 September 1813 Richmond County, NC.   (RCCR)

McSWAIN DANIEL
Born in 1757. Emigrated to America
in 1790. A farmer in Robeson County, NC,
with two children in 1812.   (1812)

McSWAIN DANIEL
Born in 1760. Emigrated to America in
1790. A farmer in Richmond County, NC,
with a wife in 1812.   (1812)

McSWAIN DANIEL
Born in 1780. Emigrated to America in
1802. A farmer in Richmond County, NC,
with a wife and child in 1812.   (1812)

McSWAIN DAVID
Born in Scotland c1700. Emigrated to
America in 1731. Married Susanna
Hamrick. Died in 1770. Buried in
McSwain Cemetery, Shelby,
Cleveland County, NC.   (Cleveland Gs)

McSWEEN DONALD MURDOCH
Born in Scotland c1725. Married
Nancy McIver. Died in Moore County, NC.   (INC60040)

McSWEEN FINLAY
Born in Scotland c1746. Emigrated
to America in 1803. A farmer in
Richmond County, NC, with a wife and
three children in 1812. Nat. 20
September 1813 Richmond County, NC.   (RCCR)(1812)

McSWEEN FINLEY
Born Inverness-shire c1746. Died at
Little Lynch's Creek, SC, in 1829.   (CJ 17.10.1829)

McSWAIN FINLAY
Born 1765. Emigrated to America in
1790. A farmer in Richmond County,
NC, with a wife and six children
in 1812.   (1812)

McSWEEN SARAH
Born in Scotland c1748. Married
John William Wadsworth. Settled in
Moore County, NC. Died there in 1822.   (INC60040)

McVANE JOHN
Jacobite soldier captured after the Siege
of Preston, Lancashire. Transported from
Liverpool to South Carolina on the
Susannah, master Thomas Bromhall, 7 May 1716.   (SPC)(CTB)

McVANE KATHERINE
30. Spinner. Glen Orchy. Argyllshire.
Emigrated from Scotland, with daughter
Mary Downie 4, and Joseph Downie - an
infant, to Wilmington, NC, on the
Jupiter of Larne, master Samuel Brown,
in September 1775.   (PRO/T47.12)

McVANE MALCOLM
Jacobite soldier captured after the Siege
of Preston, Lancashire. Transported from
Liverpool to South Carolina on the
Susannah, master Thomas Bromhall, 7 May 1716.   (CTB)(SPC)

McVEY DOUGLAS
30. Labourer. Argyllshire. Emigrated
from Greenock, Renfrewshire, to NC on
the Ulysses, master J Wilson in May 1775.   (PRO/T47.12)

McVICAR ARCHIBALD
Born in Argyllshire during 1791. A
butcher in Charleston, SC. Nat.19
October 1813 Charleston, SC.   (Nat Arch M1183.1)

McVICAR JOHN
36. Tailor. Glasgow. Emigrated from
Greenock, Renfrewshire, to Wilmington,
NC, on the Diana, master D Ruthven
in September 1774.   (PRO/T47.12)

McVICAR NEIL
Born in Argyllshire during 1794. A
butcher in Charleston, SC. Nat. 29
January 1824 Charleston, SC.   (Nat Arch M1183.1)

McWHINNIE WILLIAM
Born in Galloway during 1801. Merchant
in Charleston, SC. Nat.17 March 1828
Charleston, SC.   (Nat Arch M1183.1)

McWILLIAMS ARCHIBALD
Born in Ayr. Nat. 3 July 1797
Charleston, SC.   (Nat Arch M1183.1)

McWILLIAM WILLIAM
Born in Scotland. Nat.27 January 1825 SC(Circuit Ct J19.376)

MAIR THOMAS
Born in the Shetland Islands. Merchant.
Nat.27 May 1798 Charleston, SC.   (Nat Arch M1183.1)

MALLOY DUNCAN
53. Born in Scotland. Effie 54. Born
in NC. Archibald 28. Born in NC.
Florah 22. Born in NC. Edward 18.
Born in NC. Mary 16. Born in NC.
Daniel 14. Born in NC. Robeson County, NC.   (C)

MALLOY JOHN
Born in Kintyre, Argyllshire.
Married Catherine McCallum. Emigrated
to NC during 1804. Settled in Robeson
County, NC. Father of Duncan, Edward,
Archibald and Neill. Died 23 January
1839.   (St Paul's OPR)

MALLOY NEILL
50. Born in Scotland. Archibald 55.
Born in Scotland. Robeson County, NC.   (C)

MANSON ANDREW
Born in Ross-shire during 1786. A
merchant in Charleston, SC. Nat.
28 February 1820 Charleston, SC.   (Nat Arch M1183.1)

MANSON JANE
Emigrated from Scotland or Ireland to
SC on the ship Pearl, master Walter
Buchanan, in December 1767.
Allocated a 100 acre land grant on
12 December 1767.   (OL)

MARSHALL ANDREW
Born in Scotland. Nat.2 October 1826.(SC Circuit Ct Jl 9.435)

MARSHALL DAVID
24. Clerk. Born in Scotland. Emigrated
from London to NC on the Margaret and
Mary in February 1774.   (PRO/T47.12)

MARSHALL Mrs ISABEL
Probably from Edinburgh. Settled in
Charleston, SC.   (Pr 10.4.1767 SC)

229

MARSHALL JAMES
Aberdeen. Inn-keeper and merchant
in St Philip's parish, Charleston,
SC. Died c1765.   (APB)(Pr 6.1767 PCC)

MARSHALL JOHN
Cooper. Leith, Midlothian. Emigrated
from Kirkcaldy, Fife, to Brunswick,
NC, on the Jamaica Packet, master
T Smith, in June 1775.   (PRO/T47.12)

MARSHALL JOHN
Eldest son of Dr Hugh Marshall,
Rothesay, Bute. A merchant in
Charleston, SC. Died there on
7 June 1820.   CCG 13.6.1820)(BM 7.584)

MARSHALL JOHN T.
48. Baker. Born in Scotland. Ruth 36.
Born in England. Charleston, SC.   (C)

MARSHALL PATRICK
Son of Janet Marshall in Dundee,
Angus. A merchant in Charleston, SC.
                    Pr 13.11.1761 New Providence, Bahamas)

MARTIN ALEXANDER
Born in 1758. Emigrated to America
during 1788. A farmer in Cumberland
County, NC, with a wife and four
children in 1812.   (1812)

MARTIN ALEXANDER
Born in 1792. Emigrated to America
in 1811. A farmer in Richmond County,
NC, in 1812.   (1812)

MARTIN DANIEL
71. Farmer. Born in Scotland. Sarah
71. Born in Scotland. Flora 40. Born
in Scotland. Dorothea B. 38. Born in
Scotland. Margaret 32. Born in NC.
Cumberland County, NC.   (C)

MARTIN DONALD
Born in 1767. Emigrated to America
in 1811. A farmer in Cumberland
County, NC, with a wife and three
children in 1812.   (1812)

MARTIN FLORA
65. Born in Scotland. William P. 32.
Farmer. Born in NC. Moore County, NC.   (C)

MARTIN JOHN
Captain in the Royal North Carolina
Regiment. Administration with will to
Hector Mackay, attorney for Angus
Martin, Donald Martin and Malcolm
McLeod in Scotland.   (Pr 1.1793 PCC)

MARTIN JOHN
63. Farmer. Born in Scotland. Mary
50. Born in NC. Chesterfield County, SC.   (C)

MARTIN MARTIN
81. Farmer. Born in Scotland. Mary
70. Born in NC. Alexander 21. Farmer.
Born in SC. Margaret 17. Born in SC.
Chesterfield County, SC.   (C)

MARTIN NANCY
60. Born in Scotland.
Chesterfield County, SC.   (C)

MASON ROBERT
Born in Scotland. Deserted from HM 16th
Regiment of Foot in Charleston, SC,
during 1768. May have gone to Georgia.
                    (Ga. Procl. Bk. H.128/30)

MATHER ISABELLA
76. Born in Scotland. Christian 42.
Born in NC. Catherine 37. Born in NC.
Kenneth 35. Farmer. Born in NC.
Isabella 1. Born in NC. Moore County, NC.   (C)

MATTHESON ALEXANDER
Born in Scotland c1773. A merchant
in Camden, SC. Died on 1 May 1826.   (SC 13.5.1826)

MATHESON ALEXANDER
Son of Murdoch Matheson, Lochalsh, Ross
and Cromarty. A merchant in Carolina
during the late C18.   (HOM)

MATHIESON ALEXANDER
Son of Murdoch Mathieson and his wife
Florence MacRae, Kintail, Wester Ross.
Settled in Charleston during 1830.   (CMR)

MATHESON C
54. Merchant. Born in Scotland.
Catherine 44. Born in SC. R.H. 22.
Student. Born in SC. Thomas 2 months.
Born in SC. Kershaw County, SC.   (C)

MATHESON DANIEL
Born in Invershin, Sutherland, c1764.
Tailor. Died in Asheville,
Buncombe County, NC, 8 January 1812.   (MOT 24.2.1812)

MATHESON DONALD
Born in Ross-shire during 1811.
Emigrated from Port Glasgow to
Charleston, SC, in November 1825.
Nat. 17 April 1837 Marlborough, SC.   (SCA)

MATHESON HUGH
32. Farmer. Rimsdale, Kildonan.
Sutherland. Emigrated from Scotland,
with his sister Katherine Matheson
16, and his wife and three children
aged from 8 to 2, to Wilmington, NC,
on the Bachelor of Leith, April 1774.   (PRO/T47.12)

MATHESON JAMES
38. Labourer. New Luce, Wigtonshire.
Emigrated from Stranraer, Wigtonshire,
with his wife Jean McQuiston 27, and
child Margaret 4, to NC on the Jackie,
Master J Morris, on 31 May 1775.   (PRO/T47.12)

MATHESON JOHN
Thornhill, Dumfries-shire. A student.
Died in Manchester, SC, 9 September 1822.   (S 319.71)

MATTHIESON JOHN
Closeburn, Nithsdale, Dumfries-shire.
Covenanter. Prisoner in Canongate Tolbooth.
Banished to Carolina on 19 June 1684.
Transported from Leith by Robert Malloch,
merchant burgess of Edinburgh, August 1684.   (PC)

MATHESON DONALD
Born during 1810, fourth son of John
Matheson of Attadale and his wife
Margaret. Emigrated to America during
1825. Settled in SC. Married Christian
McLeod in 1837. Father of Hugh, Walter,
Alexander, Margaret, Mary and Sarah.
Died in 1890.   (HOM)

MATHIESON DUNCAN
Son of Donald Mathieson,1744-1845,
miller at Fernaig. Settled in
Charleston, SC.   (HOM)

MATHESON DUNCAN
Fifth son of John Matheson and his
wife Isabella, Achtaytoralan. A
merchant in Carolina. Died in 1812.   (HOM)

MATTHEWSON JOHN
Jacobite soldier captured after the Siege
of Preston, Lancashire. Transported from
Liverpool to South Carolina on the
Susannah, master Thomas Bromhall, 7 May 1716.   (CTB)(SPC)

MATHESON RODERICK
Son of Murdoch Matheson, Lochalsh. Ross
and Cromarty. Emigrated to America.
Settled in Carolina. Died during 1811.   (HOM)

MATTHEWS EFFIE
50. Born in Scotland. John 50. Farmer.
Born in NC. Norman 24. Born in NC.
Christian 21. Born in NC. Edith 18.
Born in NC. John 17. Born in NC.
William 14. Born in NC. Nancy 10.
Born in NC. Effie 8. Born in NC.
Cumberland County, NC.   (C)

MATTHEW NANCY
51. Born in Scotland. William 49.
Farmer. Born in NC. Mary 21. Born in NC.
David 18. Labourer. Born in NC. Emily
16. Born in NC. Elizabeth 14. Born in
NC. Margaret 72. Born in Scotland.
Cumberland County, NC.   (C)

MATHIS MARY
68. Born in Scotland. Hugh 71. Born in
NC. Rosa 72. Born in NC. Brunswick County, NC.   (C)

MAXTON JOHN
Born in Crieff, Perthshire, during 1787.
A baker in Charleston, SC. Nat. 4 February
1825 Charleston, SC.   (Nat Arch M1183.1)

MAXWELL JAMES
Educated at Universities of Edinburgh
and Aberdeen. Graduated M.A., and later
M.D. in Aberdeen 7 May 1790. a surgeon
in Charleston, SC.   (KCA)

MAXWELL MARGARET
Born in Dumfries during 1807.
Emigrated from Scotland to America in
1815. Settled in Columbia, SC.
Married William Martin. Poetess and
teacher. Died Columbia, SC.   (TSA)

MAXWELL PETER
Possibly born in Paisley, Renfrewshire,
c1763. Married Rebecca ....,1761-1810.
Planter in New Hanover County, NC.
Died in Brunswick County, NC, on 23
September 1812. Buried in St Philip's
Cemetery.   (Brunswick Gs)(NCA/CR.070.801)

MAXWELL ROBERT
18. Clerk. Born in Scotland.
Emigrated from London to Carolina on
the James, master Isaac Thompson, in
October 1774.   (PRO/T47.12)

MAXWELL THOMAS
Born in Scotland. Married Mary McPhail
possibly in Cumberland County, NC.
Died in Sampson County, NC, c1827.   (INC)

MAXWELL WILLIAM
Emigrated from Glasgow to SC in 1723.
Minister in Edisto Island from 1723 to
1725, later minister in Barnsted Downs.   (APC)

MAY JOHN
Born in Scotland c1700. Married Mary
Stafford in Beaufort County, NC,
c1735. Died in Pitt County, NC, 1764.   (INC)

MELVIN DAVID
Born in Scotland. Nat.1804 Craven County,NC.(Craven Co Ct Rec)

MENZIES JOHN
Born in Scotland during 1744.
Emigrated to Virginia c1772. Baptist.
Died in Rockingham County, NC, in
March 1819.   (RR 2.4.1819)

MENZIES MARY
25. Lady. Emigrated from Greenock,
Renfrewshire, to NC on the Ajax,
master R Cunningham in May 1775.   (PRO/T47.12)

MESHAW CATHERINE
65. Born in Scotland. Flora N. 33. Born
in NC. Ann Davis 26. Born in NC. Mary J.
Davis 6. Born in NC. William Davis 5.
Born in NC. Bladen County, NC.   (C)

MICHIE WILLIAM
Montrose, Angus. Merchant in
Charleston, SC.   (Pr 10.1.1772 SC)

MIDDLETON Mrs SARAH
Born c1683, widow of Arthur Middleton,
President of the Council of SC. Died
in Goose Creek, SC, in September 1765.   (SM 27.671)

MILLER ALEXANDER
Born in Kilmarnock, Ayrshire.
Nat. 12 May 1831 Craven County, NC.
Alexander Miller, 40, merchant, born in
Scotland. Henrietta 40. Born in NC.
Mary 14. Scholar. Born in NC. Alexander
10. Scholar. Born in NC. Francis 7.
Scholar. Born in NC. Henry 6. Scholar.
Born in NC. Jannet 4. Born in NC.
Henrietta 5 months. Born in NC
Craven County, NC.   (C)(Craven Co Ct Rec)

235

MILLER FRANCIS
Born in Ayrshire. Mariner.
Nat. 13 April 1797 Charleston, SC.   (Nat Arch M1183.1)

MILLER JAMES
Born in Ayrshire. Mariner.
Nat. 17 June 1796 Charleston, SC.   (Nat.Arch M1183.1)

MILLAR JAMES
Born in Dunmore, Stirlingshire, c1793.
Emigrated from London to Wilmington,
NC, in September 1815. Nat. March 1826
Cumberland County, NC.   (NCA/CR.029.301.16)

MILLER JOSEPH
Born in 1781. Emigrated to America in
1792. Resident in York District, SC,
with a family of two in 1812.   (1812)

MILLER PHILIP
Born in Scotland. Died in Edenton,
NC, during 1818.   (RM 1.1.1819)

MILLER ROBERT JOHNSTONE
Born in Baldovie, Dundee, Angus, on
11 July 1758, son of G and M Miller.
Emigrated from Scotland to America
pre 1784. Episcopalian clergyman in
NC. Died at John's River, Burke County,
NC, on 13 May 1834. Buried in Mary's
Grove Cemetery, Lenoir, Caldwell County,
NC.   (Hist of Rowan Co)(Caldwell Gs)(WC 31.5.1834)

MILLER SAMUEL
Son of Christian McKay, Thurso, Caithness.
A doctor in St Philip's parish,
Charleston, SC.   (Pr 9.6.1795 SC)

MILLER THOMAS
Minister of Kirkliston, Scotland, appointed
John Alexander, merchant in Carolina, as his
attorney there to collect goods, books,
merchandise and rent due, 8 October 1697.
                    (Records of the Province of SC 1692/1721)

MILLAR WILLIAM
Born in Scotland. A tailor and runaway
indentured servant in NC on
29 December 1773.   (CFM.204)

MILLAR WILLIAM
Born in Montrose, Angus, during 1781.
Baker. Nat. 27 May 1807 Charleston, SC.   (Nat Arch M1183.1)

MILLS ELIZABETH
Dundee, Angus. Emigrated from Kirkcaldy,
Fife, with her servant, to SC on the
Jamaica Packet, master T Smith, in
June 1775.   (PRO/T47.12)

MILLS JOHN
Joiner. Dundee, Angus. Emigrated from
Kirkcaldy, Fife, to SC on the Jamaica
Packet, master T Smith, in June 1775.   (PRO/T47.12)

MILNE ANDREW
55. Planter. Born in Scotland. Elizabeth
45. Born in SC. Eliza 11. Born in SC.
Martha 8. Born in SC. Charleston, SC.   (C)

MILNE CHARLES
Son of James Milne in Montrose, Angus.
A merchant in Georgetown, SC.   (Pr 17.1.1772 SC)

MILNE JOHN
55. Planter. Born in Scotland. Margaret
50. Born in SC. Margaret 20. Born in SC.
Christiana 18. Born in SC. Beaufort County, SC.   (C)

MILNER JAMES
Son of James Milner and his wife Margaret
Ingram, Mains of Carse, Aberdeenshire.
Emigrated to America c1759. Died in NC
c1771.   (APB)

MITCHELL ANDREW
Perthshire. Shop-keeper in Charleston, SC. (Pr 11.6.1796 SC)

MITCHELL COLIN
Born in Scotland. Nat.11 June 1805 SC.(Common Pleas Ct U3.259)

MITCHELL DAVID
Emigrated from Scotland or Ireland to SC
on the ship Pearl, master Walter
Buchanan, in December 1767. Allocated a
100 acre land grant on 12 December 1767.   (OL)

MITCHELL GEORGE
Son of Hugh and Janet Mitchell, Dalgain,
(Dalquhairn?), Ayrshire. Physician in
St Bartholemew's parish, Colleton
County, SC.   (Pr 5.1.1749 SC)

MITCHELL ROBERT
26. Tailor. Kintyre, Argyllshire.
Emigrated from Greenock, Renfrewshire,
with his wife Ann Campbell 26, to
Wilmington, NC, on the Ulysses, master
J Chalmers, in August 1774.   (PRO/T47.12)

MITCHELL Dr THOMAS
Born in Scotland. Died in Franklin
County, NC, in February 1803.   (NC Minerva 2.1803)

MITCHELL THOMAS
Born in Greenock, Renfrewshire.
Mariner in Charleston, SC. Nat. 29
September 1827 Charleston, SC.   (Nat Arch M1183.1)

MITCHELL WILLIAM
Shetland Islands. Farmer and fisherman.
Emigrated from Kirkcaldy, Fife, with
his wife and children, to Brunswick,
NC, on the Jamaica Packet, master
T Smith, in June 1775.   (PRO/T47.12)

MITCHELL WILLIAM
Born in Perthshire during 1760. Mariner
in Charleston, SC. Nat.25 July 1820
Charleston, SC.   (Nat Arch M1183.1)

MODEREN JAMES
Born in Scotland during 1776. Mariner.
Nat. 19 September 1808 Charleston, SC.   (Nat Arch M1183.1)

MOFFAT ANDREW
Born in Duns, Berwickshire, during 1795.
A merchant in Charleston, SC.
Nat.14 February 1820 Charleston, SC.   (Nat Arch M1183.1)

MOFFAT JAMES
Prisoner in Edinburgh or Canongate
Tolbooth. Banished to Carolina -
to be transported there by Robert
Malloch, merchant burgess of Edinburgh,
in August 1684.   (PC)

MOFFAT JANET
70. Born in Scotland. Keith S. 30.
Accountant. Born in Scotland.
Kershaw County, SC.   (C)

MOIR Rev JAMES
Brother of Rev Henry Moir, minister of
Auchtertool, Fife. Died in Edgecombe
County, NC, on 31 December 1766.   (SM 29.278)

MONEYDAY WILLIAM
Born in Edinburgh during 1752.
A merchant in Charleston, SC. Died in
Savanna, Georgia, on 28 September 1819.   (SR 30.9.1819)

MONIES HUGH
Born in Galloway during 1791. Settled
in Charleston, SC. Nat.19 October 1813
Charleston, SC.   (Nat Arch M1183.1)

MONIES JAMES
Born in Kirkcudbright during 1776.
Mariner. Nat.23 July 1804
Charleston, SC.   (Nat Arch M1183.1)

MONK JAMES
90. Farmer. Born in Scotland. Sarah 45.
Born in NC. Alexander 39. Born in NC.
Moore County, NC.   (C)

MUNROE ALEXANDER
Born in 1768. Emigrated to America during
1803. A farmer in Robeson County, NC, in
1812.   (1812)

MONROE ALEXANDER
51. Farmer. Born in Scotland. Charlotte
40. Born in SC. John 18. Born in SC.
George 13. Born in SC. Alexander 11.
Born in SC. James 10. Born in SC.
Kershaw County, SC.   (C)

MONROE ARCHIBALD
66. Farmer. Born in Scotland. Flora 56.
Born in Scotland. Flora 26. Born in NC.
Nancy 24. Born in NC. Mary 16. Born in
NC. Duncan 23. Farmer. Born in NC.
Richmond County, NC.   (C)

MONROE DANIEL
Born in 1770. Emigrated to America in
1790. A farmer in Richmond County,
NC, with a wife in 1812.   (1812)

MONROE DANIEL
68. Farmer. Born in Scotland. Robert 33.
Born in NC. Farmer. Margaret 21. Born
in NC. Richmond County, NC.   (C)

MUNROE DANIEL
Born in 1780. Emigrated to America in
1802. A farmer in Richmond County, NC,
with a wife and four children in 1812.   (1812)

MUNROE DONALD
Born in 1777. Emigrated to America in
1802. A fisherman in NC with a wife
and six children in 1812.   (1812)

MUNROE EFFIE
50. Born in Scotland. Daniel 21. Farmer.
Born in NC. Nancy 19. Born in NC.
Janet Shaw 60. Born in Scotland.
Montgomery County, NC.   (C)

MONRO HUGH
26. Shoemaker. Tongue, Sutherland.
Emigrated from Scotland, with his wife,
to Wilmington, NC, on the Bachelor of
Leith, in April 1774.   (PRO/T47.12)

MUNROE JAMES
Born in Fife. Mariner. Nat.6 October
1796 Charleston, SC.   (Nat Arch M1183.1)

MONROE MALCOLM
64. Born in Scotland. Florah 63. Born
in Scotland. Colin 26. Born in NC.
Duncan 25. Born in NC. Peter 23. Born
in NC. Robeson County, NC.   (C)

MONROE NANCY
60. Born in Scotland. Mary 27. Born in
NC. Bladen County, NC.   (C)

MONROE PETER
67. Born in Scotland. Isabella 67. Born
in Scotland. Malcolm 40. Born in NC.
Peter Monroe, emigrated to America in
1802, a farmer in Robeson County, NC,
with a wife and four children in 1812.   (C)(1812)

MUNROE ROBERT
Born in 1752. Emigrated to America in
1803. A farmer in Richmond County, NC,
with a wife and five children in 1812.   (1812)

MUNRO ROBERT
Born in Ross-shire(?), Scotland, c1793.
Nat. 19 November 1823 Laurens County, SC.   (Cit Bk 100)

MONRO WILLIAM
34. Shoemaker. Borgiemore, Tongue,
Sutherland. Emigrated from Scotland,
with his wife, serving maid, and
servant boy, to Wilmington, NC, on
the Bachelor of Leith, April 1774.   (PRO/T47.12)

MUNROE WILLIAM
Born in Greenock, Renfrewshire, in 1769.
Nat.6 July 1805 Charleston, SC.   (Nat Arch M1183.1)

MONTGOMERY ALEXANDER
Linlithgow, West Lothian. Covenanter.
Prisoner in Edinburgh Tolbooth.
Banished to the Plantations in America
on 27 May 1684. Transported from Leith
to Carolina by Robert Malloch, merchant
burgess of Edinburgh June 1684.   (PC)

MONTGOMERY JAMES
50. Mill superintendent. Born in Scotland.
Edgefield County, SC.   (C)

MONTGOMERY of GREVOCK ...
Emigrated from Gourock, Renfrewshire,
with his son, to Port Royal, SC, on
the Carolina Merchant 21 July 1684.   (ECJ)

MONTGOMERY AMOS
84. Shoemaker. Born in Scotland. George
44. Carpenter. Born in Scotland.
Susanna 63. Born in Scotland. Amos 18.
Clerk. Born in SC. Caroline 38. Born
in Scotland. Susan 14. Born in SC.
Arabella 12. Born in SC. Mary 9. Born
in SC. Edward 6. Born in SC.
Charleston, SC.   (C)

MONTGOMERY JOHN
Born in Scotland during 1723.
Runaway indentured servant of Thomas
Wright in 1743.   (SCGaz 5.12.1743)

MONTGOMERIE JOHN
Kilburnie, Ayrshire. Died in Charleston,
SC, on 11 September 1819.   (S 152.19)

MONTGOMERY of SKELMORLIE, Sir ROBERT
Allocated a land grant between the rivers
Altamaha and Savanna, Carolina, 18 June 1717.   (SPC)

MONTGOMERY ROBERT
Winton, NC. Serviced as Heir to his
father John Montgomery of Nettlehirst
and Mossend, Ayrshire, 4 August 1795.   (SRO/SH)

MONTGOMERIE THOMAS
Ayr. Merchant in Charleston, SC.
Nat.25 May 1787 Charleston, SC.   (Pr 11.11.1796 SC)

MONTGOMERY WILLIAM
Scottish Covenanter. Settled in SC.
Died before April 1690.   (LJ)

MOON MEREDITH WILLIAM
Born in Scotland on 24 June 1770.
Landed in Charleston, SC, on 28 January
1794. Married Mrs Sarah Robertson in
Newberry, SC. Father of Peter, Sarah,
Maria, Meredith, William, Delton L.,
Dennis F., and Elizabeth Ann.
Nat. 2 November 1807 Newberry, SC.   (SCA)

MOOR MICHAEL
Born in Scotland. Carpenter. Buried
in St Helena's parish, SC, on
26 February 1752.   (St Helena's OPR)

MOOR MILES
Jacobite soldier captured after the Siege
of Preston, Lancashire. Transported from
Liverpool to South Carolina on the
Wakefield, master Thomas Beck, 21 April 1716.   (SPC)

MORGAN GEORGE
37. Farmer. Chabster,(Scrabster?), Reay,
Caithness. Emigrated from Scotland, with
his wife and two children aged 7 and 1,
to Wilmington, NC, on the Bachelor of
Leith in April 1774.   (PRO/T47.12)

MORRISON ALEXANDER
Born in Skye, Inverness-shire, during 1717.
Doctor. Settled in Carthage, NC. Died 1777.   (SA)

MORISON ALEXANDER
60. Farmer. Kinside, Tongue, Sutherland.
Emigrated from Scotland, with his wife,
son and servant maid, to Wilmington, NC,
on the Bachelor of Leith, April 1774.   (PRO/T47.12)

MORRISON BARBARA
82. Born in Scotland. Macon County, NC.   (C)

MORRISON CATHERINE
65. Born in Scotland. Findlay 32. Farmer.
Born in NC. Duncan 30. Farmer. Born in
NC. Sarah 24. Born in NC. Cumberland County, NC.   (C)

MORRISON DAVID
67. Farmer. Born in Scotland. Nancy 60.
Born in NC. Mary 35. Born in NC.
Catherine 32. Born in NC. Anna 30. Born
in NC. Margaret 28. Born in NC. Norman
23. Farmer. Born in NC. Cumberland County, NC.   (C)

MORRISON EFFIE
60. Born in Scotland. Sally 58. Born in
Scotland. Robeson County, NC.   (C)

MORRISON EFFY
57. Born in Scotland. Marlborough County, SC.   (C)

MORRISON FLORA
51. Born in Scotland. Allan B. 56. Farmer.
Born in NC. Catherine 32. Born in NC.
Duncan 31. Born in NC. William 26. Born
in NC. Margaret 25. Born in NC Malcolm 24.
Born in NC. Christian 22. Born in NC.
Nancy 20. Born in NC. ...(m) Born in NC.
Moore County, NC.   (C)

MORRISON Mrs FLORA
Born in Scotland on 16 June 1796.
Died in NC on 8 December 1881. Buried
in Gilchrist Cemetery, NC.   (Gilchrist Gs)

MORRISON JAMES
Born in Glasgow. Grocer. Nat.1 June 1798
Charleston, SC.   (Nat Arch M1183.1)

MORRISON JAMES
Born in Scotland. Nat.5 March 1810 SC.   (Inf City Ct C4.786)

MORRISON JOHN
Born in 1745. Emigrated to America in
1802. A farmer in Richmond County, NC,
with five children in 1812.   (1812)

MORRISON JOHN
Born in 1760. Emigrated to America in
1788. A farmer in Richmond County, NC,
with a wife in 1812.   (1812)

MORRISON JOHN
Born in Scotland c1775. Emigrated to
America c1802. Nat.20 September 1813
Richmond County, NC.   (RCCR)

MORISON JOHN
Born in Fife during 1781. Merchant.
Nat.18 March 1807 Charleston, SC.   (Nat Arch M1183.1)

MORRISON JOHN
Born in 1780. Emigrated to America in
1802. A farmer in Robeson County, NC,
with a wife and two children in 1812.   (1812)

MORRISON JOHN.
80. Farmer. Born in Scotland.
Montgomery County, NC.   (C)

MORRISON JOHN
67. Born in Scotland. Catherine 57. Born
in NC. Mary S. 24. Born in NC. Alexander
19. Born in NC. Margaret 17. Born in NC.
Effie 15. Born in NC. Robeson County, NC.   (C)

MORRISON JOHN
Born in 1785. Emigrated to America in
1788. A farmer in Richmond County, NC,
with his mother, two sisters and three
orphan children in 1812.   (1812)

MORRISON JOHN McD.
Born in Scotland c1790. Emigrated to
America during 1802. Nat.20 September
1813 Richmond County, NC.   (RCCR)

MORRISON KENNETH
79. Farmer. Born in Scotland. Dorothy
27. Born in SC. Daniel 24. Born in SC.
Angus 22. Born in SC. Chesterfield County, SC.   (C)

MORRISON MALCOLM
Born in 1757. Emigrated to America in
1802. A farmer in Richmond County, NC,
with a wife and four children in 1812.   (1812)

MORRISON MALCOLM
Born in Scotland c1772. Emigrated to
America c1802. Nat.20 September 1813
Richmond County, NC. A farmer in
Richmond County, NC, with four
children in 1812.   (RCCR)(1812)

MORRISON MARGARET
65. Born in Scotland. John 35. Farmer.
Born in NC. Isabella 40. Born in NC.
Flora 35. Born in NC. Eliza 23. Born
in NC. Alexander 27. Schoolteacher.
Born in NC. Richmond County, NC.   (C)

MORRISON MARGARET
48. Born in Scotland. Daniel 39. Born
in NC. Christian 30. Born in NC.
Richmond County, NC.   (C)

MORRISON MARY
65. Born in Scotland. Florah 40. Born
in NC. Mary 26. Born in NC. Effie 24.
Born in NC. Robeson County, NC.   (C)

MORRISON MURDO
Born in 1756. Emigrated to America in
1788. A farmer in Richmond County, NC,
with a wife and two children in 1812.   (1812)

MORRISON NANCY
48. Born in Scotland. John 45. Farmer.
Born in NC. Daniel 17. Farmer. Born in
NC. Betsy 14. Born in NC. William 12.
Born in NC. John 9. Born in NC.
Margaret McLeod 50. Born in Scotland.
Sarah McLeod 60. Born in Scotland.
Richmond County, NC.   (C)

MORRISON NEIL
Born in Argyllshire before 1804.
Nat.20 November 1825 SC.   (Cit Bk 109)

MORRISON NORMAN
Born in 1752. Emigrated to America in
1790. A farmer in Robeson County, NC,
with a wife and five children in 1812.   (1812)

MORRISON NORMAN
Born in Scotland, son of Alexander
Morrison. Emigrated from Scotland
to North Carolina. Settled in
Moore County, NC, in 1773.   (AMC)

MORRISON NORMAN
Born in Scotland c1765. Emigrated to
America c1802. A farmer in Richmond
County, NC, with a wife and six
children in 1812. Nat.20 September
1813 Richmond County, NC.   (RCCR)(1812)

MORRISON SARAH
63. Born in Scotland. Richmond County, NC.   (C)

MORISON SIMON
Born in Fife during 1796.
A cabinet-maker in Charleston, SC.
Nat.13 April 1830 Charleston, SC.   (Nat Arch M1183.1)

MORRISON WILLIAM
Born in 1771. Emigrated to America
in 1788. A farmer in Richmond County,
NC, with a wife and six children in 1812.   (1812)

MORSE SARAH
46. Born in Scotland. John 46. Baptist
minister. Born in NC. Robert 18.
School-teacher. Born in NC. Flora 16.
Born in NC. Catherine 12. Born in NC.
Sarah 9. Born in NC. John 7. Born in
NC. Daniel 5. Born in NC. Flora
McMillan 51. Born in Scotland.
Catherine McMillan 48. Born in
Scotland. Richmond County, NC.   (C)

MORTON ALEXANDER
Born in Leith during 1779. Merchant.
Nat.18 May 1807 Charleston, SC.   (Nat Arch M1183.1)

MORTON THOMAS
40. Tailor. Born in Scotland.
Anderson County, SC.   (C)

MOULTRIE JOHN
Born in 1702, son of John Moultrie and
his wife Catherine Craik, Culross, Fife.
Educated at the University of Edinburgh
- graduated MA. Settled in Charleston,
SC, c1729. Co-founder of the St Andrews
Society of Charleston, SC. Married (1)
Lucretia Cooper (2)Elizabeth Matthews.
Father of John, James, William,
Thomas, and Alexander. Died in 1771.   (SCHGM.5.242)

MOWBRAY ARTHUR
Possibly from the Shetland Islands.
A surgeon in Colleton County, SC.   (Pr 6.6.1746 SC)

MOWBRAY LILIAS
Scalloway, Shetland Islands. Settled
in St Paul's parish, Colleton County,
SC.   (Pr 29.3.1765 SC)

MUDIE GEORGE
Born in Arbroath, Angus. Nat. 10 April
1820 SC.   (Circuit Ct Jl 9.56)

MUDIE JEAN
Daughter of James Mudie, physician in
Jamaica, married William Keith, SC,
in Edinburgh during March 1769.   (SM 31.167)

MUIR JAMES
Probably born in Scotland. 38. Peruke-
maker. Emigrated to Georgia on 8
November 1732. Landed there 1 February
1733. Allocated a land grant in
Savannah on 21 December 1733. Married
Mary Goodman on 29 December 1734.
Moved to Carolina in 1739. Died in
September 1739.   (ESG)

MUIRHEAD JAMES
Prisoner in Edinburgh or Canongate
Tolbooths. Banished to Carolina.
Transported there from Leith by
Robert Malloch, merchant burgess in
Edinburgh during August 1684.   (PC)

248

MUIRHEAD JAMES
Born in Edinburgh during 1792. An
accountant in Charleston, SC.
Nat.27 August 1813 Charleston, SC.   (Nat Arch M1183.1)

MUIRHEAD MARGARET
Prisoner in Edinburgh or Canongate
Tolbooths. Banished to Carolina in
1684. Transported there from Leith
by Robert Malloch, merchant burgess
of Edinburgh in August 1684.   (PC)

MUIRHEAD RICHARD M.
Glasgow. Merchant. Died in
Charleston, SC, on 3 October 1819.   (S 150.19)

MUIRHEAD ROBERT
50. Overseer. Born in Scotland.
Colleton County, SC.   (C)

MULLINGS JOHN
Born in Greenock, Renfrewshire, in
1791. Pilot in Charleston, SC.
Nat.5 July 1824 Charleston, SC.   (Nat Arch M1183.1)

MUNN DANIEL
75. Farmer. Born in Scotland. Mary 57.
Born in Scotland. Mary 26. Born in NC.
Christian 24. Born in NC. Angus 22.
Farmer. Born in NC. Daniel 13. Born in
NC. Colin 13. Born in NC. Bladen County, NC.   (C)

MUNN NANCY
75. Born in Scotland. Euphemia 40. Born
in NC. Mary 45. Born in NC.
Montgomery County, NC.   (C)

MURCHISON ALEXANDER
Born in Scotland. Died in Fayetteville,
Cumberland County, NC, 13 February 1818.   (RR 27.2.1818)

MURCHISON ALEXANDER
84. Born in Scotland. Catherine 73.
Born in NC. Mary 41. Born in NC.
Nancy 26. Born in NC.
Montgomery County, NC.   (C)

MURCHISON KENNETH McKENZIE
Emigrated from Scotland to America in
1773. Settled at Little River,
Cumberland County, NC. Father of
Duncan, Kenneth M. and David R.   (SFV)

MURCHISON MARGARET
86. Born in Scotland. Annabella 53.
Born in NC. Flora 43. Born in NC.
Kenneth 40. Farmer. Born in NC.
Martha 25. Born in NC. Margaret
F.3. Born in NC. ...(m) 1. Born
in NC. Moore County, NC.   (C)

MURCHISON MARGARET
40. Born in Scotland. Cumberland County, NC.   (C)

MURPHY C.
80. Farmer. Born in Scotland. M(f) 58.
Born in NC. E(f) 31. Born in NC. CW 25.
Farmer. Born in NC. JH 24. Civil
Engineer. Born in NC. CF 24. Physician
RH 16. Farmer. Born in NC. New Hanover County, NC. (C)

MURPHY HUGH
Born in Argyllshire in 1752. Revolutionary
soldier. Died in NC during 1835.   (LOS)

MURPHY PATRICK
Born in 1720. Married Elizabeth Kelso
in Kilmore, Arran, Bute. Emigrated
from Arran to America c1774. Settled
at Black River, Ivanhoe, NC.
Revolutionary soldier. Father of
Robert, 1765-1840. Died in 1785.   (PCM)(BAF)

MURRAY ALEXANDER
Scotland. Gentleman in Charleston, SC.   (Pr 9.1.1746 SC)

MURRAY ALEXANDER
Son of Charles Murray, Clerk of the
Bailliary of Lauderdale. Merchant
and later Naval Officer of
Charleston, SC. Serviced as Heir to
his father on 17 December 1737.
Died before 1750.   (SRO/SH)(SRO/RD3.210.491)

MURRAY Lady ANNE
Wife of John Murray, MD, Glasgow, and
daughter of George, Earl of Cromarty.
Died in Charleston, SC, 18 January 1768.   (SM 30.165)

MURRAY JAMES
Born at Unthank, Roxburghshire on
9 August 1713, son of John Murray and
his wife Annie Bennet. Emigrated from
Gravesend, Kent, to America on the
Catherine, Captain Fay, 20 September
1735. Landed at Charleston, SC, on
27 November 1735. Planter in NC.
Married Barbara, daughter of Andrew
Bennet of Chesters. Loyalist. Died 1781.   (LJM)

MURRAY JOHN, MD.
Married Lady Anne Atkins, widow of
Hon Edmond Atkins, and daughter of
George, Earl of Cromartie, in
Charleston, SC, 16 February 1764.   (SM 26.166)

MURRAY MARY
Emigrated from Scotland or Ireland on
the ship Pearl, master Walter Buchanan,
in December 1767. Allocated a 100 acre
land grant on 12 December 1767.   (OL)

MURRAY ROBERT
Born in 1721, son of John Murray.
Emigrated from Scotland to America in
1732. Married Mary Lindley in 1744.
Merchant in Pennsylvania, New York
and NC. Died 22 July 1786.   (WA)

MURRAY ROBERT
Born in Sutherland during 1782. A
tailor in Charleston, SC.
Nat. 8 February 1825 Charleston, SC.   (Nat Arch M1183.1)

MURRAY ROBERT
Born in Sutherland during 1785. A
tailor in Charleston, SC.
Nat. 15 July 1831 Charleston, SC.   (Nat Arch M1183.1)

MUSGRAVE Mrs ROBERT
Born in Scotland c1783. Settled in
Brunswick County, NC. Died in
Fayetteville on 1 January 1811.   (RR 1.1811)

MUTER MARGARET
Born in Stonehouse, Lanarkshire(?)
Died in New Hanover County, NC, 1810.   (NCA/CR 070 801)

MUTER ROBERT
Born in Scotland. Married Margaret.
Died in New Hanover County, NC, 1806.   (NCA/CR 070 801)

MYLES GEORGE
Son of John Myles, Coupar Angus. Perth-
shire. Sought in SC during 1745.   (SCGaz 22.4.1745)

NAIRN Mrs ELIZABETH
Born c1658, eldest daughter of Robert
Edward, minister of Murroes, Angus.
Married (1)Henry Quintine (2)Thomas
Nairn, Judge of the Vice Admiralty
of SC. Died 9 March 1721. Buried
St Andrews, Berkeley County, SC.   (St Andrew's OPR)

NAIRN THOMAS
Born in Scotland. Emigrated to America.
Indian Agent in SC. Killed by Indians
during April 1715.   (WA)

NAISMITH R.
Born in Scotland. Deserted from
Lt Col Cochrane's Company in April 1739.   (SCGaz)

NAPIER THOMAS
Born in Glasgow during 1778. Emigrated
to SC before July 1800. A merchant in
Charleston, SC. Nat.24 August 1813
Charleston, SC.   (Nat Arch M1183.1)

NAPIER WILLIAM
Scotland. A surgeon in Colleton County,
SC.   (Pr 16.8.1732 SC)

NEAL JOHN
45. Farmer. Born in Scotland.
Edgefield County, SC.   (C)

NEALL JOHN
48. Farmer. Born in Scotland. Elya 38.
Born in NC. George 21. Born in NC.
Mary 13. Born in NC. William 9. Born
in NC. John 7. Born in NC. Charles 2.
Born in NC. Cherokee County, NC.   (C)

NEAL PETER
75. Farmer. Born in Scotland. Janetta 20.
Born in England. Edgefield County, SC.   (C)

NEAL WILLIAM
Born in Greenock, Renfrewshire, during
1782. Mariner. Nat.2 July 1804
Charleston, SC.   (Nat Arch M1183.1)

NEALL WILLIAM
Born in Scotland. 54. Schoolteacher.
Cherokee County, NC.   (C)

NEILSON JAMES HOW
Son of George Neilson, merchant in
Glasgow. Died 28 December 1807 in
Charleston, SC.   (SM 1808)

NEILSON WILLIAM
Born in Ayrshire on 5 January 1748.
Married Jane Lewis,1753-1816, in
Virginia. Died at Hot Springs, NC,
on 30 January 1832.   (NCA/Douglas pp)

NELLES JANET
54. Born in Scotland. PD 30. Cooper.
Born in New York. Charleston, SC.   (C)

NELSON DAVID
Born in Stirlingshire. Emigrated to
America in 1825. Nat.15 April 1829
Newberry, SC.   (SCA)

NEWTON JONATHAN
Jacobite soldier captured after the Siege
of Preston, Lancashire. Transported from
Liverpool to South Carolina on the
Susannah, master Thomas Bromhill, 7 May 1716.   (SPC)(CTB)

253

NEY PETER STEWART
Born in Stirlingshire during 1787.
Nat. March 1820(?)Marlborough County,SC.   (SCA)

NICOLL ALEXANDER
46. Merchant. Born in Scotland.
Greenville County, SC.   (C)

NICHOLSON CATHERINE
86. Born in Scotland. Mary Stewart 45.
Born in Scotland. Charles Stewart 30.
Born in NC. Farmer. Malcolm Nicholson
40. Waggoner. Born in NC. Francis
Sheppard 16. Born in NC.
Richmond County, NC.   (C)

NICHOLSON DONALD
Born in Scotland c1769. Emigrated to
America c1802. Nat.20 September 1813
Richmond County, NC.   (RCCR)

NICHOLSON JOHN
Jacobite soldier captured after the Siege
of Preston, Lancashire. Transported from
Liverpool to South Carolina on the
Wakefield, master Thomas Beck, 21 April 1716.   (SPC)(CTB)

NICHOLSON JOHN
Born in Scotland on 11 May 1769.
Captain in United States Army. Died on
11 May 1814. Buried in Brown Marsh
Presbyterian Church Cemetery, Bladen
County, NC.   (Bladen Gs)

NICHOLSON MALCOLM
Born in Scotland c1756. Emigrated to
America c1802. Nat.20 September 1813
Richmond County, NC.   (RCCR)

NICHOLSON MARY
Born in Scotland. 75. Mary 53. Born in
Scotland. Margaret 49. Born in Scotland.
Peter 36. Farmer. Born in NC.
Richmond County, NC.   (C)

NICHOLSON PETER
Born in 1792. Emigrated to America
in 1802. A farmer in Robeson County,
NC, in 1812.   (C)

NICHOLSON S.
Born during 1786. Emigrated to America
in 1801. A merchant in Fayetteville,
NC, in 1812.   (1812)

NISBET OF DEAN ALEXANDER
Born son of Sir John Nisbet and his wife
Ann Myrton. Indentured as a servant to
Alexander Nisbet, a Scottish storekeeper
at Redbank, SC, from 1721 to 1726.
Married Mary Rutherford in October 1742.
Allocated a 1180 acre land grant in
Craven County, SC, 12 August 1737.
Father of Henry, John, Alexander and
Elizabeth. Serviced as Heir to his
nephew Sir Henry Nisbet of Dean on
24 March 1747. Died 7 October 1753 in
Charleston, SC. Buried in St Philip's
parish, SC.   (SCGen)(SM 15.627)(Pr 1753 SC)(SRO/GD237)(NHP)

NESBIT FRANCIS
Born in Scotland during 1760.
Emigrated to America in 1790. A
farmer in York District, SC, with
a family of nine in 1812.   (1812)

NESBIT JAMES
Born in Edinburgh. Nat.18 June 1812.(SC Circuit Ct Jl 10.79)

NESBIT ROBERT
Born in Berwick-on-Tweed on
17 November 1799. Planter. Settled
in Waccamaw, SC, during 1808. Nat.
30 March 1825 Charleston, SC. Died
on 17 October 1848.   (Waccamaw Gs)(Nat Arch M1183.1)

NIVEN DUNCAN
63. Farmer. Born in Scotland. Flora 63.
Born in Scotland. Duncan jr. Farmer.
Born in NC. Archibald. Farmer. Born in NC.
Moore County, NC.   (C)

OGILVY HENRY
Son of Henry Ogilvy of Templehall,
near Dundee, Angus. Shipmaster in
Charleston, SC. Married Hannah
Meadows. Father of Harriet. Died
in Pensacola, West Florida in 1779.   (SRO/CC8/8/126-1)

OGILVIE JAMES
Son of James Ogilvie and his wife
Mary Strachan, Aberdeen. Emigrated
to Charleston, SC, in 1744. Died in
1745.   (APB)

OGILVY WILLIAM
Possibly from Leith, Midlothian.
Settled in Pasquotank County, NC.
Died before 1774.   (NCA/CR801.7.45)

OLIPHANT ANDREW
Emigrated from Scotland to New England
c1762. Settled in Rhode Island and
later in SC.   (INE)

OLIPHANT DAVID
Born in Scotland during 1720.
Medical student c1741(?) Jacobite -
fled to America after 1746. Settled
in SC. A physician in partnership
with John Murray, and latterly
with John Linning. Died 1805.   (SA)(SRO/RD3.235.265)

OLIPHANT DAVID
Painter in Charleston, SC. Serviced
as Heir to his grandfather David Nevay,
merchant in Edinburgh, on 9 June 1828.   (SRO/SH)

OLIPHANT JEMIMA
Daughter of James Oliphant, jeweller
in Edinburgh, and Jean Nevay. Wife of
John Morison. Mother of Elizabeth Jane.
Died in Charleston, SC, pre June 1804.   (SRO/CC8/8/135)

OLIVER CATHERINE
50. Born in Scotland. Richard 71. Born
in NC. Farmer. Richmond County, NC.   (C)

ORKNEY JOHN
Born Edinburgh in November 1787.
Died in NC 1 February 1872. Buried
Washington Presbyterian Cemetery,
Beaufort County, NC.
John Orkney. Born in Scotland. 64.
Inspector. Elizabeth 48. Milliner.
Born in NC.Washington, Beaufort County, NC.(Beaufort Gs)(C)

ORR CHARLES
Born in Scotland. Died in Mecklenburg
County, NC, during 1788.   (INC60460)

ORR JAMES
68. Planter. Born in Scotland. Martha 54.
Born in Scotland. David 22. Farmer. Born
in SC. Joseph 21. Labourer. Born in SC.
Archibald 14. Born in SC. Mary 16. Born
in SC. Union County, SC.
Nat. 14 October 1823 Union County, SC.   (C)

OWENS STEPHEN
45. Clerk. Born in Scotland. Mary 34.
Born in Scotland. James 19. Born in
SC. .... 12. Born in SC. William C 8.
Born in SC. Charleston, SC.   (C)

PAGE GEORGE
Born in Scotland c1813. Died in NC
12 April 1836. Buried Raleigh City
Cemetery, NC.   (Raleigh Gs)

PAGE THOMAS
Born in Scotland c1805. Stonecutter.
Died in NC 4 September 1834. Buried
Raleigh City Cemetery, NC.   (Raleigh Gs)

PAISLY JAMES
26. Farmer. Dumfries-shire. Emigrated
from Greenock, Renfrewshire, to
Charleston, SC, on the Countess,
master R Eason, in October 1774.   (PRO/T47.12)

PAISLY JOHN
23. Weaver. Dumfries-shire. Emigrated
from Greenock, Renfrewshire, to
Charleston, SC, on the Countess,
master R Eason, in October 1774, with
his wife aged 26.   (PRO/T47.12)

PARK JEAN
Daughter of James Park, writer, and his
wife Jean Scott, Edinburgh. Married Rev
Archibald Stobo in Edinburgh on 9 July
1699. Emigrated to Darien in 1699.
Later settled in SC. Died after April 1747.   (CV)

PARSLEY ROBERT
Nat.14 April 1807 New Hanover County, NC.(New Han Sup Ct Mins)

PARSONS MARY
48. Born in Scotland. James 60. Farmer.
Born in NC. William 18. Labourer. Born
in NC. Rachel 17. Born in NC. Alexander
14. Born in NC. James 12. Born in NC.
Elizabeth 11. Born in NC. Duncan
Livingstone 76. Born in Scotland.
Montgomery County, NC.   (C)

PATTERSON ALEXANDER
Born in 1752. Emigrated to America in
1786. A farmer in Richmond County, NC,
with a wife and eight children in 1812.   (1812)

PATTERSON ARCHIBALD
Born in 1787. Emigrated to America in
1802. A farmer in Richmond County, NC,
with a wife in 1812.   (1812)

PATTERSON DANIEL
Born in 1784. Emigrated to America in
1803. A farmer in Richmond County, NC,
with his mother, brother and two
sisters in 1812.   (1812)

PATTERSON DANIEL
48. Farmer. Born in Scotland. Nancy 40.
Born in Scotland. ...(f) Born in NC.
Archibald 19. Farmer. Born in NC.
Angus 18. Born in NC. Hugh 12. Born
in NC. Euphemia 68. Born in Scotland.
Mary 55. Born in Scotland.
Richmond County, NC.   (C)

PATERSON DONALD
Emigrated from Jura, Argyllshire, to NC
before 1764.   (NCA/PC20.1/Shaw pp)

PATTERSON DUNCAN
"Came from Scotland. Got grant from the
King". Buried Patterson Cemetery, NC.   (Patterson Gs)

PATTERSON EMILIA
79. Born in Scotland. David 75. Farmer.
Born in NC. Moore County, NC.   (C)

PATTERSON GILBERT
Emigrated from Scotland to Brunswick,
NC, in September 1739.   (VOS)

PATERSON JAMES
Prisoner in Edinburgh or Canongate
Tolbooths. Transported from Leith to
Carolina by Robert Malloch, merchant
burgess of Edinburgh in August 1684.   (PC)

PATTERSON JAMES
Born in Ayrshire during 1764. Mariner.
Nat. 8 May 1806 Charleston, SC.   (Nat Arch M1183.1)

PATTERSON JOHN
Born in 1786. Emigrated to America in
1804. A farmer in Robeson County, NC,
with a wife and five children in 1812.   (1812)

PATTERSON MARGARET
64. Born in Scotland. Catherine 40.
Born in NC. Florah 38. Born in NC.
Sarah 36. Born in NC. Margaret 33.
Born in NC. John 33. Born in NC.
Hector 31. Born in NC. Robeson County, NC.   (C)

PATTERSON MARY
76. Born in Scotland. Ann 35. Born in NC.
William 32. Farmer. Born in NC.
Richmond County, NC.   (C)

PATTERSON MARY
70. Born in Scotland. Peter 45. Lawyer.
Born in Scotland. Neill 42. Farmer.
Born in NC. Mary 40. Born in NC.
Sarah 38. Born in NC. John 36. Born in
NC. Archibald 33. Born in NC.
Cumberland County, NC.   (C)

PATTERSON NEILL
Settled in NC before 1771.(Jas McAlister letter(3774)SHC/UNC)

PATTERSON PETER
Born in 1784. Emigrated to America in
1802. A farmer in Richmond County, NC,
with a wife in 1812.   (1812)

PATTERSON PETER
60. Farmer. Born in Scotland. John 30.
Farmer. Born in Scotland. Nancy 14.
Born in NC. Sarah 12. Born in NC.
Catherine 26. Born in NC. Peter 19.
Born in NC. Richmond County, NC.   (C)

PATTISON GILBERT
Emigrated from Argyllshire(?) to NC
in 1739. Allocated a 640 acre land
grant in Bladen County, NC, 4 June 1740.   (SHA.105)

PATTON JAMES
Born in Scotland. Settled in America
before 1816. Settled in Granville
County, NC. Nat. June 1821 NC.   (NCA/CR.044.311.2,3)

PATTON JAMES
61. Farmer. Born in Scotland. Nicolas B.
38. Born in Scotland. Isabel 37. Born
in NC. Jane 21. Born in NC. Ann 19.
Born in NC. Mary 17. Born in NC.
Margaret 15. Born in NC. James 14.
Born in NC. William M. 11. Born in NC.
Granville County, NC.   (C)

PATTON Dr JOHN
Born in Scotland.Settled in Camden,
Kershaw County, SC. Nat. 1815 SC.   (Cit Bk 71)

PATTULLO HENRY
Born in Scotland c1726. Emigrated to
America. Apprenticed to a merchant in
Virginia. Minister in Virginia and NC.
Teacher and scholar. Died in 1801.   (F)(SA)(HGP)

PAUL ANDREW
Born in Scotland during 1764. Nat.
4 November 1806 Marion County, SC.   (Common Pleas Ct V3.524)

PAUL ANN
Born in Arbigland, Kirkbean, Galloway,
daughter of John Paul, gardener, and
Jean McDuff. Sister of John Paul Jones.
Widow of .... in London. Emigrated to
Georgia. Merchant in Charleston, SC,
during mid eighteenth century.   ("John Paul Jones")

PAUL DUNBAR
Born in Kirkcudbright during 1790.
Emigrated to America in 1810.
Merchant in Charleston, SC.
Nat.13 September 1821 SC.
Paul Dunbar, 60, merchant, born in
Scotland. Jane 47, Born in SC. (C)(1812)(Nat Arch M1833.1)

PAUL JOHN
Born in Kirkcudbrightshire in 1785.
A grocer in Charleston, SC. Nat.
15 June 1812 Charleston, SC.   (Nat Arch M1183.1)

PAUL JOHN
Charleston, SC, married Isabella Kerr,
second daughter of William MacWhinnie,
merchant in Kirkcudbright 27 July 1829.   (BM 26.841)

PEACOCK W.
Born in Glasgow during 1768. Emigrated
to SC in 1790. Merchant's clerk in
Fayetteville.   (HGP)

PEARSON A
Born in Scotland. 50. Gardener. Eliza 48.
Born in England. Mary 18. Born in NC.
John 15. Student. Born in NC. L(f) 13.
Born in NC. Adeline 10. Born in NC.
Thomas 10. Born in NC. RobertB. 7. Born
in NC. Lesly 5. Born in NC. Elizabeth 3.
Born in NC. Buncombe County, NC.   (C)

PEDDIE ROBERT
Born in Crieff, Perthshire, in 1776.
Merchant. Died in Charleston, SC, on
15 August 1801.   (CM 21.8.1801)

PEDEN ALEXANDER
Born in Irvine, Ayrshire, on 26 July
1776. Married Mary .... Settled in
Wilmington, NC, c1800. Father of
William N. and James A.F. Died on
6 June 1830. Buried in St James's
Cemetery, Wilmington, NC.   (Wilmington Gs)(CFR 9.6.1830)
(NCA/CR 070 801)

PENMAN EDWARD
Son of George Penman, Edinburgh.
A merchant in Charleston, SC.
Nat.17 April 1784 Charleston, SC.   (SRO/RD3.245.725)

PENMAN JAMES
Edinburgh. A merchant in Charleston, SC.
Admitted a Burgess and Gildsbrother of
Glasgow on 6 May 1784.   (GBG)(Pr 26.11.1789 SC)

PERRY ISABELLA
Born in Wick, Caithness, during 1765.
Midwife. Nat.19 March 1805
Charleston, SC.   (Nat Arch M1183.1)

PHILIPSDANIEL
Born in Argyllshire during 1784.
Mariner. Nat.17 March 1806
Charleston, SC.   (Nat Arch M1183.1)

PHILPECK GEORGE
Born in Scotland. 86. Farmer. Nella 60.
Born in NC. Sarah 58. Born in NC.
Rutherford County, NC.   (C)

PHILPECK WILLIAM
Born in Scotland 70. Rutherford County, NC.   (C)

PICKEN WILLIAM
32. Farmer. Glen Orchy, Argyllshire.
Emigrated from Greenock, Renfrewshire,
with his wife Martha Huie 26, to
Wilmington, NC, on the Ulysses, master
J Chalmers, in August 1774.   (PRO/T47.12)

PITTIGREW JAMES
28. Merchant. Glasgow. Emigrated from
Greenock, Renfrewshire, to Charleston,
SC, on the Countess, master R Eason,
in October 1774.   (PRO/T47.12)

POLLOCK THOMAS
Merchant in Glasgow. Settled in the West
Indies during 1683. Later moved to NC.
A merchant in Chowan, NC. Father of
Martha, Thomas, Cullen and George.
Will dated 20 July 1722.   (PRO/C11.1135.23)

POLLOCK WILLIAM
Born in Edinburgh. Graduated from the
University of Edinburgh on 24 June
1699. Emigrated from London to
Carolina during 1706. Member of the
Council of NC.   (HSNC)(AP)

POWER CATHERINE
Emigrated from Scotland or Ireland to SC
on the ship Pearl, master Walter
Buchanan, during December 1767.
Allocated a 100 acre land grant on
12 December 1767.   (OL)

PRIDE HANNAH
Emigrated from Scotland or Ireland to SC
on the ship Pearl, master Walter
Buchanan, during December 1767.
Allocated a 100 acre land grant on
12 December 1767.   (OL)

PRIEST ANGUS
Born in 1766. Emigrated to America in
1804. A farmer in Richmond County, NC,
with a wife and seven children in 1812.   (1812)

PRIEST DAVID
71. Farmer. Born in Scotland. Catherine
74. Born in Scotland. John 37. Born in
NC. Cumberland County, NC.   (C)

PRIEST MARY
63. Born in Scotland. Cornelius 41. Born
in NC. Farmer. Duncan 33. Farmer. Born
in NC. Catherine 26. Born in NC. Mary A
28. Born in NC. Cumberland County, NC.   (C)

PRIMROSE JOHN
Born in Ayrshire. Nat.15 June 1821
Craven County, NC.   (Craven Co Ct Rec)

PRIMROSE JOHN
47. Merchant. Born in Scotland. Eliza 30.
Born in Connecticut. John 5. Born in NC.
Robert 3. Born in NC. William 1. Born in NC.
Raleigh, Wake County, NC.   (C)

PRIMROSE NICOL
Youngest son of Robert Primrose, surgeon
in Musselburgh, Midlothian. Settled in
Charleston, SC, during 1780. Merchant.
Nat.27 February 1783 SC. Died in
Charleston, SC, 13 November 1796.   (EEC.12303)(SCA)

PRIMROSE ROBERT
Born in Scotland. Emigrated to NC before
1813. Nat.20 April 1819 Craven County, NC.(NCA/CR.028.311.1)

PRIMROSE ROBERT
Only son of Nicol Primrose, Charleston,
SC, and grandson of Robert Primrose,
surgeon in Musselburgh, Midlothian.
Died in Charleston, SC, in 1824. (BM 15.494)(Pr 8.1825 PCC)

PRIMROSE ROBERT STUART
Born in Scotland during 1782. Married
Ann Stephens,1802-1863, in Newbern, NC,
during 1825. Father of four children.
Died in 1856.   (Noble pp(3849)SHC/UNC)

PRIMROSE ROBERT
53. Merchant. Born in Scotland. Ann 47.
Born in NC. Mary A. 23. Born in NC.
Robert S. 21. Student. Born in NC.
Cicero J. 19. Clerk. Born in NC. John W.
11. Born in NC. Newbern, Craven County, NC.   (C)

PRINGLE ANN
Daughter of Francis Pringle, deceased,
Lieutenant in the Royal American Regiment,
now resident in College Kirk parish,
married James Fowler Baker, Charleston,
SC, student of Physic at the University
of Edinburgh, in Edinburgh on
15 March 1772.   (EMR)

PRINGLE ROBERT
Born c1702 second son of Robert Pringle
of Symington, Stow parish. Emigrated to
Charleston, SC, c1725. A merchant on
Tradd Street, Charleston, SC. Admitted
a Burgess and Gildsbrother of Edinburgh
on 14 September 1748. Married (1) Jane
Allen 18 July 1734 (2)Mrs Judith Bull.
Father of John, Robert and Elizabeth.
Died 13 January 1776.   (SCGen)(REB)(RP)(HGP)

PROSSER DANIEL
Emigrated from Scotland or Ireland to SC
on the ship Pearl, master Walter
Buchanan, in December 1767. Allocated a
100 acre land grant on 12 December 1767.   (OL)

PURDIE ARCHIBALD
Son of James Purdie, Lanarkshire.
Settled in SC.   (Pr 17.8.1786 SC)

PURSE Mrs JENNET
Born in Scotland c1803. Wife of Thomas
E Purse, Charleston, SC. Died on
20 November 1826. Buried in St Michael's,
Charleston, SC.   (St Michael's Gs)

PURVIS JOHN
Columbia, SC. Serviced as Heir to his
father Burridge Purvis in North
Glassmount, Scotland, 16 May 1825.   (SRO/SH)

RAE JOHN
Born in 1716. Ordained in Dundee, Angus,
during 1742. Emigrated to SC in 1743.
Presbyterian minister in SC from 1743
to 1761. Died in Williamsburg, SC, 1761.   (CCVC)

R(blank)HE JAMES
Born in Auld Bay, Port Glasgow, c1754.
Merchant in Fayetteville and in
Wilmington, NC. Died in Wilmington
on 22 December 1808. Buried in
St James's Cemetery, Wilmington, NC.   (Wilmington Gs)

RALSTON JAMES
Born in Argyllshire during 1784. Wine-
merchant. Nat.9 August 1806 Charleston,
SC. Died in Charleston, SC, on
13 February 1810.   (Nat Arch M1183.1)(CCG 17.2.1810)

RALSTON ROBERT
Born in Ayrshire during 1783. A planter
on John's Island, SC. Nat.23 November
1813 Charleston, SC.   (Nat Arch M1183.1)

RAMSAY JOHN
Born in Lochore(?), Fife, son of David
Ramsay and his wife Helen Wemyss.
A shopkeeper in Charleston, SC.   (Pr 20.7.1734 SC)

RAMSAY JOHN
Born in Clackmannan during 1773.
A distiller. Nat.23 January 1804
Charleston, SC.   (Nat Arch M1183.1)

RANKIN CHARLES
Born in Scotland during 1731.
Died in Bladen County, NC, in 1807.   (HGP)

RANKIN DUNCAN
Born in Scotland. Emigrated to America
before 14 April 1802. Nat.March 1814
Richmond County, NC.   (RCCR)

RANKEN JOHN
Jacobite soldier captured after the Siege
of Preston, Lancashire. Transported from
Liverpool to South Carolina on the
Wakefield, master Thomas Beck, 21 April 1716.   (CTB)(SPC)

RASH JAMES
Jacobite soldier captured after the Siege
of Preston, Lancashire. Transported from
Liverpool to South Carolina on the
Wakefield, master Thomas Beck, 21 April 1716.   (CTB)(SPC)

RATTRAY Mrs HELEN GOVAN or
Scotland. Widow in Charleston, SC.
Will dated 4 March 1782 SC.   (SCA)

RATTRAY JOHN
Judge of the Court of the Vice Admiralty
of SC. Died in Charleston, SC, on
30 September 1761.   (SM 13.671)

RAY A.
Born in 1742. Emigrated to America in
1792. A farmer in Cumberland County, NC,
with a wife and three children in 1812.   (1812)

266

RAY ALEXANDER
62. Farmer. Born in Scotland. Barbara 62.
Born in NC. Sarah 34. Born in NC. Mary 32.
Born in NC. John 28. Farmer. Born in NC.
Neill 26. Farmer. Born in NC. Archibald
23. Farmer. Born in NC. Christian 21.
Born in NC. Moore County, NC.   (C)

RAY DANIEL
Born in Scotland. Died in NC during 1761.   (Pr 1761 NC)

RAY DANIEL
Born in Jura, Argyllshire, c1763.
Married Margaret... Emigrated to
America in 1792. Father of Catherine,
1803-1847, Mary,1800-1826, Margaret,
1818-1897. A farmer in Cumberland
County, NC, with a wife and six
children in 1812. Died in NC on
9 March 1826. Buried in Longstreet
Presbyterian Cemetery, Fort Bragg,
Hoke County, NC.   (1812)(Hoke Gs)

RAY DUNCAN
Born in 1765. Emigrated to America in
1791. A farmer in Moore County, NC,
with a wife and eleven children in 1812.   (1812)

RAY DUNCAN
76. Farmer. Born in Scotland. Flora 44.
Born in NC. Angus 36. Farmer. Born in NC.
Mary 31. Born in NC. Cumberland County, NC.   (C)

RAY DUNCAN
55. Farmer. Born in Scotland. Mary 58.
Born in Scotland. Cumberland County, NC.   (C)

RAY JOHN
Born in Scotland c1723. Died in
Fayetteville, NC, 20 March 1808.   (RR 3.1808)

RAY JOHN A.
Born in Scotland during 1744. Died
in NC during 1821. Buried in Ray
Cemetery, Moore County, NC.   (Ray Gs)

RAY JOHN
86. Born in Scotland.
Cumberland County, NC.
John Ray, emigrated to America in
1792. A farmer in Cumberland County,
NC, with a wife and three children
in 1812.   (C)(1812)

RAY JOHN
73. Farmer. Born in Scotland.
Archibald 28. Farmer. Born in NC.
Cumberland County, NC.   (C)

RAY JOHN
Born in 1780. Emigrated to America in
1792. A farmer in Cumberland County,
NC, in 1812.   (1812)

RAY MARGARET
45. Born in Scotland. Catherine 72.
Born in NC. Duncan 25. Farmer. Born
in NC. Archibald 26. Schoolmaster.
Born in NC. Sarah A. 23. Born in NC.
Anna 22. Born in NC. Alexander 19.
Farmer. Born in NC. Lauchlin 17.
Student. Born in NC. Martin 15.
Student. Born in NC. Neill 11. Born
in NC. Margaret 8. Born in NC.
Cumberland County, NC.   (C)

RAY MARGARET
Born in Islay, Argyllshire, during 1719.
Died in NC on 8 October 1809. Buried in
Longstreet Cemetery, Fort Bragg, Hoke
County, NC.   (Hoke Gs)

RAY MARY
50. Born in Jura, Argyllshire. Angus 65.
Born in Robeson County, NC. Margaret 29.
Born in Robeson County, NC. Laughlin 27.
Born in Robeson County, NC. Sally 21.
Born in Robeson County, NC. Neill 22.
Born in Robeson County, NC. Angus 18.
Born in Robeson County, NC. Robeson County, NC.   (C)

RAY MARY
47. Born in Scotland. Daniel 50. Farmer.
Born in NC. Neill 14. Born in NC.
Margaret 12. Born in NC. Daniel 10.
Born in NC. Archibald 8. Born in NC.
David 6. Born in NC. Isabel 4. Born
in NC. Cumberland County, NC.   (C)

RAY PETER
51. Tailor. Born in Scotland. Margaret
50. Born in NC. Neill 23. Farmer.
Born in NC. Margaret 21. Born in NC.
Catherine 18. Born in NC. John 12.
Born in NC. Cumberland County, NC.   (C)

RAY SARAH
87. Born in Scotland. Archibald 58.
Farmer. Born in Scotland. Jane 53.
Born in NC. Mary 21. Born in NC.
Sarah 19. Born in NC. Gilbert 17.
Farmer. Born in NC. Cumberland County,NC.   (C)

READ CATHERINE
Widow of John Douglas, SC.
Serviced as Heir to her sister Isabel
Read in Drumgeath, Scotland, on
10 February 1789.   (SRO/SH)

REECE THOMAS
Born in Scotland. 70. Tailor. Mary 70.
Born in Virginia. Rockingham County,NC.   (C)

REGISTER MARY
Born in Scotland. 60. Norman McLeod 49.
Farmer. Born in Scotland. Bladen County, NC.   (C)

REID DAVID
Born in Forfar, Angus. Nat.8 August 1825
Craven County, NC.   (Craven Co Ct Rec)

REID DAVID
Born in Scotland. 83. Pauper. Macon County, NC. (C)

REID JAMES
Captain of the Charles of Charleston, SC.
Admitted a Burgess and Gildsbrother of
Edinburgh, gratis, 12 May 1737.   (REB)

269

REID JAMES
Born in Ayrshire. Mariner. Nat.3 April
1798 Charleston, SC.   (Nat Arch M1183.1)

REID MALCOLM
Jacobite soldier captured after the Siege
of Preston, Lancashire. Transported from
Liverpool to South Carolina on the
Susannah, master Thomas Bromhall, 7 May 1716.   (CTB)(SPC)

REID ROBERT
Emigrated from Scotland or Ireland to SC
on the ship Pearl, master Walter
Buchanan, in December 1767. Allocated a
100 acre land grant 12 December 1767.   (OL)

RENWICK WILLIAM
Born in Scotland. Nat.5 September 1823
Granville County, NC.   (NCA/CR.044.311.4)

RESTON FRANCIS C.
Born in Scotland. A merchant in
Wilmington, NC. Died in Fayetteville,
NC, on 25 October 1825.   (RR 1.11.1825)

RESTON Rev JOHN
Edinburgh. Died in Wilmington, NC,
on 11 August 1829.   (BM 27.134)

RESTON THOMAS C.
Born in 1790. Emigrated to America in
1811. Nat.February 1811 Wilmington,NC.   (1812)

REYNOLDS BENNET
46. Farmer. Born in SC. Nancy 45. Born
in Scotland. Angus B. 21. Born in SC.
Benjamin F. 17. Student. Born in SC.
Catherine 2. Born in SC. Alexander 10.
Born in SC. Bennet 8. Born in SC.
John 6. Born in SC. Abbeville County, SC.   (C)

RHIND DAVID
Aberdeen. Emigrated to America. A
teacher at the Academy of Charleston,SC,
c1765.   (APB)

RICE ISABELLA
75. Born in Scotland. Martha 40. Born in
SC. Ludwell 20. Born in SC. Harriet 16.
Born in SC. Priscilla 14. Born in SC.
John 12. Born in SC. Edgefield County, SC.   (C)

RICHARDSON ANN
Daughter of Thomas Richardson in Linton,
Roxburghshire. Died in Charleston,
North America, during 1796.   (SRO/CC8/8/143)

RICHARDSON JOHN
Jacobite soldier captured after the Siege
of Preston, Lancashire. Transported from
Liverpool to South Carolina on the
Wakefield, master Thomas Beck,21 April 1716.   (SPC)(CTB)

RICHARDSON JOHN
Born in Oxnam, Roxburghshire, eldest son
of Rev James Richardson, Morebattle,
Roxburghshire, on 29 July 1765. Died in
SC on 14 March 1818. Buried in St Michael's
Cemetery, Charleston, SC.   (S 71.18)(St Michael's Gs)

RICHARDSON ROBERT
Jacobite soldier captured after the Siege
of Preston, Lancashire. Transported from
Liverpool to South Carolina on the
Wakefield, master Thomas Beck,21 April 1716.   (CTB)(SPC)

RICHARDSON THOMAS
Edinburgh. Carpenter in Charleston, SC.   (Pr 7.4.1792 SC)

RIGG ALEXANDER
Born in Scotland. Gentleman in
Charleston, SC.   (Pr 23.10.1771 SC)

RITCHIE JAMES
Born in Auld Bay, Port Glasgow, in 1755.
A merchant in Wilmington and Fayetteville,
NC. Died on 28 December 1808. Buried in
St James's Cemetery, Wilmington, NC.
          (Wilmington Gs)(RM)(RR 5.1.1809)

RITCHIE WILLIAM
Merchant in Washington. Died in
Fayetteville, NC, 26 November 1796.   (EEC.12306)

ROBB JAMES
Jacobite soldier captured after the Siege
of Preston, Lancashire. Transported from
Liverpool to South Carolina on the
Susannah, master Thomas Bromhall,7 May 1716.   (SPC)(CTB)

ROBB JAMES
60. Grocer. Born in Scotland. Martha 59.
Born in Scotland. Louisa 25. Born in
Scotland. Caroline 20. Born in SC.
Amelia 18. Born in SC. Charleston, SC.
James Robb, born in Stirling, settled
in Charleston. Nat.24 May 1830
Charleston, SC.   (C)(Nat Arch M1183.1)

ROBB JOHN
Jacobite soldier captured after the Siege
of Preston, Lancashire. Transported from
Liverpool to South Carolina on the
Susannah, master Thomas Bromhall, 7 May 1716.   (CTB)(SPC)

ROBB THOMAS
Jacobite soldier captured after the Siege
of Preston, Lancashire. Transported from
Liverpool to South Carolina on the
Susannah, master Thomas Bromhall, 7 May 1716.   (CTB)(SPC)

ROBERSON JANE
63. Born in Scotland. Samuel 68. Born in
NC. Farmer. Ellen 26. Born in NC.
Harriet 22. Born in NC. Gaston County, NC.   (C)

ROBERTS JAMES
Born in Fife during 1798. An actor in
New York c1826. Died in Charleston,
SC, in 1833.   (TSA)

ROBERTSON DONALD
Jacobite soldier captured after the Siege
of Preston, Lancashire. Transported from
Liverpool to South Carolina on the
Susannah, master Thomas Bromhall, 7 May 1716.   (CTB)(SPC)

ROBERTSON DONALD
Born in Scotland during 1770. Emigrated
to America c1802. Nat.20 September 1813
Richmond County, NC.   (RCCR)

ROBERTSON JAMES
60. Born in Scotland. Charleston, SC.   (C)

ROBERTSON JAMES
Born in Fife during 1796. A merchant in
Charleston. Nat.5 April 1823 Charleston,SC.(Nat Arch M1183.1)

ROBERTSON JAMES
50. Merchant. Born in Scotland. Ellen 40.
Born in SC. Catherine 17. Born in SC.
Margaret 13. Born in SC. Charles 15.
Born in SC. Mary Jane 7. Born in SC.
John F. 6. Born in SC. Dunbar Paul 5.
Born in SC. Peter 3. Born in SC.
Charleston, SC.   (C)

ROBINSON DUNCAN
Jacobite soldier captured after the Siege
of Preston, Lancashire. Transported from
Liverpool to South Carolina on the
Susannah, master Thomas Bromhall,7 May 1716.   (CTB)(SPC)

ROBINSON JAMES
Born in Argyllshire c1761. Died near
Salisbury, NC, on 23 July 1821.   (WC 31.7.1821)

ROBINSON JOB
Born in Scotland c1738. Married Charity
... Father of five children. Settled in
Tryon County, NC.   (ALR)

ROBINSON JOHN
Jacobite soldier captured after the Siege
of Preston, Lancashire. Transported from
Liverpool to South Carolina on the
Susannah, master Thomas Bromhall. 7 May 1716.   (CTB)(SPC)

ROBINSON RICHARD
Born in Scotland c1762. Married (1)Eliza
Stowe (2)Catherine Lively. Father of
John, Joseph, Richard, Mary and Evelyn.
Settled in SC c1799.   (GWS)

RODICK JAMES
Born in Annan, Dumfries-shire. Nat.
4 May 1799 Charleston, SC.   (Nat Arch M1183.1)

RODEAK WILLIAM
35. Farmer. Dumfries-shire. Emigrated
from Greenock, Renfrewshire, to
Charleston, SC, on the Countess, master
R Eason, in October 1774.   (PRO/T47.12)

ROGERS JAMES
Probably from Roxburghshire. A shop-
keeper in Charleston, SC.   (Pr 1.8.1794 SC)

ROLLAND HENRY
Son of James Rolland, coppersmith in
Culross, Fife. A carpenter in
Charleston, SC, before 1774.   (HGP)

ROME Mr GEORGE
Covenanter. Prisoner in Edinburgh or
Canongate Tolbooths. Transported from
Leith to Carolina by Robert Malloch,
merchant burgess of Edinburgh, in
August 1684.   (PC)

RONALD GEORGE
Glasgow. Merchant. Settled on Cape Fear,
Brunswick County, NC, 26 February 1738.
In Bladen County, NC, during 1757.
                (SRO/CC8/8/107)(Bladen Co Deed Book 23)

ROSE ALEXANDER
Born in Inverness during 1738. Emigrated
from Scotland to America before 1755.
Merchant in Virginia and NC. Married
Eunice Lea in Caswell County, NC, on
5 May 1774. Died in Person County, NC,
on 12 May 1807.   (INC19177)(RSA)

ROSE Captain DAVID
Shipmaster in Inverness, Scotland,
purchased land in Craven County, SC,
from William Poole, on 15 October 1743.   (SC Deeds V2.p72)

ROSS AGNES
Spinner. Kirkcaldy, Fife. Indentured for
four years service in NC on 8 July 1736.
Aged 21.   (LGR)

ROSS ANDREW
Born in Galloway during 1771. Mariner.
Nat.13 December 1803 Charleston, SC.   (Nat Arch M1183.1)

ROSS CHARLES
Jacobite soldier captured after the Siege
of Preston, Lancashire. Transported from
Liverpool to South Carolina on the
Wakefield, master Thomas Beck, 21 April 1716.   (CTB)(SPC)

ROSS CHARLES
62. Farmer. Born in Scotland.
Catherine 41. Born in NC. Cumberland County, NC.   (C)

ROSS JAMES
Born in the Shetland Islands during 1785.
Settled in Charleston. Nat.25 March 1823
Charleston, SC.   (Nat Arch M1183.1)

ROSS JAMES
Born in Scotland. Emigrated from
Scotland to Philadelphia, Pennsylvania,
22 May 1819. Settled in Charleston, SC,
on 24 May 1820. Nat.29 March 1826
Chester County, SC.   (Chester Nats A.225)

ROSS JAMES
40. Port-worker. Born in Scotland.
Charleston, SC.   (C)

ROSS JOHN
47. Farmer. Widower. Kabel, Farr,
Sutherland. Emigrated from Scotland,
with his six children aged 20 to 5,
to Wilmington, NC, on the
Bachelor of Leith in April 1774.   (PRO/T47.12)

ROSS JOHN
Born in 1783, son of Henry Ross, writer
in Lerwick, Shetland. A merchant in
Charleston, SC. Serviced as Heir to
his father on 25 February 1808.
Nat.24 August 1810 Charleston, SC.(SRO/SH)(Nat Arch M1183.1)

ROSS PATRICK
35. Schoolmaster. Unmarried. Farr,
Sutherland. Emigrated from Scotland to
Wilmington, NC, on the Bachelor of Leith,
in April 1774.   (PRO/T47.12)

ROSS THOMAS
Jacobite soldier captured after the Siege
of Preston, Lancashire. Transported from
Liverpool to South Carolina on the
Susannah, master Thomas Bromhall, 7 May 1716.   (CTB)(SPC)

ROSS WILLIAM
Born in Ayr during 1771. A merchant.
Nat. 7 September 1803 Charleston, SC.   (Nat Arch M1183.1)

ROSS WILLIAM
75. Farmer. Born in Scotland. Mary 55.
Born in Scotland. Chesterfield County, SC.   (C)

ROSS WILLIAM
60. Planter. Born in Scotland. Sarah 50.
Born in NC. William 25. Labourer. Born
in SC. Maria 26. Born in SC. James 18.
Labourer. Born in SC. Sarah 15. Born in
SC. Catherine 13. Born in SC. Daniel 10.
Born in SC. Sumter County, SC.   (C)

ROWAND WILLIAM
Glasgow. Established a saddler's shop
near Wilmington Court House, NC, in 1774.
                    (NCGaz 15.5.1774)(CFM.224)

RUS JOHN
Born in Scotland(?) Nat.10 October 1822
New Hanover County, NC.   (NH Sup Ct Mins)

RUSSELL WILLIAM
Born in Ayrshire during 1770. A merchant.
Nat.24 May 1804 Charleston, SC.   (Nat Arch M1183.1)

RUTHERFORD ANNE
Daughter of James Rutherford of Bowland
and his wife Isabella Simpson, married
R Shaw, Wilmington, NC. Died in
Wilmington during 1766.   (RTI)

RUTHERFORD BARBARA
Daughter of James Rutherford of Bowland
and his wife Isabella Simpson, married
Alexander Chapman, Wilmington, NC.
Died in Wilmington during 1763.   (RTI)

RUTHERFORD JAMES
Edinburgh. Gold and silver-smith in
Charleston, SC. Advertisement 1751.   (SCGaz.18.11.1751)

RUTHERFORD JOHN
Born in Scotland. Emigrated to Cape Fear, NC,
with his cousin James Murray in 1739.
Public official, planter and merchant.
Married Frances, widow of Gabriel
Johnston, during 1754. Died in Cork,
Ireland, during 1782.   (NCA)

RUTHERFORD WALTER
Sixth son of Sir John Rutherford of
Edgirston and his wife Elisabeth
Cairncross. Married Mary, daughter
of General Alexander, Earl of Stirling.
Settled in Rutherford County,
America, during the eighteenth century.   (RTI)

RUTHERFORD WALTER B.
Born in Jedburgh, Roxburghshire.
Emigrated to America during 1815.
Nat.16 April 1819 SC.   (Cit Book 82)

RUTHERFORD WALTER
Born in Scotland. Emigrated to America
in 1815. Settled in Rutherford County,
NC, in 1819. Nat.April 1827
Rutherford County, NC.   (Rutherford Co Ct Rec)

RUTHERFORD WALTER
53. Farmer. Born in Scotland. Sarah 57.
Born in SC. Walter 27. Lawyer. Born in
NC. William 23. Printer. Born in NC.
Margaret 21. Born in NC. Amelia 19.
Born in NC. George W. 17. Born in NC.
Elizabeth 10. Born in NC.
Rutherford County, NC.   (C)

RUTHVEN DAVID
58. Farmer. Born in Scotland. Sarah 58.
Born in Scotland. Hugh 25. Teacher.
Born in NC. Sarah 21. Born in NC.
Cornelius 17. Farmer. Born in NC.
Chesterfield County, SC.   (C)

RYBURN JOHN
45. Ditcher. Born in Scotland. Cumberland County, NC.   (C)

RYMER JAMES
Born in St Andrews, Fife. Emigrated to
SC during 1753. Presbyterian minister in
SC from 1754 to 1755. Died in
Walterborough, SC, on 8 July 1755.   (CCVC)(SCGaz 10.7.1755)

SALMOND THOMAS
67. Bank officer. Born in Scotland.
WJ 63. Born in SC. LA 32. Born in SC.
BB 29. Born in SC. NJ 23. Born in SC.
MJ 3. Born in SC, Edward 1. Born in SC.
Kershaw County, SC.   (C)

SANDERS JOHN
Born in Glasgow during 1772. A merchant.
Nat.16 May 1805 Charleston, SC.   (Nat Arch M1183.1)

SANDS JAMES
A merchant. Died in Charleston, SC,
on 3 August 1767.   (SM 31.502)

SANGSTER JOHN
Born in Scotland. Nat.8 February 1796
Charleston, SC.   (Nat Arch M1183.1)

SANGSTER WILLIAM
Born in Stirlingshire. Mariner.
Nat.27 October 1797 Charleston, SC.   (Nat Arch M1183.1)

SAWERS WILLIAM
Born c1779, youngest son of Robert
Sawers of Drumteack, East Monkland,
near Glasgow. Died on Sullivan's
Island, America, 30 August 1800.   (GC 1426)

SCOLLAY SAMUEL
Probably from Lerwick, Shetland. Married
Elizabeth .... Father of two daughters.
Settled in Bertie County, NC. Died c1751.   (NCA)

SCOTT ANDREW
Son of Andrew Scott, merchant in
Glasgow. Legatee in the will of his
uncle George Henderson.   (Pr 27.11.1736 Bertie, NC)
Settled in NC.

SCOTT GEORGE
Son of Andrew Scott, merchant in
Glasgow. Settled in NC. Legatee in the
will of his uncle George Henderson. (Pr 27.11.1736 Bertie, NC)

SCOTT HUGH
Son of Andrew Scott, merchant in
Glasgow. A merchant in NC. Received
land on the Cashai River, NC, in the
will of his uncle George Henderson. (Pr 27.11.1736 Bertie, NC)

SCOTT MARGARET
16. Spinner. Born in Scotland. Emigrated
from London to NC in February 1774 on
the Margaret and Mary.   (PRO/T47.12)

SCOTT WALTER
Son of John Scott, Letham, Fife.
Partner in firm of Scott and Clerk,
merchants in Camden, SC. Died
during August 1798.   (EA 3648.383)

SCOTT WILLIAM
Son of Rev John Scott, minister of
Dumfries. A merchant in Charleston,
SC.   (Pr 26.4.1765 SC)

SCOTT WILLIAM
21. Maltster. Born in Scotland.
Emigrated from London to NC during
February 1774 on the Margaret and Mary.   (PRO/T47.12)

SCOULER THOMAS
Born in Haddington, East Lothian, in 1765.
Ships carpenter in Charleston, SC.
Nat.26 June 1812 Charleston, SC.   (Nat Arch M1183.1)

SEAMAN GEORGE
Leith, Midlothian. Gentleman in
Charleston, SC.   (Pr 10.2.1769 SC)(Pr 24.7.1769PCC)

SERJEANT HENRY
Jacobite soldier captured after the Siege
of Preston, Lancashire. Transported from
Liverpool to South Carolina on the
Susannah, master Thomas Bromhall,7 May 1716.   (CTB)(SPC)

SEYMOUR JOHN
Aberdeenshire. Planter in St Stephen's
parish, SC.   (Will 11.6.1775 SC)

SHARPE JAMES
Born in Scotland. Died in Anson County,
NC, during June 1830.   (RR 17.6.1830)

SHAW ALEXANDER
Jacobite soldier captured after the Siege
of Preston, Lancashire. Transported from
Liverpool to South Carolina on the
Susannah, master Thomas Bromhall,7 May 1716.   (CTB)(SPC)

SHAW ANGUS
Born in 1756. Emigrated to America in 1792.
A farmer in Robeson County, NC, with a wife
and five children in 1812.   (1812)

SHAW Mrs ANNE
Daughter of James Rutherford of Bowland,
and wife of Robert Shaw, in Wilmington,
NC. Died in Wilmington 11 January 1767.   (SM 29.166)

SHAW ARCHIBALD
Born in 1764. Emigrated to America in
1802. A farmer in Cumberland County,
with a wife and two children in 1812.   (1812)

SHAW COLIN
Emigrated from Jura, Argyllshire, to
NC before 1764. A merchant in
Cumberland County, NC, c1764.   (NCA/PC20.1)

SHAW DANIEL
Born in Scotland in 1758. Emigrated to
America during 1790. A farmer in
Robeson County, NC, with a wife and
two children in 1812. Died in Robeson
County, NC, 16 July 1826.   (RaNCSw 28.7.1826)(1812)

SHAW DANIEL
70. Born in Scotland. Catherine 59.
Born in NC. Robeson County, NC.   (C)

SHAW EFFIE
80. Born in Scotland. Flora 78. Born in
Scotland. Cumberland County, NC.   (C)

SHAW FLORA
56. Born in Scotland. Chesterfield County,SC.   (C)

SHAW GILBERT
81. Farmer. Born in Scotland. Catherine
70. Born in NC. Margaret 26. Born in NC.
Mary 24. Born in NC. Cumberland County, NC.   (C)

SHAW GRIZEL
80. Born in Scotland. Raleigh, NC.   (C)

SHAW ISOBEL
Born in Glasgow c1715. Runaway indentured
servant of Joseph Dapson, tailor,
Middle Street, Charleston,SC, in
February 1734.   (SCGaz 16.2.1734)

SHAW JAMES
Born in Muirkirk, Ayrshire. Settled in
Newbern, NC, during 1822. Died there
on 4 June 1828.   (RR 17.6.1828)

SHAW JAMES
Born in Ayrshire. Nat.23 October 1823
Craven County, NC.   (NCA/CR.028.928.15)

SHAW JOHN
Jacobite soldier captured after the Siege
of Preston, Lancashire. Transported from
Liverpool to South Carolina on the
Wakefield, master Thomas Beck, 21 April 1716.   (CTB)(SPC)

SHAW JOHN
Jacobite soldier captured after the Siege
of Preston, Lancashire. Transported from
Liverpool to South Carolina on the
Wakefield, master Thomas Beck, 21 April 1716.   (CTB)(SPC)

SHAW JOHN
Born in 1762. Emigrated to America in
1791. A farmer in Robeson County, NC,
with a wife and seven children in 1812.   (1812)

SHAW JOHN
Emigrated from Jura, Argyllshire, to NC
before 1764. Brother of Colin Shaw, a
merchant.   (NCA/PC20.1)

SHAW KITT
Sister of Colin Shaw, merchant.
Emigrated from Jura, Argyllshire, to
NC before 1764. Settled in NC.   (NCA/PC20.1)

SHAW LACHLAN
LIeutenant of an Independent Company
in SC. Married Mary ... Father of
Bridget and Lachlan. Died in Prince
William parish, SC, during 1761.
            (Pr 7.7.1761 SC)(Pr 2.1765 PCC)(SRO/CCі/8/119-1)

SHAW MARIAN
74. Born in Scotland. Christian 42.
Born in NC. Bladen County, NC.   (C)

SHAW MATTHEW
Born in 1762. Emigrated to America during
1804. A grocer and spirits-maker in
Raleigh, NC, with a wife and six
children in 1812.   (1812)

SHAW MATTHEW
51. Lawyer. Born in Scotland. Hannah 41.
Born in NC. Elizabeth 19. Born in NC.
Helen 13. Born in NC. Laura 12. Born
in NC. William 11. Born in NC. Robert
9. Born in NC. Matthew 5. Born in NC.
Washington Town, Beaufort County, NC.   (C)

SHAW MATHEW
Born in Bute. Nat.4 April 1820 SC.   (Circuit Ct Jl 9/54)

SHAW NANCY
91. Born in Scotland. Catherine 55. Born
in NC. Christian 50. Born in NC. Sarah
57. Born in NC. Robeson County, NC.   (C)

SHAW NEIL
Born during 1743. Emigrated to America in
1802. A farmer in Robeson County, NC, with
a wife and four children in 1812.   (1812)

SHAW PETER
Jacobite soldier captured after the Siege
of Preston, Lancashire. Transported from
Liverpool to South Carolina on the
Susannah, master Thomas Bromhall, 7 May 1716.   (CTB)(SPC)

SCHAW ROBERT
Emigrated from Scotland to NC before 1751.
Settled in New Hanover County. Merchant,
planter and public official. Died 1786.   (WTB)

SHAW SARAH
54. Born in Scotland. Neill 64. Born in
NC. Robeson County, NC.   (C)

SHAW THOMAS
48. Merchant. Born in Scotland. Sarah E
34. Born in NC. Washington Town,
Beaufort County, NC.   (C)

SHAW WILLIAM
Jacobite soldier captured after the Siege
of Preston, Lancashire. Transported from
Liverpool to South Carolina on the
Susannah, master Thomas Bromhall, 7 May 1716.   (CTB)(SPC)

SHAW WILLIAM
Born in Ayrshire c1763. A merchant and
postmaster in Raleigh, Wake County, NC.
Presbyterian. Died on 27 December 1827.
Buried in Raleigh City Cemetery. (RRsw 1.1.1828)(Raleigh Gs)

SHAW WILLIAM
Born in 1778. Emigrated to America during
1800. A merchant in Washington, NC, in 1812.   (1812)

SHAW WILLIAM
65. Farmer. Born in Scotland. Mary 64.
Born in NC. Alexander 34. Farmer. Born
in NC. Mary 30. Born in NC. Jane 28.
Born in NC. Catherine 26. Born in NC.
Eliza 20. Born in NC. Dugald 12. Born
in NC. Moore County, NC.   (C)

SHELBURNE MARGARET
Emigrated from Scotland or Ireland to SC
on the ship Pearl, master Walter Buchanan,
in December 1767. Allocated a 100 acre
land grant on 12 December 1767.   (OL)

SCOTS IN THE CAROLINAS

SHEPHERD EFFIE
Born in Argyllshire during 1790.
Married Augustus Shepherd in Virginia.
Mother of Frederick, Mary Ann and Sarah.
Died 19 February 1863. Buried in East
View Cemetery, Wadesboro, Anson County,NC.   (Wadesboro Gs)

SHEPHERD JOHN
75. Born in Scotland. Richland County, SC.   (C)

SHIELDS ELIZABETH
52. Born in Scotland. Jane 45. Born in
Scotland. John A. 16. Clerk. Born in SC.
Richland County, SC.   (C)

SHIELDS HENRY
Born in 1777, son of Henry Shields, farmer
in Coaltown of Balmull. Emigrated to
America during 1803. A grocer and
merchant in Charleston, USA. Nat.
6 October 1813 Charleston, SC.
Serviced as Heir to his father on
6 October 1819.   (Nat Arch M1183.1)(1812)(SRO/SH)

SHINNIE ALEXANDER
Born in Aberdeenshire or Kincardineshire
during 1782. Settled in Charleston, SC,
c1821. Millwright. Nat. 27 July 1831
Charleston, SC. Died 31 October 1834.
                (Nat Arch M1183.1)(Telescope 8.11.1834)

SHIRRAS ALEXANDER
Born in Old Deer, Aberdeenshire, c1753.
Merchant in Charleston, SC, c1781 to 1811.
Died 20 October 1811. Buried in
St Michael's, Charleston, SC.   (St Michael's Gs)

SHUTTARD BERNARD
Jacobite soldier captured after the Siege
of Preston, Lancashire. Transported from
Liverpool to South Carolina on the
Susannah, master Thomas Bromhall, 7 May 1716.   (CTB)(SPC)

SILLAR HUGH
55. Farmer. Kintyre, Argyllshire.
Emigrated from Greenock, Renfrewshire,
with his wife Catherine Currie 62, and
children Mary 27 and Catherine 23, to
Wilmington, NC, on the Diana, master
D Ruthven, in September 1774.   (PRO/T47.12)

SCOTS IN THE CAROLINAS

SIM WILLIAM
24. Husbandman. Born in Scotland.
Emigrated from London, with his wife
Jane 24, to NC on the <u>Margaret and
Mary</u> in February 1774.   (PRO/T47.12)

SIMMONS CHRISTIAN
60. Born in Scotland. Pleasant 51.
Farmer. Born in NC. Archibald 20.
Labourer. Born in NC. Martha 19.
Born in NC. Deborah 17. Born in NC.
Christian 16. Born in NC. James jr 22.
Farmer. Born in NC. Montgomery County, NC.   (C)

SIMMONS JEREMIAH
Emigrated from Scotland or Ireland to
SC on the ship <u>Pearl</u>, master Walter
Buchanan, in December 1767. Allocated
a 100 acre land grant 12 December 1767.   (OL)

SIMPSON ARCHIBALD
Born in Glasgow on 1 March 1734, son of
William Simpson, merchant in Perth, and
his wife Susannah Gardner. Married Jane,
daughter of William Muir, in August 1752.
Emigrated to SC 6 March 1753.   (HPC)

SIMPSON HUGH
Born in Scotland during 1770. Emigrated
to America in 1792. A farmer in York
District, SC, with a family of 11 in 1812.   (1812)

SIMSON JAMES
Jacobite soldier captured after the Siege
of Preston, Lancashire. Transported from
Liverpool to South Carolina on the
<u>Susannah</u>, master Thomas Bromhall, 7 May 1716. (CTB)(SPC)

SIMPSON JAMES
Charleston, SC, Serviced as Heir to his
grandfather James Sim Tibbers 1 August 1770.   (SRO/SH)

SIMPSON JAMES M.
55. Carpenter. Born in Scotland.
Brunswick County, NC.   (C)

SIMPSON JOHN
Born in Glasgow on 9 March 1747.
Merchant. Died 9 March 1800. Buried
in Washington, Beaufort County, NC. (Beaufort Gs)

SIMPSON JOHN
Port Glasgow. Emigrated from Scotland
to Washington, NC, during 1780s.
Settled in Newbern, NC, during 1797
with his family. Father of Jackie,
Margaret, Eleanor and John. (DU/Josiah C Trent pp)

SIMPSON JOHN
Born in the Orkney Islands.
Nat. 10 June 1823 SC. (Circuit Ct Jl 9.295)

SIMPSON PATRICK
John's Island, SC. Died pre 1794.
(Pr 3.1792 PCC)(SRO/CC8/8/129.2)

SIMPSON ROBERT
Born in 1777. Emigrated to America in
1811. In Wilmington, NC, with a wife
and four children in 1812. (1812)

SIMPSON Miss
Daughter of John Simpson, Edinburgh.
Died in Brunswick County, NC, on
10 December 1826. (RRw 5.1.1827)

SINCLAIR ALEXANDER
A Scottish indentured servant who
absconded in SC during March 1735. (SCGaz 4.1735)

SINCLAIR ALEXANDER
36. Farmer. Dollochlogy, Reay,
Caithness. Emigrated from Scotland,
with his wife and three children aged
from 18 to 2 years, to Wilmington, NC,
on the Bachelor of Leith, April 1774. (PRO/T47.12)

SINCLAIR ALEXANDER
Born in Perthshire. Nat.10 January 1804 SC(Common Plea Ctu3.232)

SINCLAIR ANN
65. Spinner. Glen Orchy, Argyllshire.
Emigrated from Scotland, with his
daughter Margaret 25, a spinner, to
Wilmington, NC, on the Jupiter of Larne,
master Samuel Brown, in September 1775.   (PRO/T47.12)

SINCLAIR DANIEL
57. Farmer. Born in Scotland. Flora 53.
Born in Scotland. John 30. Born in
Marion County, SC. Alexander 21. Born
in Marion County, SC. Archibald 18. Born
in Marion County, SC. Duncan 16. Born in
Marion County, SC. Sarah 14. Born in
Marion County, SC. Daniel 12. Born in
Marion County, SC. Margaret 10. Born in
Marion County, SC. Joseph 7. Born in
Marion County, SC. Marion County, SC.   (C)

SINCLAIR DUNCAN
24. Farmer. Glen Orchy, Argyllshire.
Emigrated from Greenock, Renfrewshire,
with his wife Isobel McIntyre 24, to
Wilmington, NC, on the Ulysses, master
J Chalmers, in August 1774.   (PRO/T47.12)

SINCLAIR HUGH
60. Farmer. Born in Scotland. Margaret
62. Born in Scotland. John 23. Farmer.
Born in Scotland. Isabella 19. Born in
Scotland. Effie 25. Born in Scotland.
Cumberland County, NC.   (C)

SINCLAIR JAMES
21. Farmer. Forsenan, Reay, Caithness.
Emigrated from Scotland, with his wife,
to Wilmington, NC, on the Bachelor of
Leith in April 1774.   (PRO/T47.12)

SINCLAIR JOHN
32. Farmer. Glen Orchy, Argyllshire.
Emigrated from Greenock, Renfrewshire,
with his wife Mary 33, to Wilmington,
NC, on the Ulysses, master J Chalmers,
in August 1774.   (PRO/T47.12)

SINCLAIR JOHN
71. Born in Scotland. Robeson County, NC.   (C)

SINCLAIR MARY
70. Born in Scotland. Nancy 62. Born
in Scotland. Christian 25. Born in
Robeson County, NC. Peter 22. Born
in Robeson County, NC. Duncan 21.
Born in Robeson County, NC.
Robeson County, NC.   (C)

SINCLAIR NEIL
Born during 1794 in Tarbert, Kintyre,
Argyllshire. Emigrated from Glasgow
to Wilmington, NC, in August 1804.
Married Catherine McMillan. Settled
in Robeson County, NC. Father of
Duncan and Mary. Died 18 August 1880.
NEIL SINCLAIR, 56, Born in Argyllshire.
Catherine 50. Born in Cumberland County,
NC. Duncan 27. Born in Robeson County,
NC. John C. 26. Born in Robeson County,
NC. Isabella 24. Born in Robeson County,
NC. Mary 22. Born in Robeson County, NC.
Thomas 20. Born in Robeson County, NC.
Elizabeth 15. Born in Robeson County,
NC. Flora A. 10. Born in Robeson County,
NC. Catherine 12. Born in Robeson County,
NC. Margaret G. 7. Born in Robeson County,
NC. Robeson County, NC.   (St Paul's OPR)(PCM)(C)

SINCLAIR PATRICK
Jacobite soldier captured after the Siege
of Preston, Lancashire. Transported from
Liverpool to South Carolina on the
Wakefield, master Thomas Beck, 21 April 1716.   (SPC)(CTB)

SINCLAIR PEGGY
Emigrated from Jura, Argyllshire,
(probably)on the General Wolfe, master
J MacLean, to America. Landed at
Brunswick, NC, 4 November 1767.
Allocated a 100 acre land grant in
Cumberland or Mecklenburg Counties.   (SCGaz.1671)(SHA.1671)

SINCLAIR RICHARD
Born in Scotland. Merchant in
Charleston, SC.   (Pr 18.7.1733 SC)

SKENE GEORGE
Son of Andrew Skene in Aberdeen(?)
Minister in Prince Frederick parish,SC.   Pr 14.11.1766 SC)

SKENE JAMES
Son of Professor Francis Skene.
Physician in Charleston. Honorary
MD of Aberdeen University
13 November 1766.   (MCA)

SKENE THOMAS
Angus. Granville County, SC.   (Pr 18.1.1760 SC)

SLOAN ALEXANDER
89. Farmer. Born in Scotland. Chloe 58.
Born in NC. William 57. Born in NC.
Andrew 21. Born in NC. Mary 19. Born in
NC. Chatham County,NC.   (C)

SMITH ALEXANDER
Angus. Tailor in Charleston, SC.
Allocated a 700 acre land grant in
Berkeley County, SC, 13 July 1737.   (Pr 15.10.1745 SC)

SMITH ANDREW
Born in Banff during 1762. Emigrated to
America in 1775. A farmer in St George's,
Dorchester, in 1814. A farmer in
Greenville, SC, with a wife in 1812.(Nat Arch M1183.1)(1812)

SMITH ARCHIBALD
Born in 1778. Emigrated to America in
1802. A farmer in Richmond County, NC,
with a wife and two children in 1812.   (1812)

SMITH D.
57. Farmer. Born in Scotland. Catherine
46. Born in NC. John 25. Cooper. Born in
NC. David 23. Cooper. Born in NC. Robert
20. Cooper. Born in NC. James 19.
Labourer. Born in NC. Matilda 17. Born
in NC. Margaret 15. Born in NC. George
13. Born in NC. Elizabeth 12. Born in
NC. Colin 10. Born in NC. Jane 5. Born
in NC. Benjamin 3. Born in NC.
Sampson County, NC.   (C)

SMITH DANIEL
61. Born in Scotland. Catherine 56.
Born in Scotland. John 22. Born in NC.
Neill 21. Born in NC. Joseph 20. Born
in NC. Margaret 18. Born in NC.
Elizabeth 16. Born in NC. Christian 16.
Born in NC. Florah 14. Born in NC.
Absalom 66. Born in Scotland.
Robeson County, NC. (C)

SMITH DAVID
Jacobite soldier captured after the Siege
of Preston, Lancashire. Transported from
Liverpool to South Carolina on the
Susannah, master Thomas Bromhall, 7 May 1716. (CTB)(SPC)

SMITH DONALD
Jacobite soldier captured after the Siege
of Preston, Lancashire. Transported from
Liverpool to South Carolina on the
Wakefield, master Thomas Beck, 21 April 1716. (CTB)(SPC)

SMITH DUNCAN
90. Born in Scotland. Margaret 80. Born
in Scotland. Effie 54. Born in NC.
Mary 50. Born in NC. Margaret 40. Born
in NC. Catherine 38. Born in NC.
Nancy 36. Born in NC. Robeson County, NC.
DUNCAN SMITH, emigrated to America 1786.
A farmer in Robeson County, NC, with a wife
and ten children in 1812. (C)(1812)

SMITH GEORGE
Emigrated from Scotland or Ireland to SC
on the ship Pearl, master Walter Buchanan,
in December 1767. Allocated a 100 acre land
grant on 12 December 1767. (OL)

SMITH GEORGE
Born in Scotland. 60. Sailmaker. Mary 40.
Born in NC. Newbern, Craven County, NC. (C)

SMITH JAMES
Emigrated from Scotland or Ireland to SC
on the ship Pearl, master Walter Buchanan,
in December 1767. Allocated a 100 acre land
grant on 12 December 1767. (OL)

SMITH JAMES
Born in Banffshire. Nat.21 January 1799
Charleston, SC. (Nat Arch M1183.1)

SMITH JAMES
Born in Ayr. Nat.13 August 1829
Craven County, NC.   (Craven Co Ct Rec)

SMITH JANET
Adopted daughter of Lachlan MacNeill,
Breakachie. Settled near Little
River, Cumberland County, NC, in
1784. Died 1785.   (NCA/PC726)

SMITH JOHN
Prisoner - transported from Glasgow to
SC on the brigantine John and Robert,
master Thomas Clark. Landed 22 July
1730. Indentured servant.   (SRO/JC27)

SMITH JOHN
Emigrated from Scotland, with his wife
Margaret Gilchrist (who died on the
voyage) and children Malcolm and
Janet, to America. Settled in NC pre 1736. (HGP)

SMITH JOHN
Emigrated from Scotland to Brunswick,
NC, in September 1739.   (VOS)

SMITH JOHN
Son of Susanna Smith in Dumfries.
Settled in Prince George's parish,
Winyah County, SC.   (Pr 23.1.1767 SC)

SMITH JOHN
Emigrated from Scotland or Ireland on the
ship Pearl, master Walter Buchanan, in
December 1767. Allocated a land grant
of 100 acres on 12 December 1767.   (OL)

SMITH JOHN
Born in Scotland. A merchant in Frederica.
Married Elizabeth Williamson in
St Helena's, Beaufort County, SC, on
11 June 1749.   (St Helena's OPR)

SMITH JOHN
Born in Argyllshire c1789. Died in
Charleston, SC, on 15 October 1816.
Buried in the Presbyterian Cemetery.   (CCG 16.10.1816)

SMITH JOHN
Born in 1752. Emigrated to America in
1791. A farmer in Robeson County, NC,
with a wife and six children in 1812.   (1812)

SMITH JOHN
Born in Ayrshire. Settled in Charleston.
Nat.19 October 1813 Charleston, SC.   (Nat Arch M1183.1)

SMITH MALCOLM
64. Farmer. Kintyre, Argyllshire.
Emigrated from Greenock, Renfrewshire,
with his wife Mary McAlester 64, and
children Peter 23 and Mary 19, to
Wilmington, NC, on the Ulysses, master
J Chalmers, in August 1774.   (PRO/T47.12)

SMITH MATTHEW
Shipscarpenter. Irvine, Ayrshire.
Settled in Pasquatank, NC. Died
before 1771.   (SRO/CC8/8/122.1)

SMITH MICHAEL
Born in Scotland c1740. Married Judith
Rice. Settled in Rockingham County, NC.
Died in Virginia.   (INC60519)

SMITH NEIL
Born during 1752. Emigrated to America
in 1802. A farmer in Robeson County,
NC, with a wife and two children in 1812.   (1812)

SMITH NEAL
Born in Scotland. A merchant in
Camden, SC. Died in August 1822.   (SC 28.8.1822)

SMITH PATRICK
Jacobite soldier captured after the Siege
of Preston, Lancashire. Transported from
Liverpool to South Carolina on the
Susannah, master Thomas Bromhall, 7 May 1716.   (CTB)(SPC)

SMITH PETER
Born in Campbelltown, Argyllshire,
during 1768. Mariner. Nat.9 July 1806
Charleston, SC.   (Nat Arch M1183.1)

SMITH ROBERT
Born in Scotland. Died in Edenton, NC,
on 28 March 1824.   (RaNCSw 9.4.1824)

SMITH SAMUEL
Born during 1779. Emigrated to America
in 1808. A shoemaker in Fayetteville,
NC, in 1812 with a wife and child.   (1812)

SMITH THOMAS LOUGHTON
SC. Admitted a Burgess and Gildsbrother
of Edinburgh on 18 October 1769.   (REB)

SMITH WHITEFORD
Born in Orkney. Nat.17 October 1794 SC.
                              (Court of Wardens Y3.160)

SMITH WILLIAM
Born in Scotland. A merchant.
Nat.9 May 1803 Charleston, SC.   (Misc Rec V3.30)

SMITH WILLIAM
Born in Longside, Aberdeenshire, during
1750. A merchant in Charleston, SC,
from c1784 to 1814. Died 9 April 1814.
Buried St Michael's, Charleston, SC.   (St Michael's Gs)

SMITH WILLIAM
Born in Kilmarnock, Ayrshire. A merchant
in Charleston, SC. Nat.1799(?)SC.   (Misc Rec 03.205)

SMYTH Dr
Born in Scotland. Educated in Edinburgh
c1700. Physician in NC.   (SC)

SMYLIE MATTHEW
Emigrated from Scotland to Brunswick,
NC, in September 1739.   (VOS)

SMYLIE NATHANIEL
Emigrated from Scotland to Brunswick,
NC, in September 1739.   (VOS)

SMILY PATRICK
Emigrated from Scotland or Ireland to SC
on the ship Pearl, master Walter
Buchanan, in December 1767. Allocated
a 100 acre land grant on 12 December 1767.   (OL)

SOMERVILLE DAVID
Born during April 1742, eldest son of
John Somerville and his wife Margaret
Cunningham, Shothead, Currie,
Midlothian. Married Jean Telfer in
Strathavon, Lanarkshire, on
14 October 1770. Emigrated from
Scotland to SC in 1790. Father of
John and William. Presbyterian
minister in Charleston, SC. Died
there in 1792.   (Col Fams V3.534)(SRO/CC8/8/131.1)

SOMMERVILLE MARGARET
Emigrated from Scotland or Ireland to SC
on the ship Pearl, master Walter
Buchanan, in December 1767. Allocated
a 100 acre land grant 12 December 1767.   (OL)

SOMMERS JAMES
Born in Scotland during 1713.
Shoemaker. Buried on 11 December 1753,
in St Helena's parish, Beaufort, SC.   (St Helena's OPR)

SONGSTER ANDREW
Jacobite soldier captured after the Siege
of Preston, Lancashire. Transported from
Liverpool to South Carolina on the
Wakefield, master Thomas Beck, 21 April 1716.   (CTB)(SPC)

SPARKS ALEXANDER
70. Farmer. Born in NC. Jane 60. Born
in Scotland. Samuel 22. Born in SC.
Darlington County, SC.   (C)

SPEIR ALEXANDER
19. Clerk. Glasgow. Emigrated from
Greenock, Renfrewshire, to Wilmington,
NC, on the Diana, master D Ruthven
in September 1774.   (PRO/T47.12)

SPENCE JOHN
Born in Scotland. Settled in Granville
County, NC. Heir to Ninian Spence, dec'd.,
in Scotland. Power of attorney on
5 May 1801 Granville County, NC.   (NCA/CR.044.928.7)

SPRADLING ANN
Emigrated from Scotland or Ireland to SC
on the ship Pearl, master Walter
Buchanan, in December 1767. Allocated
a 100 acre land grant 12 December 1767.   (OL)

STALKER EFFIE
Born in Argyllshire during 1804.
Married John McLaurin. Died on
18 September 1881. Buried in
Stewartsville Cemetery, Laurinsburg,
Scotland County, NC.   (Laurinburg Gs)

STALKER JOHN
Argyllshire. Emigrated from Scotland
to America during 1824. Buried in
Sutherland Cemetery, SC.   (SHC)

STEEL Captain DAVID
Born in Scotland c1762. Settled in
Georgetown SC, c1818. Died on
28 June 1838.   (Georgetown Union 1.9.1838)

STEELE GORDON
Born in Greenock, Renfrewshire,
during 1786. Nat.15 March 1819
Charlestown, SC.   (Nat Arch M1183.1)

STEEL or THOMSON THOMAS
Emigrated from Gourock, Renfrewshire,
to Port Royal, SC, on the Carolina
Merchant, master Walter Gibson,
21 July 1684.   (ECJ)

STEEL WILLIAM
Born in Scotland. 51. Carpenter.
Martha 34. Born in NC. Edward 2.
Born in NC. Gates County, NC.   (C)

STEPHEN JAMES
Son of David Stephen and his wife Elspet
Gavin, Peterculter, Aberdeenshire.
Emigrated from Scotland to America.
Cooper in Charleston, SC. Died c1766.   (APB)

STEVEN JAMES
27. Farmer. Inch, Wigtonshire. Emigrated
from Stranraer, Wigtonshire, with his
sisters Christian 23 and Sarah 16, also
his brother Thomas 11, to NC on the
Jackie, master J Morris, 31 May 1775.   (PRO/T47.12)

STEVENS JAMES
Born in Galloway (?), Scotland.
Emigrated to NC before 1775. Married
Mary Dalrymple, a Scot, who died on
12 June 1824. Settled in Robeson
County, NC. Father of Margaret, Ann
and Elizabeth. Died pre 1824.   (St Paul's OPR, RobesonCo)

STEVENS WILLIAM
Emigrated from Scotland to Brunswick,
NC, in September 1739.   (VOS)

STEPHENSON JANE
60. Born in Scotland. Alexander 24.
Farmer. Born in NC. Stokes County, NC.   (C)

STEWART ALEXANDER
Born in Scotland c1691. Registrar of
the Court of Chancery. Gentleman in
Charleston, SC. Died there on
18 May 1763.   (SM 25.415)(Pr 5.8.1763 SC)

STEWART ALEXANDER
Born 9 December 1725, son of Rev James
Stewart of Clunie, MA, and his wife
Elizabeth Campbell. Emigrated to
America c1744. Settled in Bath, NC.
Married a daughter of Colonel William
Spiers in NC during 1756. Clerk of the
County Court in 1758. Planter and
timber merchant. Father of Anne,
Elizabeth, Dorothy, William Spiers,
James and Alexander. Died on 30 July
1772. Buried at Yankee Hall, Pitt
County, NC.   (SFG)

STEWART ALEXANDER
35. Gentleman-farmer. Breadalbane,
Perthshire. Emigrated from Scotland,
with his son Charles 15, to
Wilmington, NC, on the Jupiter of
Larne, master Samuel Brown, during
September 1775.   (PRO/T47.12)

STEWART ALLAN
44. Former Lieutenant in Fraser's
Regiment. Breadalbane, Perthshire.
Emigrated from Scotland to
Wilmington, NC, on the Jupiter of
Larne, master Samuel Brown, during
September 1775.   (PRO/T47.12)

STEWART ANDREW
Born in Scotland. HM Printer in NC
before 1765.   (HSNC)

STEWART ARCHIBALD
30. Shoemaker. Glen Orchy, Argyllshire.
Emigrated from Scotland to Wilmington,
NC, on the Jupiter of Larne, master
Samuel Brown, in September 1775.   (PRO/T47.12)

STEWART CHARLES
Son of Rev James Stewart of Clunie, MA,
(1683-1735), and his wife Elizabeth
Campbell. Emigrated to NC.   (SFG)

STEWART DANIEL
Born in 1757. Emigrated to America in
1791. A farmer in Cumberland County,
NC, with a wife and six children
during 1812.   (1812)

STEWART DONALD
Jacobite soldier captured after the Siege
of Preston, Lancashire. Transported from
Liverpool to South Carolina on the
Wakefield, master Thomas Beck, 21 April 1716.   (CTB)(SPC)

STEWART DOUGAL
Emigrated from Argyllshire(?) to NC
during 1739. Allocated a 640 acre
land grant in Bladen County, NC,
on 4 June 1740.   (SHA.106)

STEWART DOUGALD
40. Labourer. Glen Orchy, Argyllshire.
Emigrated from Scotland, with his wife
aged 40, and children John 16, James
10, Thomas 6, and Alexander 4, to
Wilmington, NC, on the Jupiter of Larne,
master Samuel Brown, in September 1775.   (PRO/T47.12)

STEWART DUGALD
69. Farmer. Born in Scotland. Mary 40.
Born in NC. Robert 28. Farmer. Born in
NC. Margaret 26. Born in NC. Richmond County, NC.   (C)

STEWART DUNCAN
Jacobite soldier captured after the Siege
of Preston, Lancashire. Transported from
Liverpool to South Carolina on the
Susannah, master Thomas Bromhall, 7 May 1716.   (CTB)(SPC)

STEWART DUNCAN
61. Farmer. Born in Scotland. Harriet 40.
Born in SC. Lucious B. 5. Born in SC.
James C. 2. Born in SC. Colleton County, SC.   (C)

STEWART HUGH
Jacobite soldier captured after the Siege
of Preston, Lancashire. Transported from
Liverpool to South Carolina on the
Susannah, master Thomas Bromhall, 7 May 1716.   (CTB)(SPC)

STEWART JAMES
Son of John Stewart of Dalguise, Dunkeld,
Perthshire. Emigrated via Gravesend, Kent,
to Charleston, SC, during 1749.
Shipwright. Died in Charleston in 1755.
                         (Pr 10.1755 PCC)(SRO/GD38)

STEWART JAMES
Born in Scotland on 11 November 1775.
Settled in Richmond County, NC.
Merchant, farmer and politician.
Died in NC on 29 December 1821.   (WA)

STEWART JOHN
In Carolina c1712 - described as 'very
old and very poor'. His family had been
banished from Scotland by the
Presbyterians.   (SPC/1712/440)

STEWART JOHN
Jacobite soldier captured after the Siege
of Preston, Lancashire. Transported from
Liverpool to South Carolina on the
Susannah, master Thomas Bromhall, 7 May 1716.   (CTB)

STEWART JOHN
Born in Scotland. Sheriff of Cumberland
County, NC, after 1758.   (HSNC)

STEWART JOHN
48. Clothier. Glen Orchy, Argyllshire.
Emigrated from Scotland, with his wife
Elizabeth 46, and children John 15,
Margaret 13, Janet 12, Patrick 6, and
Elizabeth 3, to Wilmington, NC, on the
Jupiter of Larne, master Samuel Brown
in September 1775.   (PRO/T47.12)

STEWART KENNETH
40. Former shipmaster. Breadalbane,
Perthshire. Emigrated from Scotland,
with his wife Isobel 30, and children
Alexander 14, John 5, Banco 3,
Christian 3, and William - an infant,
to Wilmington, NC, on the Jupiter of
Larne, master Samuel Brown, during
September 1775.   (PRO/T47.12)

STEWART MALCOLM
Born in 1761. Emigrated to America in
1791. A farmer in Robeson County, NC,
with a wife and nine children in 1812.   (1812)

STEWART MARY
61. Born in Scotland. Neill 59. Hatter.
Born in NC. Effy 27. Born in NC.
Alexander 26. Farmer. Born in NC.
Roderick 24. Farmer. Born in NC. John 20.
Farmer. Born in NC. Charles 18. Born in
NC. Farmer. Anna 17. Born in NC. Mary A
6. Born in NC. Sampson County, NC.   (C)

STEWART NEIL
Jacobite soldier captured after the Siege
of Preston, Lancashire. Transported from
Liverpool to South Carolina on the
Susannah, master Thomas Bromhall, 7 May 1716.   (CTB)(SPC)

STEWART NEIL
Jacobite soldier captured after the Siege
of Preston, Lancashire. Transported from
Liverpool to South Carolina on the
Susannah, master Thomas Bromhall, 7 May 1716.   (CTB)(SPC)

STEWART PATRICK
Jacobite soldier captured after the Siege
of Preston, Lancashire. Transported from
Liverpool to South Carolina on the
Susannah, master Thomas Bromhall, 7 May 1716.   (CTB)(SPC)

STEWART PATRICK
Lederich, Perthshire. Married
Elizabeth Menzies. Emigrated from
Scotland to Cape Fear, NC, during
1739. Died in SC during 1772.   (VG)

STEWART PATRICK
Emigrated from Argyllshire(?) to NC
in 1739. Allocated a 320 acre land grant
in Bladen County, NC, 4 June 1740.   (SHA.106)

STEWART PETER
Born in 1759. Emigrated to America in
1811. A farmer in Richmond County, NC,
with a wife and five children in 1812.   (1812)

STEWART PETER D.
Born in Scotland. 48. Merchant. Mary 21.
Born in NC. Charles W. 3. Born in NC.
Robert 1. Born in NC. Beaufort, Carteret County,NC.   (C)

STEWART SALLY
83. Born in Scotland. Jennett 32.
Born in NC. Robeson County, NC.   (C)

STINNESS ADAM
53. Farmer. Born in Scotland. Elizabeth
55. Born in Scotland. Isabella 25. Born
in Scotland. Jane 22. Born in SC. John
21. Born in SC. Elizabeth 20. Born in SC.
Greenville County, SC.   (C)

STIRLING JAMES
Born in Scotland on 13 October 1702. As a
widower he married Jane Wood, widow, on
6 November 1747. Buried at St Helena's
parish, Beaufort County, SC, on
25 September 1757.   (St Helena's OPR)

STOBIE JAMES
Son of James Stobie, merchant in Charleston,
apprenticed to John Young, locksmith in
Edinburgh, for six years, on 3 May 1773.   (REA)

SCOTS IN THE CAROLINAS

STOBO ARCHIBALD
Born in Scotland c1674. Graduated MA from
the University of Edinburgh 25 June 1697.
Married Elizabeth Jean Park. Father of
Jean. Emigrated from Scotland to
Darien in September 1699 - landed on
30 November 1699. Sailed from Darien to
Charleston, SC, on the Rising Sun in
1699. Settled in Charleston, SC.
Presbyterian minister. Founded the
Scots Presbyterian Church there.
Allocated a 900 acre land grant on the
Savanna River, SC, during 1737. Died
c1740.   (SHR)(F)

STOCKARD JAMES ANDREW
Born in Scotland during 1745. Married
Ellen Trousdale. Settled in Orange
County, NC. Died Tennessee 1818.   (INC27441)

STORIE JAMES
Prisoner in the Tolbooth of Edinburgh.
Transported from Scotland to Carolina
by Walter Gibson, 21 May 1684.   (PC)

STRACHAN CHARLES
Jacobite soldier captured after the Siege
of Preston, Lancashire. Transported from
Liverpool to South Carolina on the
Wakefield, master Thomas Beck, 21 April 1716.   (CTB)(SPC)

STRACHAN THOMAS
Born in Scotland c1718. Mason.
Indentured servant who absconded in
March 1744.   (SCGaz 12.3.1744)

STRANG WILLIAM F.
Born in Glasgow c1804.
Nat.September 1825 Cumberland County, NC.(NCA/CR.029.301.16)
WILLIAM F STRANGE. Born in Scotland.
45. Chief Clerk in US Mint, Charlotte.
Mecklenburg County, NC.   (C)

STRONACH WILLIAM
46. Stonecutter. Born in Scotland.
Sarah 38. Born in Virginia. Anna M. 12.
Born in NC. Mary E. 11. Born in NC.
George F. 8. Born in NC. Willis C. 6.
Born in NC. Alexander 2. Born in NC.
Raleigh, Wake County, NC.   (C)

STRONG DAVID
Born in Scotland. Nat.21 April 1827 SC(Circuit Ct Jl 2.243)

STRONG LAWRENCE
Born in the Shetland Islands during 1782.
Mariner. Nat.27 January 1804 Charleston,SC.(Nat Arch M1183.1)

STUART FRANCIS
Born in Scotland. A merchant.
Married Anne Reeve in St Helena's,
Beaufort County, SC, on
28 December 1752.   (St Helena's OPR)

STUART JOHN
Emigrated from Scotland or Ireland on the
ship Pearl, master Walter Buchanan, in
December 1767. Allocated a 100 acre land
grant on 12 December 1767.   (OL)

STUART JOHN
Probably from Edinburgh. A merchant in
Carolina. Married Henrietta Burnett,
who died in Edinburgh during 1718.
Father of John and Charles - both
merchants in Carolina. Died pre 1718.   (SRO/CC8.8.87)

SULLIVAN FLORAH
55. Born in Scotland. Robeson County, NC.   (C)

SUTHERLAND BARBARA
Emigrated from Scotland or Ireland to SC
on the ship Pearl, master Walter
Buchanan, in December 1767. Allocated
a 100 acre land grant 12 December 1767.   (OL)

SUTHERLAND DANIEL
Born in Scotland on 9 May 1755. Married
Anne McDowell, Edgecombe County, NC, in
1777. Father of Isabel, P..., Elizabeth
and Margaret. Revolutionary artilleryman.
Died in Edgecombe County, NC, during
January 1793.   (LOS)

SUTHERLAND JAMES
Born in Elgin, Morayshire, during 1773.
A merchant. Nat.21 March 1803
Charleston, SC. (Nat Arch M1183.1)

SUTHERLAND MARY
80. Born in Scotland. Daniel 70. Born in
NC. Sarah Dawson 84. Born in Scotland.
Cumberland County, NC. (C)

SUTHERLAND WILLIAM
40. Farmer. Strathaladale, Reay,
Caithness. Emigrated from Scotland,
with his wife and five children aged
from 19 to 9, to Wilmington, NC, on
the Bachelor of Leith in April 1774. (PRO/T47.12)

SUTHERLAND WILLIAM
24. Latheron parish, Caithness.
Emigrated from Scotland, with his
wife (left only child at home), to
Wilmington, NC, on the Bachelor of
Leith, in April 1774. (PRO/T47.12)

SWINHOE JAMES
Jacobite soldier captured after the Siege
of Preston, Lancashire. Transported from
Liverpool to South Carolina on the
Susannah, master Thomas Bromhall, 7 May 1716. (CTB)(SPC)

SWINTON WILLIAM
Born in Scotland. Planter in Craven
County, SC. (Pr 29.3.1742 SC)

TAILFER Dr PATRICK
Physician and surgeon in Edinburgh.
Emigrated to America with his wife
Mary. Landed in Georgia 1 August 1734.
Surgeon in Savanna. Allocated a 500
acre land grant on River Nese, Georgia,
15 October 1733. Moved to Carolina on
31 August 1740. (SPC)(ESG)

TAIT GEORGE
Son of James Tait, Exciseman in Glasgow.
Died on Sullivan's Island, Charleston,
SC, 30 August 1801. (GC.1583)

TATE JOHN
Born in Galloway. Nat.9 February 1796
Charleston, SC.   (Nat Arch M1183.1)

TAIT PETER
Born during 1781 in Whitsome,
Berwickshire. Married Agnes Hogarth,
c1779 -13 March 1817. Tenant farmer
in Hordean. Settled in Charleston, SC.   (Whitsome Gs)

TAIT WILLIAM
Born in Scotland. Died on 2 August 1806
in Columbia, SC.   (SCHGM.30.68)

TAYLOR Mr
Born in Scotland. Baker. Died in
Wilmington, NC, during August 1811.   (RR 8.1811)

TAYLOR ALEXANDER
Born in Scotland. Nat.5 February 1793
Charleston, SC.   (Nat Arch M1183.1)

TAYLOR ALEXANDER
Born in Brechin, Angus. Mariner.
Nat.22 February 1797 Charleston, SC.   (Nat Arch M1183.1)

TAYLOR ANGUS
71. Farmer. Born in Scotland. Flora 68.
Born in NC. Bladen County, NC.   (C)

TAYLOR Mrs ANN
Born in Scotland. Settled in
Fayetteville, Cumberland County, NC.
Methodist. Died in Raleigh, Wake County,
NC, on 27 November 1829.   (RR 3.12.1829)

TAYLOR ISAAC
Born in Marykirk, Kincardineshire, c1762.
Died in Newbern, NC, 4 July 1846. Buried
Cedar Grove Cemetery, Craven County, NC.   (Cedar Grove Gs)

TAYLOR ISABEL
Emigrated from Scotland or Ireland to SC
on the ship Pearl, master Walter
Buchanan, in December 1767. Allocated a
100 acre land grant on 12 December 1767.   (OL)

SCOTS IN THE CAROLINAS

TAYLOR JOHN
Born in Fife during 1767. Mariner.
Nat.18 March 1799 Charleston, SC.   (Nat Arch M1183.1)

TAYLOR WILLIAM
Emigrated from Scotland or Ireland to SC
on the ship Pearl, master Walter Buchanan,
in December 1767. Allocated a 100 acre
land grant on 12 December 1767.   (OL)

TAYLOR WILLIAM
Born in Scotland. Died in Newbern, NC,
on 28 October 1835.   (Bibical Recorder, Wake Forest, NC)

TELFAIR THOMAS
Emigrated to America. Settled in NC c1793.
Nat.August 1812 Edgecombe County, NC. (Edgecombe Co Ct Rec)

TENNANT JAMES
Covenanter. Prisoner in Canongate or
Edinburgh Tolbooth. Banished to the
Plantations in Carolina on 6 August 1684.
Transported from Leith to Carolina by
Robert Malloch, merchant burgess of
Edinburgh.   (PC)

TENNANT ROBERT
Born in Glasgow during 1787.
A shopkeeper in Charleston, SC.
Nat.15 October 1813 Charleston, SC.   (Nat Arch M1183.1)

TENNANT WILLIAM
Born in Stirlingshire. Indian trader
in SC.   (Pr 29.5.1734 SC)

THOM ROBERT
Born in Lanark. Nat. 1798 Charleston, SC. (Nat Arch M1183.1)

THOMSON ANDREW
Stirling. Silversmith. Settled in NC
during early 1730s. Married (1) Ann
Hicks (2)Lucretia Hicks. Father of Ann.   (SNC)

THOMPSON DANIEL
Born in Scotland. Married Ann ... Father
of Richard. Died in Wilmington, NC, 1803.   (NCA/CR.070.801)

THOMSON DAVID
Stirling. Settled in NC during early 1730s. (SNC)

THOMSON DAVID
Possibly from Jedburgh, Roxburghshire.
A merchant in NC and Virginia. (Pr 29.12.1749 NC)

THOMSON DAVID L.
45. Farmer. Born in Scotland. CM 37.
Born in SC. John 12. Born in SC.
David 10. Born in SC. William 9.
Born in SC. Elspeth 7. Born in SC.
Robert 6. Born in SC. Anne 5. Born
in SC. James 3. Born in SC.
Beaufort County, SC. (C)

THOMSON GEORGE
Lanarkshire. Settled in Charleston, SC. (Pr 22.6.1796 SC)

THOMSON GEORGE
Born in Kincardineshire. Shipscarpenter
in Charleston. Nat.15 January 1828
Charleston, SC. (Nat Arch M1183.1)

THOMSON GRIZEL
Daughter of Andrew Thomson in Baad,
Serviced as Heir to her uncle David
Henderson, Bertie, NC, 16 August 1737. (SRO/SH)

THOMSON ISOBEL
Daughter of Andrew Thomson in Baad,
Serviced as Heir to her uncle David
Henderson, Bertie, NC. 16 August 1737. (SRO/SH)

THOMPSON JAMES
Born in Perthshire during 1782. A
merchant. Nat.7 July 1800 Charleston, SC. (Nat Arch M1183.1)

THOMPSON JOHN
21. Tailor. Born in Scotland. An
indentured servant who absconded from
his master Hugh Evans in Charleston,
SC, during November 1734. (SCGaz 12.11.1734)

THOMSON JOHN
Son of Andrew Thomson in Baad,
Serviced as Heir to his uncle David
Henderson, Bertie, NC, 16 August 1737.   (SRO/SH)

THOMSON JOHN
Born in Scotland during 1690.
Emigrated, via County Down, Ireland,
to New York in 1715. Presbyterian
minister in Delaware, Pennsylvania,
Virginia and North Carolina. Died
in Centre, NC, during 1753.   (CCMC)

THOMSON JOHN
Son of Margaret Thomson, Grassmarket,
Edinburgh. A merchant in Charleston,SC.   (Pr 23.9.1763 SC)

THOMPSON JOHN
Possibly from Colvend, Kirkcudbrightshire.
Died in Charleston, SC.   (Pr 24.12.1790 SC)

THOMSON JOHN BLANE
Born in Kilmarnock, Ayrshire. Settled
in Charleston, SC. Member of the Bar
of SC. Married Ann Elizabeth, daughter
of Alexander Christie, Charleston, SC,
in Charleston on 31 May 1827.
Nat.5 November 1827 Charleston, SC.
                    (S 787.472)(Nat Arch M1183.1)

THOMSON JOHN
40. Shopkeeper. Born in Scotland.
Catherine 36. Born in Ireland. John 21.
Engineer. Born in SC. Jane 19. Born in
SC. Ellen 17. Born in SC. Richard 15.
Cabinetmaker. Born in SC. Charleston, SC.   (C)

THOMSON NEIL
23. Farmer. Kintyre, Argyllshire.
Emigrated from Greenock, Renfrewshire,
to Wilmington, NC, on the Ulysses,
master J Chalmers, in August 1774.   (PRO/T47.12)

THOMPSON NINIAN
60. Farmer. Born in Scotland. Mary 59.
Born in Scotland. Abbeville County, SC.   (C)

THOMSON MARY
Daughter of Andrew Thomson in Baad,
Serviced as Heir to her uncle David
Henderson, Bertie, NC, 16 August 1737.   (SRO/SH)

THOMSON THOMAS
Son of Andrew Thomson in Baad,
Serviced as Heir to his uncle David
Henderson, Bertie, NC, 16 August 1737.   (SRO/SH)

THOMSON WILLIAM
Born in Fife during 1800. A clockmaker
and watchmaker in Raleigh and
Wilmington, NC, from 1834 to 1850.
Died in 1850 Buried in Oakdale Cemetery,
Wilmington, NC.   (Wilmington Gs)(SNC)

THOMPSON WILLIAM
53. Watchmaker. Born in Scotland. Anna
40. Born in NC. William A. 28. Watchmaker. Born in Jamaica. Frederick 14.
Born in NC. AS 11. Born in NC. James 7.
Born in NC. Wilmington, New Hanover County, NC.   (C)

THORNSON ANDREW
20. A merchant. Born in Glasgow.
Emigrated from Greenock, Renfrewshire, to
Charleston, SC, on the Countess, master
R Eason, in October 1774.   (PRO/T47.12)

TODD JAMES
Born in Scotland c1707. An indentured
servant who absconded on SC during
October 1734.   (SCGaz 19.10.1734)

TODD WILLIAM
Emigrated from Scotland or Ireland to SC
on the ship Pearl, master Walter
Buchanan, in December 1767. Allocated
a 100 acre land grant 12 December 1767.   (OL)

TORREY BEATRICE
Born in Scotland during 1757. Married
Malcolm Purcell, c1770, possibly in NC.
Settled in Cumberland County, NC. Died
in Robeson County, NC, in 1828.   (INC27566)

TORRY JAMES
Born in 1745. Emigrated to America in
1789. A farmer in Cumberland County,
NC, with a wife and three children
in 1812.   (1812)

TORREY JOHN
Born in Scotland c1720. Married
Margaret ..., in Scotland, c1744.
Settled in Robeson County, NC.
Probably died in Cumberland County, NC.   (INC27566)

TORRY JOHN
Born in Paisley, Renfrewshire.
Married Margaret ... Emigrated via
Pennsylvania to NC c1765. Father of
three sons and three daughters.   (LRS)

TROTTER NANCY
45. Born in Scotland. Joshua 48.
Coachmaker. Born in Virginia.
Adeline 22. Born in Virginia. Ann 18.
Born in Ohio. Emily 16. Born in Ohio.
Charlotte, Mecklenburg County, NC.   (C)

TULLOCH CHARLES
Born in 1782. Emigrated to America in
1808. A millwright in Robeson County,
NC, during 1812.   (C)

TURNBULL Dr ANDREW
Born in Annan, Dumfries-shire c1719.
Expedition leader to Florida in 1768.
Physician in SC c1781. Died in
Charleston, SC, 13 May 1792.   (SM 54.309)(SA)

TURNBULL GAVIN
Born in Berwickshire during 1765.
A teacher in Charleston, SC.
Nat.23 October 1813 Charleston, SC.   (Nat Arch M1183.1)

TURNBULL JAMES
Born in Scotland. An indentured servant
who absconded from his master J Fraser
in Charleston, SC, during June 1734.   (SCGaz 22.6.1734)

TURNBULL JOSEPH
Born in Scotland. Nat.14 June 1823 SC(Circuit Ct Jl 9.296)

TWEED ALEXANDER
Son of William Tweed, merchant in Banff,
1683-1760, and his wife Jean Jaffrey.
A planter and merchant in Carolina.
Admitted as a Burgess of Banff 1776.   (Banff Gs)(AOB)

URE ALEXANDER
A weaver. Emigrated from Gourock,
Renfrewshire, to Port Royal, SC,
on the Carolina Merchant, master
Walter Gibson, 21 July 1684.   (ECJ)

URE JOHN
Son of David Ure, Haddington, East
Lothian. A housecarpenter in SC.   (Pr 20.10.1797 SC)

URQUHART ALEXANDER
Born in Scotland c1765. A merchant in
Wilmington, NC. Brother of Henry
Urquhart. Died 10 October 1792.
Buried in St James's Cemetery,
Wilmington, NC.   (Wilmington Gs)

URQUHART Mrs ANNA
Born in Scotland during 1777.
Settled in Wilmington, NC, pre 1804.
Widow of Henry Urquhart. Died on
22 December 1844. Buried in St James's
Cemetery, Wilmington, NC.   (Wilmington Gs)

URQUHART LENNARD
Edinburgh. A carpenter in SC.   (Pr 6.1.1758 SC)

VEITCH WILLIAM
Born in Scotland. Married Jane O'Riley
Ferguson in Charleston, SC, on
1 January 1818.   (CCG 3.1.1818)

VESEE ROBERT
55. Merchant. Born in Scotland. Charleston, SC.   (C)

VOICE(VAUS?) JANE
Emigrated from Scotland or Ireland to SC
on the ship Pearl, master Walter
Buchanan, in December 1767. Allocated a
100 acre land grant 12 December 1767.   (OL)

WACHOPE JOHN
Son of John Wachope, Camestone, Scotland.
A merchant in Charleston, SC.   (Pr 26.10.1739 SC)

WADDELL JAMES
Born in Scotland. Nat.16 September 1828
Carteret County, NC.   (Carteret Co Ct Rec)

WALKER ALEXANDER
Edinburgh. Died in Charleston, SC.   (Pr 10.10.1792 SC)

WALKER CATHERINE
New Luce, Wigtonshire. Emigrated from
Stranraer, Wigtonshire, to NC on the
Jackie, master J Morris, 31 May 1775.   (PRO/T47.12)

WALKER JOHN
54. Born in Scotland. Isabel 45. Born
in NC. Margaret 21. Born in NC.
Sarah 18. Born in NC. Isabel 16. Born
in NC. Mary 15. Born in NC. John 20.
Born in NC. Betsy 8. Born in NC.
Florah 5. Born in NC. Robeson County, NC.   (C)

WALKER PATRICK
18. Covenanter. Prisoner in Edinburgh
Tolbooth. Banished to Carolina on
24 July 1684. Transported from Leith
to Carolina by Robert Malloch,
merchant burgess of Edinburgh.   (PC)

WALKER THOMAS
Born in Edinburgh. Nat.20 September 1796
Charleston, SC.   (Nat Arch M1183.1)

WALLACE ANDREW
67. Born in Scotland. Sarah 53. Born in
Virginia. Eliza 16. Born in SC. Alfred
15. Born in SC. Edward 12. Born in SC.
Richland County, SC.   (C)

WALLACE JAMES
Born in Scotland during 1788.
Emigrated to America in 1791. A
farmer in York District, SC, with
a family of three in 1812.   (1812)

WALLACE JOHN
Second son of John Wallace, merchant
burgess of Aberdeen, and his wife
Margaret Mair, Fyvie, Aberdeenshire.
Emigrated to America. Died in SC
during late eighteenth century.   (TOF)

WALLACE MARY
50. Born in Scotland. William 65.
Farmer. Born in NC. Mary 16. Born
in NC. Esther 12. Born in NC.
Richmond County, NC.   (C)

WALLACE WALTER
Born in Scotland. A painter. An
indentured servant who absconded from
his mistress Mrs Mary Stevenson in SC
during March 1735.   (SCGaz 29.3.1735)

WARD HUGH
Emigrated from Scotland to Brunswick,
NC, during September 1739.   (VOS)

WARD MILES
Emigrated from Scotland to Brunswick,
NC, during September 1739.   (VOS)

WARDROPE DAVID
Born in Edinburgh. Mariner.
Nat.2 July 1804 Charleston, SC.   (Nat Arch M1183.1)

WATSON ALEXANDER
Born in Fife during 1795. A planter.
Nat.17 October 1825 Charleston, SC.   (Nat Arch M1183.1)

WATSON DANIEL
66. Born in Scotland. Sarah 70. Born in
SC. Anny 39. Born in NC. Sarah Ingraham
7. Born in NC. Robeson County, NC.   (C)

WATSON DANIEL
Born in 1777. Emigrated to America in
1803. A shoemaker in Richmond County,
NC, with a wife and two children in 1812.   (1812)

WATSON DAVID
Leith. Wigmaker in Charleston, SC.   (Pr 17.8.1732 SC)

WATSON DAVID
Born in Scotland. Married ...Hamby in
Wilkes County, NC. Died there c1822.   (INC)

WATSON J.
Born in Scotland. Deserted from Lt Col
Cochrane's Company in SC April 1739.   (SCGaz 4.1739)

WATSON JAMES
50. Merchant. Born in Scotland.
Charleston, SC.   (C)

WATSON JAMES
Born in Fife during 1782. A mariner.
Nat.16 March 1807 Charleston, SC.   (Nat Arch M1183.1)

WATSON JOHN jr
Born in Scotland. Died in SC.   (Pr 29.7.1748 SC)

WATSON JOHN
Nat.3 November 1809 Cumberland County, NC.(NCA/CR.029.311.1)

WATSON JOHN jr
Edinburgh. A merchant in Charleston, SC.
Died before December 1756.   (SRO/CC8/8/116.1)

WATSON JOHN
Born in Musselburgh, Midlothian, c1751.
Settled in Charleston, SC, c1782.
Died 10 December 1812. Buried in
St Michael's, Charleston, SC.   (St Michael's Gs)

WATT ALEXANDER
Born in Carron, Stirlingshire, during
1767. A mariner. Nat.2 November 1803
Charleston, SC.   (Nat Arch M1183.1)

WATT JAMES
Son of Hugh Watt, baker, and Ann Cook
in Perth. Emigrated to Charleston, SC.
Died 19 September 1811. (Greyfriars Perth Gs)

WEDDERBURN JAMES
Younger son of Sir PH Wedderburn, MP
for Fife. Settled in SC during 1733.
Appointed Clerk of the Common Pleas
in SC on 30 April 1733. Allocated
1000 acres in Craven County, SC, on
12 February 1737, and 500 acres on
the Savannah River, SC, 12 April 1738. (SPC)

WHITE CATHERINE
60. Born in Scotland. Richmond County, NC. (C)

WHYTE DANIEL
Born in Argyllshire during 1779. A
butcher in Charleston. Nat. 28
December 1813 Charleston, SC. (Nat Arch M1183.1)

WHITE Rev DONALD
Born in Scotland during 1776.
Emigrated to America during 1808.
A Baptist minister and farmer in
Richmond County, NC, with a wife
and three children in 1812.
Died in New Hanover County, NC,
28 October 1824. Buried in
Springfield Cemetery, Wagram,
Scotland County, NC. (1812)(RRw 19.11.1824)(Wagram Gs)

WHITE JOHN
59. Stone-cutter. Born in Scotland. Jane
48. Born in SC. William 26. Stone-cutter.
Born in SC. Isabel 23. Born in SC.
James E. 22. Student. Born in SC.
Euphemia 21. Born in SC. Robert 17.
Stone-cutter. Born in SC. Ruthven 15.
Born in SC. Marion 13. Born in SC.
Charleston, SC.
JOHN WHITE, born in Edinburgh during 1790,
stonecutter in Charleston, nat.10 October
1826 Charleston, SC. (Nat Arch M1183.1)(C)

WHITE JOHN
44. Farmer. Born in Scotland. Flora 42.
Born in NC. Daniel 21. Farmer. Born in
NC. Mary 19. Born in NC. Rebecca 17.
Born in NC. Eliza 15. Born in NC. Neill
13. Born in NC. Catherine 9. Born in NC.
Flora 6. Born in NC. Margaret 3. Born in
NC. Anna 77. Born in Scotland.
Richmond County, NC.   (C)

WHITE SUSAN
Wife of D White in SC, Serviced as Heir
to her mother Florence Fullerton, wife
of Peter Kermack in Greenock,
Renfrewshire, on 21 January 1813.   (SRO/SH)

WHITE WILLIAM
Fraserburgh, Aberdeenshire. A shop-
keeper in Charleston, SC.   (Pr 19.7.1793)(Pr 1.1795 PCC)

WHITLEY ROGER
Possibly from Scotland. Died at Fort
King George, SC, before February 1729.   (Pr 12.1729 PCC)

WHITNEY Captain JOHN B.
Born in Fochabers, Morayshire.
Settled in Charleston, SC, during 1803.
Died 18 December 1817.   (CCG 27.12.1817)

WICKER JANE
38. Born in Scotland. Lewis 48. Farmer.
Born in NC. Nancy 19. Born in NC.
Archibald 11. Born in NC. Sarah 10.
Born in NC. Benjamin 9. Born in NC.
Frances 7. Born in NC. Mary 5. Born
in NC. Margaret 4. Born in NC.
Bertram 2. Born in NC. James 8 months.
Born in NC. Moore County, NC.   (C)

WIGHTMAN WILLIAM
57. Merchant. Born in Scotland. Ann 62.
Born in England. Edgefield County, SC.   (C)

WILKERSON JOHN
Born in Scotland. Settled in SC 1785.
Nat.14 November 1809 Laurens County,SC.   (Laurens Roll 34)

WILKIE JAMES
Jacobite soldier captured after the Siege
of Preston, Lancashire. Transported from
Liverpool to South Carolina on the
Wakefield, master Thomas Beck, 21 April 1716.   (SPC)

WILKIE WILLIAM
Rantoles Bridge, SC. Serviced as Heir to
his father Peter Wilkie, grocer in
Glasgow, 12 October 1832.   (SRO/SH)

WILKINS JAMES
Born in Scotland. Mariner.
Nat.26 March 1797 Charleston, SC.   (Nat Arch M1183.1)

WILKINSON ALEXANDER
Born in Scotland. Settled in SC 1785.
Nat.17 April 1810 Laurens County, SC.(Laurens Court Roll 35)

WILKINSON DANIEL
80. Born in Scotland. Sarah 52. Born in
NC. James 51. Born in NC. Jane 49. Born
in NC. Daniel 35. Born in NC. Edward 30.
Born in NC. Robeson County, NC.   (C)

WILLIAMS JOHN
Son of Isabel Marshall or Williams in
Glasgow. Emigrated from Scotland to
America c1800. Settled in Wilmington,
NC. A merchant. Married in 1805.
Father of William Augustus, born 1810.
Nat.24 February 1814.Newhaven, NC. (Williams pp(787)SHC/UNC)

WILLIAMS JOHN
70. Born in Scotland. William A. 41.
Distiller. Born in NC. SC(f) 36. Born
in NC. JF 13. Born in NC. RD 10. Born
in NC. E(f) 8. Born in NC. T(f) 6. Born
in NC. Wilmington, New Hanover County, NC.   (C)

WILLIAMS MARY
78. Born in Scotland. John McLeod 48.
Farmer. Born in NC. Elizabeth 45. Born
in NC. William 10. Born in NC.
Archibald 5. Born in NC. Richmond County, NC.   (C)

316

WILLIAMSON ANDREW
Farmer and fisherman. Shetland Islands.
Emigrated from Kirkcaldy, Fife, with
his wife and children, to Brunswick,
NC, on the Jamaica Packet, master
T Smith, in June 1775.   (PRO/T47.12)

WILLIAMSON ANGUS
63. Farmer. Born in Scotland. Elizabeth
49. Born in NC. Chatham County, NC.   (C)

WILLIAMSON JAMES B.
Born in Scotland(?) Nat.30 October 1825
New Hanover County, NC.   (New Han Sup Ct Mins)

WILSON ALEXANDER
Born in Scotland. A planter in
St Bartholemew's parish, SC.   (Pr 8.3.1798 SC)

WILSON DAVID
Born in Stirlingshire. Settled in SC
during 1825. Nat.25 April 1829
Newberry, SC.   (Cit Book 119)

WILSON DAVID
58. Teacher. Born in Scotland. Jane M. 60.
Born in Pennsylvania. Beaufort County, SC.   (C)

WILSON ELIZABETH
45. Born in Scotland. Angus 27. Teacher.
Born in Ireland. Joseph 24. Student.
Born in SC. Charleston, SC.   (C)

WILSON GEORGE
Son of David Wilson, merchant in Coupar
Angus, Perthshire. Surgeon in SC.   (Pr 14.1.1791 SC)

WILSON GEORGE
Born in Edinburgh during 1803. A pilot
in Charleston. Nat.19 August 1826
Charleston, SC.   (Nat Arch M1183.1)

WILSON HUGH
Born in Ayrshire during 1778. Married
Janet ..., born in East Lothian during
1781. Father of William, born in
Ayrshire in 1803, John, born in Ayrshire
in 1812, Hugh, born in Ayrshire in 1820.
Emigrated to SC in October 1822. Nat.
15 November 1827 Laurens County, SC.   (Laurens Ct Roll 84)

WILSON HUGH
Born in Ayr during 1785.
Nat.30 November 1823 SC.   (Cit Book 99)

WILSON JACOBINA
Wife of Pate Mills Milner, planter in
NC. Serviced as Heir to her father
John Wilson, storekeeper in Virginia,
during February 1771.   (SRO/SH)

WILSON JAMES
Jacobite soldier captured after the Siege
of Preston, Lancashire. Transported from
Liverpool to South Carolina on the
Wakefield, master Thomas Beck, 21 April 1716.   (SPC)

WILSON JAMES
Born 14 September 1742, near St Andrews,
Fife. Educated at the Universities of
St Andrews, Glasgow and Edinburgh -
graduated LL.D. Emigrated from Scotland
to New York during 1765. Settled in
Philadelphia, Pennsylvania, during 1766.
Married Rachel Bird in 1772. Academic,
judge and politician. Died in Edenton,
NC, on 21 August 1798.   (AP)

WILSON JAMES
Eldest son of John Wilson in Stirling.
Died in Charleston, SC, on 7 September 1804.   (SM 66.973)

WILSON JAMES jr
Born in Angus during 1780. A merchant.
Nat.10 December 1805 Charleston, SC.   (Nat Arch M1183.1)

WILSON JAMES
Born in Leith, Midlothian, during 1774.
Nat.13 July 1807 Charleston, SC.   (Nat Arch M1183.1)

318

WILSON JANETTE
49. Born in Scotland. Abbeville County, SC.   (C)

WILSON JOHN
Born in Lanarkshire during 1789.
An engineer and surveyor in Charleston.
Nat.7 May 1814 Charleston, SC.   (Nat Arch M1183.1)

WILSON ROBERT
Born in Cupar, Fife(?), on 2 April 1736.
Apprenticed to Dr Martin Eccles of the
Royal College of Physicians of Edinburgh.
An apothecary and surgeon in Burntisland,
Fife. Emigrated from London to SC as an
indentured servant in September 1753.
Married Ann Chisholm in Charleston, SC,
on 8 April 1759. Father of Robert, 1770-
1821. Died 26 August 1815.   (BAF)(SA)(LGR)

WILLSON ROBERT
Emigrated from Scotland or Ireland on the
ship Pearl, master Walter Buchanan, in
December 1767. Allocated a 100 acre land
grant on 12 December 1767.   (OL)

WILSON SAMUEL
Born in Castle Douglas, Kirkcudbrightshire,
c1802. Settled in SC c1819. Died on
20 October 1828. Buried in Columbia
Presbyterian Cemetery.   (SC State Gaz 25.10.1828)

WILSON WILLIAM
Born in Scotland during 1746. Married
Nancy Green. Died in Rowan County, NC,
during 1806.   (INC27631)

WILSON WILLIAM
Born in Edinburgh during 1788. A
butcher in Charleston. Nat.23 October
1813 Charleston, SC.   (Nat Arch M1183.1)

WISHART Mr WILLIAM
Covenanter. Prisoner in Edinburgh or
Canongate Tolbooths. Banished to
Carolina. Transported from Leith to
Carolina by Robert Malloch, merchant
burgess of Edinburgh, during 1684.   (PC)

WITHERSPOON JOHN
Born in Glasgow. Presbyterian minister
in SC from 1710 to 1734. Died on James
Island, SC, 14 August 1734.   (CCVC)

WODDROP JOHN
Born in Edinburgh on 8 July 1756. A
merchant in Charleston, SC. Died on
31 July 1828. Buried in St Michael's,
Charleston, SC.   (St Michael's Gs)

WOOD ANDREW
Born in Scotland. Collector of Beaufort.
Buried in St Helena's, Beaufort, SC, on
9 December 1755.   (St Helena's OPR)

WOOD DANIEL
Born in Scotland. Buried in St Helena's,
Beaufort, SC, on 2 February 1734.   (St Helena's OPR)

WOTHERSPOON ROBERT
55. Merchant. Born in Scotland. Sarah 52.
Born in England. Charleston, SC.
ROBERT WOTHERSPOON, born in Glasgow,
nat.27 July 1831 Charleston, SC.   (C)(Nat Arch M1183.1)

WRIGHT DUNCAN
Born in Scotland c1724. Died in
Cumberland County, NC, during
September 1827.   (RR 11.9.1827)

WRIGHT JAMES
Possibly from Grantown on Spey,
Moravshire. Settled in St Thomas's
parish, SC.   (Pr 12.6.1790 SC)

WYLLIE HUGH
Eldest son of Hugh Wyllie, merchant
and former Lord Provost of Glasgow.
A merchant in Williamsburgh,
Granville County, NC, c1787.   (SRO/RD2/242.1/757)

YATES ANDREW
Born in Aberdeen c1776. Died on
25 January 1804. Buried at Old
Fourth Creek, Statesville,
Iredell County, NC.   (Statesville Gs)

SCOTS IN THE CAROLINAS

YEAMAN FRANCIS
Jacobite soldier captured after the Siege
of Preston, Lancashire. Transported from
Liverpool to South Carolina on the
Susannah, master Thomas Bromhall, 7 May 1716.   (CTB)(SPC)

YOUL THOMAS
Born in Mellarstain, Gordon parish,
Berwickshire. Died 14 April 1813.
Buried at Cedar Grove, Craven County, NC.   (Cedar Grove Gs)

YOULE THOMAS
Nat. June 1814 Craven County, NC.   (Craven Co Ct Rec)

YOUNG ALEXANDER
Born in Fife. Settled in Baltimore,
Maryland. Moved to Camden, SC.
Nat.22 January 1808 SC.   (Cit Book 59)

YOUNG of NETHERFIELD JAMES
Son of James Young of Nethersfield
and his wife Lilias Carmichael.
Settled in Halifax, NC, during
mid eighteenth century.   (RSLanarkshire)

YOUNG JAMES
Born in Edinburgh. Settled in
Columbia, SC. Nat.5 December 1806 SC.   (Cit Book 54)

YOUNG MARY
59. Born in Scotland. Richland County, SC.   (C)

YOUNG ROBERT
Jacobite soldier captured after the Siege
of Preston, Lancashire. Transported from
Liverpool to South Carolina on the
Wakefield, master Thomas Beck, 21 April 1716.   (SPC)

YOUNG SAMUEL
Born in Scotland during 1721. Educated
at the University of Edinburgh.
Emigrated to America in 1748. Settled
in Rowan County, NC. Married Susan Young
in Brunswick County, Virginia, during
1776. Politician. Died during 1793.
Buried in Third Creek Presbyterian
Cemetery, Cleveland, Rowan County, NC.   (Rowan Gs)(LOS)

SCOTS IN THE CAROLINAS

YOUNG THOMAS
21. Surgeon. Glasgow. Emigrated
from Greenock, Renfrewshire, to
Wilmington, NC, on the Ulysses,
master J Chalmers, in August 1774.   (PRO/T47.12)

YUNGBALL D.M.
52. Shopkeeper. Born in Denmark.
Elizabeth 48. Born in Scotland.
Frederick 7. Born in SC.
Beaufort County, SC.   (C)

ADDENDA

BOWMAN JOHN
Son of Lord Provost Bowman of Glasgow.
Emigrated from Scotland to Carolina in
1769. A planter in Carolina.   (H 23.4)

BURN Mrs ANN
Widow of John Burn, SC, and
formerly the widow of Alexander
Baron, SC, also mother of Ann
Baron and James Burn, c1788.   (SRO/RD4/253/747)

CHARLES JAMES
Probably from Musselburgh, Midlothian.
A baker in Charleston, SC, c1793.   (SRO/RD4/254/393)

CLELAND JOHN
Born in Scotland. A Member of HM Council
in SC from 1740 to 1760. Father of Nancy.
Died during 1760.   (H 23.4)

GIBB ROBERT
Born in Edinburgh. Physician - educated
in Edinburgh. Settled in Georgetown, SC,
during 1754. Died during 1777.   (H 23.4)

GRANT HARRY
Son of Robert Grant in Leith, Midlothian.
A merchant in Charleston, SC.   (SRO/RD4/252/1272)

WITHERS JAMES
Born in Scotland. Builder. Settled in
Charleston, SC, in early eighteenth century.   (H 23.4)

CPSIA information can be obtained
at www.ICGtesting.com
Printed in the USA
FFOW04n0832280515
13738FF